Routledge Revi

Uganda: A Modern History

Uganda: A Modern History (1981) provides a comprehensive political, social and economic history of Uganda from the beginnings of colonial rule in 1888. It focuses particularly on the development of the Ugandan economy and demonstrates how the economy became structurally dependent on world capitalism during the colonial period and how this has affected its subsequent development. The book also deals with the political and social tendencies which shaped Ugandan society in both the colonial and postcolonial period. The first four chapters examine the initial colonial occupation and the colonial state's role in the rural nexus of chiefs, peasants and migrant workers. They also look at the colonial state and the context of the wider national, regional and international economy and analyse the African nationalist response and the formation of political parties to take control of the post-colonial state. The second part of the book considers the political alliances and economic strategies of the Obote regime and the events of Amin's military regime. The epilogue looks at events since the fall of the Amin regime and suggests ways in which Uganda may be able to tackle its underlying economic problems.

Uganda: A Modern History

Jan Jelmert Jørgensen

Routledge
Taylor & Francis Group

First published in 1981
by Croom Helm

This edition first published in 2024 by Routledge
4 Park Square, Milton Park, Abingdon, Oxon, OX14 4RN

and by Routledge
605 Third Avenue, New York, NY 10017

Routledge is an imprint of the Taylor & Francis Group, an informa business

© 1981 Jan J. Jørgensen

Publisher's Note
The publisher has gone to great lengths to ensure the quality of this reprint but points out that some imperfections in the original copies may be apparent.

Disclaimer
The publisher has made every effort to trace copyright holders and welcomes correspondence from those they have been unable to contact.

A Library of Congress record exists under LCCN: 82217907

ISBN: 978-1-032-59090-5 (hbk)
ISBN: 978-1-003-45291-1 (ebk)
ISBN: 978-1-032-59102-5 (pbk)

Book DOI 10.4324/9781003452911

UGANDA
A Modern History

JAN JELMERT JØRGENSEN

CROOM HELM LONDON

Croom Helm Ltd, 2-10 St John's Road, London SW11

British Library Cataloguing in Publication Data

Jørgensen, Jan Jelmert
   Uganda – History
   I. Title
   967.6'1   DT431.U2
   ISBN 0-85664-643-1

Portions of Chapter 5 appeared earlier as 'Structural Dependence and the Move to the Left' in Timothy Shaw and Kenneth Heard (eds.), *The Politics of Africa; Dependence and Development* (London: Longman for Dalhousie University Press, 1979). Reprinted by permission.

Printed and bound in Great Britain
by Billing and Sons Limited
Guildford, London, Oxford, Worcester

CONTENTS

MAPS AND FIGURES

Maps

Figures

TABLES

ACKNOWLEDGEMENTS

This study grew out of a doctoral thesis for McGill University ("Structural Dependence and Economic Nationalism in Uganda, 1888-1974"), but my interest in Africa goes back much earlier, to my father's love of warm climates where flowers could thrive, his faith in Africa as the continent of the future, and my mother's story of two aunts who went by sail to Madagascar at the turn of the century. At Chapel Hill, the civil rights movement and courses by William G. Fleming nurtured the early interest. A brief marriage to the great-granddaughter of Dr. E. J. Baxter, one of the early CMS missionaries in Mpwapwa, narrowed my focus to East Africa. Upon delving into Uganda's history, I realized that here was the story worth telling.

The research for the study has received generous support from several institutions and individuals to whom I owe thanks. The Centre for Developing Area Studies at McGill University sponsored my initial field-work in Uganda during the 1970-71 academic year. A grant from the Norwegian Agency for International Development to study multi-national firms in Kenya enabled me to make two brief, but valuable, visits to Uganda in 1974. Additional support for writing came from the McConnell Foundation, the Centre for Foreign Policy Studies at Dalhousie University, the Norwegian Council for Research in the Sciences and Humanities, and the University of Waterloo Social Sciences and Humanities Grant Fund. On occasion, 'private fellow-ships' from my brothers Vidar and Frank helped to bridge the gap between grants.

My intellectual debts are many, but I note the earlier works on Uganda by the authors listed in the bibliography, and the new theoretical perspectives by Samir Amin, Johan Galtung, and Immanuel Wallerstein. Special thanks are due Baldev Raj Nayar for his detailed suggestions, pointed criticism and patient super-vision of the original thesis. Gerald Kibirige proved very competent as a research assistant in Kampala. Congenial and stimulating environments were provided by the Makerere Institute of Social Research, the International Peace Research Institute (Oslo), the Centre for Developing Area Studies, and the Royal Norwegian Embassy in Nairobi. I am grateful also to the many individuals who provided me with interviews in Kampala, London and elsewhere.

Acknowledgements

The staffs at the Entebbe National Archives, the London Public Records Office, and the libraries at Makerere, McGill, Harvard, and the University of Waterloo were both helpful and forgiving. The University of Waterloo Computing Centre and the Cartographic Unit headed by Gary Brannon made possible the preparation of graphs and maps for the book. I am indebted to Carolyn McConnell for the index. Final revisions to tables and text were made easier by the Uganda microfilm collection of the Centre for Research Libraries and by three indispensable sources on African current events: *Africa Research Bulletin, Africa Confidential,* and *Africa Contemporary Record.*

For their useful comments and criticism of portions of the book and thesis, I must thank Edward A. Brett, Bonnie Campbell, David Cohen, Irving Gershenberg, Peter C.W. Gutkind, Anthony G. Hopkins, Moses Kiggundu, Omari Kokole, Frank Kunz, Storrs McCall, Ali Mazrui, Godfrey Okoth, Peter Omara-Ojungu, Timothy Shaw, Yash Tandon, J. Burtin Webster and the Ugandan graduate students in the History Department of Dalhousie University. With such aid, any errors of fact and interpretation that remain in the final product are obviously my responsibility. Friends who provided encouragement and sounding boards for ideas include Malcolm Alexander, Ellen Baxter, Rosalynd Boyd, Beverley Gartrell, Al Hausfather, Rhoda Howard, Miriam Lukwago, Claude Maire, Per Olav Reinton and Henry Srebrnik.

But above all, it is my best friend and wife, Frances J. Ezzy, who has been most generous with her support, gentle prodding, and material contributions. The latter include organising workable timetables for completing the manuscript, editing awkward passages, criticising convoluted logic, and typing and retyping successive drafts. For five years Fran has patiently put up with lonely weekends and evenings and with the creeping imperialism of charts and drafts overflowing the study into the dining and living rooms. Having lived and breathed Uganda's history so long, she is relieved to see this "other woman" finally leave our home and go out into the world.

Jan J. Jørgensen
Montreal

FOR FRAN AND FOR SIGVART AND SOLVEIG

PREFACE

We live in a world of economically interdependent nation-states, a world in which the disparity in average income between rich and poor nations exceeds forty to one. Yet within some of the richest nations many are unemployed, and some suffer from malnutrition, while within the poorest nations some drive a Mercedes and employ many servants. With a per capita income of $280 in 1978, Uganda ranks among the 25 poorest nations in the world. This study examines the roots of poverty and inequality in Uganda by focusing on six major themes: (1) the interplay of international, regional and domestic forces in shaping Uganda's role in the international division of labour; (2) variations in peasant response to incorporation into the world economy; (3) the changing structures of dependence and inequality; (4) the post-1945 emergence of a small but integrated manufacturing sector; (5) the political base and economic strategies of post-1938 movements, parties and regimes; and (6) the ebb and flow of political violence in Uganda.

The emergence of newly-independent nations after the Second World War generated fresh approaches to study the new diversity in the international system. The first of these were largely unidisciplinary, reflecting the traditional division of labour among the social sciences in universities. In political science, structural-functionalism and modernisation focused on the means by which political systems evolved to expand capabilities, diversify roles, develop secular patterns of authority and widen the range of choice, while maintaining stability and cohesion. The concepts of choice and equilibrium were clearly derived from classical liberalism. In economics, developmental economics emerged to stress the importance of trade and foreign investment in generating growth and maximising the benefits gained from specialisation according to Ricardo's theory of comparative advantage. In sociology and anthropology, the new paradigms of modernisation and acculturation emphasised the importance of external agents of social change and of intercultural contacts as stimulants to the diffusion of modernisation and Westernisation. Conversely, the obstacles to change were seen to be the persistence of traditional beliefs and customs.

The Six Phases of the Structural Dependence Paradigm

The 'structural dependence' paradigm emerged as a nationalist response by intellectuals in the new nations to the liberal paradigms and to orthodox Marxism, which posited its own Eurocentric model of linear stages of development. The new structural dependence paradigm countered these with a view of the world system 'from below'. Since its inception in the 1950s, the paradigm has passed through six overlapping phases: (1) the Prebisch-Singer phase; (2) the metropole-satellite phase; (3) the 'new dependency theory' phase; (4) the unequal exchange debates; (5) the 'negation' phase; and (6) the 'modes of production' debates.

Raul Prebisch's 1950 manifesto on the structural causes of inflation in Latin America heralded the start of the first phase.[1] Whereas orthodox (monetarist) economists cited inflation as the cause of balance of payments problems in Latin America, the structuralists argued that the international divison of labour between exporters of manufactured goods and exporters of raw materials contributed to rigidities of supply and thus to inflation in raw-material-exporting nations. Rejecting the monetarist cure of currency devaluation as a prescription for transferring productivity gains from the periphery to the centre, the structuralists urged the imposition of export taxes to capture productivity gains in production of export commodities and the erection of import tariffs to encourage industrialisation based on import substitution, which would eventually expand to export markets. Dynamic technocrats and domestic entrepreneurs were to be the agents of social change in the structuralist vision of the future.[2]

Rejecting the reformist recommendations of the structuralists as utopian, Andre Gunder Frank attacked the unilinear 'stages of development' model which the structuralists had retained from the orthodox developmental economics. Like Paul Baran, Frank drew a distinction between *un*development, a pristine stage found only in pre-industrial Europe and Japan, and *under*development, the consequence of the poriphery's subordinate incorporation into an already existing world capitalist system.[3] Frank also repudiated the 'dualist' model which portrayed development as a process of penetration of an isolated, traditional, rural sector by the dynamic, modern, urban sector in the developing nation. On the contrary, according to Frank, the capitalist system had, over the course of several centuries of expansion, penetrated the most remote and isolated areas of the world. In place of the dualist and stages-of-development models, he proposed the

metropolis-satellite model in which the metropolis or centre of the
world system sucked capital or economic surplus from the remotest
areas through a chain of monopolistic and exploitative relationships. To
break the chain of exploitation, Frank called for revolution in the
periphery, led by the peasants and their allies.

It was precisely this contradiction between a capitalist world system,
which apparently required transformation at the global level, and the
framework of nation-states, which must form the 'immediate arena of
struggle', that led to the schisms among theorists in phases four, five and
six.

Although sympathetic to Frank's radical approach, many found his
initial formulation inadequate and mechanistic. In the third phase,
then, the 'new dependency theory' set out to improve on Frank's
original model by focusing on the following phenomena: the diversity
of social formations in the periphery;[4] the 'infrastructure of
dependency';[5] periodisation of the uneven and unequal development of
the world system since 1500;[6] the nature and role of the state in both
the centre and periphery;[7] the role of multinational firms in maintaining and reproducing the vertical international division of labour;[8]
dependent industrialisation;[9] and the role of primitive accumulation
(forcible appropriation) in the initial incorporation of Asia, Latin
America and Africa into the world system.[10]

The exuberance of research activity in the third phase masked
underlying disagreements regarding theories of imperialism, strategies
of 'autonomous development', definitions of socialism, and identification of primary obstacles to development. The illusion of harmony was
shattered by the publication of Emmanuel's theory of unequal
exchange.[11] Starting with the initial assumptions of international
mobility of capital, relative international immobility of labour, relative
equalisation of rates of profit both between nations and between
branches of industry, and the fundamental assumption of higher wages
in the centre than in the periphery, Emmanuel demonstrated that trade
between the centre and the periphery initially entailed unequal
exchange in that the centre exported commodities containing fewer
hours of paid labour in exchange for commodities from the periphery
containing more hours of paid labour. Moreover, high wage rates forced
firms in the centre to industrialise to reduce the amount of paid labour
per unit of output. Given the resulting differences in capital stock
between the centre and the periphery, the initial level of unequal
exchange arising from wage disparities would be further magnified by
unequal productivity. What was revolutionary about Emmanuel's

theory was its return to the labour theory of value. What was discon-
certing about his conclusions was the rejection of any material basis
for solidarity between the proletariat in the centre and the proletariat
and peasantry in the periphery. According to the theory, the proletariat in the centre benefited from unequal exchange. The primary
contradiction was therefore between rich and poor nations rather than
between the proletariat and the bourgeoisie at either the national or
global level.

Charles Bettelheim and Samir Amin criticised Emmanuel's theory
of unequal exchange on two grounds: first, it assumed rather than
explained the inequality in wages between centre and periphery;
second, it focused on exploitation in terms of the circulation of commodities rather than the relations of production.[12] Turning to the
relations of production, both Bettelheim and Amin noted that the
capitalist mode of production had completely dissolved pre-capitalist
modes in the centre (except for unpaid housewives); in the periphery,
however, the capitalist mode of production overlay pre-capitalist
modes. The disparity in wages between centre and periphery could
therefore be explained by relations of production. Whereas wages in the
centre had to cover the entire cost of the maintenance and reproduction of labour-power, wages in the periphery need cover only part of
the cost. The remainder was shoved onto the so-called subsistence or
pre-capitalist rural sector, which bore the cost of the migrant worker's
childhood and retirement and the peasant's entire subsistence.[13]

Far from being the barrier to modernisation, as depicted in the dualistic model of the developmental approach, the pre-capitalist 'subsistence' sector was recast by Bettelheim and Amin as the wretched prop
supporting the modern capitalist system. But it was both prop and
barrier, for the survival of pre-capitalist social formations in the
periphery hindered industrialisation by depressing wages. Low wages
limited the domestic market for means of subsistence and reduced the
impetus for increasing the productivity of labour. What remained
ambiguous in this synthesis was the solution. Did it lie in increased
integration of the rural sector into the international division of labour
or in some form of withdrawal from that division of labour through
'autonomous development?'[14]

The appearance of Amin's grand theory of unequal development
marked the transition from the fourth to the fifth phase. Attempting
to synthesise and extend the findings of phases one through four,
Samir Amin produced a skilful work of eclecticism, but not a unified
theory. Indeed, there could be no unified theory because the capit-

alist world system did not entail homogeneity. In the centre one found a close approximation to the 'pure' model of the capitalist mode of production. In the periphery one found a diversity of social formations, which obscured the dominance of the capitalist mode. The social structure of the periphery was a truncated structure which could only be comprehended by situating it within the world social structure. In short, the unity of the world system was characterised by its inequality and diversity, in which domination by the capitalist mode of production constituted the basis for linking the heterogeneous periphery with the homogeneous centre.[15]

This brings us to the sixth phase in the structural dependence paradigm: the debates over modes of production and articulation of (hierarchical relations between) modes of production.[16] These debates antedate and crosscut the structural dependence paradigm. The Dobb-Sweezy exchange regarding Europe's transition from feudalism to capitalism, the Frank-Laclau dispute over whether Latin America was feudal or capitalist, and the similar Rudra-Patnaik-Chattopadhyay-Banaji debate over Indian agriculture have become celebrated battles in this complex and multifaceted controversy. Parallel to the unequal exchange debate, the most hotly contested points centre on the proper unit of analysis: relations of production vs. relations of exchange vs. relations of exploitation; the world system vs. the social formation vs. the nation-state vs. 'on farm'/'in firm' relations between producers and non-producers. As Foster-Carter observed, at one extreme are Frank and Wallerstein, for whom everything is capitalism after 1500, including socialism; at the other extreme are micro-view studies in which 'each Andean valley has its own mode of production, and individuals may change them two or three times a week like underwear'.[17]

I have abdicated to others the task of outlining and periodising the mode(s) of production in Uganda.[18] There is, however, one important point in the debate which should be mentioned. Rey notes that the capitalist mode of production entered the periphery from the outside 'already fully-grown and well-armed'.[19] According to Foster-Carter, this inside/outside distinction — the fact of conquest — helps explain the resistance to dissolution of pre-capitalist modes of production in the periphery. Nationalism emerges as an unexpected dimension in the partial dissolution/partial conservation of pre-capitalist modes of production.

Coming from a different direction, Nairn offers a similar view.[20] Uneven development meant that the spread of 'Progress' from the centre to the periphery took the form of imperial conquest rather than

peaceful diffusion. To mobilise resistance against centre-based domination, even the most westernised elites in the periphery had to resort
to *national*ism as a unifying force. Hence, even as the spread of
capitalism united the human race into a single division of labour, it
generated a new political fragmentation. So far, Nairn's view parallels
Samir Amin's view of homogeneity in the centre, heterogeneity in the
periphery, united by capitalist domination. But Nairn argues that it was
in the centre and the semi-periphery that national*ism* attained its most
terrifying forms: imperialism and fascism. Today, nationalism even
threatens to undo nations in the centre: Britain, Spain, France.
*National*ism (Welsh, Norwegian, Québéçois, Cuban, Polish, Kiganda,
etc.) is more culturally and psychically satisfying than the austere ration-
ality of proletarian internationalism. Nairn concludes on an optimistic
note. While nationalism arsing from uneven development has sabotaged
the emergence of international class solidarity, it has displaced socialism
from the centre to the periphery as the (economic) ideology of catching
up. But is socialism merely a populist *étatiste* strategy for catching up?

Applications and Critiques of the Paradigm

Aside from analysing the diversity of social formations in the periphery,
one of Amin's more important contributions was the elaboration of a
model which contrasted the centre and the periphery in terms of the
key economic sectors in each. As shown in Figure 1, the key

Figure 1: Samir Amin's Model of Production and Distribution

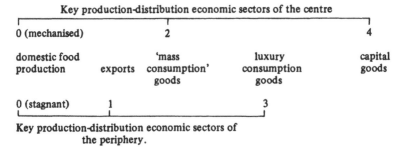

Key production-distribution economic sectors of the centre

0 (mechanised)		2		4
domestic food production	exports	'mass consumption' goods	luxury consumption goods	capital goods
0 (stagnant)	1		3	

Key production-distribution economic sectors of
    the periphery.

Source: Samir Amin, 'Accumulation and Development: A Theoretical Model',
Review of African Political Economy, no. 1 (1974), p. 10, with modifications
suggested by Dieter Senghaas.

production and distribution sectors in the centre were the 'mass consumption' sector, the capital goods sector and the mechanised food production sector. By contrast, the export commodities sector and the luxury goods sector constituted the key economic activities in the periphery, where food production remained relatively stagnant and unmechanised.

Amin's model of the periphery is that of a disarticulated domestic economy which must export raw materials to import machinery, and whose income distribution is so badly skewed that only the urban elite and rural landowners have sufficient buying power to support local manufacturing. To some extent, this picture fits Uganda.

Direct analysis of the disarticulation of the Ugandan economy would require an input-output analysis. The last such attempt was abandoned in the economic chaos following the 1972 expulsion of Asians. In a 1974 interview, a Ministry of Commerce and Industry official (a person with a solid education in economic planning) questioned the value of such an analysis, since the gaps in intersectoral linkages were so numerous in Uganda. One turns therefore to indirect indicators of the disarticulation of the economy: the composition of the gross domestic product and the composition of external trade.

Throughout the 1963-74 period, the primary sector (agriculture, forestry, mining and the subsistence sector) accounted for 55 per cent of Uganda's output of goods and services, not surprising since 90 per cent of the population of 12.6 million (1980) lives in rural areas. Manufacturing accounted for only 8 per cent of the output. Industry was often heavily dependent on imported inputs as well as machinery and technology. The paper industry imported pulp from Scandinavia; the superphosphate fertiliser industry imported sulphur; and the match factory used imported raw materials. But we cannot have it both ways, arguing that imports of raw materials are a sign of dependence in a poor country and a sign of development in a rich country. Using the SITC commodity classifications, Galtung and Hungrø developed a trade composition index so that a totally industrialised country, which imported only raw materials and exported only finished goods, had an index of +1.00, whereas a totally dependent country, which imported only finished goods and exported only raw materials, had an index of -1.00.[21] A comparison of the trade composition index for Uganda (-0.77), Kenya (-0.46), and Tanzania (-0.63) for 1973 reveals that all three exhibit a high degree of dependence, but Uganda more so than the others. Uganda's raw material exports were highly concentrated. Coffee, cotton and copper accounted for 73 per cent of exports in

1968; in 1975, coffee, cotton and tea accounted for 93 per cent. By contrast, in Norway and Canada — two industrialised nations renowned for raw material exports — the top three raw materials accounted for only 18 per cent of all exports in 1968.

Yet, contrary to Samir Amin's model, the small manufacturing sector in Uganda produced a significant range of mass-consumption goods (cotton and rayon piece-goods, edible vegetable oil, soap, sugar, hoes, fishing nets, corrugated iron roofing, bicycle tyres, matches and fertiliser) as well as simple luxury goods (beer, spirits and cigarettes). More importantly, there were some intersectoral linkages beyond crop-processing. Not only was the textile industry based on local cotton, but soap, edible oil and cattle feed were produced from the cotton seed. The sugar industry had spawned an engineering works and a small steel industry which produced construction materials, spare parts and hoes for the growers. The economic problems of Idi Amin's regime demonstrated that sharp declines in investment in non-agricultural sectors could create severe bottlenecks in agricultural production.

Elsewhere, one finds other exceptions to the basic model of the periphery, notably countries which mainly export labour (Upper Volta, Niger, Mozambique, Haiti), and those (Singapore, Taiwan, Hong Kong, South Korea) which served as sites for 'off-shore manufacturing' by 'runaway industries' from the centre seeking cheap, but disciplined, non-union labour.[22] Because of the heterogeneity of the periphery, there was no single cluster of characteristics which distinguished nations in the periphery from those in the centre. Any search for such a definition would be based on an atomistic view of the world system more characteristic of the 'stages of growth' approach than of the holistic view of the world system as a set of unequal relationships between the centre and the periphery within a changing vertical international division of labour. Structural dependence was therefore not a self-sufficient concept.[23] To rise above description, the concept has to be placed within the context of a more comprehensive theory of the capitalist world system. This entailed formulating a theory of imperialism. By the same token, attempts to test empirically the dependency 'theory' were doomed to failure if based on cross-sectional analyses which assumed an underlying homogeneous model. Senghaas suggested that one first map the heterogeneity of the periphery in both time and space, using monographic studies, before embarking on statistical tests of nomothetic hypotheses.[24] This history of Uganda therefore tests the 'fit' of the structural dependence paradigm to a single case.

Aside from empirical tests of the paradigm and theoretical critiques by both orthodox and 'gauchiste' Marxists, there have been liberal critiques which merit examination, such as Cohen's *The Question of Imperialism*.[25] Since Cohen correctly situates the dependency paradigm within the broader context of theories of economic imperialism, an assessment of his critique must necessarily briefly deal with his arguments concerning imperialism as well. In Cohen's case against radical and Marxist theories of imperialism, there are two major themes: the first that economic imperialism is not necessary for the survival of capitalism, and the second that political explanations of imperialism are more adequate than economic explanations. But this argument requires a mechanistic distinction between economic and political imperialism. If one defines economic imperialism as the expansion of the world market to new territories and control of that world market by oligopolistic firms backed by state intervention, one has a definition of economic imperialism which includes the necessary political dimension.

The history of capitalism abounds with examples of such economic imperialism. Yet was this imperialism necessary for the survival of capitalism? Or, was it merely a convenience or even an aberration? It is important to note that refutation of the necessity of economic imperialism would not negate the existence of the phenomenon.

For Lenin, imperialism was necessary economically in that the most advanced capitalist nations had to export surplus capital to find profitable outlets and necessary politically in that imperialism made possible the alliance between the bourgeoisie and the 'labour aristocracy' in the advanced industrial nations. For Rosa Luxemburg and for Wallerstein, geographical expansion of the capitalist system is necessary to stave off a 'realisation crisis', a crisis caused by the overproduction of commodities which cannot be sold to realise a profit on investment. For Samir Amin, imperialism has been an expedient rather than a necessity in the history of capitalism. For him, imperialism is not a requirement of the economic laws of capitalism but rather a political product of class antagonisms and alliances at both the national and global levels. Periods of expansion and contraction in the world economy are marked by changes in the membership of both the centre and the periphery, changes in the function of each within the vertical international division of labour, and changes in the class alliances required for the maintenance and reproduction of the system.[26]

Cohen attributes overcoming the chronic underconsumption of the late nineteenth century to capitalism's unbounded capacity for reform.

Nevertheless, higher wages, the welfare state, pollution control and similar reforms have a fundamental outer limit, namely the capitalist requirement that the ownership of capital continue to be rewarded through profit.

Cohen is correct in asserting that there is a political dimension to economic imperialism, but incorrect in arguing that Marxists and radicals have ignored it. Cohen ultimately reduces imperialism to a purely political phenomenon inherent in an 'anarchic system of nation-states' ruled by inherently greedy human beings. Yet the nation-state, which he assumes to be an eternal feature of human society, only emerged with the rise of capitalism in the fifteenth and sixteenth centuries.[27] Even if one accepts Cohen's assertion that human beings are inherently greedy (a fundamental tenet of economic liberalism), one must recognise that the economic system influences the form which greed will take.

Cohen's critique of the dependency paradigm embodies two closely related themes: the first that the dependency paradigm exaggerates the negative consequences of the periphery's incorporation into the world system and ignores positive effects, and the second that the world system is a 'non-zero-sum game' in which all participants benefit absolutely though the benefits be distributed in a relatively unequal manner.

The accusation of exaggeration is certainly true, but it is sometimes necessary to exaggerate a feature of reality that has heretofore been ignored. Cohen uses the 'vent for surplus' theory to argue that poor nations benefit from specialising in the export of primary commodities produced by surplus labour which would otherwise be idle. Nevertheless, the authority (Caves) cited for this theory is far more pessimistic. Caves contrasts the surplus of natural resources position of Canada, Australia and New Zealand to the surplus of labour situation found in most poor countries. He notes that development with 'unlimited supplies of labour' is predicated on low wages for labour and excess profits for investing firms. Caves foresees a secular deterioration in the terms of trade for surplus labour nations, whereas no comparable negative effects are predicted for nations with surplus natural resources.[28]

Moreover, Cohen ignores the historical factors which brought into being 'unlimited supplies of labour' in parts of the periphery and returns to explanations of lack of development in the periphery based on internal factors: lack of entrepreneurship and lack of receptivity to change. As this history of Uganda demonstrates, it was the colonial state which restricted African entrepreneurial activity to commodity production and wage-labour until the blocking strategy ceased being politically feasible after the Second World War. Furthermore, resistance to change on the part of peasants was often solidly rooted in the labour requirements of food crops.

Cohen's description of the world economy as a non-zero-sum game is useful for two reasons.

First, by distinguishing between absolute and relative gains (and losses) in a growing economy, Cohen pinpoints a key disagreement between liberals and radicals. For the former (including Cohen), increased relative inequality is not unjust as long as each participant receives a larger absolute amount than before.[29] For the latter (including myself), increased relative inequality is itself unjust, notwithstanding absolute gains.

Second, the fact that most participants enjoy some absolute gains in a growing economy helps explain why few are willing to opt out of the unequal division of labour and unequal division of gains. By expanding the social production of commodities, import substitution is at least marginally better than no industrialisation. Colonial transport systems geared to promote exports of raw materials are better than no roads or railroads. Colonial health measures designed to safeguard commodity production and ensure the continued flow of migrant labour have obvious positive side effects. Generally it is better to be badly paid but employed than to be unemployed. So too, it is generally better to be badly developed than be outside the international division of labour.

To say that structural dependence entails underdevelopment is therefore simplistic. All development under the capitalist mode of production entails underdevelopment in the sense that capitalist production is motivated by the accumulation of capital through production for profit on an ever-expanding scale rather than by production for human needs. In both centre and periphery there is sub-optimal production of use-values. In the centre sub-optimal production may take the form of waste: military spending, proliferation of brand names and of disposable commodities. Metaphorically one speaks of 'over-development' in the centre since 6 per cent of the world's population consumes or wastes 30 to 40 per cent of the world's annual output. Yet it is the sub-optimal production of use-values which underlies this so-called overdevelopment. Galtung has described the gap between what is feasible with a given set of resources and technology and what actually exists as 'structural violence', as distinct from personal physical violence.[30] We shall find evidence of both in the history of Uganda.

To temper the mechanistic tendencies inherent in the structural

dependence paradigm, this history emphasises the indigenous response
to domination. The attempt by any indigenous group to win a higher
status for itself in the domestic or international division of labour can
be labelled *economic nationalism*. Those attempts, however, which con-
sign other indigenous groups to lower status can be termed *bourgeois*
economic nationalism.

Between 1888 and 1980 the following Ugandan strata have pursued
strategies of bourgeois economic nationalism: landlords, capitalist
tenant farmers,[31] merchants, traders, professionals, the state salariat
(including chiefs and the military), and white-collar workers. Collec-
tively these strata may be labelled the *national bourgeoisie*. Some may
argue that this is an overly Eurocentric term for a group in the
periphery that is comparatively weak in both economic and political
power. None the less, since political independence, the state has served
the interests of these strata in opposition to both domestic and foreign
groups. As Sklar observed, those who control the state bureaucracy in
the newly independent states exercise control of the means of compulsion and thus enjoy relative autonomy *vis-à-vis* foreign and domestic
groups.[32] The state protects the bourgeois basis of their appropriation
of surplus from domestic productive strata and aids their attempts to
wrest a larger share of the domestic surplus from foreign interests.

Although petty bourgeois and *comprador* tendencies exist among
members of the national bourgeoisie, we must not lose sight of the
reality of conflicts between them and foreign interests. It is not because
of their intermediary position *vis-à-vis* foreign firms that they enjoy
their appropriation of surplus; it is rather because their own appropriation of domestic surplus is based on the export of raw materials
that they benefit foreign firms. Similarly, it is not because members of
the state salariat and ruling party own shops or transport firms that
they control the state; it is because they control the state that they are
able to enter commerce.

The link (or lack of it) between bourgeois economic nationalism and
the problem of structural transformation may be illustrated by delineat-
ing four levels of analysis and action, as shown in Figure 2: Level I,
the world; Level II, the nation; Level III, economic sub-sectors within
the nation; and Level IV, firms and institutions within each sub-sector.

Although bourgeois economic nationalism is primarily concerned
with indigenisation of high-status positions within existing firms and
institutions (Level IV) and with indigenisation of ownership and
control of firms in key economic sub-sectors (Level III), examples of
bourgeois economic nationalism at Level II include industrialisation

Figure 2: Four Levels of Analysis and Action in the Periphery

Unit of Analysis	Method of Analysis	Strategies of Action (Bourgeois and Radical)
I. The World	Focus on vertical international division of labour. Analysis of international division of labour and capitalist mode of production within capitalist world system.	Class struggle at global level. Transition from capitalist to socialist world system. Commodity producer cartels. Regional autonomy and collective self-reliance.
II. The Nation	Focus on structure of domestic economy. Input-output analysis; analysis of composition of external trade; study of intersectoral links; study of basic human needs and available resources at national level.	Structural transformation or socialism at national level. Class struggle at the national level. Strategies of self-reliance. Income redistribution to expand domestic market. Auto-centred accumulation. Import-substitution industrialisation. Sub-imperialism to expand market.
III. Economic sub-sectors	Focus on control of units of production and distribution within economic sub-sectors. Analysis of nationality of owners of individual firms within each sub-sector.	Nationalisation. Joint ventures or semi-nationalisation. Expulsion of foreigners. State aid to indigenous entre-preneurs. Restrictions on foreign ownership in certain sub-sectors. State corporations.
IV. The Firm	Focus on division of labour by ethnic or national identity within individual firms or institutions. Analysis of ethnic and national identity of holders of high-status positions within firms or institutions.	Indigenisation of positions within firms and institutions. Expansion of technical, commercial and managerial education. Immigration restrictions on, or expulsion of, foreigners.

Structural Transformation

Bourgeois Economic Nationalism

Adapted from Dharam P. Ghai, 'Concepts and Strategies of Economic Independence,' *Journal of Modern African Studies*, vol. 11, no. 1 (1973), pp. 21-42.

through import substitution (India, Uganda), industrialisation by invitation to foreign firms (Kenya, Ivory Coast), and regional sub-imperialism (South Africa, Brazil).[33] At the world level (Level I), bourgeois economic nationalism appears to be limited to the formation of commodity producer cartels and verbal appeals for a new international economic order, neither of which has succeeded in altering the international division of labour so far.[34] Although actions at Levels IV and III may involve heated disputes with foreign interests, only Levels II and I involve structural transformation.

Does this mean that structural transformation is to be equated with revolutionary socialism? Not necessarily. The day after the revolution the problem of structural dependence remains. Few revolutionary governments are prepared to emulate Pol Pot's bold, or foolhardy, attempt to withdraw completely from the international division of labour. The revolutionary government therefore has to adapt the economy to the realities of the capitalist world market and the vertical international division of labour. The revolution in and of itself cannot undo the skewed allocation of resources created and reproduced by previous decades of peripheral capitalist development. Cuba continues to produce sugar for the world market, while attempting to diversify and increase the autonomy of its economy. Vietnam continues to produce rubber and coal for the world market and encourages off-shore oil exploration by capitalist firms. Mozambique continues to export migrant labourers to South Africa. Angola sells petroleum to Gulf Oil. Zimbabwe is forced to trade with South Africa. Initially these countries have tackled more pressing problems: control of the means of production and allocation of state services, particularly education, agriculture and health. Only gradually can changes be made to the role of the economy in the vertical international division of labour. As both Wallerstein and Sweezy have noted,[35] for small countries the prospects may be very limited — socialism or no socialism — for a substantially better role in the global division of labour, though it may be possible to guarantee at least a minimum decent standard of living for the poorest strata under 'peripheral socialism'.

If the prospects for small countries are dim, and if, as Cox suggests,[36] national self-reliance runs the risk of becoming a slogan for the ennobling of poverty rather than its eradication, where does hope for the future lie? For Clive Thomas and Samir Amin, it lies in collective (regional) self-reliance.[37] Such south-south co-operation would have to be on a scale sufficiently large to allow increased regional disengagement from the vertical north-south division of labour. Whether the forces of nationalism described by Nairn can be harnessed or transcended to achieve these aims remains to be seen.

The foregoing theoretical excursion is longer than I intended, and some may wonder how the structural dependence paradigm will be applied to Uganda's history in the following chapters. To avoid burdening the general reader with unwanted jargon, I have applied the paradigm beneath the surface, so to speak, and used 'natural language' as much as possible. The study has been organised into four broad parts corresponding to the four political regimes in Uganda since the onset of the colonial occupation. The analysis of the colonial regime is itself divided into four chapters. The first examines the initial colonial occupation and Uganda's incorporation into the capitalist world system. Chapter 2 examines the colonial state's role in the rural nexus of chiefs, peasants and migrant workers. Chapter 3 looks at the colonial state in the wider national, regional and international context, emphasising changing constraints and priorities. Chapter 4 analyses the African nationalist response and the formation of political parties which contest for control of the post-colonial state. The social base, political alliances and economic strategies of the Obote regime (1962-71) are examined in Chapter 5, while Chapter 6 does the same for the Amin regime (1971-9). Implications of the study for the problems facing the post-Amin regimes can be found in the epilogue (Chapter 7).

Notes

1. Cf. Raul Prebisch, 'The Economic Development of Latin America and Its Principal Problems', *Economic Bulletin for Latin America*, vol. 7 ((February 1962), pp. 1-22; and Hans W. Singer, 'The Distribution of Gains Between Investing and Borrowing Countries', *American Economic Review; Papers and Proceedings*, vol. 40, no. 2 (May 1950), pp. 473-85. The Singer-Prebisch thesis regarding declining terms of trade for primary commodity producers continues to be a subject of controversy. Samir Amin suggests that a distinction be made between the external terms of trade experienced by countries and the internal terms of trade faced by local producers/consumers, *Unequal Development* (New York: Monthly Review Press, 1976), pp. 163-71. See also Appendix Table A.5.

2. Raul Prebisch, 'The System and the Social Structure of Latin America',' *Latin American Radicalism*, ed. I.L. Horowitz, J. de Castro and J. Gerassi (New York: Random House, 1969), pp. 29-60.

3. Cf. Andre Gunder Frank, 'The Development of Underdevelopment', and Paul Baran, 'On the Political Economy of Backwardness', *Imperialism and Underdevelopment*, ed. R.I. Rhodes (New York: Monthly Review Press, 1970), pp. 4-17 and 285-301 with W.W. Rostow, *The Stages of Economic Growth*, 2nd edn. (Cambridge: Cambridge University Press, 1966), pp. 4-16.

4. Samir Amin, *Accumulation on a World Scale* (New York: Monthly Review

Press, 1975).

5. Susanne Bodenheimer, 'Dependency and Imperialism', *Politics and Society*, vol. 1, no. 3 (May 1971), pp. 327-57.

6. Celso Furtado, *Economic Development of Latin America* (Cambridge: Cambridge University Press, 1970); Samir Amin, 'Underdevelopment and Dependence in Black Africa', *Journal of Peace Research*, vol. 9, no. 2 (1972), pp. 105-19; and Immanuel Wallerstein, *The Modern World System* (New York and London: Academic Press, 1974).

7. Charles Tilly, 'Western State-Making and Theories of Political Transformation', *The Formation of National States in Western Europe* (Princeton: Princeton University Press, 1975), pp. 601-38; Hamza Alavi, 'The State in Post-Colonial Societies', *New Left Review*, no. 74 (July-August 1972), pp. 59-81; Michaela von Freyhold, 'The Post-Colonial State and Its Tanzania Version', *Review of African Political Economy*, no. 8 (January-April 1977), pp. 75-89; and W. Ziemann and M. Lanzendörfer, 'The State in Periphery Societies', *Socialist Register, 1977*, ed. Ralph Miliband and John Saville (London: Merlin Press, 1977), pp. 143-77.

8. Stephen Hymer, 'The Multinational Corporation and the Law of Uneven Development', *Economics and World Order*, ed. J.N. Bhagwati (London: Macmillan, 1972), pp. 113-40; Christian Palloix, *L 'économie mondiale capitaliste et les firmes multinationales* (Paris: Maspero, 1975); Richard Barnet and Ronald E. Müller, *Global Reach* (New York: Simon and Schuster, 1974); and Carl Widstrand (ed.), *Multinational Firms in Africa* (Uppsala: Scandinavian Institute for African Studies, 1975).

9. Fernando Henrique Cardoso, 'Associated Dependent Development', *Authoritarian Brazil*, ed. Alfred Stephan (New Haven: Yale University Press, 1973), pp. 142-76; and Philip Ehrensaft, 'Polarized Accumulation and the Theory of Economic Dependence', *The Political Economy of Contemporary Africa*, ed. Peter Gutkind and Immanuel Wallerstein (Beverly Hills: Sage Publications, 1976), pp. 58-89.

10. Giovanni Arrighi, 'Labour Supplies in Historical Perspective', *Journal of Development Studies*, vol. 6, no. 3 (April 1970), pp. 197-234; and Walter Rodney, *How Europe Underdeveloped Africa* (Washington, DC: Howard University Press, 1974), pp. 95-146, 164-72.

11. Arghiri Emmanuel, *Unequal Exchange* (New York: Monthly Review Press, 1972).

12. Charles Bettelheim, 'Appendix I', in *Unequal Exchange*, pp. 297-98; and Samir Amin, *L 'échange inégal et la loi de la valeur* (Paris, Éditions anthropos-IDEP, 1973), pp. 91-6.

13. Immanuel Wallerstein, 'The Rural Economy in Modern World Society', *The Capitalist World-Economy* (Cambridge: Cambridge University Press, 1979), pp. 119-31.

14. Cf. Geoffrey Kay, *Development and Underdevelopment* (London: Macmillan, 1975), p. x; and Samir Amin, 'Le tiers-monde et la division internationale du travail', *Le Monde Diplomatique*, February 1977, p. 26.

15. Samir Amin, *L 'échange inégal et la loi de la valeur*, pp. 49-62, 91-6; and *Unequal Development*, pp. 148-9, 293-5.

16. Ernesto Laclau, 'Feudalism and Capitalism in Latin America', *New Left Review*, no. 67 (May-June 1971), pp. 19-38; Claude Meillassoux, 'From Reproduction to Production', *Economy and Society*, vol. 1, no. 1 (1972), pp. 93-105; Pierre-Phillippe Rey, *Colonialisme, néo-colonialisme et transition au capitalisme* (Paris: Maspero, 1971); R. Hilton (ed.), *The Transition from Feudalism to Capitalism* (London: New Left Books, 1976); Perry Anderson, 'The "Asiatic Mode of Production" ', *Lineages of the Absolutist State* (London: New Left Books, 1974), pp. 462-95; Immanuel Wallerstein, 'The Rise and Future Demise of

the World Capitalist System', *The World Capitalist-Economy*, pp. 1-36; and Hamza Alavi, 'India and the Colonial Mode of Production', *Socialist Register, 1975*, ed. Miliband and Saville, pp. 160-97.

17. Aiden Foster-Carter, 'Can We Articulate "Articulation"?', *The New Economic Anthropology*, ed. John Clammer (London: Macmillan, 1978), p. 239.

18. Mahmood Mamdani, 'On the Colonial State and the Articulation of Modes of Production', *Politics and Class Formation in Uganda* (New York: Monthly Review Press, 1976), pp. 138-46; and E.A. Brett, 'Relations of Production, the State and the Ugandan Crisis', *West African Journal of Sociology and Political Science*, vol. 1, no. 3 (1978), pp. 249-84.

19. Pierre-Phillippe Rey, *Les alliances de classes* (Paris: Maspero, 1973), p. 70, as cited in Foster-Carter, 'Can We Articulate "Articulation"?', p. 229.

20. Tom Nairn, 'The Modern Janus [Nationalism]', *New Left Review*, no. 94 (November-December 1975), pp. 3-29.

21. Johan Galtung, 'A Structural Theory of Imperialism', *Journal of Peace Research*, vol. 8, no. 2 (1970), pp. 81-117.
The trade composition index =

$$\frac{(a + d) - (b + c)}{a + d + b + c},$$

where

a = the value of raw materials imported,
b = the value of raw materials exported,
c = the value of processed goods imported, and
d = the value of processed goods exported.

The index tends to be very crude with respect to the degree of processing; moreover, it relies on trade to infer the internal structure of an economy. Hypothetically, a nation could be highly self-reliant and still have a negative trade composition index.

22. On the latter phenomenon, see Otto Kreye, *World Market-Oriented Industrialization of Developing Countries* (Starnberg, FRG: Max Planck Institute, 1977).

23. Sanjaya Lall, 'Is "Dependence" a Useful Concept in Analysing Underdevelopment?', *World Development*, vol. 3, nos. 11-12 (1975), pp. 799-810.

24. Dieter Senghaas, 'Reflections on a Contextual Analysis of Dependency Structure', Paper presented to the International Peace Research Institute Seminar on Dependency Structures, Oslo, March 1975.

25. Benjamin Cohen, *The Question of Imperialism* (New York: Basic Books, 1973).

26. Samir Amin, 'Towards a New Structural Crisis of the Capitalist System?', *Multinational Firms in Africa*, ed. Widstrand, pp. 3-25.

27. Wallerstein, 'The Rise and Future Demise', pp. 4-5, 19.

28. Richard Caves, ' "Vent for Surplus" Models of Trade and Growth', *Trade, Growth and the Balance of Payments*, ed. Robert Baldwin and others (Chicago: Rand McNally, 1965), pp. 95-115.

29. Cohen, *The Question of Imperialism*, pp. 214-15.

30. Johan Galtung, 'Violence, Peace and Peace Research', *Journal of Peace Research*, vol. 6, no. 3 (1969), pp. 167-91.

31. Capitalist (tenant) farmers are growers who regularly employ wage-labour on their own or rented land to produce commodities. Although these capitalist farmers are rarely wealthy and usually operate on a small scale with rudimentary techniques, the alternate labels of kulaks, yeomen and progressive farmers have even more unfortunate connotations.

32. Richard Sklar, 'Post-Imperialism', *Comparative Politics*, vol. 9, no. 1

(October 1976), p. 83.

33. Immanuel Wallerstein, 'Dependence in an Interdependent World', *The Capitalist World-Economy*, pp. 66-94.

34. Robert W. Cox, 'Ideologies and the New International Economic Order', *International Organization*, vol. 33, no. 2 (Spring 1979), pp. 257-302; and Geoffrey Barraclough, 'Waiting for the New Order', *New York Review of Books*, vol. 25, no. 16 (26 October 1978).

35. Paul M. Sweezy, ' Socialism in Poor Countries', *Monthly Review*, vol. 28, no. 5 (October 1976), pp. 1-13; and Wallerstein, 'Dependence in an Interdependent World'.

36. Cox, 'Ideologies and the New International Economic Order', p. 283.

37. Samir Amin, 'Strategies for the Future of Africa', Discussion Paper, Council for the Development of Economic and Social Research in Africa (CODESRIA), Dakar, July 1980; and Clive Y. Thomas, *Dependence and Transformation* (New York: Monthly Review Press, 1974).

1 TRANSFORMATION INTO DEPENDENCE, 1888-1922

The economic history of Uganda since 1888 has several dimensions. At one level it is the history of struggles over ownership and control of the means of production. At the same time it is the history of the emergence of new socio-economic strata and of changes in the social relations of production. Finally, it is the history of the transformation of the economic structure itself, of shifts in the orientations of the economy, and of changes in what was produced, how and for whom. The great transformation of Uganda's economic structure in the period 1888-1922 marked both its unification and its incorporation into the capitalist world system.

Map 1: Peoples and States of Nineteenth-century Uganda (1967 boundaries for reference only)

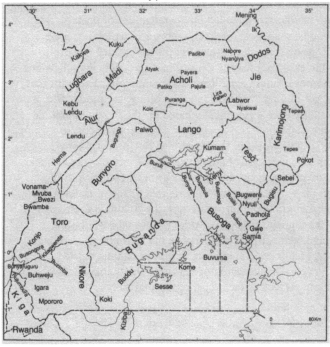

It is misleading to speak of *the* Ugandan economy prior to 1888, for there were many economies, each with its own division of labour. Although largely self-sufficient, these economies were not isolated. They were linked by local and regional trade (and tribute) in salt, iron, hoes, cattle, grain, dried fish, bananas, copper, tobacco, coffee, pottery, barkcloth and domestic slaves.[1] The prevalence of non-indigenous crops in Uganda demonstrates the extent of indirect contact with the outside world over the centuries. Supplementing indigenous sorghum and millet, cultivators had succeeded in adapting bananas, cassava, yams, sweet potatoes, maize, groundnuts, pulses, gourds, sesame (sim-sim) and ficus (for barkcloth) to local conditions. Many cultivators mulched their crops and practised intercropping and crop rotation; in areas of low population density some could afford the luxury of shifting cultivation. The extension of cultivation had altered the landscape of Uganda, permitting animal husbandry on grazing land freed from the tsetse fly and sleeping sickness (trypanosomiasis).[2] Blacksmiths in Bunyoro, Nkore, Kakwa, Lugbara, Koki, Acholi and Labwor made hoes, spears and knives from local or imported iron. Salt from Katwe and Kibero was exported over a wide area and often served as currency, as did hoes. In Acholi and other areas salt was manufactured from plant ashes. In northern Uganda, grain cultivators built granaries and milled flour. Other Ugandan handicrafts included the manufacture of pottery, fish-nets, leather goods, soap, beer, baskets, canoes and barkcloth. State formation in Uganda from the thirteenth century onward was itself linked to the increased population density made possible by indigenous technological innovations in agriculture and handicrafts. Yet, with the exceptions of salt-mining, iron-working and fishing, the production of the means of subsistence was generally based on the family household rather than on social labour. Compulsory social labour or *corvée* built roads and public works in the kingdoms. Reciprocal communal labour, by which neighbouring households helped one another at busy times in the agricultural cycle, appeared to be most common among the Langi with their prodigious use of *wang tic* (village work line), the Iteso, the Bagisu in *kibaga* and work parties, the Acholi in their *awak*, the Alur, and, excluding tillage, the Bakiga (house-raising, hunting, beer-brewing and water-trough digging) and the Karimojong (herding associations). A highly eclectic mixture of labour regimes existed among the Alur: *corvée* cultivation of fields for chiefs and chieflets, domestic serfdom, as well as reciprocal communal labour.[3]

Peoples and Polities of Nineteenth-century Uganda

Because of migrations, conquests, intermarriage and assimilation over
the past two millennia and the increasing tempo of political and technological change during the past five centuries, there are no pure ethnic
groups in Uganda in the colonial sense of 'tribes' or 'physiognomic
races'. The present 'tribes' of Uganda are at least partially the product
of amalgamations and divisions imposed by the colonial occupation.
Nevertheless, the diversity of peoples and polities in nineteenth-century
Uganda can be illustrated in terms of languages and socio-political
structures.

Within the present boundaries of Uganda there were at least 63
distinct languages in the nineteenth century, spoken by groups ranging
in size from a few thousand (the Ik) to a million (the Baganda).
According to Greenberg's taxonomy of African languages, the 26
languages in northern and eastern Uganda belong to six sub-groups of the
Nilo-Saharan family of languages: Lwoo (Luo), Central Paranilotic,
Kalenjin, Nyangia, Bari and Moru-Madi, of which the first five are
Eastern Sudanic and the sixth, Central Sudanic, sub-groups of the extensive Chari-Nile group. The 37 Bantu languages in southern and western
Uganda belong to the Niger-Congo group of the Congo-Kordofanian
family of languages.

Within Uganda, the Lwoo sub-group includes the Alur (also Jonam
dialect), Acholi and Palwo in the northwest and north and Padhola in
the southeast (Budama). The Central Paranilotic sub-group in the northeast quarter is represented by Teso (Iteso-Iworopom), Jie, Dodos,
(Ngadotho), Napore and Karimojong (Ngakarimojong). Lango, Kumam
(Ikokolemu), Nyakwai and Labwor in central Uganda are probably Lwoo-
Central Paranilotic hybrid languages. The Kalenjin sub-group includes
Pokot (Suk) and Sebei (Kupsabiny), both in the east. Nyangiya, Tepes
(Tepeth) and Ik (Teuso) in the northeast belong to the Nyangiya
sub-group. Kakwa and Kuku in the northwest and Mening (Kaabong,
a Lotuho dialect) in the northeast belong to the Bari cluster of Eastern
Sudanic languages. In the northwest are also languages of the Central
Sudanic Moru-Madi sub-group: Lugbara (Terego, Marach and Aringa
dialects), Madi (Okollo, Ogoko, Moyo and Oyuwi dialects), Lendu, and
Kebu, plus Mvuba in western Uganda.

From west to east the Bantu languages in Uganda include the
following (listed by name of the state or people, with language in parentheses): Rwanda (Runyarwanda), Kiga, Rujumbura, Bunyaruguru,
Busongora, Konjo, Bwamba (Kwamba), Bwezi (Lubwisi), Vonama,

Mpororo (Ruhororo), Igara, Buhweju, Toro (Rutooro), Kitagwenda, Buzimba, Nkore (Runyankore), Bunyoro (Runyoro), Bugungu, Kiziba, Koki (Lukooki), Buddu, Buganda (Luganda), Buruli, Bunyara, Sesse, Kome, Buvuma, Busoga (Lusoga), Bugabula (Ludiope), Bulamogi, Busiki, Kenyi, Bugwere, Nyuli (Lunyole), Samia, Gwe and Bugisu (Masaba).[4]

In terms of socio-political structures, nineteenth-century Uganda contained at least 200 distinct political entities. Busoga and Acholi each contained more than 50 mini-states, as did Alur-land stretching into Zaire.[5] Polities in Uganda ranged in size and complexity from centralised feudal kingdoms and loose confederations of mini-states to egalitarian, or at least less hierarchical, segmentary societies based on clans, lineages or age-sets.

Although it is true that the strongest states emerged in the Bantu-speaking south, one must reject the generalisation that the division between segmentary societies and hierarchical kingdoms coincided with the north-south division between Nilo-Saharan and Bantu language groups.[6] Kingdoms with feudal relations of production emerged in the north in the nine major kingdoms of the Acholi and among the Alur and the Palwo (Jo-pa-Lwoo or Chobe).[7] On the other hand, some Bantu-speakers, the Bagisu in the southeast and the Amba (Bwamba), Bakonjo and Bakiga in the southwest, organised themselves into segmentary clans and lineages with no internal *corvée*, although the latter two paid tribute to larger feudal kingdoms.[8]

On the whole, one can make a stronger case for an east-west rather than a north-south division in socio-political structures. The feudal-like kingdoms were concentrated in a western corridor extending from northern Uganda southward into Rwanda, Burundi and northwestern Tanzania. East and west of this corridor, which lay astride one of the major migration routes through Uganda, socio-political structures tended to be more egalitarian and less centralised. Within the north-south corridor arose the kingdoms in Acholi, Alur and Palwo as well as the better known Bantu interlacustrine kingdoms of Bunyoro-Kitara, Buganda, Nkore and Toro, plus Karagwe, Kiziba, Rwanda and Burundi beyond the southern borders of Uganda.

None the less, the more centralised kingdoms in the nineteenth century were the Bantu successor states of the legendary Kitara empire that had extended from Bunyoro to Karagwe in the fifteenth century. While the identity of the Chwezi rulers of Kitara remains shrouded in controversy, the subsequent Babito, Bahinda (Bahima) and Watusi dynasties of the Kitara successor states of Bunyoro, Nkore, Buganda,

Karagwe and Rwanda have been linked with the Jo-Bito, the royal
clan of Acholi and Palwo.[9] In Buganda the Babito dynasty was over-
thrown in the process of breaking away from Kitara, while in the óther
successor states the pastoral Jo-Bito aristocracy adopted the Bantu
languages of their subject cultivators. On the basis of the Jo-Bito
dynastic link plus trade and strategic factors, Bunyoro maintained
fairly good relations with Palwo, Acholi and Lango throughout the
nineteenth-century struggle between Bunyoro and Buganda for regional
supremacy. But even the two rival kingdoms engaged in trade with each
other as well as brief wars. Bunyoro exported salt from Kibero and,
when under its control, Katwe and iron hoes in return for Buganda's
barkcloth and *matoke* (plantain).[10]

According to one interpretation, the fact that Bunyoro had a time-
and labour-consuming culture based on grain, sweet potatoes and cattle,
while Buganda enjoyed a *matoke* culture, gave Buganda a cumulative
advantage in manpower and organisation.[11] Whatever the validity of
this hypothesis, Buganda was the stronger, more aggressive power when
the capitalist world economy penetrated the region in the nineteenth
century, despite Bunyoro's favourable access to ivory, control of major
salt-works and superiority in iron-working.

The Expansion of the World Economy into Uganda, 1800-88

It was the penetration of the Uganda economies by African (Nyamwezi,
Swahili, Baqqàra and Danàqla), Egyptian and Arab (Zanzibar-based
Umani) long-distance traders that marked the start of direct links with
the outside world economy. This external trade, consisting of exports
of ivory and some slaves and imports of firearms, cotton cloth and
trumpery (beads and copper wire), strengthened the already strong
states of Buganda and Bunyoro over the course of the nineteenth
century, to the general detriment of neighbouring states.

Sporadic trade between Buganda and the external world economy
dates to Kabaka (King) Kyabbugu's acquisition of plates and cups in
the mid-eighteenth century.[12] Until the 1830s Nyamwezi long-distance
traders enjoyed a virtual monopoly on southern routes between the
western interlacustrine kingdoms and Indian Ocean coast. In 1811
Captain Thomas Smee reported the Nyamwezi to be the major source
of ivory and slaves at Zanzibar.[13] However, notwithstanding the
increased demand between 1830 and 1873 for slave labour by Zanzibar
plantations producing cloves for the world economy, ivory became the

major export from southern Uganda, where the external demand for
its slaves was a function of the need for ivory porters and the singular
but steady market for Bahima concubines.[14]

But in northern Uganda the penetration by the world economy had
more disruptive effects, notably in West Nile, Madi and northern
Acholi. Between 1840 and 1862, the Khartoum-based plunder of
southern Sudanese ivory and slaves which helped finance Eygpt's entry
into the capitalist world system gradually extended beyond the natural
Sudd barrier into northern Uganda. The Khedive Ismā'īl (1863-79)
placed northwestern Uganda under nominal Egyptian control as part of
the Equatorial Province of the Sudan that included also northeast Zaire
and the Sudan south of Bahr al-Ghazāl. Egyptian attempts to suppress
the slave trade following the 1877 Slave Trade Convention failed. Emin
Pasha, governor of the Equatorial Province, complained that the
Egyptian government appeared more interested in 'the exploitation of
Africa for pecuniary ends' than in suppression of the slave trade.[15]
Greatly overextended, the Egyptian administration in the Sudan
imposed heavy grain taxes and 'nationalised' the ivory trade. This alienated the Danāqla traders, who joined the Mahdist rebellion (1881-98)
against Egyptian and British overrule.[16] By 1886 the slave trade in Bahr
al-Ghazāl and the Equatorial Province had ended, disrupted not by
Egyptian edicts but by upheavals in the wake of the Mahdist
rebellion.[17] By blocking Emin Pasha's export of ivory and import of
needed supplies, this rupture of the northern trade route reduced his
hitherto sympathetic but ineffectual administration to bands of
pillagers. That Madi and northern Acholi were the *only* areas in Uganda
infested by the tsetse fly prior to 1900 attests to the disruption of
agriculture caused by the northern trade and by the marauders of the
collapsing Equatorial Province administration.[18]

To the south, external trade left the pattern of domestic production
intact, while introducing cowrie-shell currency as the money of account
in internal and external trade.[19] External demand for ivory stimulated
such entrepreneurial activity as was required for hunting elephants and
collecting ivory by means of domestic trade, plunder and tribute.
Buganda, being densely populated, had few elephants and thus
plundered widely, extending its boundaries in the process. Trade with
the coast stimulated the demand for luxury goods among the dominant
strata of Buganda and Bunyoro. The introduction of firearms after
1840, and especially after 1860, although detrimental to the weaker
states of the region, helped Buganda and Bunyoro consolidate and
maintain state power in a time of rapid change and uncertainty caused

by the Egyptian threat and the influx of explorers, traders and missionaries. However, the proliferation of weapons among subordinates and
rival states also increased internal instability as did the introduction of
new ideologies and new belief systems. Christian missionaries and
Islamic traders sometimes functioned more as military attachés than as
earnest proselytisers.[20]

The rulers of Buganda armed their followers and allowed them and
the court pages to be taught the ideology of the foreigners: Islam,
Protestantism and Catholicism. Buganda court politics, traditionally
rife with factionalism, acquired a new overlay of religious conflict. It
was perhaps inevitable that the royal pages of Kabaka Mutesa's court
would eventually adopt a 'holier than thou' attitude towards the
Kabaka and the value system of his regime. Moreover, since the administrative *bakungu*[21] chiefs of the kingdom were recruited from the court
pages, within a generation (1850-85) the factionalism of the royal court
spread to the entire countryside.

These *bakungu* chiefs ultimately deposed Kabaka Mutesa's successor,
Kabaka Mwanga II, in the long revolution of 1888-1900. The revolution transformed relations of production in Buganda by making land
a commercial commodity, whose market value depended on its suit-
ability for production of commodities for the world market. The
success of this revolution was in turn dependent on external factors,
notably British overrule and the reduction in transport costs effected
by the completion of a railway to the Indian Ocean. None the less, it
was the success of the *bakungu* chiefs in controlling changes in land
tenure between 1890 and 1900 that determined the *form* of Uganda's
incorporation into the capitalist world system.

External Factors: Pre-emptive Imperialism and the Uganda Railway, 1873-1902

The external impetus for the initial penetration of Uganda by the world
economy originated in the European industrial expansion of 1815-73,
specifically the strong demand for African ivory in India, Europe and
the United States, and the integration of Egypt and Zanzibar into the
vertical international division of labour as producers of cotton and
cloves, respectively.[22] The external impetus for Uganda's final incorporation into the world system came from the attempts of leading
European industrial nations to surmount the crisis of 1873.

British textile manufacturers were able to escape the worst effects of the crisis by continuing to shift exports of cotton piece-goods from the intensely competitive European and American markets to the protected market in British India. In the 1880s exports of cotton textiles still accounted for one-third of total British exports; in terms of volume, India absorbed between 40 and 45 per cent of British exports of cotton piece-goods.[23] The cotton mills of Lancashire, having been shielded from the rigours of competition in the depression, were subsequently even less able to compete with the textile industries emerging in China, Japan and even India itself. Similar problems faced other leading branches of British industry *vis-à-vis* competitors in Europe and the United States. Manufacturing interests in other European nations sought to emulate British manufacturers' privileged access to the markets and raw materials of British India by obtaining their own colonies in Africa in the 1880s and 1890s.

Yet the European partition of Africa was largely a pre-emptive scramble, in that the fear of being shut out of potential future markets weighed more heavily than the prospects of immediate commercial gain.[24] Once under colonial occupation, the colonies had to be integrated into the international division of labour, if only to pay for the costs of administration. Rather than turning African colonies into protected markets on the British India model, the Congo Basin Treaties (1885 and 1919) allowed relatively free trade on the part of Britain, Belgium, Japan, Portugal, Italy and the United States in the Congo Basin and East Africa, while the Anglo-French Convention of 1898 extended the arrangement to West Africa.[25]

British interest in control of Uganda stemmed primarily from strategic considerations: guarding the trade route to India via Suez and ensuring Lancashire's supply of Egyptian long-staple cotton. From a commercial perspective, control of Uganda, British East Africa (Kenya) and Zanzibar would, it was argued, expand trade between India and East Africa to the benefit of British trade and investments in India and British shipping in the Indian Ocean. In the opinion of the London Chamber of Commerce:

> As long as England continues to hold India, her interest in the Red Sea, the Suez Canal and in Egypt, can hardly diminish. As long as England is interested in Egypt she cannot remain indifferent to the state of the Nile, on the fertilizing waters of which so much of the prosperity of Egypt depends. The retention of Uganda is thus as much connected with Egypt as with East Africa. Moreover, the trade of India with Africa is growing rapidly, and it is probable that in a

few years East Africa, Uganda and Zanzibar will be more valuable to India than directly to ourselves. If India is prosperous, its prosperity will react on our markets . . . There should be no hesitation on the ground of present cost . . . It is mainly a matter of international competition . . . We can tolerate no other power on the Nile . . . unless we decide also to retire from Egypt and to have access to India and Australasia only via the Cape.[26]

But there was hesitation on the part of the British government, particularly the Colonial Office, precisely on the ground of present cost.[27] The government granted a royal charter to the Imperial British East Africa Company (IBEA) in 1887 to open East Africa to legitimate commerce to replace the allegedly widespread slave trade. Financial backing and public support for the IBEA came from many sources, notably persons active in the anti-slavery movement and the Church Missionary Society (CMS). The CMS, which had established an Anglican mission in Buganda in 1877, viewed the IBEA as an important ally in the increasingly violent political factionalism in Buganda in the 1890s. The vice-president and treasurer of the CMS, Thomas Fowell Buxton, served as a director of the IBEA. When the IBEA threatened to withdraw from Uganda at the end of 1891 because of the British government's refusal to provide subsidies for administration and the planned railway, it was the CMS which raised £16,500 to postpone the withdrawal and launched the publicity campaign which ultimately persuaded the government to assume the financial burdens of empire in Uganda in 1894.[28]

The IBEA's attempt at private colonialism ended in bankruptcy, but shareholders succeeded in obtaining partial compensation from Parliament. More importantly, the other companies in the IBEA-Mackinnon group survived both the death of William Mackinnon in 1893 and the disappearance of the IBEA. Having succeeded in shoving the costs of administration and railway building onto the British government and the people of Uganda, these private firms reaped profits from the eventual incorporation of Uganda into the world economy. The surviving Mackinnon firms were based in India (Mackinnon, Mackenzie and Company), Zanzibar (Smith-Mackenzie and Company) and in shipping (British and India Steam Navigation Company).[29]

The barrier to the integration of Uganda into the world economy prior to 1900 was not the lack of a suitable export, for samples of agricultural produce from Uganda had already proven their ability to fetch world prices in the London market, but rather the extraordinarily high cost of transportation. Prior to completion of the railway in 1902, transportation of goods between Uganda and Mombasa relied primarily on caravans of human porters, supplemented by teams of ox-drawn carts in the late 1890s. These caravans were in effect slave caravans since most of the porters in any given caravan were not free wage-labourers but slaves hired from their masters. Slave porters were required to remit up to three-fourths of their wages to their owners. Lugard described as a 'paltry subterfuge' the European pretence that rented slave porters were voluntary wage-labourers. 'Rent-a-slave' caravans were used by Burton, Speke, the missionary societies, the IBEA, the railway survey party, Arabs, Indians, Germans and others. Even the British naval vessels based at Zanzibar to suppress the slave trade employed slaves to load coal.[30]

Aside from moral aspects, the 'rent-a-slave' system was odious to the employer because of its expense. In addition to paying a 'wage' to the slave, which was primarily a rent passed on to the slave owner for use of his property, the employer had to provide the slave with subsistence in kind. In the competititon among European, Arab, Swahili and Indian trading caravans, employers shaved costs where possible, namely on the subsistence in kind to the slave porter.

Human porters and ox-drawn carts limited the goods that Uganda could export to luxury goods, such as ivory, which could bear the transport charge of £130 to £300 per ton between Uganda and the coast. Even ignoring the cost of production in Uganda and transport from Mombasa to London or Bombay, the world price of staples, say coffee at £70 to £90 per ton, could cover only a fraction of the Uganda-Mombasa transport cost by caravan. Hence it was the railway which allowed Uganda to be integrated into the world economy as a producer of staples by cutting the Kisumu-Mombasa transport cost to £2.40 per ton and the Kampala-Kisumu-Mombasa transport time from three months to six days.[31]

The Uganda Railway, surveyed and built between 1891 and 1902, cost the British government £5.3 million. Yet why did the British government in 1895 assume the financial burden of building the railway, *prior* to the establishment of the cash-crop economy in Uganda which would make it viable? Debates in the British House of Commons regarding the railway would lead one to believe the railway was motivated almost solely by the desire to eliminate the slave trade, as pledged at the Brussels Conference in 1890, and by expectations of commercial gain following completion of the railway.[32] The first motive strains credulity in the basic practicality of British politics; the second strains credulity in the basic short-sightedness of parliamentary politics. Clearly expectations of more immediate benefit must have remained unstated.

Three unstated motives, one strategic and two commercial, lay behind the 1895 decision to complete the railway. The strategic motive was to secure the Nile River against the French, Germans and Belgians.[33] The first commercial motive was the desire to gain British control over the Indian-financed Arab and Swahili trading networks in East Africa by building the British-controlled railway.[34] However, the building of the railway provided even more immediate financial gain to British suppliers of steel, locomotives and rolling stock and to the British shipping interests.

As in the contemporary case of 'foreign aid', the building of the Uganda Railway was a form of export subsidy rather than a form of capital-money transfer.[35] Fully £2.3 million was spent in Britain for rails and locomotives. Less than £1 million was spent in India for rolling stock and labour recruitment; less than £0.2 million in the United States for locomotives; and finally the remainder in East Africa for wages and local food supplies. British shipping firms transported 305,000 tons of material from west of Suez and 41,000 tons of material and 32,000 indentured labourers from India for the project. The costs of the railway were ultimately borne by the British taxpayer.[36]

The use of Indian contract labour rather than African labour was dictated by the fact that Africans were, for presumably perverse reasons, 'unable to discriminate between contract labour and slavery', whereas India appeared to be a bottomless source of this cheap form of labour, thanks to years of the British civilising mission. The replacement of the African slave-porter caravans by the railway resulted in the death of 2,493 Indian labourers and the disabling of a further 6,454.[37] Such was the human cost of the transport revolution in East Africa.

Hence the establishment of British overrule in Uganda consisted of a series of events between 1886 and 1902: the declaration of IBEA control in 1890; the division of spheres of influence between Britain and Germany in 1886 and 1890; the establishment of a Protectorate over Uganda in 1893-4; the exclusion of French influence in the Fashoda incident of 1898; and the completion of the railway which ensured British military control. The economic transformation of Uganda in the period 1900-22 resulted from the interplay of these external factors and the long revolution in Buganda.

Consolidation of British Overrule and African Resistance and Collaboration

Although Britain's sphere of influence in East Africa had been demarcated in treaties with the Umani Sultan of Zanzibar and in agreements with Germany in 1896 and 1890, the course and pace of Britain's fitful occupation of Uganda was determined more by the unfolding pattern of local African resistance and collaboration and by the pressure to make the occupation self-financing, than by lines drawn on maps in Zanzibar and Europe.

Northern Uganda's 'Egyptian' period of administration ended in 1899, when Stanley engineered Emin Pasha's ragged retreat to Zanzibar.[38] Left behind were remnants of the Equatorial Province's military force, the Sudanese or 'Nubian' soldiers. These survived, as they had under Emin, by pillaging the countryside. Omukama (King) Kabalega (1870-99) of Bunyoro had maintained correct and even friendly relations with Emin Pasha's administration. Yet Kabalega was viewed as anti-British because Bunyoro had successfully resisted incorporation into the Equatorial Province following the 1872 clash between Baker and Kabalega at Masindi.[39] Under Kabalega, Bunyoro attempted to regain its former dominant status in the northern interlacustrine region. The *Abarusura*, the standing army founded by Kabalega, reconquered Toro in 1876 and staged raids into Palwo, both of which had seceded in 1830. By occupying the salt-works at Lake Katwe in Toro, Bunyoro regained its virtual monopoly on the salt trade in the region. Buganda made two unsuccessful attempts to extort salt from Bunyoro, demanding 1,000 loads of salt in the 1880s and 500 loads of salt in 1892.[40]

Although Bunyoro successfully exploited its salt monopoly and its superior iron products in the northern interlacustrine trade, its weak access to external trade routes prevented it from fully exploiting the ivory resources of the Lake Albert region. The expansion of the northern trade route via the Nile to Khartoum was hampered by the difficulty of navigating through the vast swamp of the Sudd and by the Egyptian nationalisation of the ivory trade. The Mahdist rebellion completely blocked the northern route between 1882 and 1896. As for the southern routes, these were controlled by Buganda and Nkore. Not only did Buganda control the land routes through Buddu and Koki to Karagwe and the lake route to Uzinza, but Kabakas Mutesa and Mwanga shrewdly used this control of the southern routes to regulate the entry of Arab and Swahili traders into Bunyoro. The Nkore route was closed by Omugabe (King) Ntare V in 1885, possibly in retaliation against *Abarusura* raids.[41]

In 1890 Lugard forced Kabaka Mwanga to sign a treaty giving the IBEA formal control over Buganda's external relations in return for IBEA 'protection'.[42] The Baganda chiefs and the IBEA launched a joint military campaign in the following year to drive Kabalega's forces out of Toro. The *Abarusura* fled before the Maxim gun of the invaders. For the Baganda chiefs, the expedition served to end Bunyoro's control over Toro and the Katwe salt-works by installing Prince Kasagama as 'puppet' Omukama of Toro with Yafeti Byakweyamba, a Buganda 'citizen' of Bunyoro extraction, as royal adviser. For the IBEA, the campaign achieved three goals: (1) securing desperately needed additional sources of revenue through control of the salt and ivory trade in the region; (2) linking up with the remnants of Emin Pasha's military force on the western shore of Lake Albert to reduce the IBEA's military dependence on Buganda; and (3) setting up a string of forts between Toro and Bunyoro, guarded by the 1,000 Sudanese troops, to check Bunyoro's resurgence southward. Signing a standard IBEA treaty, Kasagama agreed to IBEA sovereignty over Toro, an IBEA monopoly in the ivory trade and Toro's assumption of the cost of IBEA administration and garrisons.[43] Buganda and Toro were now nominal IBEA dependencies.

Kabalega's attempts to recapture Toro led to the 1892 ultimatum in which Buganda and the IBEA demanded an end to Bunyoro's raids in Toro and a recompensation tribute of 80 tusks, 600 hoes and 500 sacks of salt. Against the advice of his mother and three generals of the *Abarusura* (Rwabudungo, Ireeta and Nyakamutura), Kabalega rejected the ultimatum and continued the raids. It was in late 1893, during the transition from IBEA company rule to direct British overrule,[44] that a combined Baganda-British force launched a massive retaliatory invasion of Bunyoro. Colonel Colvile led the British officers and Sudanese troops, while Semei Kakungulu led a force of 14,000 Baganda irregulars. Major battles continued until early 1895, with Kabalega being forced to retreat north and finally east into Lango. By April 1894 the British controlled the Kibero salt-works on Lake Albert and had allowed Buganda to annex large areas of southern and eastern Bunyoro, which became known as the 'lost counties'. Most Banyoro chiefs surrendered to the British by mid-1895, but Kabalega and a small band of monarchist followers switched to guerrilla tactics and continued harrassing both occupation forces and collaborators.[45]

Kabaka Mwanga, whose control of Buganda had become dependent

on the *bakungu* administrative chiefs following a rebellion in 1888,
staged his own rebellion in 1897 against the increasingly dominant
coalition of British officials and Baganda chiefs. With a group of Muslim
supporters, he too turned to guerrilla warfare against British overrule.
However, the fact that the *bakungu* chiefs, led by the Regency of
Apolo Kagwa, Stanislaus Mugwanya and Zarkaria Kisingiri, were able to
continue administering Buganda, unimpeded by Mwanga's defection,
demonstrated the hollowness of the post-1888 Kabakaship.

A more substantial challenge to British overrule erupted in
October, 1897, when the Sudanese troops employed by the Protectorate also rebelled. Fatigued by constantly changing assignments, bitter
over pay in arrears and angry at being ordered to abandon their families
and link up with the British expedition against the Mahdist government
in the Sudan, the Sudanese garrisons in eastern Uganda mutinied and
marched on Kampala. They were stopped at Luba's Fort east of Jinja
by 3,000 Baganda irregulars and 'loyal' Sudanese, led from the rear
by British officers and CMS missionaries. The mutiny was then crushed
by reinforcements from Machakos (near Nairobi) and Indian troops
travelling inland via the partially completed railway.[46]

Meanwhile, following his escape from German captors in Tanganyika,
Mwanga and his followers made their way through Nkore and the
Buganda-Bunyoro border zone into Lango and linked up with Kabalega,
his old foe. They were both captured there in 1899 and deported to the
Seychelles.[47] The extension of British occupation forces into Nkore
and Lango was largely a consequence of the campaign against Mwanga
and Kabalega. Between 1901 and 1907, Buganda's control over the
remainder of Bunyoro expanded rapidly under the 'Ganda agent'
administration organised by Jemusi (James) Miti.[48]

Semei Kakungulu, frustrated in his quest for high office in Buganda,
persuaded Johnston to dispatch him into eastern Uganda to eliminate
remaining pockets of mutineers and rebels. Kakungulu proceeded to
build his own eastern empire, proclaiming himself Kabaka of Bukedi,
which embraced Bukedi, Bugisu and Teso. His garrisons and colonies
effectively set the eastern boundaries of Uganda by limiting the 1902
land transfer to British East Africa (Kenya) to territory east of his
empire. Following the 1905 Budama uprising against his oppressive
tax collectors, he was transferred to Busoga, where he presided over the
local Lukiko and transformed the administrative system, making it
highly lucrative for the colonial state, chiefs and headmen. In 1913
Kakungulu was effectively retired to Mbale in the down-graded but
well-paid role of *saza* chief. The remaining boundaries of the Uganda

Protectorate were determined by a series of transfers among the European powers between 1910 and 1915 and by a final transfer of Rudolph Province to Kenya in 1926.[49]

Revolution in Buganda, 1888-1900

The temporary overthrow and exile of Kabaka Mwanga in 1888 by Muslim chiefs in alliance with Christian chiefs marks the start of the bourgeois revolution in Buganda which was to replace the absolute monarchy with a constitutional monarchy and transform land into a commodity. The Muslim chiefs soon drove away their Christian allies. However, the Christian chiefs formed an alliance with the exiled Kabaka, staged a raid on an Arab trading caravan to secure arms and succeeded in returning Mwanga to the throne in 1889 as a nominal Catholic. The Muslim chiefs and their supporters were exiled to the northwestern fringes of the kingdom.[50]

The power of the restored Kabaka was diminished by his indebtedness to the Christian *bakungu* chiefs. For their part, the Christian chiefs were aware that their newly achieved supremacy would be tenable only if the exiled Muslims failed to strike an alliance with the Omukama Kabalega in Bunyoro or with soldiers of the crumbling Egyptian administration in the Equatorial Province. The Christian chiefs themselves sought external allies against this threat but disagreed as to whether aid should be sought from the French or the English. The Catholic and Protestant chiefs were divided into the *Bafalanza* (French) and *Bangereza* (English) factions, respectively.[51]

When Lugard arrived at Mengo, the capital, in 1890 as agent of the IBEA, the Christian chiefs were deeply embroiled in disputes about control of land and usufruct. These disputes demonstrate that possession of land and usufructuary rights rather than possession of political office was the base of economic and political power in Buganda. Notwithstanding the Kiganda proverb that 'a chief does not rule land, he rules people',[52] rule over people in Buganda depended on control of land and usufruct. The common people were neither serfs bound to the land nor slaves owned by chiefs. They were free to move to the domain of another chief if a ruler placed overly onerous demands on them in terms of rent, taxes and *corvée*. Competing Protestant and Catholic factions began to view land as a commodity in that the better agricultural land with reliable rainfall would attract and keep subjects willing to pay rent and taxes.[53] The competition for land took the form of competition for *bakungu* administrative offices associated with particular tracts of land at the county (*saza*) and sub-county (*gombolola*) levels.

A treaty between the Protestants and Catholics in October 1889 had divided chiefly offices, hence land and subjects, approximately equally between the two factions. However, whether due to Kabaka Mwanga's adhesion to Catholicism in this period or due to the general ascendancy of the Catholic faction at the time, the Protestant faction in 1891 found its position eroding as commoners and sub-chiefs converted to Catholicism. The converts, though still cultivating 'Protestant' land, paid their rent and taxes to Catholic chiefs and would perform *corvée* only for Catholic chiefs. Seeking to arrest its political and economic decline, the Protestant faction proposed that a total of 600 chiefly offices and associated tracts of land be permanently divided between the two factions and that conversion be grounds for eviction or dismissal (in the case of a chief) unless the convert continued contributing surplus to his former allegiance. Nothing came of the proposal.[54]

With the assistance of IBEA troops and CMS missionaries, the Protestant faction defeated the Catholic faction in the 1892 Battle of Mengo. Katikiro (Prime Minister) Apolo Kagwa led the Protestant forces, while Stanislaus Mugwanya, in Mwanga's absence, led the Catholic forces.[55] Kabaka Mwanga returned after peace was restored and ruled until his 1897 uprising with two Katikiros, Kagwa and Mugwanya, representing the two factions.

By 1896 the two Katikiros and the Kabaka had commercial plantations producing coffee, rice and wheat. On British advice, they encouraged other chiefs to plant coffee, rice, cotton, tobacco, groundnuts, sesame and sunflowers to supplement declining ivory exports. However, the embryonic British colonial administration at Entebbe blocked Kabaka Mwanga's purchase of a sawmill from the CMS, citing the poor condition of the equipment and the general shortage of labour and engineers. Fear of African competition in manufacturing might well have been the real reason behind this decision since the Kabaka had access to *corvée* labour and could easily bid Asian and Arab engineers away from the colonial administration. Small tracts of land were given or sold to Europeans, particularly the missions, but European firms attempted with little success to obtain larger land concessions for plantations.[56] What is important is not so much the magnitude of the early African commercial plantations and land sales as their demonstrative effects in accelerating the commercialisation of land tenure.

When Harry Johnston arrived in Buganda in 1900, with instructions from the Foreign Office to negotiate an agreement with the Regents (Kagwa, Mugwanya and Kisingiri) and the *bakungu* chiefs on land tenure and fiscal support for the colonial administration, the now dominant Protestant faction shifted from its 1891 position of ownership by faction to ownership of land by individuals. Both Johnston's original proposal and the *bakungu* chiefs' counter-proposals implicitly recognised that land would henceforth be a marketable commodity. What were at issue were the following points: (1) how much land would be allocated to the chiefs and their supporters; (2) how much land would be allocated to the colonial administration as forest reserves and as 'Crown Land' for future sale to non-African planters, settlers and concession companies; (3) whether the Baganda or the British would get first choice in the selection of land; (4) whether the colonial state or African landowners would retain mineral rights on private land; and (5) under what conditions land owned by Africans could be alienated to non-Africans.

Johnston wanted the bulk of land in Buganda, and for that matter Uganda, to be Crown Land as a source of revenue to the colonial administration. Accordingly, he initially offered the chiefs 156 square miles (40,435 hectares) of freehold estates for the royal family, ministers and county chiefs, with the remainder being Crown Land, alienable 'tribal' land on which the colonial state retained mineral rights.

Recognising that this proposal would amount to the semi-proletarianisation of all but the immediate royal family, the Regents and the 20 county (*saza*) chiefs, the *bakungu* chiefs led by Kagwa rejected Johnston's proposal. By dint of their bargaining skills, backed by the veiled threat of anarchy, bloodshed and chaos, the chiefs eventually won recognition of allodial ownership, rather than ordinary freehold, of private estates totalling 8,385 square miles (2.17 million hectares), including mineral rights and control over the location and allocation of these private *mailo* estates, plus 573 square miles (0.15 million hectares) of non-inheritable *ex-officio mailo* estates for chiefs, ministers and royal officials, on which the colonial state retained mineral rights. The '1,000 chiefs and private landowners' thereby won control of over half the land in Buganda, including the better agricultural land with reliable rainfall totalling at least 30 inches annually. The Lukiko, the Buganda legislature established by the agreement, was not only charged with the task of allocating *mailo* estates but also reserved for itself ultimate control over alienation of *mailo* land to non-Africans.[57]

Those who berate Johnston for having misunderstood the traditional form of land tenure in Buganda and for having imposed a Western capitalist system of land tenure on a traditional society have themselves missed the point that it was the *bakungu* chiefs who imposed their bourgeois concept of land tenure on Johnston.[58] Johnston's 'generosity' was dictated by the weakness of the British colonial state in the aftermath of the 1897-9 rebellions.

The colonial state's military force consisted of two battalions totalling 1,520 troops and 45 officers, plus 1,060 policemen. For their part, the *bakungu* chiefs had at least 3,000 and possibly as many as 12,000 armed supporters. Even with the Maxim gun, the colonial state would have faced formidable odds and a costly, lengthy guerrilla war had the negotiations failed.[59] By securing its base in Buganda, the colonial administration could afford to take a tougher stance in negotiating land agreements elsewhere in Uganda, backed by the willingness of the Baganda chiefs to be sub-imperial conquerors and tax-farming administrators in Toro, Bunyoro, Busoga, Bukedi, Lango, Teso and Bugisu.[60]

The gun tax of three rupees (four shillings) per annum in the 1900 agreement was probably designed to have a confiscatory effect on all but the largest landowners. Political and administrative notables and those holding more than 500 acres were exempt from the tax. The agreement also confirmed the political ascendancy of the administrative chiefs by transforming the Kabakaship into a constitutional monarchy in which a major share of power rested with the Lukiko, which was to be filled largely on an *ex officio* basis by administrative chiefs.[61]

By imposing a hut tax of three rupees per annum on any dwelling (later changed to a poll tax on all adult males), the agreement solved at one stroke both the problem of making the colonial occupation self-financing and the problem of creating a 'voluntary' labour force. A performance clause (Article 20) bound the Kingdom of Buganda, in effect the Regents and the *bakungu* chiefs, to collect a minimum level of taxes annually proportionate to the estimated population or face abrogation of the land settlement, while guaranteeing a bonus if collections exceeded £45,000 per annum in two consecutive years. This level of tax collection was achieved in the 1905-6 fiscal year and all subsequent years. The fact that the total specie available in the whole of Uganda was only Rs. 650,000 (£48,750) as of 1 April 1903, illustrates the magnitude of the hut tax and later poll tax in relation to the monetary economy.[62]

Integration of Uganda into the International Division of Labour, 1900-22

In their dual capacity as landlords and administrative cadres, the *bakungu* chiefs put direct pressure on their tenant-subjects to produce for the world market. During the primitive capital accumulation of 1900-5, the chiefs in Buganda and Ganda agents and collaborators elsewhere stripped away from their tenant-subjects cattle, goats and anything else of commercial value to enrich themselves directly as tax farmers and landlords and to fulfil the performance clause in the 1900 agreement, guaranteeing the Buganda land settlement.[63]

The completion of the railway made available a vast array of imported goods in shops, further stimulating the acquisitive spirit of Buganda's status-conscious ruling class and collaborators elsewhere. Retail prices fell with lower transport costs, while control of trade shifted from Arabs and Swahilis to Indian and European immigrants. Former luxuries such as cotton piece-goods became simple necessities, and a new pattern of imported luxury consumption was brought into vogue: steel cutlery, corrugated iron roofing, enamelled ware, blankets, clocks, watches, boots, suits, linen and bicycles. By the end of 1904 hides and skins had supplanted ivory as the Protectorate's major export, supplemented by chillies and raw rubber. Between 1895 and 1904/5 total exports increased four-fold from £16,315 to £66,991; however, imports increased ten-fold from £14,800 to £149,737.[64]

Despite the strenuous and ruthless tax-collecting efforts of the African chiefs, the growing revenues of the colonial state fell far short of expenditures until 1914/15. The annual deficit fluctuated widely, averaging £52,821 between 1893/94 and 1896/97; £246,894 during the mutiny and wars against Kabalega and Mwanga, 1897/98-1900/01; £120,486 between 1901/02 and 1909/10, during final punitive expeditions against opponents of the new order; dropping to £57,148 between 1910/11 and 1913/14. Deficits were covered by grants-in-aid from Great Britain totalling £2.5 million between 1894 and 1915.[65]

Any British hopes of basing Uganda's future on European settlers and plantations, already precarious following the 1900 land settlement in Buganda, received a further setback in 1902, when the territory east of Bukedi, including the Kisumu terminus of the Uganda Railway and the highlands between Kisumu and Nairobi, was transferred to British East Africa (Kenya) for exploitation by its growing population of European settlers. By this transfer the Uganda Protectorate lost its revenue from the hut tax on Africans in the densely populated

Kavirondo area of what became Nyanza Province, Kenya.[66] In an effort
to increase both exports and revenues, the colonial state demanded
that the hut tax in the remainder of Uganda be paid in money or
corvée rather than by produce in kind (mainly cattle, hides and foodstuffs). This measure forced Africans producing solely for their own
consumption or for simple barter trade to enter the monetary economy
by either working one month on roads and buildings for the colonial
state or cultivating produce for sale in the world market.

The British commissioner at Entebbe viewed the imposition of the
money hut tax as a means of forcibly integrating Africans into the
international division of labour:

> With regard to products generally, the great difficulty is to get the
> native to cultivate the right kind, and in sufficient quantities. They
> live under such easy conditions as regards food that there has
> hitherto been no necessity, and but little inducement, for exertion.
> In this I have great hopes of the hut tax, which obliges those who
> cannot pay in cash to do a month's work for the Government, and if,
> as I trust, Uganda becomes a producing country on a large scale,
> it will be largely due to the effects of this measure . . . When once the
> people see that it is easier to bring a load of produce for sale to the
> merchants than to do a month's work on buildings and roads, and
> that there is money to be made, the inducement to extend cultivation
> will follow.[67]

Economic behaviour based on the rational requirements of the subsistence economy was labelled as laziness and indolence by colonial
administrators and planters, who took it for granted that production
for the world market was more rational than production for direct use
and appropriation by the producer. The economic behaviour demanded
by the new order must have seemed irrational, at least initially, to the
African peasant. Consider the case of cotton. The chief gives the
cultivator a quantity of seeds and orders him to grow an amount of
cotton which the cultivator knows to be far in excess of his own or
even the chief's requirements for consumption, a product which cannot
be eaten, but which requires that resources of land and labour be
shifted from food production, a product which requires much labour
and which is easily spoiled by rain. Why grow it at all? If the cultivator
protests, the chief beats him and informs him that the great *Kabaka ba
Bangereza* (King of the English) across the waters, whose troops wield
the terrible Maxim gun, demands this inedible product as tribute.

Reluctantly the cultivator grows the cotton, only to learn that he must also headload it into town. In return for this effort he receives some round pieces of metal, most of which are promptly confiscated by the chief as rent and taxes.[68]

Despite the understandable initial resistance of tenants to cotton cultivation, cotton production expanded rapidly in Uganda from 1903 onward, replacing hides and skins as the major export by 1907/08, thanks largely to the coercive methods employed by the chiefs and headmen. But why did Uganda initially specialise in cotton, rather than other staples such as cocoa, tea, rubber or coffee? Although Uganda may not have enjoyed any absolute advantage in the production of cotton, cotton enjoyed a comparative advantage over many staples in that it yielded the earliest return, a single crop season rather than several years. Time appeared scarce to both the administrative chiefs and the colonial state in the initial years after the 1900 agreement. Cotton seemed a logical choice for a crash programme of planting a commercial export crop. Moreover, the period 1902-5 was auspicious for cotton in the world market, whereas, to take one counter-example, coffee was at the bottom of its price cycle.[69]

By the turn of the century the United States had shifted from being primarily a semi-peripheral staple producer to being an industrial power and core-state in the world system. The growth of industry in the northern cities of the United States bid labour away from the cotton plantations of the southern states. In order to reduce its dependence on American cotton, the British textile industry established the British Cotton Growing Association in 1902 to promote cotton cultivation throughout the Empire for Lancashire textile mills. Africa, rather than India, was viewed as the area offering the best prospects for expanding long-staple cotton production.[70] Having been politically incorporated into the Empire to protect British access to the markets of India, Uganda was now to be economically integrated into the Empire to protect and expand Lancashire's supply of raw materials.

It was the Uganda Company, a commercial offshoot of the Church Missionary Society, which, in conjunction with the British Cotton Growing Association, the Uganda Protectorate government and the Baganda chiefs, initiated widespread cotton production in Uganda. With financial backing from wealthy CMS sympathisers in London, K. Borup launched the Uganda Company in 1903 around the nucleus of the former CMS Industrial Mission in Buganda. The previous year Borup had entered into discussions with the ministers of the Kingdom of Buganda to enlist their support in cotton promotion and to work out a system for seed distribution and cotton marketing. Borup obtained 2.5 tons of various varieties of cotton seeds from the British Cotton Growing Association in 1903 for distribution by 27 leading chiefs in Buganda. The Uganda Company entered into written contracts with the chiefs, the former agreeing to supply seeds and to buy the entire crop and the latter agreeing to distribute the seeds and encourage its cultivation by their tenant-subjects. A key aspect of the scheme was that the grower received a label with each seed packet that had to be returned with the harvested cotton to enable the company to identify the varieties most suitable for Uganda. At the same time the colonial state imported 1.5 tons of cotton seeds from Egypt for distribution by chiefs and headmen in Buganda and surrounding districts.[71]

The first cotton crop was harvested in 1904. Exports rose from 10 metric tons worth £236 in 1904/05 to 717 metric tons in 1908/09 worth £41,223. By 1915/16 cotton exports amounting to 4,768 metric tons earned £245,426, or 48.7 per cent of total exports. Grants-in-aid from Great Britain ended as revenues rose to £285,412, of which fully 65.8 per cent was derived from the poll tax on African males and 18.3 per cent from customs duties.[72]

Yet, despite the confident assumption by colonial administrators that 'even a very small field of cotton would give [the native] a yield in cash exceeding his greatest hopes', African tenant-farmers clearly regarded cotton cultivation as a duty imposed by the chiefs and the colonial administration rather than a boon in these early years.[73] At best cotton cultivation was viewed as a less arduous and demeaning way of paying taxes and rent and buying cloth for Sunday worship than the alternative of wage-labour for the colonial Public Works Department or European plantations. Significantly, the largest relative increases in cotton production occurred in 1906, 1910 and 1920 *following* correspondingly large increases in taxes and rent. In 1905 the Regents of Buganda succeeded in adding a poll tax of two rupees per adult male to the three-rupee hut tax to eliminate the tax-evading practice of crowding several families into a single hut. The chiefs and the colonial state in that year began demanding that rent of two rupees be paid in cash on plots on *mailo* estates and Crown Land. The hut tax was replaced in 1909 by a five-rupee poll tax on adult males in Buganda and Busoga and three rupees elsewhere. In Buganda rent was raised to three and one half rupees per holding in early 1910. Moreover, in the face of the rising demand for porters to carry cotton to market and for labourers to build roads and the increasing unwillingness on the part of Africans to do either, the colonial state in 1909 introduced the *kasanvu* system of coerced labour. Tenants who were not elsewhere employed were obligated to work one month for the Public Works Department at an arbitrarily set wage, which in turn tended to depress the market rate for voluntary wage-labour. By 1920 the *kasanvu* wage rate was 38 per cent below the depressed market wage.[74] Several avenues emerged for avoiding the unpopular *kasanvu* labour obligation: (1) working in alternate employment on European plantations, in cotton ginneries or as a last resort as a porter; (2) fleeing to Kenya; (3) bribing the chief to avoid being recruited; (4) establishing oneself as a self-employed artisan; and (5) saving enough money to buy a plot of land, thereby becoming an exempt landowner. The peasant could no longer engage only in subsistence food production, but had to increase his production of cash crops or enter the labour force. Cotton production doubled between 1909 and 1910. A substantial increase in cotton production also followed the 1919 increase in the poll tax to 7½ rupees in Buganda, Busoga, Teso, Bukedi and Bunyoro.[75]

Just as the high cost of human porterage had prevented Uganda's incorporation into the world market as a staple producer prior to the completion of the railway, so now it became apparent that the high cost of human porterage within Uganda limited the further expansion of cotton production to areas within walking range of the cotton ginneries. On a tour of outlying areas in Buganda in 1909, Governor Bell observed many plots of unharvested cotton.

> In answer to my enquiries, I was informed by some of the peasants that they had planted the cotton some months before in deference to the advice or orders of their chiefs, and that they had properly cultivated the plots. The idea of having now to carry their crops on their heads all the way to the ginneries at Kampala, ninety miles off, was, however much more than they were prepared to do, even to please their chiefs or the Government, and they declared that they would far sooner let the cotton rot on the bushes than be put to such intolerable trouble. I was furthermore assured that the price which the produce would fetch at Kampala would hardly pay for its transport, calculated at the current rates paid for porterage.[76]

Beyond Buganda, which at least had a good pre-colonial network of dry weather roads radiating from Mengo-Kampala, the situation was even worse. The magnitude of the transport problem can be illustrated by the Department of Agriculture's estimate that the 1914 crop in the Eastern Province (Busoga, Lango, Teso and Bukedi) represented ½ million porter loads. The demand for porters seriously threatened the precarious food supply in Busoga by drawing labourers away from the fields during the food planting season.[77]

It thus became necessary to expand the internal road network and to build cotton ginneries nearer areas of cotton cultivation. Although the use of motor transport did not become widespread until the mid-1920s, as early as 1909 motor vans supplemented ox carts and porters in bringing the cotton crop from growers to the ginneries. The development of Uganda's internal road network – extensive by African standards – owes much to the sheer bulkiness of seed cotton and the growers' refusal to headload the crop free of charge to the market. Ginneries which were scattered through the countryside required roads both to the growers and to the urban entrepôts and railways, roads built largely by *kasanvu* labour. Under the *kyalo* transport system which evolved in the 1920s, lorries owned by independent drivers and increasingly by the ginneries brought both the grower and his seed cotton to the ginnery market. The cost of this transport was initially borne by the ginneries, but was passed on to the growers in the form of lower prices.[78] The *kyalo* system failed to protect the grower from being short-changed, in that once he was at the ginnery the grower had to accept the weight and price determined by the ginnery or pay for transport elsewhere. However, it was a boon to the chiefs, who merely had to station themselves at the ginnery to collect both rent and taxes, as well as under-the-counter payments from the ginnery.

Areas beyond the expanding network of roads and ginneries, namely West Nile, Madi and Acholi, and areas not suitable for cotton or plantations, such as Ankole, became the labour reserves of the Protectorate, exporting migrant labourers to the urban centres and rural cotton areas and plantations to earn the required poll tax. The great boom in European and Asian-owned plantations between 1909 and 1922 was due primarily to the *kasanvu* labour obligation, which depressed wage rates. By 1920 there were 204 European plantations and at least 16 Asian plantations producing coffee, rubber and sugar. Yet cotton produced by African peasants continued to be the dominant export crop, and European plantations collapsed following the abolition of *kasanvu* labour in 1922. Increasing numbers of Baganda landowners started their own coffee plantations, while Baganda commoners began shunning all unskilled forms of wage-labour, preferring clerical and technical work. By 1919 two-thirds of the male population in Buganda had succeeded in obtaining exemption from *kasanvu* labour, the burden of which fell on the very old, the very young and the very poor. In response to the unpopularity of *kasanvu* and in response to their own desire for more labourers, the chiefs in the Lukiko joined the campaign against *kasanvu* in 1921.[79]

Meanwhile, the number of cotton ginneries in Uganda increased from 8 in 1905, to 20 in 1915, 37 in 1919 and 83 in 1922. The ginneries were located as follows in 1919, roughly in proportion to the size of the crop in each area: 6 in Kampala, 1 at Entebbe, 11 in Jinja and rural Busoga, 5 in Bukedi, 12 in Teso and 2 in Lango.[80] Whereas British firms and the colonial state owned the ginneries in 1905, other European firms and an Indian firm had entered the ginnery business by 1913. Control of the cotton ginning industry and the destination of cotton exports shifted dramatically during and following the First World War. Whereas almost the entire crop had been shipped to Liverpool in the first decade, the share of cotton shipped to Bombay rose from 12.5 per cent in 1915 to 54.3 per cent in 1918/19 and a peak of 91.5 per cent in 1935. Narandas Rajaran and Company, a Bombay textile firm, established its first ginnery in Uganda in 1916, buying and ginning cotton for its cloth mills in India. Of the 37 ginneries operating in Uganda in 1919, 20 were owned by British firms; 14 by Indian and India-based British firms; and 3 by a French firm. By 1923 Indian firms owned 59 of the 101 ginneries in Uganda.[81] Because of substantially lower salaries paid to Indian managerial and technical staffs, the Indian-owned ginneries were generally more profitable than their European competitors. Attempting to reduce costs, both European and Indian-owned ginneries increasingly resorted to child labour, even on night shifts.[82]

Although the growth of cotton exports to Bombay between 1914 and 1919 can be attributed to the First World War shipping crisis, which severely reduced direct trade between Europe and East Africa, this temporary interruption cannot account for the continuation of the trend after the war. At the end of the war, imported hoes from Europe once again supplanted the indigenous Bunyoro hoe industry, which had enjoyed a revival during the shipping crisis, but exports of cotton to Bombay continued to increase relative to direct exports to Liverpool.[83] Bombay became the entrepôt for Ugandan cotton destined for Lancashire and Japan as well as for Indian textile mills. The cause of this long-term shift in the direction of Uganda's cotton exports lay in the secular decline of Lancashire textiles, the rise of Japanese and Indian textiles and the penetration of the Ugandan cotton ginning industry by Indian firms.[84]

Despite Governor Bell's exaggerated fear that the entry of Indian firms into cotton ginning might lead to the establishment of Indian textile mills in Uganda, the Indian ginneries were far more interested in supplying India, Japan and England with long-staple cotton than in establishing a competitive textile industry in East Africa.[85] Ironically, it was the United States rather than Britain that initially dominated the textile import market in Uganda. From the late nineteenth century to 1916, unbleached calico cloth, or 'Americani', constituted the single most important import, accounting for approximately 10 per cent of Uganda's total imports betwee 1907 and 1917. Imports of Americani rose from 1.1. million yards in 1904/05, to 2.7 million yards in 1906/07 and 7.6 million yards in 1913/14. However, Britain fared better in higher quality bleached, printed, dyed and coloured textiles for which demand proved to be highly income elastic, while Japan and India supplanted the United States as the major supplier in the relatively stagnant market for Americani between 1916 and 1922. Holland displaced Germany in imports of cotton blankets after 1914. Overall, the British Empire accounted for 60.1 per cent of Uganda's total imports between 1907/08 and 1916/17, primarily from Britain and India.[86]

Costs of the New Order

The new order brought about by Uganda's integration into the vertical international division of labour as a producer of cotton and importer of manufactured goods brought general prosperity to the domestic ruling class of chiefs, provided they maintained the delicate balance between protecting their own interests and demonstrating loyalty to the colonial state. Benefits of the new order to the common man and woman were more mixed and unequally dispersed. Integration into the world system was accompanied or preceded by epidemics, wars of pacification, famine, forced labour, increased taxes and rent, conscription for war service and a sharp drop in population as well as by higher incomes for some, more consumer goods and the introduction of schools and hospitals.

Uganda's pre-colonial and early colonial contact with the external world economy brought severe consequences in the area of health. The introduction of new diseases created much of the havoc which figured prominently in the European explorers' accounts. Between 1876 and 1920 successive waves of black-quarter disease, pleuro-pneumonia, East Coast fever, rinderpest and sleeping-sickness reduced Uganda's cattle herds to a small fraction of their former size, causing havoc among the pastoral peoples in Karamoja, Acholi, Lango, Bunyoro and Ankole.[87] Weakened by food shortages caused both by cattle diseases and by the ravaging of grain crops by locusts, the pastoral peoples succumbed to smallpox and sleeping-sickness epidemics. Survivors resorted to cattle-raiding and inter-ethnic warfare in their attempts to rebuild their herds. The Jie survivors in Karamojong were saved by hunters from the northeast who supplied them with rifles, enabling them to hunt elephants and trade ivory for cattle.[88] According to Lugard, the Bahima in Nkore in southern Uganda were less fortunate. Large numbers starved after their cattle perished in the great rinderpest epidemic of the 1890s.[89] While many of the cattle epidemics which swept through eastern and southern Africa in the late nineteenth century seem to have been an unfortunate by-product of contact with the outside world, the famines and sleeping-sickness which befell much of the population of Uganda were the result of human as well as natural factors.

According to Kjekshus, containment of the tsetse-fly vector which carries sleeping sickness is dependent on the ability of agriculturalists to extend cultivation and control the migration of game.[90] Disruptions in cultivation caused by Emin Pasha's administration enabled the tsetse fly to obtain a foothold in the West Nile, Madi and northwest Acholi by the late nineteenth century. Following the Buganda-Bunyoro wars and the colonial campaigns against rebellions and mutinies in the 1890s, the tsetse fly spread quickly southward to the shores of Lake Victoria. Between 1895 and 1906 a massive sleeping-sickness epidemic struck southern Busoga and parts of Buganda, killing an estimated 200,000 people of a total population of 300,000 in southern Busoga.[91] The colonial state responded by ordering the chiefs to evacuate the entire population from the Buvuma and Sese Islands and from within two miles of the shores of Lake Victoria and the Nile. Settlement, hunting and fishing were banned in the affected areas. While these measures saved some lives in the short run, abandonment of the affected areas to brush and game provided ideal breeding conditions for the tsetse fly.[92]

A new disaster, famine, struck Busoga in 1908. In their eagerness to reap maximum personal benefits from the *bwesengeze* administrative system set up by Kakungulu, the chiefs and headmen pushed ahead with cotton cultivation to the neglect of food supplies. On their *bwesengeze*, or personal estates, the chiefs used *corvée* labourers to cultivate cotton and to transport the crop to market. The adult male population, already decimated by the sleeping-sickness epidemic, was thereby withdrawn from food production during the planting season. Furthermore, in their capacity as tax farmers for the colonial state, the chiefs and headmen compelled peasants to grow cotton on the remaining non-*bwesengeze* land to generate cash income for rent and taxes; a percentage of taxes accrued to the chiefs and headmen as income. The colonial state not only encouraged this single-minded policy of expanding cotton cultivation but also demanded *kasanvu* for road construction in Busoga. With one fifth the area and one third the population of Buganda, Busoga cultivated just 20 per cent less cotton than Buganda between 1911 and 1920. Serious food shortages were reported in Busoga in 1908, 1914, 1918, 1920, 1927 and 1928. The population declined from about one million in 1890 to 400,000 in 1908 and 220,000 in 1923, before recovering.[93] The chiefs prospered to the extent that the incomes of some exceeded those of the highest European administrators. In 1924 the *saza* chief of Bugabula county, Busoga, earned an estimated £3,500 from his estates and tax farming.[94] Although peasants could not eat cotton, Busoga demonstrated that cotton could devour peasants.

The ordinary peasant in Buganda was only slightly better off. Between 1900 and 1927 the land tenure system in Buganda combined the oppressive features of the feudal pre-colonial relations of production with the 'free' contractual obligations of emerging capitalist relations of production and new obligations to the European-controlled, European-administered colonial state. In contrast to the *métayage* system of early modern Europe, in which landlords provided tenants with seeds and implements as well as access to land in return for a share of the crop, the landlord in Buganda provided the tenant only with access to land in return for a tithe (*envujo*), ranging from 10 to 25 per cent of the crop, and rent (*busulu*), originally the *mpalo* obligation to work one month in the year on the chief's estate. Between 1902 and 1927 the *busulu* was gradually transformed from a labour obligation to money-rent equivalent to one month's wage. The fact that *envujo* tended to be higher on cash crops such as cotton and coffee than on food crops may have been a factor limiting cash-crop production in Buganda. In any event there were few food shortages reported in Buganda. On top of the tithe and rent came the communal *corvée*: unpaid *luwalo* for the Kingdom of Buganda and poorly-paid *kasanvu* for the colonial state, each amounting to one month's labour. The *luwalo corvée* involved work on local roads and buildings, but was sometimes misappropriated by the chief for his estate, leading to objections by European planters that the chiefs had unfair advantages. Between 1920 and 1930 *luwalo* was commuted to a money tax to the

Kingdom of Buganda. Finally, on top of these burdens and obligations
came the poll tax paid to the colonial state via the chief.[95] The size of
the total burden on the tenant in Buganda was a powerful incentive for
the more ambitious to save money to buy land and become a landowner, an option not readily available in other districts of the Protectorate, where apart from Toro and Ankole, there were only official,
not private, estates for chiefs. The high cost of establishing the new
order was reflected in Buganda's population statistics. Not only had the
population declined from a pre-1888 estimate of well over one million
to 650,000 in 1920, but the death rate of 30 per thousand greatly
exceeded the birth rate of 17 per thousand. Until the mid-1930s, the
death rate continued to surpass the birth rate in Buganda's Mengo
District, as well as in Bunyoro and in Bugwere (Bukedi).[96]

Despite the claim by imperial apologists that colonial rule brought
peace to warring tribes, there was less peace between 1893 and 1920
than in any previous period. Following the massive upheavals of the
1890s, scattered resistance to the new colonial order continued until
1920. Eastern Uganda recorded at least 17 tax revolts and punitive
expeditions between 1903 and 1911. In Ankole the British Sub-
Commissioner was assassinated in 1905. A campaign of passive resistance
in Bunyoro in 1907-8, the *Nyangire* revolt, protested British imposition
of Baganda chiefs. The *Nyabingi* cult in Kigezi led the Bakiga rebellion
against Rwandan, then British, overrule between 1900 and 1920. The
Bakonjo in Toro rose against Batoro agents and British overrule in
1919, the same year the Kakwa prophet Rembe and collaborative chiefs
turned resisters led the *Yakan* revolt of the Lugbara in West Nile.
Punitive expeditions were almost annual events in Lango and Acholi
between 1907 and 1919. The onset of the First World War disrupted a
massive punitive expedition against the Turkana in what was then the
Rudolph Province of Uganda.[97]

Between 1914 and 1917 nearly 200,000 Africans were called into
the military, or almost a third of Uganda's adult male population.
Over half served as job porters, transporting food supplies and ammunition within Uganda. Not only were nearly a third of the men removed
from food production for months at a time, but the remaining population was required to continue cotton production and contribute food
for the war effort. The generally poor state of health among the African
population was starkly illustrated by the 1917 call up of 41,706 men
from Lango, Teso and Bukedi; only 5,763 were deemed medically fit
to serve as carriers. Of the 50,315 carriers who served outside Uganda,
4,418 were reported dead, maimed or missing in action. Dysentery due

to poor food, pneumonia and influenza were the leading causes of
death. At the war's end, the colonial state rewarded its European and
Indian employees with a bonus to compensate them for war hardships
and the higher cost of imported goods, but excluded African employees
from the war bonus because imported food and clothes were considered
beyond the aspirations of Africans.[98]

Although cotton production declined slightly during the war, high
world prices more than compensated for the decline. When peace finally
came, cotton production rapidly increased to over twice the pre-war
level: 23,273 metric tons of lint in 1923. Tax and rent increases in
1919 were more than offset by higher prices to cotton producers.
Cotton cultivation was sufficiently more remunerative than wage-
labour to create a severe labour shortage. To maintain supplies of
labour, European and Asian planters pressured the colonial state to
slow down cotton promotion in outlying districts, such as West Nile
and Acholi; however, the colonial state rebuffed the planters' more
Draconian suggestions for increasing the labour supply through expansion of the *kasanvu* system. When cotton prices declined sharply in
1921, small producers expanded their cotton acreage to maintain their
incomes, while farmers with large estates switched from cotton to more
lucrative crops.[99]

The colonial state in 1920 for the first time spent as much on agriculture, health and education as it did on the military, police and
prisons; however, few of these services benefited the general population.
As the otherwise hostile European planter community noted with satisfaction in 1920, practically the entire research effort of the agricultural
staff was devoted to plantation crops rather than food crops or
cotton.[100] Health services funded by the state were overwhelmingly
geared to the needs of the European and Asian community; mission
hospitals and dispensaries did handle about 100,000 African outpatients
annually. Mission schools, aided by state subsidies, had 93,370 pupils
enrolled at the end of the war. These limited social services for Africans
tended to be concentrated in Buganda.[101]

Conclusion

By 1922 the main structural features of the modern Ugandan economy
were in place. Until 1945 there would be few structural changes in the
economy: alterations in land tenure in Buganda and Busoga in the late
1920s, the emergence of coffee as a secondary African cash crop and

the rise of Asian-owned sugar plantations. Based on peasant production of primary commodities for the world market, the newly unified economy was no longer self-sufficient but structurally dependent on the external economy for processing domestic raw materials into consumer and capital goods. In terms of colonial measures of progress — increased exports and self-financing administration — the Uganda Protectorate was a successful colony. Exports totalled £2.4 million and state revenues £1 million in 1923. The African poll tax and the new cotton export tax together accounted for half of state revenues with import duties, which fell heavily on cotton piece-goods, providing most of the rest.[102] However, the new order brought negligible benefits to the average peasant between 1893 and 1922, beyond a few yards of imported cloth, an occasional blanket and the iron hoe. The sharp decrease in population that accompanied Uganda's integration into the capitalist world system was the most damning evidence of the cost of establishing the new order. Only through substantial use of force and coercion had the British administrators and collaborative chiefs attained political hegemony, established cotton production and expanded the transportation network.

Nevertheless, had the alliance between the Baganda *bakungu* chiefs and British administrators failed to induce peasants to grow commercially viable export crops, Uganda would still have been integrated into the world system, only on a different basis and at an even higher initial cost to the population. The post-1900 economic integration of Africa into the capitalist world system owed its external impetus to four factors: (1) the financial burden of formal empire, which made it imperative that colonies become administratively self-financing as quickly as possible; (2) the growth of socialist political parties in Europe, whose revolutionary potential coud be lessened by providing European workers with better living conditions through imports of cheaper raw materials and increased export earnings; (3) the transportation revolution effected by the introduction of steamships in the late nineteenth century; and (4) the exceptionally high world prices for agricultural commodities between 1900 and 1920. However, local factors determined the form of integration into the world economy.

Essentially there were four alternative paths by which Africa was integrated into the world system after 1900: the economy of peasant production and colonial trade; the economy of settlers and plantations; the economy of labour reserves; and the economy of concession companies.[103]

In Algeria, South Africa, Southern Rhodesia, Kenya and Angola, the introduction of the settler and plantation economy necessitated the semi-proletarianisation of the peasantry. By concentrating the African population into reserves and imposing taxes, peasants were transformed into a reserve army of cheap migrant labour to be exploited first by European settlers and planters and later by industry. By paying the labourer a wage only equivalent to the cost of subsistence for a single adult, the settlers and planters shoved the costs of reproduction of labour and retirement onto the reserves. From the point of view of metropolitan capital, the economy of settlers and plantations proved to be a costly and politically awkward alternative. Not only did settlers and plantation owners demand direct and indirect subsidies which reduced the surplus available to metropolitan capital, but settlers sooner or later demanded political autonomy and economic self-determination, erecting tariff barriers to imports from the metropole.[104] In Uganda, the colonial state's motive for not encouraging plantations and settlers lay in its contentment with the *status quo* of peasant production and the realisation that settlers posed an alternative which was economically and politically more costly. Most of the European plantations in Uganda were financially crippled after the First World War by unfavourable currency fluctuations, the sharp drop in commodity prices following the 1920 boom, and the abolition of *kasanvu* in 1922.[105] A further weeding out of European plantations occurred during the slump in the 1930s. By the 1950s plantations in Uganda were limited to two enormous Asian-owned sugar plantations producing for the East African market and a few coffee and tea plantations.

A second alternative entailed becoming a pure labour reserve, exporting migrant labourers to other territories for employment by mines, plantations, settlers and even African commercial farmers. This was the transformation advocated by Johnston as Uganda's last resort, should peasant production have failed to develop.[106] Despite its location within what Samir Amin has termed the macro-region of labour reserves (eastern and southern Africa), Uganda escaped such a fate. On the contrary, by the very success of African commercial production, southern Uganda attracted migrant labourers from the labour reserves of Rwanda-Burundi and the southern Sudan.

A third alternative would have been to turn vast areas in Uganda over to concession companies for exploitation, as was done in the Congo Free State (Zaire), Congo-Brazzaville and Namibia. This option was opposed by Johnston both because of the rapacious reputation of concession companies and because he feared that British firms would not be as adventurous as German, Belgian or French firms in staking out concessions. One significant concession was granted for a large natural rubber venture in the Mabira forest, but it collapsed, as did the plantations, because of the rise in wages following the abolition of *kasanvu* and the lower world prices for agricultural commodities in the early 1920s.[107]

Ultimately, then, it was the economic nationalism of the *bakungu* chiefs in Buganda that determined the form of Uganda's integration into the capitalist world system by setting the parameters for land and labour policy and by compelling their tenant-subjects to cultivate cash crops for the world market. The claim by both British imperialists and Marxists that Britain consciously created a landed gentry in Buganda must be seen as an *ex post facto* rationalisation. It was the *bakungu* chiefs who staged the bourgeois revolution in Buganda which initiated the commercialisation of agriculture and land tenure prior to the 1900 agreement, prior to the completion of the railway and prior to the introduction of cotton. More specifically, it was the Protestant faction, in a sense the faction which became Protestant in order to collaborate, which seized the chance offered first by Lugard and then by Johnston to ally themselves with a militarily superior external power to defeat domestic rivals and to transform themselves into *rentier* landlords. The colonial state required almost three decades from the signing of the 1900 agreement to undermine the political and economic power of the *bakungu* chiefs and form a new, more unequal, collaborative alliance with Ugandans, based on capitalist tenant-farmers, capitalist landowners and state-appointed chiefs, an alliance which was subordinated to the alliance between the colonial state and non-African commercial interests formalised in the 1921 establishment of the Legislative Council.

Notes

1. Eduard Schnitzer (Emin Pasha), *Emin Pasha in Central Africa*, ed. by G. Schweinfurth and others (London: George Philip and Son, 1888), pp. 10-16, 25, 73-82, 111-23, 176-80, 265-76 and 284-8; Lars Sundström, *The Exchange Economy of Pre-Colonial Tropical Africa* (London: C. Hurst and Company, 1974), pp. 130, 138, 214 and 250; Okete Shiroya, 'Northwestern Uganda in the Nineteenth Century: Inter-Ethnic Trade', paper presented to the Universities of East Africa Social Science Conference, Dar es Salaam, December 1970; G.N. Uzoigwe, 'Pre-colonial Markets in Bunyoro-Kitara', paper presented to the Universities of East Africa Social Science Conference, Dar es Salaam, December 1970; John Lamphear, *The Traditional History of the Jie in Uganda* (Oxford: Clarendon Press, 1976), pp. 165-8, 195-201; and John Tosh, 'The Northern Inter-lacustrine Region', *Pre-Colonial African Trade; Essays on Trade in Central and*

Eastern Africa before 1900, ed. Richard Gray and David Birmingham (London: Oxford University Press, 1970), pp. 103-18. On material life in pre-colonial Uganda, see Margaret Trowell and K.P. Waschmann, *Tribal Crafts of Uganda* (London: Oxford University Press, 1953), pp. 5-307.

2. Helge Kjekshus, *Ecology Control and Economic Development in East African History: the Case of Tanganyika, 1850-1950* (London: Heinemann, 1977), pp. 51-79.

3. Aidan W. Southall, *Alur Society* (Nairobi: Oxford University Press, 1953), pp. 33-4, 81 and 197-9; T.T.S. Hayley, *The Anatomy of Lango Religion and Groups* (Cambridge: Cambridge University Press, 1947), pp. 58-60; Joan Vincent, *African Elite* (New York: Columbia University Press, 1971), pp. 187-208; J.S. La Fontaine, *The Gisu of Uganda* (London: International African Institute, 1959), pp. 17-18; F.K. Girling, *The Acholi of Uganda* (London: HMSO, 1960), p. 193; May Mandelbaum Edel, *The Chiga of Western Uganda* (New York: Oxford University Press, 1957), pp. 85-8; Neville Dyson-Hudson, *Karimojong Politics* (Oxford: Clarendon Press, 1966), pp. 68-73; and Uganda, 'Communal Labour', *Report on Uganda Census of Agriculture* (Entebbe: Government Printer), vol. I (1965): 63.

4. J.E.G. Sutton, 'The Settlement of East Africa', *Zamani; A Survey of East African History*, 2nd edn, ed. B.A. Ogot (Nairobi: East African Publishing House and Longman, 1974), pp. 82-3; Joseph H. Greenberg, *The Languages of Africa*, 3rd edn (Bloomington: Indiana University Press, 1970); Peter Ladefoged, Ruth Glick and Clive Criper, *Language in Uganda* (London: Oxford University Press, 1972), pp. 65-84; G.N. Uzoigwe, 'Towards Updating the History of Uganda', *Tarikh* (Ibadan), 3, No. 2: *The Peoples of Uganda in the Nineteenth Century* (London: Longman, 1970), pp. 1-5; M.A.E. Odada, 'The Kumam: Langi or Iteso?', *Uganda Journal*, vol. 35, no. 2 (1971), pp. 139-52; J.B. Webster, 'Noi! Noi! Famines as an Aid to Interlacustrine History', paper presented at the Canadian Association of African Studes Conference, Halifax, Nova Scotia, February 1974; H.F. Morris, *A History of Ankole* (Nairobi: East African Literature Bureau, 1962), pp. 9-13; Kenneth Ingham, *The Kingdom of Toro in Uganda* (London: Methuen, 1975), pp. xii-xiii; Edward H. Winter, *Bwamba* (Cambridge: W. Heffer & Sons, 1955), pp. 4-5; and Lamphear, *The Traditional History of the Jie*, p. 64.

5. David William Cohen, *The Historical Tradition of Busoga* (Oxford: Clarendon Press, 1972), Map II, p. 14; Girling, *The Acholi*, pp. 8-9, 112, 205-6 and Map II, p. 238; and Southall, *Alur Society*, Map 3, p. 16. By contrast, fifteenth-century Europe contained about 500 'more or less independent' polities, Charles Tilly, *The Formation of National States in Western Europe* (Princeton University Press, 1975), p. 15.

6. Whether any interlacustrine social formations were truly feudal is a tangled question that hinges on one's choice of the 'key' features of European and Japanese feudalism. If one focuses simply on the relationship between the immediate producer and appropriator, between villein and lord, then clearly the tribute and corvée given by the former to the latter in exchange for protection and access to land constituted feudal relations of production not only in Buganda, Bunyoro, Nkore, Toro and the kingdoms of Busoga, but also in Palwo and the kingdoms of Acholi and Alur-land. For Mamdani, the feudal social formation consists of such a villein-chief economic nexus and the hierarchical kingdoms superstructure. Following Mukherjee, he considers the northern social formations to be transitional because their nineteenth-century superstructures were not yet as centralised·as in· the southern kingdoms. Much to the contrary, the complex definition employed by Bloch and by Anderson·specifies the following as essential features of feudalism: (a) a subjected peasantry juridically bound, not so much to the land, but to the chief(s); (b) the identity of the warrior class with the class of

chiefly nobles who, in return for military service, enjoyed at first conditional but later hereditary landownership and seigneurial jurisdiction over villeins on the manorial estate; (c) the distinctive ties of obedience and protection, known within the warrior-noble class as vassalage; (d) non-centralised political authority, fragmented sovereignty, and the absence of monopoly in judicial and fiscal competence, which together allowed the emergence of towns; and (e) the survival of anterior forms of association: family and state. By this definition, ironically it was the centralised and hierarchical structure of interlacustrine kingdoms, their absolutism, which prevents them from being considered feudal in the European sense. Moreover, whereas land, with the partial exception of clan estates, remained under the ultimate control of the interlacustrine kings until the colonial period, in Europe the transition from feudalism to absolutism was accompanied by the important survival of landed property which could not be seized by the king, without the consent of the landed nobility itself. Compare the following: Mahmood Mamdani, *Politics and Class Formation in Uganda* (New York: Monthly Review Press, 1976), pp. 20-35; Ramkrishna Mukherjee, *The Problem of Uganda; A Study in Acculturation* (Berlin: Akademie-Verlag, 1956), pp. 48-101; Marc Bloch, *Feudal Society* (London: Routledge & Kegan Paul, 1961), vol. II, pp. 441-7; Perry Anderson, *Lineages of the Absolutist State* (London: New Left Books, 1974), pp. 20-21, 28-9, 49-51, 397-431; and Audrey I. Richards, "Feudalism" in the Interlacustrine Kingdoms', *East African Chiefs* (London: Faber and Faber, 1959), pp. 378-93.

7. According to Ocheng, the feudal claims of the Acholi *rwodi* (kings) to corvée and rent in kind were being eroded in the nineteenth century by a resurgence in clan rights, while Atkinson maintains the *rwodi*, at least in the western kingdoms, were making inroads on clan rights by monopolising the sale of ivory to Sudanese traders. Compare D.O. Ocheng, 'Land Tenure in Acholi', *Uganda Journal*, vol. 19, no. 1 (March 1955), pp. 57-61; and R.R. Atkinson, 'Adaptation and Change in Acholi, 1850-1900', Seminar Paper 23/1971-72, Makerere Department of History, mimeo. cited in Ralph Herring, 'Centralization, Stratification and Incorporation: Case Studies from Northeastern Uganda', *Canadian Journal of African Studies*, vol. 7, no. 3 (1973), p. 504. Atyak, Pabo, Padibe, Puranga, Pajule, Koic, Payera, Patiko and Lira Palwo are the major Acholi kingdoms or 'chiefdoms' listed by Cherry Gertzel, *Party and Locality in Northern Uganda, 1945-1962* (London: The Athlone Press, 1974), p. 57.

8. La Fontaine, *The Gisu*, pp. 14-34; E.H. Winter, *Bwamba Economy* (Kampala: East African Institute of Social Research, 1955), pp. 5-16; Edel, *The Chiga*, pp. 79-111; and Ingham, *The Kingdom of Toro*, pp. 27, 37. Doornbos suggests that transactions between a majority of Bairu cultivators and the Bahima pastoralists who dominated the Nkore political system were sufficiently inter-mittent to justify regarding the Bairu as being outside the effective domain of the Nkore kingdom even though they lived within its physical boundaries. If so, the unequal exchange of goods and services between some Bairu and some Bahima and between the Bairu and the Nkore state should be regarded as external relations analogous to the relations between the Bwamba and Toro. Martin Doornbos, 'Images and Reality of Stratification in Pre-Colonial Nkore', *Canadian Journal of African Studies*, vol. 7, no. 3 (1973), pp. 477-95.

9. On the controversy surrounding the origins of the Chwezi and the Babito, see the following: Eduard Schnitzer, *Die Tagebücher von Dr. Emin Pasha*: 31 October 1879, cited in Sir John Gray, 'Diaries of Emin Pasha; Extract IV', *Uganda Journal*, vol. 26, no. 2 (September 1962), pp. 121-39; J.P. Crazzolara, 'The Lwoo People', *Uganda Journal*, vol. 5, no. 1 (1937/38), pp. 1-21; Merrick Posnansky, 'Kingship, Archeology and Historical Myth', *Uganda Journal*, vol. 30, no. 1 (1966), pp. 1-12; Samwiri Rubaraza Karugire, *A History of the Kingdom of*

Nkore in Western Uganda to 1896 (Oxford: Clarendon Press, 1971), pp. 118-49;
M.S.M. Kiwanuka, *A History of Buganda from the Foundation of the Kingdom to 1900* (London: Longman, 1971), pp. 44-63; and Cohen, *The Historical Tradition of Busoga*, pp. 79-196.

10. Both Kiwanuka and Emin Pasha emphasise that relations between Buganda and Bunyoro were generally peaceful until 1886. Bunyoro's blacksmiths at Masindi produced iron hoes in such quantities that smelting was abandoned in northern Lango. John Tosh, 'The Langi of Northern Uganda', *Tarikh*, vol. 3, no. 2: *The Peoples of Uganda*, p. 66. Buganda's iron from Kyagwe and Koki was softer than the iron Bunyoro obtained. Schnitzer, *Emin Pasha*, p. 122.

11. Jan Vansina, 'Inner Africa: A.D. 500-1800', *The Horizon History of Africa*, ed. Alvin M. Josephy, Jr. (New York: American Heritage Publishing Co., 1971), pp. 272-3.

12. Tosh, 'The Northern Interlacustrine Region', p. 111.

13. Richard F. Burton, *Zanzibar; City, Island and Coast* (London: Tinsley Brothers, 1872), vol. II, p. 510; and Andrew Roberts, 'Nyamwezi Trade', in Gray and Birmingham (eds.), *Pre-Colonial African Trade*, pp. 39-74.

14. Since the weight of imported trade goods equalled one-half to two-thirds the weight of exported ivory, Roberts maintains there was a limited demand for additional porters on the return journey. Roberts, 'Nyamwezi Trade', p. 61. The demand for slaves at Zanzibar ranged between 2,000 and 6,000 annually between 1800 and 1830 rising to a peak of almost 20,000 annually between 1858 and 1873. During the peak period most of the slaves were taken from the Lake Malawi region, far south of modern Uganda. Edward A. Alpers, *Ivory and Slaves in East Central Africa* (London: Heinemann, 1975), pp. 87, 159, 192-3, 239, 247; Abdul Sheriff, 'The Rise of a Commercial Empire: An Aspect of the Economic History of Zanzibar, 1770-1873', University of London PhD Thesis, 1971; G.N. Uzoigwe, 'Pre-colonial Markets in Bunyoro-Kitara', pp. 28-9; and Schnitzer, *Emin Pasha*, pp. 116-17.

15. Schnitzer, *Emin Pasha*, p. 425; and Samir Amin, 'Underdevelopment and Dependence in Black Africa: Historical Origin', *Journal of Peace Research*, vol. 9, no. 2 (1972), pp. 111-12.

16. P.M. Holt, *The Mahdist State in the Sudan, 1881-1898* (Oxford: Clarendon Press, 1958).

17. Schnitzer, *Emin Pasha*, p. 501.

18. Uganda Tsetse Control Division, 'Tsetse Control', *Atlas of Uganda*, 2nd edn (Kampala: Department of Lands and Surveys, 1967), p. 58.

19. The external exchange rate, via the Maria Theresa thaler, was 500 cowries (*simbi*) for three shillings and sixpence in 1879, and 250 cowries for three shillings and five pence in 1885. Emin Pasha quoted the following prices for goods traded between Bunyoro and Buganda (all prices 1883, except where noted):

One ox	6,000 to 7,000 cowries
Fat goat	1,200 to 1,500 cowries
One sheep	1,000 to 1,200 cowries
Maize	400 to 600 cowries per packet
Flour (1879)	10 cowries for a very small basketful
Matoke (plantain)	40 to 50 cowries per bunch
Gonje (sweet banana)	1 cowrie each
Salt (1895)	400 cowries for a 25 pound load
Soda (medicinal)	10 to 20 cowries for small quantity from Uzinza
Mbugu (undyed barkcloth)	300 to 400 cowries per cloth

Schnitzer, *Emin Pasha*, pp. 81, 114-15, 120, 122, 180. Uganda demonetised cowrie shells in 1901.

20. Alexander Mackay, the Protestant missionary, gained entrée to Kabaka Mutesa's court by spending much of his time operating a firearms repair service and by promising to build a cannon. Father Siméon Lourdel of the Catholic White Fathers challenged Muslims to join Christians in a walk through fire with each side carrying the Koran and Bible, respectively. Kambi Mbaya (sic), a devout Muslim from the coast, staged a spectacular mock battle before the Kabaka's palace, complete with real gunpowder, to impress the Kabaka with the military prowess of the faithful of Allah. John A. Rowe, 'Revolution in Buganda 1856-1900; Part One: The Reign of Kabaka Mukabya Mutesa, 1856-1884', University of Wisconsin PhD Thesis, 1966, pp. 121, 175-7.

21. There were three categories of chiefs in Buganda. The *bakungu* were territorial administrative chiefs appointed by the Kabaka. The *bataka* were heads of ancestral clans and were custodians of *butaka* land belonging to the clan. The *batongole* were the king's officials in the countryside, charged with maintaining internal security, supervising royal estates and military duties. David Kiyaga-Mulindwa, 'Social Change in Pre-Colonial Buganda', p. 16; and John A. Rowe, 'The Pattern of Political Administration in Pre-colonial Buganda', p. 13, both papers presented to the Canadian Association of African Studies Conference, Halifax, Nova Scotia, February 1974.

22. Alpers, *Ivory and Slaves*; Samir Amin, 'Underdevelopment and Dependence in Black Africa'; and Immanuel Wallerstein, 'The Three Stages of African Involvement in the World-Economy', *The Political Economy of Contemporary Africa*, ed. Peter C.W. Gutkind and I. Wallerstein (Beverly Hills: Sage Publications, 1976), p. 38.

23. Albert H. Imlah, *Economic Elements in the Pax Britannica: Studies in British Foreign Trade in the Nineteenth Century* (Cambridge: Mass.: Harvard University Press, 1958), p. 104; and Eric J. Hobsbawm, *Industry and Empire* (Harmondsworth: Penguin Books, 1969), pp. 135-53. As Redford pointedly commented, 'The Lancashire cotton trade leaned heavily on the Indian peasant . . . ' Arthur Redford, *Manchester Merchants and Foreign Trade*, 2: *1850-1939* (Manchester: Manchester University Press, 1956), p. 22.

24. Arghiri Emmanuel, 'White-Settler Colonialism and the Myth of Investment Imperialism', *New Left Review*, vol. 73 (May-June 1972), pp. 35-57.

25. Edward A. Brett, *Colonialism and Underdevelopment in East Africa; The Politics of Economic Change, 1919-39* (London: Heinemann, 1973), p. 151.

26. London Chamber of Commerce, *Eleventh Annual Report: Transactions of the Year 1892*, pp. 36-7. For its part, the Manchester Chamber of Commerce had initially opposed the timing of the construction of the Suez Canal because it diverted labour from cotton production in Egypt at the height of the cotton famine caused by the Civil War in the United States. Later it became the staunchest defender of the importance of maintaining British control of the Suez route to India. Egypt itself was Lancashire's most important African market for cotton piece-goods. Redford: *Manchester Merchants*, 2: 62, 75, 167.

27. On the conflict between the Foreign Office and the Colonial Office regarding control of the Nile and the financial viability of further colonisation, see A.J.P. Taylor, 'Prelude to Fashoda: The Question of the Upper Nile, 1894-95', *English Historical Review*, vol. 65 (1950), pp. 52-80. The hawkishness of the Foreign Office in the period 1889-98 regarding the importance of the Nile is well documented in Ronald Robinson, John Gallagher and Alice Denny, *Africa and the Victorians; The Climax of Imperialism* (New York: St Martin's Press, 1961), pp. 247-348. Hence it was the Foreign Office that assumed the financial burden of Ugandan overrule between 1894 and 1905.

28. H. Gresford Jones, *Uganda in Transformation* (London: Church Missionary Society, 1926), pp. 42-3; Donald Anthony Low, 'British Public Opinion and the Uganda Question: October-December 1892', *Uganda Journal*, vol. 18 (September 1954), pp. 81-100; Leonard Woolf, *Empire and Commerce in Africa; A Study in Economic Imperialism* (London: George Allen and Unwin, 1920), pp. 242-302; John S. Galbraith, *Mackinnon and East Africa, 1878-1895* (Cambridge: Cambridge University Press, 1972); and Robinson, Gallagher and Denny, *Africa and the Victorians*, pp. 48, 307-38.

29. Today these firms are part of the Inchcape Group, headed by Kenneth James William Mackay, Lord Inchcape, who also heads the P & O shipping group.

30. Frederick D. Lugard, *The Rise of Our East African Empire: Early Efforts in Nyasaland and Uganda* (Edinburgh and London: William Blackwood and Sons, 1893), vol. 1, pp. 482-3.

31. *Hansard*, 4th Series, *I* (1892), 3rd March, cols. 1841-42; Christopher C. Wrigley, 'Buganda: An Outline Economic History', *Economic History Review*, 2nd series, vol. 10, no. 1 (1957), p. 75; and A.M. O'Connor, *Railways and Development in Uganda* (Nairobi: Oxford University Press for EAISR, 1965), pp. 36-7.

32. *Hansard*, 4th Series, *I* (1892), 3rd March, cols. 1853-85; XLII (1896), 2nd July, cols. 553-70; and XLIII (1896), 27th July, cols. 705-724.

33. Robinson, Gallagher and Denny, *Africa and the Victorians*, pp. 307-78.

34. Richard D. Wolff, *The Economics of Colonialism; Britain and Kenya, 1870-1930* (New Haven and London: Yale University Press, 1974), pp. 42-3.

35. The British drive to build railways in far-flung corners of the Empire in the latter half of the nineteenth century can be explained in terms of the Marxist concept of overproduction of capital goods (steel, locomotives) rather than in terms of Lenin's nebulous concept of overripened capital being forced to export surplus capital.

36. Great Britain, *Parliamentary Papers* (Commons) *1904* (LXII 763), Cd. 2164, 'Final Report of the Uganda Railway Committee', pp. 8, 11, 31; and Christopher C. Wrigley, 'Kenya: Patterns of Economic Life, 1902-1945', *History of East Africa*, ed. Vincent Harlow, E.M. Chilver and Alison Smith (Oxford: Clarendon Press, 1965), vol. 2, p. 211.

37. See 'Final Report of the Uganda Railway Committee', Cd. 2164, p. 8. A small force of 2,800 Africans did work at various times on the railway, but no records were kept regarding casualties among them.

38. A.J. Mounteney-Jephson, *Emin Pasha and the Rebellion at the Equator* (New York: Charles Scribner's Sons, 1890), pp. 314-480.

39. Kabalega's distrust of Baker stemmed from the fact that the latter was accompanied by Khartoum-based slave raiders. J.W. Nyakatura, *Anatomy of an African Kingdom* (Abakama ba Bunyoro-Kitara), ed. by Godfrey N. Uzoigwe (Garden City, New York: Anchor Books, 1973), pp. 104, 119-23.

40. Schnitzer, *Emin Pasha*, p. 176. Bunyoro also controlled the Kibero salt mine in Bugahya county.

41. Norman R. Bennett, 'The Arab Impact', in Ogot (ed.), *Zamani*, p. 222; and Schnitzer, *Emin Pasha*, p. 489.

42. Lugard, *The Rise of Our East African Empire*, vol. 2, pp. 39, 41; and John A. Rowe, *Lugard at Kampala*, Makerere History Papers No. 3 (Kampala: Longman Uganda, 1969).

43. Nyakatura, *Anatomy of an African Kingdom*, pp. 147-50; and Edward I. Steinhart, *Conflict and Collaboration: The Kingdoms of Western Uganda, 1890-1907* (Princeton: Princeton University Press, 1977), pp. 42-52.

44. Although Gerald Portal had declared a British Protectorate over Buganda

and Toro in April 1893, Parliament did not ratify his *fait accompli* until June 1894, when it appropriated an annual sum of £50,000 for administration of the Protectorate.

45. Nyakatura, *Anatomy of an African Kingdom*, pp. 132, 150-63; Steinhart, *Conflict and Collaboration*, pp. 64-95, 157-77; A.D. Roberts, 'The "Lost Counties" of Bunyoro', *Uganda Journal*, vol. 26 (September 1962), pp. 194-9; and John Beattie, *Bunyoro: An African Kingdom* (New York: Holt, Rinehart and Winston, 1960), pp. 22-3.

46. Putting aside imperialist rivalry, German stations in northwest Tanganyika sent ammunition to British forces during the Mutiny. George Wilson to Salisbury, 7 December 1897, F.O. 2/134, Public Records Office, London. See also Great Britain, 'Report by Her Majesty's Commissioner in Uganda on the Recent Mutiny of the Sudanese Troops in the Protectorate', C. 9027 (LX 525), 1898; and Albert Cooke, 'Kampala During the Closing Years of the Last Century', *Uganda Journal*, vol. 1, no. 2 (April 1934), pp. 91-5.

47. Nyakatura, *Anatomy of an African Kingdom*, pp. 162-9. Mwanga died in exile in 1903, while Kabalega died in Jinja in 1923, en route from exile to his homeland.

48. Steinhart, *Conflict and Collaboration*, pp. 157-77; and Godfrey N. Uzoigwe, *Revolution and Revolt in Bunyoro-Kitara*, Makerere History Papers No. 5 (Kampala: Longman Uganda, 1970).

49. John Gray, 'Kakunguru in Bukedi', *Uganda Journal*, vol. 27, no. 1 (1963), pp. 52-3; Andrew Roberts, 'Evolution of the Uganda Protectorate', *Uganda Journal*, vol. 27, no. 1 (1963), pp. 95-106; and H.B. Thomas, 'The Evolution of Uganda's Boundaries', *Atlas of Uganda*, 2nd edn, pp. 74-5.

50. Rowe, *Lugard at Kampala*, pp. 2-9; and Donald Anthony Low and R. Cranford Pratt, *Buganda and British Overrule, 1900-1955* (London: Oxford University Press for the East African Institute of Social Research, 1960), pp. 7-8.

51. F.B. Welbourn, *Religion and Politics in Uganda, 1952-62* (Nairobi: East African Publishing House, 1965), p. 6; and Rowe, *Lugard at Kampala*, p. 24.

52. '*Omwami tafuga ttaka, afuga bantu.*' Henry W. West, *Land Policy in Buganda* (Cambridge: Cambridge University Press, 1972), p. 11.

53. '*Abakopi mayenje; gagwa walime.*' Peasants are like cockroaches, which settle on cultivated land. C.S. Nason, 'Proverbs of the Baganda', *Uganda Journal*, vol. 3, no. 4 (April 1936), p. 251.

54. Frederick Lugard, *The Diaries of Lord Lugard*, ed. by Margery Perham, vol. 2: *December 1890-December 1891* (Evanston: Northwestern University Press, 1959), pp. 89, 112-13.

55. Rowe, *Lugard at Kampala*.

56. E.J.L. Berkeley to Salisbury, 2 November 1896, 'Report on the Trade and Industry of Uganda', Great Britain, Foreign Office, *Diplomatic and Consular Reports on Trade and Finances, 1897*, No. 1844, C. 8277; and Lugard, *Diaries of Lord Lugard*, vol. 2, pp. 89-113.

57. The land tenure system that evolved from the settlement became known as the 'mailo' land system because the original tracts were measured in square miles (Luganda: *mailo*). The process of allocating, surveying and registering mailo estates took far longer than expected. The number of original mailo claimants rose from the anticipated 1,030 chiefs and landowners to 3,650 (West, *Land Policy in Buganda*, p. 19) or even 3,945 individuals (Low and Pratt, p. 115) in the first allotment list. The number of original mailo owners represented far less than 1 per cent of the total population of Buganda. Of the approximately 20,000 square miles of land in Buganda, less than half was eventually allocated to the colonial state as Crown Land. Low and Pratt, *Buganda and British Overrule*,

pp. 3-159 (full text of 1900 Agreement in Appendix II, 350-64); West, *Land Policy in Buganda*, pp. 11-47; A.B. Mukwaya, *Land Tenure in Buganda* (Kampala: East African Institute of Social Research, 1953), pp. 23-4; and Henry W. West, *The Transformation of Land Tenure in Buganda Since 1896* (Leiden: Afrika Studiecentrum, 1971), pp. 3-18.

58. The following works, although correct in noting that the 1900 agreement deprived clanheads (*bataka*) of traditional common land and in observing the inconsistency between the private estates and traditional land tenure, none the less ascribe the final agreement either to Johnston's ignorance, Baganda self-conscious tribalism or Britain's goal of creating a comprador class of landowners. Cf. West, *Land Policy in Buganda*, p. 16; Low and Pratt, *Buganda and British Overrule*, pp. 42-3, 49-50 and 52; and Mahmood Mamdani, *Politics and Class Formation in Uganda* (New York and London: Monthly Review Press, 1976), pp. 41-3.

59. Low and Pratt, *Buganda and British Overrule*, p. 94; H.B. Thomas, 'Capax Imperii: The Story of Semei Kakuguru', *Uganda Journal*, vol. 6; no. 3 (January 1939), pp. 125-36; and Uganda Protectorate, *Blue Book, 1901-02*, p. 29.

60. Andrew D. Roberts, 'The Sub-Imperialism of the Baganda', *Journal of African History*, vol. 3, no. 3 (1962), pp. 435-50; Thomas, 'Capax Imperii'; John Gray, 'Kakunguru in Bukedi', *Uganda Journal*, vol. 27, no. 1 (1963), pp. 31-59; G. Emwanu, 'The Reception of Alien Rule in Teso, 1896-1927', *Uganda Journal*, vol. 31, no. 2 (1967), pp. 171-82; and Steinhart, *Conflict and Collaboration*, pp. 42-52, 157-77.

61. Chiefs accounted for 60 of the 89 seats in the 1902 Lukiko. By religious faction, there were 49 Protestants, 35 Catholics and 5 Muslims. Donald Anthony Low, 'The Composition of the Buganda Lukiko in 1902', *Uganda Journal*, vol. 23 (March 1959), pp. 64-8.

62. George Wilson to A.J. Turnbull, 5 March 1906, 'National Bank of India: Proposed Branch at Entebbe', File 197/06, Item 2, National Archives, Entebbe.

63. J.A. Atanda, 'The Bakopi [Peasants] in the Kingdom of Buganda, 1900-1912', *Uganda Journal*, vol. 33, no. 2 (1969), pp. 151-62.

64. E.J.L. Berkeley to Salisbury, 2 November 1896, 'Report on the Trade and Industry of Uganda', Great Britain, Foreign Office, *Diplomatic and Consular Reports on Trade and Finances*, 1897, No. 1844, C. 8277; Uganda, *Blue Book 1904/05*, C.O. 613/4; J. Hayes-Sadler, 'General Report on the Uganda Protectorate for the Year Ending 31 March 1903', Cd. 1839, as printed in C.O. 613/18, p. 17; and George Wilson to A.J. Turnbull, 5 March 1906, 'National Bank of India: Proposed Branch at Entebbe'. Wilson lists the following firms as the principal traders in the Protectorate in 1906:

Entebbe	*Kampala*	*Jinja*
1. Alidina Visram	1. Uganda Company	1. Alidina Visram
2. Societa Coloniale Italiana	2. L. Besson & Cie.	2. Mohamed Elias Jousey
3. Souza Junior and Dias	3. Max Klein	3. Mazhar Ali Khan
4. Victoria Nyanza Agentur	4. Soc. Col. Italiana	4. Tamachi Suliman
5. A. de Figueirede	5. Alidina Visram	5. Mohamed Noor Barawa
6. Campbell Dowse & Co.	6. Dharamsi Katae & Co.	6. Gulam Hussein
7. East Africa Trading Co.	7. Ahmed bin Rashid	7. Said bin Amir
8. A. E. Bertie-Smith	8. Khimji Bhanji	8. Abdulla Nathu
9. A. Fritz	9. Hajee Adam & Sons	9. Mohamed Bakar
10. Entebbe Bakery	10. Baljee Bhanjee	10. Max Klein

65. H.B. Thomas and Robert Scott, *Uganda* (London: Humphrey Milford and Oxford University Press, 1935), p. 504; and Uganda, *Report of the Uganda*

Development Commission, 1920, p. 7.

66. H.R. Wallis, *The Handbook of Uganda*, 2nd edn (London: Crown Agents for the Colonies, 1920), pp. 236-43.

67. J. Hayes-Sadler, 'General Report on the Uganda Protectorate for the Year Ending 31 March 1903', p. 20.

68. This anecdotal account of the peasant's view of cotton cultivation has been borrowed, with permission, from William G. Fleming's description of the introduction of cotton cultivation in the West Nile area.

69. Despite heavy rains and an insufficiently hot ripening season, conditions in southern and central Uganda guaranteed that there would never be a total crop failure with cotton. Christopher C. Wrigley, *Crops and Wealth in Uganda; A Short Agrarian History* (Kampala: East African Institute of Social Research, 1959), pp. 15-16, 25.

70. Arthur Redford, *Manchester Merchants and Foreign Trade, 1850-1939*, vol. 2, p. 77. Although Uganda's output of cotton, even at its peak, comprised an insignificant portion of the total world production of cotton lint, Uganda's specialisation in long-staple cotton earned it third place in the category. In 1933-4 staple longer than 1 1/8 inch represented between 8 and 10 per cent of world cotton production, the largest producers of long-staple being Egypt (285,400 metric tons), the United States (170,000 metric tons) and Uganda (51,800 metric tons). Based on data in Imperial Economic Committee, *Industrial Fibres, 1937* (London: HMSO, 1937), pp. 15-18.

71. Harry Johnston, *The Uganda Protectorate* (London: Hutchinson and Company, 1902), vol. 1, pp. 273-4; Christopher C. Wrigley, 'Buganda: An Outline Economic History', *Economic History Review*, 2nd series, vol. 10, no. 1 (1957), p. 75; Thomas and Scott, *Uganda*, p. 127; Cyril Ehrlich, 'Cotton and the Uganda Economy, 1903-09', *Uganda Journal*, vol. 21, no. 2 (September 1957), p. 168; and H. Hesketh Bell, 'Report on the Introduction and Establishment of the Cotton Industry in the Uganda Protectorate', Great Britain, *Parliamentary Papers* (Commons) *1909*, Cd. 4910, November 1909, pp. 2-3.

72. Uganda, *Blue Book, 1915/16*.

73. Bell, 'Report on the . . . Cotton Industry in the Uganda Protectorate', pp. 10-11.

74. Uganda, *Annual Report of the Department of Agriculture, 1920*, p. 23.

75. Philip Geoffrey Powesland, *Economic Policy and Labour*, ed. by Walter Elkan (Kampala: East African Institute of Social Research, 1957), pp. 13-34.

76. Bell, 'Report on the . . . Cotton Industry in the Uganda Protectorate', p. 12.

77. Uganda, *Annual Report of the Department of Agriculture, 1913/14*, p. 7.

78. At an early stage the ginneries began eliminating independent driver-owners by establishing their own lorry fleets and persuading the colonial state to ban independent buyers from doing business within a five-mile radius of existing ginneries (1918). See Cyril Ehrlich, 'The Marketing of Cotton in Uganda, 1900-1950; A Case Study of Colonial Government Economic Policy', University of London PhD Thesis, 1958, pp. 137-42. The ginneries used the heavy expenditure on *kyalo* transport and secret payments to chiefs and cotton touts as a justification for the universal practice of cheating growers in the weighing of cotton. Uganda, *Report of the Commission of Enquiry into the Cotton Industry, 1929* (Entebbe: Government Printer, 1929), pp. 24-5; and Uganda, *Report of the Uganda Cotton Commission, 1938* (Entebbe: Government Printer, 1939), pp. 43-5.

79. Powesland, *Economic Policy and Labour*, pp. 13-34; and Uganda, *Annual Report of the Department of Agriculture, 1920*.

80. Uganda, *Blue Book, 1918/19*; Uganda, *Report . . . into the Cotton*

Industry, 1929, p. 35.

81. Uganda, *Blue Book, 1918/19*; Ehrlich, 'The Marketing of Cotton in Uganda', pp. 116, 146; Thomas and Scott, *Uganda*, p. 136; and Uganda, *Report of the Uganda Cotton Commission, 1938*, p. 118.

82. The Department of Agriculture's concern over child labour stemmed from the reduction in quality of ginned cotton caused by the fact that 'quite small children are employed by so many ginneries to feed the gins'. Uganda, *Annual Report of the Department of Agriculture, 1923*, p. 5. Only in 1929 did the colonial state even begin to consider limiting the hours children could work in ginneries. At the time 50 hours per week was standard. Uganda, *Report of the Commission of Enquiry into the Cotton Industry, 1929*, p. 28; and Uganda, *Blue Book, 1928*, p. 108.

83. Uganda, *Blue Book, 1918/19*.

84. D.H. Buchanan, *The Development of Capitalistic Enterprise in India*, 2nd Edition (London: Frank Cass & Co., 1966), pp. 194-230; and Redford, *Manchester Merchants and Foreign Trade, 1850-1939*, vol. 2, p. 289.

85. Bell, 'Report on the . . . Cotton Industry in the Uganda Protectorate', p. 11.

86. According to J. Hayes-Sadler,

Here the American article easily holds the supremacy it has established over Northern and Eastern Africa under the name of Americani. It is admirably adapted for ordinary wear in these countries, and, in point of durability and absence of sizing, it has no equal . . . Eventually some two or three million people will have to be clothed, and these will wear cotton. It will be a race between Manchester and the United States, with the advantage at present to the latter, unless the cotton industry of the Protectorate develops, and mills are started to meet local requirements.

'General Report on the Uganda Protectorate for . . . 1903', p. 15. Import statistics from Uganda, *Blue Books*, selected years, 1904/05-1916/17. Because of the consolidation of Kenya's and Uganda's import statistics, separate trade statistics are not available for Uganda between 1917 and 1923. Commissioner of Customs, *Annual Trade Report of Kenya and Uganda*, 1923.

87. John Lamphear, *The Traditional History of the Jie of Uganda* (Oxford: Clarendon Press, 1976), pp. 215-62; Frederick Lugard, *The Rise of Our East African Empire*, vol. 1, pp. 359, 525-9; and Helge Kjekshus, *Ecology Control and Economic Development*, pp. 126-32.

88. Lamphear, *The Traditional History of the Jie of Uganda*, pp. 221-6.

89. Lugard, *The Rise of Our East African Empire*, vol. 1, pp. 359, 525-9.

90. Kjekshus, *Ecology Control and Economic Development*, pp. 51-79, 161-78.

91. Thomas and Scott, *Uganda*, pp. 298-301; and Albert R. Cook, 'Further Memories of Uganda', *Uganda Journal*, vol. 2, no. 2 (October 1934), pp. 112-13.

92. Kjekshus, *Ecology Control and Economic Development*, pp. 165-78.

93. Bishop Alfred R. Tucker to the Parliamentary Committee on Emigration from India to the Crown Colonies and Protectorates, 7 September 1909, Cd. 5194 (XXVII 563), 1910, pp. 152-54; Uganda, *Annual Report of the Department of Agriculture*, selected years, 1914-27; Wallis, *The Handbook of Uganda*, pp 302-3; Lloyd A. Fallers, *Bantu Bureaucracy; A Century of Political Evolution Among the Basoga of Uganda*, 2nd edn (Chicago: University of Chicago Press, 1965), pp. 57, 148-50; and Uganda, *Blue Books*, 1912 through 1923.

94. Fallers, *Bantu Bureaucracy*, p. 149.

95. Atanda notes that even the Christian missions used corvée labour in building churches and schools in the first decade of the century. Atanda, 'The Bakopi in the Kingdom of Buganda, 1900-1912', pp. 151-62; Low and Pratt, *Buganda and British Overrule, 1900-1955*, pp. 233-4; Philip Geoffrey Powesland, 'History of the Migration in Uganda', in Audrey I. Richards (ed.), *Economic Development and Tribal Change; A Study of Immigrant Labour in Buganda* (Cambridge: W. Heffer and Sons for the East African Institute of Social Research, 1954), pp. 17-26, 43; Wrigley, *Crops and Wealth in Uganda*, pp. 48-55; and West, *Land Policy in Buganda*, p. 69, 90-1.

96. Wallis, *The Handbook of Uganda*, pp. 127, 266, 302-3; H. Hesketh Bell to the Secretary of State, 15 April 1909, Cd. 5194, 1910, p. 152; and S.J.K. Baker, 'The Population Map of Uganda', *Uganda Journal*, vol. 1, no. 2 (April 1934), p. 144. Citing the 'alarming decrease' in the African population, Bell advocated the large-scale importation of Indian agricultural labourers. Although colonial administrators attributed the high infant mortality rate to syphilis, it was not until 1935 that medical researchers realised that kwashiorkor, a severe form of protein malnutrition in infants and children, was the cause of the pigment discoloration which had mistakenly been diagnosed as congenital syphilis. H.C. Trowell, 'Food Protein and Kwashiorkor', *Uganda Journal*, vol. 21, no. 1 (March 1957), pp. 81-90.

97. Wallis, *The Handbook of Uganda*, passim; Morris, *A History of Ankole*, pp. 41-5; Uzoigwe, *Revolution and Revolt in Bunyoro-Kitara*, pp. 30-64; P.T.W. Baxter, 'The Kiga', *East African Chiefs*, ed. Audrey I. Richards (London: Faber and Faber, 1959), pp. 287-8; Edel, *The Chiga*, pp. 108, 148-59; Uganda, *Report of the Commission of Inquiry into the Recent Disturbances amongst the Baamba and Bakonjo People of Toro* (Entebbe: Government Printer, 1962), pp. 2-3; John Middleton, *The Lugbara of Uganda* (New York: Holt, Rinehart and Winston, 1965), pp. 3-4; Anne King, 'The Yakan Cult and Lugbara Response to Colonial Rule', *Azania* (Nairobi), vol. 5 (1970), pp. 1-25; John Tosh, 'Small-scale Resistance in Uganda: The Lango Rising at Adwari in 1919', *Azania*, vol. 9 (1974), pp. 51-64; and D.A. Low, 'Uganda: The Establishment of the Protectorate, 1894-1919', *History of East Africa*, vol. II (1965), pp. 103-10.

98. Wallis, *The Handbook of Uganda*, pp. 250-62; Anthony Clayton and Donald C. Savage, *Government and Labour in Kenya, 1895-1963* (London: Frank Cass, 1974), pp. 81-107; Nizar A. Motani, *On His Majesty's Service in Uganda: The Origins of Uganda's African Civil Service, 1912-1940* (Syracuse: Maxwell School of Citizenship and Public Affairs, 1977), pp. 11-24.

99. Uganda, *Annual Report of the Department of Agriculture, 1921*, p. 43; Uganda, *Report of the Commission of Enquiry into the Cotton Industry of Uganda, 1929*, p. 35; and Uganda, *Report of the Uganda Development Commission, 1920* (Entebbe: Government Printer, 1920), pp. 13-20.

100. Wallis, *Report of the Uganda Development Commission, 1920*, p. 36; and Uganda, *Blue Book, 1920*.

101. Wallis, *The Handbook of Uganda*, pp. 263-71.

102. Ehrlich, 'The Marketing of Cotton in Uganda', p. 365.

103. This four-fold typology is adapted from Samir Amin, 'Underdevelopment and Dependence in Black Africa: Historical Origin', *Journal of Peace Research*, vol. 9, no. 2 (1972), pp. 105-19.

104. Arghiri Emmanuel, 'White-Settler Colonialism and the Myth of Investment Imperialism', *New Left Review*, no. 73 (May-June 1972), pp. 35-48; Giovanni Arrighi, 'Labour Supplies in Historical Perspective: A Study of the Proletarianization of the African Peasantry in Rhodesia', *Journal of Development Studies*, vol. 6, no. 3 (April 1970), pp. 197-234; and Edward Brett, *Colonialism and Underdevelopment in East Africa, 1919-1939* (London: Heinemann, 1973),

pp. 77, 205, 209-10.

105. Powesland, *Economic Policy and Labour*, p. 33. Regarding the underlying economic weakness of European settlers in Kenya, see Paul van Zwanenberg,
'Kenya's Primitive Colonial Capitalism', *Canadian Journal of African Studies*,
vol. 9, no. 2 (1975), pp. 277-92.

106. Johnston, *The Uganda Protectorate*, vol. 1, pp. 282-6.

107. 'The Mabira Forest Company', Secretariat Minute Paper 344/10, 1910,
National Archives, Entebbe; Johnston, *The Uganda Protectorate*, vol. 1, p. 296;
and Mamdani, *Politics and Class Formation in Uganda*, pp. 58-9.

2 THE COLONIAL STATE IN THE RURAL NEXUS: CHIEFS, PEASANTS AND MIGRANT LABOUR

The history of the colonial state in Uganda can be divided into three phases, each characterised by a distinct political constellation and economic thrust. The first phase, 1893-1922, was characterised by the political dyarchy of the colonial state and collaborative chiefs, which integrated Uganda into the vertical international division of labour. In the second phase, 1922-45, state-appointed salaried chiefs replaced the self-recruited collaborative chiefs, and resident European and Asian firms gained representation within the Legislative Council (1921). The economic thrust of the second phase was simply the maintenance of the colonial pattern of trade. However, although the colonial state reinforced ethnic-tribal divisions in this period and restricted African entry into commerce, Africans made some gains in education and political organisation which set the stage for political decolonisation. Similarly, the creation of a protected Kenya-Uganda market for scheduled locally-produced commodities in 1923, and its enlargement to include Tanganyika and Zanzibar, laid the economic foundation for the manufacturing strategy of the third phase. During the third phase, 1945-62, the transition to formal decolonisation was marked by the gradual Africanisation of the colonial bureaucracy, the manoeuvring of African political factions for control of the post-colonial state and a decline in the formal political role of European and Asian commercial interests. The economic thrust of the third phase was the modernisation of dependence through minor adjustments in the colonial pattern of trade and in the domestic division of labour. Specifically, this involved state-assisted import substitution and state-assisted formation of a small African commercial stratum.

We examine first the rural nexus of political control, the propagation of cash crops and the production of migrant labour. In the subsequent chapter we turn to the changing role of the colonial state within the wider economy.

Conflicts Within the Dyarchy

British colonial administration from 1893 to 1900 was largely an exercise in expanding and securing military control over Uganda with the aid of Baganda chiefs and Sudanese and Indian troops. Over half the colonial expenditures in this period were allocated to military purposes. Only following the capture of Kabalega and Mwanga and the signing of the 1900 agreement in Buganda could the colonial state be considered *the state* in the Weberian sense of successfully claiming a monopoly on the legitimate use of force within a given territory.

Although the colonial security force of 2,625 soldiers and police[1] was well-armed and able to draw on reinforcements from British East Africa (Kenya) and India, its ability to police the territory was in large part dependent on the energetic collaboration of African chiefs and their followers. As noted in the previous chapter, the chiefs played a central role in incorporating Uganda into the world economy after the focus of state policy shifted from extension of effective occupation to the attainment of self-financing administration through imposition of taxes, the promotion of agricultural exports and the installation of the infrastructure required by the colonial pattern of trade.

Thanks to the sub-imperialism of Baganda chiefs and agents and the colonial state's desire for a uniform, centralised pattern of administration, the hierarchical Buganda model of county (*saza*) administration was imposed wherever possible, even over segmentary societies. By 1920 the Protectorate had been divided into five provinces (Buganda, Eastern, Northern, Western and Rudolph), which were subdivided into districts and counties. At the time, there were approximately 85 county chiefs: 20 in Buganda, 14 in Ankole, 10 each in Bukedi and Toro, 8 each in Busoga and Lango, 6 in Bunyoro, 5 in Teso and at least 4 in Kigezi.[2] Below these *saza* chiefs were hundreds of chiefs and headmen at the sub-county (*gombolola*), parish (*muruka*) and village levels.

Conflicts between the chiefs and the colonial state centred on five issues: lines of authority, allocation of freehold estates outside Buganda, control over *corvée*, income to chiefs from commissions on collected taxes, and education. The common element in these disputes was the question whether the dyarchy should continue. For their part, the chiefs wished to continue the dyarchy and transform themselves into a hereditary landed nobility. The colonial state, on the other hand, viewed the demands of the chiefs for greater privileges as a threat to colonial hegemony and sought therefore to reduce the autonomy of the chiefs, in effect to end the dyarchy.

Under the dyarchy, the multiple roles of the chiefs blurred the institutional boundaries of the colonial state. On the one hand, the chiefs formed part of the administrative cadres of the colonial state, bearing responsibility for tax assessment and collection, maintenance of law and order, promotion of cotton production, conscription of *luwalo* labour for the construction and maintenance of local roads and public buildings, and conscription of *kasanvu* labour (1909-22) for the colonial state.[3] On the other hand, in their capacity as landlords on official and personal estates, the chiefs functioned as a social class rather than as agents of the state. They derived income from commissions on tax collection, from sale of produce from their estates and from rent, tithes and *corvée* from their tenant-subjects. In tax collection the chief was directly accountable to the colonial state; in other official duties he was indirectly accountable via the Kabaka's government in Buganda[4] and the local Lukiko, or council of county chiefs, elsewhere. It was the issue of whether chiefs could deal directly with the colonial state without going through the Kabaka's government that was to precipitate the downfall of Katikiro Apolo Kagwa in 1925.

In Busoga, Bunyoro, Ankole and Toro the chiefs pressed unsuccessfully for inheritable freehold estates modelled on the *mailo* estates established by the Buganda agreement of 1900. Except for non-hereditary official estates, the colonial government was willing to allocate only a few hundred square miles of freehold estates to the 'ruling families' in Busoga, Bunyoro, Ankole and Toro, in contrast to the thousands of square miles of *mailo* estates allocated to the royal family, chiefs and followers in Buganda. With its base secure in Buganda, the colonial state could afford to drive a hard bargain elsewhere.

In Busoga, the colonial state deemed chiefly estates in *bwesengeze* sub-counties to be non-inheritable official estates rather than inheritable freehold. The initial colonial state opposition to large-scale freehold grants to chiefs outside Buganda sprang from the desire to keep open the European plantation option. In the early 1920s, however, the fall in world commodity prices and the rise in African wages, caused by currency fluctuations (the Indian rupee's advance against the pound) and the abolition of *kasanvu*, temporarily undermined European plantations and confirmed the resiliency of peasant production. Thereafter, colonial opposition to extension of African freehold shifted to new ground, namely that Buganda lagged behind other areas in cotton production. Over the period 1911-20, Buganda averaged only 17 hectares under cotton per thousand population compared to 49 hectares per thouand in Busoga and 73 in Teso.[5] Over the period 1921-31, Buganda narrowed the gap somewhat, planting an average 85 hectares of cotton per thousand population, compared to 123 in Busoga and 175 in Teso.[6] Yet the persisting gap demonstrated that freehold estates were not the optimal form of land tenure for expanding cotton production. From the colonial state's perspective, the problem with freehold estates lay not only in relatively low output of export crops but in the undesirable autonomy such estates afforded chiefs.

In labour policy the maintenance of colonial rule and the expansion of export commodity production required the creation of a class of wage-labourers to be employed in cotton ginneries, on plantations, in the transport of commodities and in the construction of roads, administrative buildings and expatriate housing. When the labour force failed to materialise at the wages deemed appropriate for subject races, the colonial state resorted to the forced labour *kasanvu* system, paying wages below the market rate and thereby depressing the market rate. It was the chiefs who conscripted *kasanvu* labour and granted exemptions. By 1920 the colonial state demanded 20,500 *kasanvu* recruits per month in Buganda alone for public works and, occasionally, for private employment on plantations.[7] Viewing this as a drain on their own supply of labour, the chiefs in the Buganda Lukiko demanded the abolition of *kasanvu*. When Britain ordered a ban on forced labour in 1922 because of scandalous mistreatment of forced labourers in Kenya, the ban included *kasanvu* but did not extend to the traditional *corvée* obligations of tenant-subjects to chiefs in Uganda.[8] Since the prestige and authority of chiefs was maintained in large part by *corvée* obligations of subjects and since the income of chiefs was in part derived from commissions on tax collection and from various forms of tribute from tenant-subjects, the chiefs, particularly in Buganda and Busoga, had a vested interest in preventing the out-migration of their subjects. Hence, rightly or wrongly, non-African employers felt that the chiefs were responsible for the reduced supply of wage-labour following the abolition of *kasanvu*.

When chiefs in Buganda, Busoga and Toro petitioned the colonial state in the 1920s to allow their sons to attend university abroad, colonial officials discouraged such proposals and recalled some students who had already gone abroad, arguing that university-educated Africans could not accommodate themselves to colonial society upon their return.[9] What the European administrators feared was the return of university-trained Africans demanding high-level positions within the state apparatus and equality with Europeans. While rudimentary social equality between African chiefs and European administrators might have been a necessary part of the initial 'pacification' of Uganda, it jarred the European vision of the 'proper' racial order in East Africa as a new generation of British administrators filled the ranks of the civil service of the Protectorate. The highest ranking African administrators, the powerful *saza* chiefs, were formally excluded from the ranks of the colonial civil service proper and were segregated into ethnically compartmentalised Native Administrations, which, with the partial exception of Buganda, increasingly fell under the control and direction of the European Provincial and District Commissioners.[10] The removal of Baganda agents from administrative posts outside Buganda in response to popular discontent against the Ganda-agent system completed the process of ethnic compartmentalisation. At the centre, the colonial civil service emerged as a three-tier structure in which Europeans held the highest posts, Asians filled the intermediate clerical and artisanal positions, and Africans were relegated to the lowest, usually non-pensionable posts as messengers, file clerks, interpreters and labourers.[11]

Yet, in the 1920s the incomes of many county chiefs from tax commissions and commercial farming surpassed the fixed salaries of European administrators. The case of the *saza* chief of Bugabula county, Busoga, has already been mentioned. His estimated 1924 income of £3,500 compared favourably with the £3,000 annual salary, plus £1,000 duty allowance, of the Governor and the £1,300 salary, plus £200 duty allowance, of the Chief Secretary; it greatly exceeded the £1,000 salary of the Provincial Commissioner for the Eastern Region.[12] Moreover, the annual salary of the lowest paid Europeans in the colonial service ranged between £300 and £315 plus free housing, or roughly one-tenth the income of *saza* chiefs in the major commodity-producing areas. Perhaps it is not so surprising that Chief Gideon Obaja of Kibulu County, Busoga, contemptuously referred to European administrators as *his* employees.[13] Nor is it surprising that European administrators used every means to bring about the dismissal of Chief Obaja and other self-recruited or hereditary collaborative chiefs who viewed themselves as the equals or betters of the European newcomers. The colonial state's policy towards the income of the chiefs was not unlike a factory owner's policy regarding the wages of workers and salesmen. As long as their productivity was low, it was cheaper to pay by piecework or commission. When, however, productivity rose, it became cheaper to shift to fixed wages and eliminate commissions.[14]

Termination of the Dyarchy

The colonial state's dismantling of the dyarchy had in a sense begun in
1906 with the initial exile of Kakungulu from Mbale to Busoga and
Governor Jackson's abrupt condemnation of the use of Ganda agents in
1911. By 1914 the Ganda agents had been or were being withdrawn
from Bunyoro, Busoga, Bukedi and Bugisu. However, Ganda agents
were used as advisers and even county chiefs in Lango, Acholi and
Teso at least through 1919 and in Kigezi until 1928-30. When local
chiefs, whether self-recruited or appointed, failed to meet the requirements of the colonial order, the Protectorate Government installed
Ganda agents in their place, as in Ankole (1905-8), Toro (1923-4) and
Teso (1927-30). Not all the 'agents' were Baganda. Toro chiefs served as
sub-imperial agents in Bwamba; the Munyoro general Kazana ruled as
agent over Kumam and parts of Lango from 1902 to 1919; and a
Munyoro chief and several Sudanese or 'Nubian' soldiers left behind by
Emin Pasha functioned as agents among the West Nile Lugbara. In
much of Uganda, the colonial state created *ex nihilo* 'traditional' chiefs
to administer territorial units that were often equally artificial. Even
where traditional chiefs predated colonial rule, the British distorted
their original functons and domain, demoting former kings to *saza*
chiefs (Buhweju in Ankole, Bulamogi in Busoga) or even to *gombolola*
chiefs (in Kigezi), elevating segmentary clan heads to hierarchical
county chiefs (Lango, Teso, Bugisu), enlarging and amalgamating
chiefdoms (West Nile) or kingdoms (Buganda, Busoga, Toro, Ankole,
Acholi), and severing one kingdom (Bunyoro, which lost territory to
Buganda).[15]

Furthermore, authentic traditional chiefs holding hereditary posts
outside Buganda were transformed into appointed civil servants by a
four-stage process. First, the traditional chief would be recognised as
a chief within the terms of the Native Authority Ordinance of 1919,
which defined the duties and powers of chiefs and confirmed the
colonial state's authority to appoint, transfer and dismiss chiefs and to
regulate their conditions of service. Second, the traditional chief would
be retired and replaced by a mission-trained son or relative chosen by
the colonial state. Third, the new chief would be transferred to a post
other than the traditional one. Fourth, having separated the chief from
his traditional political base, the original post would be made appointive
rather than hereditary. By this lengthy process the colonial state
eliminated hereditary county chiefs in Busoga (the kings of Bugabula,
Luuka, Bulamogi, etc.), hereditary chiefs among the Alur in West Nile

and hereditary *rwodi* (the kings of Atyak, Padibe, Puranga, Patiko, Pajule, etc.) in Acholi.[16] Village headmen in Busoga, by contrast, retained their hereditary positions by refusing both official status and salaries.

In Buganda, *saza* chiefs were guaranteed a salary under the 1900 agreement and *gombolola* chiefs were salaried by 1916. But in Buganda and elsewhere the bulk of chiefs' incomes was derived, as noted earlier, from tribute, rent, *corvée* and tax commissions. Beginning in Toro in 1923 and in other areas after 1926, the colonial state instituted fixed salaries for all grades of chiefs in lieu of tribute, rebates and rent. Tribute, rebates and sometimes rent formerly pocketed by *saza* chiefs, *gombolola* chiefs and private landowners were now to be paid into the European-supervised coffers of the district Native Administration. Except in Buganda, the district Native Administration Treasury was but a central government fund for local salaries, public works and services controlled by the Provincial Commissioner and the District Commissioner.[17] With this transfer of resources for social services and patronage from African chiefs to European officials, the role of chiefs was reduced to essentially negative tasks which did little to enhance their popularity: tax assessment and collection; maintenance of law and order including imprisonment of minor offenders; enforcement of rules for cotton cultivation; enforcement of rules for cultivation of famine root crops (cassava and sweet potatoes); control of manufacture and consumption of alcoholic beverages; recruitment of communal labour; supervision of weed and brush control; restriction of tree-cutting; regulation of grazing; waste disposal and prevention of water pollution; provision of food and porters for visiting European officials; arbitration and adjudication of local disputes; and promulgation of orders as dictated by the District Commissioner or Provincial Commissioner.[18]

Self-recruited collaborative chiefs within Buganda became expendable in the 1920s. Not only had the chiefs outlived their initial political usefulness as collaborators and sub-imperialist agents, but they now posed a barrier to the consolidation of the colonial state's political hegemony. Moreover, they constituted a *rentier* class which, according to colonial officials, stifled expansion of commodity production by appropriating an ever larger share of economic surplus for its own consumption. Dominated by *bakungu* landlord-chiefs, the Buganda Lukiko authorised landlords to collect a 10 per cent *envujo* (tithe) from *kibanja* tenants on cotton and coffee cash crops. Although the Governor vetoed this measure in 1921 as well as a similar 5 per cent

levy in 1924, landlords continued to collect *envujo* on cash crops, with
the rate ranging from 10 per cent in 1921 to as much as 35 per cent on
cotton and 20 per cent on coffee in 1926.[19] On the political side,
popular protests led by Josuwa Kate forced Apolo Kagwa to shelve his
proposal for a House of Lords to enable large landowners to dominate
the Lukiko and Kabaka.[20]

The arrogance of the *bakungu* chiefs led by Katikiro Kagwa gave
rise to organised political protest in the form of the *bataka* movement
led by the Bataka Association. It was this movement founded in 1921
which both enabled and compelled the colonial state to liquidate
vestiges of the dyarchy with semi-autonomous chiefs. The base of the
bataka movement consisted of peasants aggrieved by the multiple
burdens of enforced cotton cultivation, the high rate of *envujo* on
cash crops, the *busulu* rent, the *luwalo corvée*/tax and the colonial poll
tax on adult males collected by chiefs. The *busulu*, at Shs. 5 to Shs. 12
per tenant, represented the cash commutation of the pre-1902 *mpalo
corvée* of one month's labour for the chief. *Luwalo*, originally a
communal obligation of one month's unpaid labour on local roads and
buildings, had since 1920 been commutable, at the chief's discretion,
to payment of Shs. 10 tax to the Buganda Government Treasury. In
addition, there were the less visible burdens of export duties on cotton
and import duties on consumer goods such as textiles.

Widespread discontent on the part of subject-tenants enabled one
element in the pre-1888 ruling class, the *bataka* heads of hereditary
clans, to form a populist alliance with the peasants to challenge the
privileges conferred on *bakungu* chiefs by the 1900 agreement. The
alliance was led by James Miti, a former Ganda agent in Bunyoro, and
by 16 heads of clans, including Josuwa (Yosya) Kate, who was both the
Mugema or head of the important Nkima (monkey) clan and county
chief of Busiro. Kate had previously clashed with the Katikiro over the
proposed House of Lords in 1912 and over preserving the Nkima clan's
central ceremonial role in the Kabaka's investiture in 1914.[21]

Invoking claims to legitimacy based on tradition, the Bataka Association argued that the 1900 agreement had wrongfully deprived clans of
their ancestral communal land. Although major *bataka* estates had been
allocated to heads of clans under the agreement, such land had been
allocated to clan heads as individuals, thereby becoming alienable
outside the clan under court interpretations of the Land Law of 1908.
Furthermore, many minor *bataka* estates had been allocated to *bakungu*
chiefs and even the colonial state rather than to clan heads.[22] Since
every Muganda is a member of one of the 30 or more Kiganda clans,

the Bataka Association was able to mobilise extensive popular support for its cause.

After being rebuffed by the Lukiko, the Bataka Association presented its case to the Governor and then to Kabaka Daudi Chwa, who was also *Sabataka*, or head of all clans. Rejecting a compromise formulated by the Kabaka, the *bakungu*-dominated Lukiko claimed exclusive right to resolve land allocation disputes arising from the 1900 agreement. The Bataka Association responded by asking the Kabaka to broaden representation in the Lukiko to eliminate its *bakungu* bias, but Kabaka Chwa ignored the request.[23]

Ultimately, the colonial state re-entered the *bataka* land controversy, establishing a commission of inquiry and referring the dispute to the British Secretary of State for the Colonies, who ruled in 1926 that the rightful historical claims of the *bataka* were outweighed by the practical difficulty of reverting to the pre-1888 *status quo*.[24] None the less, the colonial state soon demonstrated that it hardly considered sacrosanct the existing land tenure system in Buganda.

First, the colonial state forcibly retired Katikiro Apolo Kagwa, the dominant political figure in Buganda for three decades, the man who symbolised the dyarchical alliance between the older *bakungu* chiefs and the colonial state. The issue that precipitated Kagwa's downfall in 1926 was his conflict with Provincial Commissioner Postlethwaite, who insisted that lower chiefs be allowed to bypass the government of Buganda and deal directly with the colonial state.[25]

Second, with Kagwa out of the way, the colonial state used the threat of outright abolition of *envujo* to force the Lukiko in 1927 to enact a rent control measure, the Busulu and Envujo Law. With effect from 1 January 1928, the law limited the amount of *busulu* (rent) and *envujo* (tithe) that a *mailo* owner could exact from the tenant of a traditional *kibanja* holding. *Busulu* was fixed at Shs. 10 per annum for the entire *kibanja*, and *envujo* restricted to Shs. 4 per acre per annum for the first three acres planted in cotton and coffee.[26] Moreover, subject to the condition that the *kibanja* remain under continuous cultivation, the new law guaranteed the *kibanja* tenant the security of *inheritable* tenancy, regardless of changes in ownership of the *mailo* containing the *kibanja.*

Hitherto, the colonial state had tolerated landlords collecting ever-increasing levels of *envujo* on export crops as their incentive for prodding tenants to take up cash crop cultivation. Henceforth, freezing the tithe at a low level was to be the instrument for encouraging *bibanja* tenants to grow more cash crops. Certainly in their arguments defending *envujo*, the *bakungu* chiefs and the Kabaka recognised that maximising cotton production was a central concern of the colonial state.[27] What was also at issue was the growing income of the landlords, income which colonial administrators firmly believed should accrue instead to the colonial state.[28]

One must discount claims that it was the colonial state's solicitude for the plight of ordinary peasants that prompted passage of the Busulu and Envujo Law.[29] The *bataka* agitation fueled by underlying agrarian discontent may well have spurred the colonial state into action, but low peasant income by itself did not. As far as colonial officialdom was concerned, 'with the possible exception of 1927, . . . the native had usually obtained more than he should for his cotton'.[30]

Apolo Kagwa's retirement and the changes in land tenure satisfied immediate peasant grievances, thereby undermining the popular base of the Bataka Association. Although claims to lost *bataka* land faded, clan heads remained symbolically linked with opposition to autocratic administrative chiefs. Clans continued to be an important factor in land tenure in other ways: lineage and clan councils screened individual heirs to land, including individually-owned *bataka* land; and shared clan membership afforded the buyer a discount in ordinary land purchases.[31]

As for the original collaborative *bakungu* chiefs, Kagwa's retirement accelerated the process of transforming them from semi-autonomous political entrepreneurs into appointed servants of the colonial state. Already in 1913, the colonial state, after barring *bakungu* chiefs from holding double chieftancies as *saza* chief in one county and *gombolola* chief in another, had intervened in the selection of the 20-odd probationers to fill the *gombolola* vacancies.[32] Throughout the 1920s and early 1930s it moved to dismiss or to retire forcibly self-recruited *bakungu* chiefs and replace them with appointees drawn from the ranks of African clerks in the Protectorate government. The colonial state thus achieved two aims: the taming and bureaucratisation of the Buganda government and removal from the Protectorate government of African clerks who were activists in the mildly syndicalist BGNEA. The BGNEA (British Government Native Employees' Association) was founded by African employees of the Uganda Government in 1922-3 to campaign for African equality with Asian and European government employees in conditions of service and to protest against the paternalistic racism of colonial officials. Serwano Kulubya, Sepiriya Kadumukasa, Joswa Kamulegeya, Yusufu Bamuta, Sulemani Waligo, Erasito Bakaluba, Yosiya Sewali, Serwanga Sadulaka and Michael Kintu were but a few of the colonial government interpreters and clerks who were later appointed to Buganda government posts ranging from *gombolola* chief to Katikiro.[33] Even so, with 145 of 212 *saza* and *gombolola* chiefs being replaced between 1921 and 1933,[34] the high turnover meant that less than half of the new chiefs could have previously served in the Uganda government. Whether the high turnover of chiefs was due mainly to colonial state interference or simply illness and age, it had a striking effect: the Buganda government that faced the colonial state in the 1930s was as docile and subordinate as the District 'Native' Adminstrations in other provinces, notwithstanding Buganda's unique legal status[35] and its special economic status as the commercial centre of Uganda.

As shown in Table 2.1, by the late 1940s, *saza* (county) chiefs in Buganda earned salaries that differed but little from salaries of *saza* chiefs in most districts in other provinces. Significantly, the average salary of a Buganda *saza* chief in 1948 was equal to what had been the lowest salary of European employees of the colonial state in 1923: about £300 per annum. Despite the reduction in the number of *gombololas* (sub-counties) in Buganda from about 190 in the 1920s to 135 in 1948, *gombolola* chiefs' salaries were, if anything, lower in Buganda than elsewhere. But what continued to separate chiefs in Buganda from chiefs elsewhere was the fact that the former could and did own private estates, whereas private estates were the exception elsewhere.[36] And what separated Buganda in general from the rest of Uganda was the fact that in Buganda the combination of the 1900 agreement and the Busulu and Envujo Law had created a unique land-tenure system, the *mailo-kibanja* system, under which the more ambitious peasants could rise from tenant status to that of capitalist farmer.

Variations in Land Tenure in Uganda over Time and Space

Whatever complex motives had occasioned the enforced passage of the Busulu and Envujo Law in 1927, it was for its colonial context a remarkably progressive measure, one which transformed rural relations of production, though often in ways not foreseen by the colonial state. For example, its immediate effect was not the hoped-for expansion of cotton production but a land-buying spree by tenants and a sudden spurt in coffee production in Buganda.

As Buganda Finance Minister Serwano Kulubya reported in 1931,

Table 2.1: Colonial Hierarchy of Chiefs in Uganda, 1947-8

Province District	County level		Sub-county level		Parish (*muruka*) level		Sub-parish (*mutala*) level	
	Number	Annual[a] salary (pounds)	Number	Annual[b] salary (pounds)	Number	Annual[c] salary (pounds)	Number	Annual salary (pounds)
Buganda	20	240-600[d] av. 329	135	av. 73[e]	1,328	9-20	_[f]	—
Eastern								
Busoga	8	250-570	52[g]	70-192	265	24-54	1,200[g]	None[h]
Bukedi	6	250-570	27	70-192	117	24-54	250	11-36
Bugisu	4	250-570	26	70-192	98	24-54	258	11-36
Teso[i]	7	250-570 av. 291	44	70-192 av. 124	185	24-54 av. 38	377	14-35 av. 20
Western								
Bunyoro	4	200-300	24	30-120	65	9-30	160	6-9
Toro	7	120-350[j]	37	30-180[k]	214	10-20	462[l]	6-9
Ankole	10	150-350	55	30-132	333[m]	15-21	449[m]	8
Kigezi	5	180-350	35[n]	42-84	151[n]	12-15	311	3.12s
Northern								
Acholi	6	105-170	22	75-123	71	21-45	143	15
Lango	7	285-390	37	105-147	74	12-45	226	12-15
West Nile[o]	15	80-420	51	27-180	n.a.	12-52	n.a.	6
Karamoja	6	60	32	30	n.a.	18	n.a.	—
Total No.	105		577		2,901 excluding W. Nile and Karamoja			

Notes:

[a] County-level chiefs also enjoyed free housing and a pension.

[b] Sub-county level chiefs enjoyed free housing and either a pension or a lump-sum gratuity upon retirement.

[c] Parish level chiefs received neither housing nor retirement benefits.

[d] Each *saza* chief in Buganda also enjoyed the usufruct from official estates totalling nearly 8 square miles.

[e] Each *gombolola* chief in Buganda enjoyed the usufruct from official estates totalling 49 acres, located on the *saza* chief's official *mailo*.

[f] Officially there were no chiefs below the level of *muruka* chief in Buganda. However, a *muruka* chief might appoint assistants as *batongole* chiefs, the *musigire* (steward) appointed by a *mailo* owner functioned as a local headman; and landowners themselves were considered *batongole*.

[g] Lloyd A. Fallers, 'The Soga', *East African Chiefs*, ed. by Audrey I. Richards (London: Faber and Faber, 1959), p. 83. Data from 1950-2.

[h] The Basoga headmen at the *mutala* (ridge or 'village') and *kisoko* (sub-village) levels held unsalaried, hereditary posts which were not officially recognised by the colonial state. The headmen had rejected official salaried status in 1936, continuing instead to collect land allocation fees (*nzibuzi* or *nkoko*) from new *bibanja* tenants.

[i] 1950 Teso data from African Studies Branch, Colonial Office, 'Uganda; A Survey of Local Government Since 1947', *Journal of African Administration*, vol. 4, no. 2 (April 1952), p. 30.

[j] The county chiefs of the five counties recognised in the Toro Agreement of 1900 enjoyed the usufruct of 10-square mile official estates. The other two county chiefs enjoyed lifetime usufruct from 100-acre official estates. The Toro Landlord and Tenant Law of 1937 limited rent to Shs. 4 per annum per tenant.

[k] Each sub-county chief in Toro enjoyed lifetime usufruct from a 49-acre official estate.

[l] There was a fifth level of chiefs below the *bakungu* village chiefs: namely the unsalaried headmen of *migongo* (sub-villages). A.I. Richards and B.K. Taylor, 'The Toro', *East African Chiefs*, p. 136.

[m] D.J. Stenning, 'The Nyankole', *East African Chiefs*, p. 160, number of chiefs in 1957.

[n] P.T.W. Baxter, 'The Kiga', *East African Chiefs*, p. 291, number of chiefs in 1955.

[o] A.W. Southall and A.I. Richards, 'The Alur', *East African Chiefs*, p. 322, salaries of chiefs in 1950.

Source: Lord Hailey, *Native Administration in the British African Territories* (London: HMSO, 1950), vol. I, pp. 1-85, except as otherwise noted.

'There is a big movement now. People are buying land. Anybody who gets some money wants to buy his own land . . . from the chiefs.'[37] Despite the security of tenure afforded by the new law, many status-conscious tenants preferred buying full title to the *kibanja*, thereby becoming a small-scale *mailo* owner (*nannyini ttaka*). Although such purchases diverted capital from agricultural improvements, they did enable the new owner to undertake future improvements without seeking permission from the landlord, permission which might not have been forthcoming under the new law. Landownership also conferred on the owner of even a few acres the right to participate in local councils (*nkiko*) and the opportunity, however slim, to be appointed *muruka* chief, the lowest rung on the ladder of political success in Buganda.[38]

Moreover, since land reform had reduced the rental income and thus the market value of large *mailo* tracts encumbered by customary tenants, *mailo* owners were suddenly more willing to sell *bibanja* holdings to current tenants. By selling small land parcels to tenants, large large *mailo* owners temporarily shielded themselves from the income-reducing effects of land reform. In addition, landlords were permitted to levy commercial rents and tithes on inheritable *bibanja* holdings with more than three acres planted in cash crops and could charge ample rent on non-inheritable holdings, or leased land known as *bupangisa*. The *mailo* owner could also levy an 'entrance fee' on a *kibanja* allocated to a new tenant. Although the Buganda Lukiko, the colonial state and the British Colonial Office had, by a series of measures between 1906 and 1922,[39] severely restricted the sale of lease of *mailo* land to non-Africans, attempts by more zealous Baganda to bar non-Baganda Africans from *mailo* purchases, *bupangisa* leases and *bibanja* tenancies failed to become law. However, migrants from outside Buganda tended to be charged higher rent on *bupangisa* leases and *envujo* far above legal limits on new *bibanja* holdings and faced social obstacles in buying *mailo* land.[40]

But one of the most important consequences of the Busulu and Envujo Law was that, over time, it made possible the rise of small-scale capitalist farmers who, given the secure tenure required for bringing coffee trees to maturity (two to three years), shifted from cotton to producing coffee for the world market, using migrant labour from outside Buganda. Robusta coffee acreage on African holdings in Buganda rose from less than 1,000 acres in 1925 to 16,170 in 1930, 32,255 in 1938, 62,636 in 1944 and 142,523 in 1946.[41]

By 1962 the size of individual holdings farmed by this new stratum varied greatly, from the original *kibanja* of three acres, possibly five, to very large holdings with 80 or more acres planted in coffee. For example, in Masaka District only 3.7 per cent of rural households farmed holdings larger than 25 acres; nevertheless, with an average holding of 68 acres of which 15 to 30 acres might be coffee, this group alone accounted for one-third of the district's cultivated acreage. Yet we must include as capitalist farmers some with very small holdings containing only 1½ to 8 acres of coffee. The average farmer in a sample of such holdings in Masaka District cultivated only 2.9 acres of coffee; even so, he (or she) employed 27 man-months of wage-labour during the year.[42]

Whether individual members were tenants, landowners or a bit of both and whether cultivated holdings were large or small, this upwardly mobile stratum could be labelled *capitalist tenant-farmers*. They were farmers, as distinct from landlords, both because they derived income primarily from the cultivation of cash crops rather than from rent and because family members themselves laboured in the fields. Unlike simple cultivators who produced for the world market using only family labour, they were capitalist farmers who regularly employed wage-labour. Finally, 'tenant' describes not only their humble origins but also the fact that they frequently rented land to expand production. The archetypal antecedents of these capitalist tenant-farmers in Buganda include the yeomen of sixteenth-century England, the kulaks of nineteenth-century Russia and the rich peasants of twentieth-century China.[43] As Barrington Moore observed, although basically similar in economic function, their respective emotive legacies — progressive heroes in England, reactionary villains in the Soviet Union and China — hinged both on their political roles *vis-à-vis* the state and on the nation's course in the world system.[44]

In the five decades after 1927, capitalist tenant-farmers in Buganda played a dualistic political role: progressive nationalists struggling against the colonial economic order, yet conservative, even reactionary, neo-traditionalists defending Buganda's privileged status within Uganda. But unlike yeomen and kulaks, Buganda's capitalist tenant-farmers and their imitators in other districts may reap neither honour nor abuse from future generations. For Uganda's peripheral role in the world economy as a small raw material producer circumscribes the scope and impetus for continued rationalisation of agricultural production by such capitalist farmers. Instead, they face the danger of sliding *en masse* into semi-subsistence cultivation for the world market on increasingly fragmented family plots.

Already in 1954 a committee investigating agricultural productivity warned that soil fertility on *bupangisa* tenancies in Buganda had declined so sharply that it could be said 'the land is being mined and not farmed'.[45] Land purchases and inheritance increased the number of landowners in Buganda from less than 4,000 in the initial *mailo* allocation after the turn of the century to approximately 112,000 in 1967, or from less than 1.0 to 6.1 per cent of the population.[46]

But whether there was a trend towards significant democratisation of landownership or a slide towards excessive land fragmentation is a matter of interpretation, which hinges on the choice of the unit of analysis. Because the unit of landownership in Buganda is not necessarily coterminous with the unit of cultivation, trends in concentration or fragmentation of landownership may be only dimly reflected in patterns of land cultivation by households, and vice versa.

Examining the disposition over time of 55 original *mailo* titles covering 23,053 acres west of Kampala and 43 titles covering 28,574 acres northwest of Masaka, Mukwaya found the number of landowners increased as follows: 135 in 1920, 225 in 1930, 476 in 1940 and 687 in 1950.[47] Had this curvilinear trend continued, the average size of an estate would have declined from 382.4 acres in 1920 and 75.2 acres in 1950 to 13.0 acres in 1980. But these averages conceal the extreme inequality in the size of estates. While inequality in landownership among all *taxpayers* declined only slightly between 1920 and 1950, as measured by the Gini index (1920: 0.98; 1950: 0.97), inequality among *landowners* actually increased due to the sharp rise in the number of landowners with less than 20 acres (Gini index of original *mailo* titles: 0.53; 1920: 0.58; 1930: 0.68; 1940: 0.74; 1950: 0.73).[48] The great increase in the number of landowners was due primarily to purchases rather than to inheritance, but inherited estates tended to be far larger than purchased estates.[49] Despite the absence of primogeniture in Buganda, it was the custom to leave the major portion of an estate to one heir. Mukwaya concluded that inheritance had tended to preserve the large *mailo* estates while land purchases had tended to create a substantial number of small landowners.

Using another type of data drawn from a later time period, the 1950-65 records of the *Ddiiro* or Buganda Standing Committee on Succession, West emerged with the strikingly different conclusion that continued unregulated inheritance would result in excessive fragmentation rather than perpetuation of large holdings, whereas only land purchases could achieve the consolidation 'by private enterprise' necessary for rationalisation and improved productivity. Noting that the major heir's portion was in practice treated as the residual portion by first parcelling out bequests to other heirs, West calculated that the share of the total estate received by the designated 'successor' declined from an average 53.6 per cent in 1956 to 36.5 per cent in 1965. As the size of estates of deceased landowners declined from an average 185.7 acres in 1950-2 to 123.4 acres in 1963-4, the average size of estates acquired by all beneficiaries declined from 34.7 to 24.4 acres. Notwithstanding these trends, West concluded that, in contrast to Kigezi, Bugisu and Bukedi, land fragmentation was not yet a serious problem in Buganda.[50] The average size of the successor's estate in 1964 was a respectable 45 acres, in a kingdom in which, according to the 1963 agricultural census, the household unit of cultivation averaged only 6.3 acres and the median size holding was a mere 4.5 acres.

It is necessary to place changes in land tenure in Buganda within a wider context. For Uganda as a whole, there were three major phases in official colonial policy towards land tenure between 1891 and 1962. In the first phase, the colonial state attempted to set aside as much Crown Land as possible for forest reserves, mineral concessions and future alienation to European planters and settlers, while allowing collaborative chiefs substantial autonomy in extracting surplus from subjects both for themselves and for the pressing financial requirements of the colonial state. The variations in this policy across Uganda have already been noted.[51] World market fluctuations between 1920 and 1922 reduced the number of European-owned plantations from 204 to 146 and confirmed the resilience of peasant-based production of cash crops. In order to undercut the economic independence of chiefs and to remove the real or imagined fetters placed on peasant production by landlordism, the colonial state restricted the prerogatives of landlords in Buganda and their far less numerous counterparts in Toro and Ankole and attempted to extinguish the economic claims of landlords upon tenant-subjects in Bunyoro and Busoga. Tribute from peasants was redirected from landlords to district treasuries to pay the salaries of chiefs. The emergence of capitalist farmers in Buganda during this second phase was an entirely fortuitous consequence of colonial policy. Only in the third phase, from 1950 or perhaps only 1955, did the colonial state abandon the ideal of peasant producers in secure tenure but without marketable land title and foster the ideal of peasant proprietors who could buy and sell land. At the apex of the new rural social order stood the capitalist farmer, or yeoman or progressive farmer, who was to be the stabilising force in the transition to independence and post-colonial society.[52] However, it could be argued that the colonial state had done much to hinder the formation of this stratum by severely depressing the price to producers for export crops between 1943 and 1952.

Even so, colonial policy was but one element in the matrix of factors affecting land tenure. For land tenure was the product of at least four factors: (1) traditional land tenure, whose diversity across Uganda evolved from the interplay of social and environmental forces; (2) changes wrought by the incorporation of Uganda into the capitalist world economy, in particular the commercialisation of agriculture and the enforced appearance of wage-labour; (3) variations in colonial policy from district to district, as well as over time; and (4) the response of African groups and strata to opportunities and obstacles presented by variations in colonial policy.

The interaction of traditional land tenure and commercialisation of agriculture can be illustrated by comparing the Sebei in eastern Uganda with the Bwamba in western Uganda. Among the Sebei on the northern slopes of Mt Elgon, domestic animals ranging from hens to cattle were traditionally the private property of individual men, who by *contractual* agreements exchanged, leased and sold animals in order to build up a herd of cattle. Goldschmidt reports the Sebei entertained Horatio Alger myths of building a sizeable cattle herd from a single hen through a series of advantageous contracts. (The neighbouring Bagisu went a step further with (field) rats-to-riches stories of success.) The Sebei held a Lockean view of private property, namely that things in nature are common property until a person mixes his labour with the natural object to make something useful, then that product becomes the private property of the person whose effort went into making it.[53] However, just as Locke barred the servant from ownership of the turf he had cut, so too did Sebei men bar women from ownership of the land they tilled.[54] With the sale of cattle and grain to Swahili trade caravans in the mid-nineteenth century, the traditional concept of private property in cattle became more generalised, paving the way for the commercialisation of agriculture. Following the introduction of arabica coffee around 1922, land in western Sebei quickly became private property, though the use of plants to demarcate permanent boundaries of individual plots was reported as early as 1910. By the 1920s land was being bought and sold for money rather than cattle as the Sebei transferred the concept of private property in cattle to private property in land, extinguishing clan control over land allocation. By 1962 there was a population density of approximately 1,000 persons per square mile in southwest Sebei (Sasur), with individual households

cultivating an average 2.3 to 2.5 acres of food and cash crops for an
average annual cash income of Shs. 750, of which two-thirds came from
coffee sales.[55] Land was extremely scarce, and the price of land high,
higher than in the prime coffee-growing areas in Buganda.[56] Although
smaller-scale cultivators might employ only family labour, those with
two or more acres planted in arabica coffee employed seasonally both
wage-labour and *moyket*-labour (work paid in beer or meat), and were
therefore capitalist farmers. A landless proletariat only began appearing
in 1972; hence the bulk of wage-labourers came from smaller farmers
and cultivators.[57] The emergence of capitalist farmers in Sebei was thus
the product of traditional cattle tenure and the opportunities opened by
Uganda's integration into the world market. It was a development owing
nothing to a colonial land-tenure policy which did not recognise individual property rights on Crown Land in Bugisu-Sebei until after 1955.

A very different land-tenure system emerged among the Amba,
inhabitants of the Western Rift Valley between the Semliki River and
the northern slopes of the Ruwenzori mountains. Traditional Bwamba
land tenure was grounded in actual use of the soil, rather than in
permanent individual land rights and contracts. The partrilineage of a
given ridge or 'village' regulated land allocation. Every adult male had
the right to be allocated land for cultivation. Any land left uncultivated
for longer than the normal fallow period gradually reverted to the
patrilineage, thus becoming available for reallocation. Partly because of
a sleeping-sickness epidemic and partly for commercial reasons, the
colonial state designated half the Bwamba areas as a Forest Reserve after
the First World War and closed it to habitation. Toro agent-chiefs introduced robusta coffee in the 1920s, appropriating both Bwamba land
and *corvée* for its cultivation on the chiefs' estates. The Amba were also
required to grow robusta on their own plots to pay taxes. They had to
headload the coffee, and after 1930 seed cotton as well, 50 miles to
Fort Portal. Only in 1938 was a road built, replacing porters with
lorries.[58]

In spite of this harsh introduction to the world economy, Bwamba
land tenure survived largely unchanged, as Winter discovered in 1950-2.
Since there were no registered titles to land on what was in colonial
law Crown Land, land could not be used as collateral for loans, but
coffee groves could be mortgaged. Moreover, coffee groves could be
bought and sold, and therewith rights to the land. Another innovation
was that the Toro chiefs gained some control over land allocation,
particularly, to non-Amba. With a population density of 400 persons
per square mile in 1948, land in Bwamba was not as scarce as in south-

western Sebei, but disputes did arise over 'borrowed' land when the borrower refused to return land to the lender. Seen from the colonial goal of maximising export crop production, the only flaw in the traditional Bwamba system was a fortuitous product of a high divorce rate and the way the sexual division of labour evolved after Bwamba's incorporation into the world economy. Although the husband and wife each contributed labour to growing the new cash crops, men controlled the product and kept the proceeds from the sale of coffee and cotton. In a stable marriage this inequality might be partially offset by the husband's purchase of cloth for his wife. But, given the high divorce rate, women resented contributing labour to crops which enriched the husband, especially coffee, a perennial crop whose productivity might far outlast the marriage. Women preferred working on food crops, whose product they controlled, including rice which was a cash/food crop. Winter concluded that a lower divorce rate or a more equitable sexual division of labour might well boost coffee and cotton production. On the whole, though, the Bwamba land-tenure system represented the ideal of the colonial state's tenure policy in phase two: peasants in secure tenure, but without title, and tenure linked to continuous cultivation. The system was self-regulating and required no outlays by the colonial state for expensive cadastral surveys and land-title registers. And, although the Amba were willing to work for persons of higher socio-economic status, such as Europeans, their adamant refusal to work as wage-labourers for fellow-Amba added a further barrier to the emergence of the capitalist farmer of phase three.[59]

The three cases so far have been coffee-producing areas: Bantu-speaking Buganda and non-Bantu-speaking Sebei, both with capitalist farmers, and Bantu-speaking Bwamba without capitalist farmers. Whether through permanent individual ownership or through traditional rights based on continuous cultivation, growers in each of the three areas enjoyed the security of land tenure necessary for cultivating a perennial cash crop. We turn then to two potential coffee-growing areas which were deficient in this security: Busoga and Bunyoro.

Although the *bwesengeze* system started by Kakungulu was formally abolished in 1926 with the elimination of private chiefly estates and the abolition of tax rebates for chiefs, this was but one step in the longer 1922-36 transition from tribute-based incomes to fixed salaries for chiefs in Busoga. Before 1922 the labour obligation of subject-tenants for chiefs had been as high as 52 days a year. The labour obligation was reduced to one month in 1922, commutable to a cash payment of Shs. 10. With the abolition of tax rebates in 1926, this obligation was divided into two parts: twelve days of *corvée* for the chief, commutable to a cash payment of Shs. 4, and a cash payment of Shs. 6 to the Busoga Native Administration to finance the system of salaries and pensions being introduced for chiefs. In 1930 the colonial state made a final offer of 85 square miles of private estates to the chiefs and nobility in Busoga, who rejected the offer as inadequate. Finally, in 1936 the colonial state abolished *corvée* and tribute for salaried chiefs. However, the hereditary *mutala* (ridge or 'village') and *kisoko* ('sub-village') headmen at the bottom of the chiefly hierarchy refused to exchange their traditional claims to tribute for salaried, appointive status. They argued, 'If you pay me to wash my table it will then become your table.'[60]

When *corvée* for chiefs was banned, unsalaried headmen continued to control land allocation and derived income from charging an allotment fee for each new *kibanja* holding. This *nkoko* fee, literally meaning a chicken, ranged from Shs. 25 to Shs. 1,000 depending on economic conditions and the size and location of the *kibanja*. By 1961 the average *nkoko* fee ranged from Shs. 40 per acre near Kamuli to Shs. 200 per acre in newly settled areas near Jinja. As Fallers pointed out, the fact that the allotment fee was the headman's only source of tribute proved to be a strong incentive for increasing the turnover in *bibanja* tenants through evictions. Though contrary to custom as long as the land remained under cultivation, evictions usually succeeded because of the headman's stature in court hearings on land disputes.[61]

Hence the headmen's response to colonial policy had the fortuitous effect of reducing the security of *kibanja* tenure, which in turn delayed the introduction of coffee as a cash crop. Although a *kibanja* holder in Busoga normally cultivated bananas as a perennial food crop, annual crops such as cotton and groundnuts were a more prudent choice for cash crops than the perennial coffee. The latter might tempt the headman to evict the holder when the coffee reached maturity. Despite the allegedly favourable foundations laid by a quasi-feudal past, the emergence of capitalist farmers in Busoga was thus retarded by insecure land tenure.[62] Indeed, the headmen opposed the shift to phase three, because permanent individual ownership of land would end their control over land allocation and eliminate their *nkoko* income. When capitalist coffee farmers did emerge in significant numbers in the late 1950s and early 1960s, they were found primarily in the newly-opened southern areas which had been closed following the 1901-6 sleeping-sickness epidemic.[63]

Bunyoro presents another example of the importance of the African response to colonial land-tenure policy. Here too all land was officially Crown Land, with some exceptions: mission land, administrative townships and a few thousand acres of European coffee and Asian sisal plantations. Behind the official façade of Crown Land stood the real world of a traditional land-tenure system greatly changed by the commercialisation of agriculture. In a manner not unusual in land-tenure history, key Bunyoro terms had developed opposite meanings from similar words in Buganda and Busoga. In Bunyoro, the *ekibanja* was a private estate covering five acres to many square miles rather than a small tenant holding; and the *obwesengeze* was the official estate of the chief rather than a private estate. Upon retirement, a portion of a chief's *obwesengeze* would become his *ekibanja*, in lieu of pension. A landowner was the *de facto* petty-chief over his tenants. By 1931 the chiefs and 600 landowner-chiefs had converted the best cultivated land into *obwesengeze* and *ekibanja* estates. Of the 22,000 taxpayers in Bunyoro, 18,000 were tenants, two-thirds on official estates and one-third on private estates. In the Bunyoro Agreement of 1933, the colonial state refused to recognise an African landed gentry. It abolished official estates and commuted rent and tribute due the landowner-chiefs into cash payments to the Bunyoro Native Administration to fund salaries and pensions for chiefs. Diverging slightly from this familiar pattern, the colonial state did agree to issue certificates of occupancy to actual cultivators. Landlords seized this loophole to secure 'titles' to their *ekibanja* estates, thereby pre-empting their tenants from taking out certificates of occupancy.[64] Although officially *ekibanja* estates could be inherited but not sold, there evolved a brisk market in *ekibanja* titles. Beattie estimated in 1954 that 1,500 of 5,000 certificates of occupancy were for tenanted estates rather than simple peasant holdings. Despite the abolition of rent and tribute, landlords retained many prerogatives: high social status, deference from tenants, the right to allocate tenancies, the power of eviction and the right to prohibit tenants from erecting permanent structures.[65] As Beattie noted, cultivation of perennial crops was sufficient cause for eviction as late as 1953. Hence annuals – cotton and tobacco – were the major cash crops in Bunyoro. Tobacco proved an especially lucrative crop – for foreign firms and for the colonial state, which levied an excise duty on tobacco ten times greater than the price received by the grower.[66] Although less than half the households in Bunyoro were still tenants in the early 1950s, it was the landlords who stood to gain most from the phase three legitimation of marketable private titles to land.

Finally, we compare Acholi, Lango and Teso, three districts of the interior plateau in which climate rather than land tenure restricted the choice of cash crops to annuals. Here the severe December-March dry season precludes coffee cultivation. Finger millet, often interplanted with sorghum, and cattle form the basis of the food system. The externally-induced introduction of cotton as a cash crop led to seasonal labour shortages because of the conflicting labour demands of finger millet. To what extent did the colonial promotion of cotton production lead to changes in traditional land tenure in each of the three districts?

In the pre-colonial Acholi kingdoms, the Rwot (king) was *won lobo*, guardian of the land, by virtue of being head of the aristocratic lineage or *kal*. Apart from the royal village (*gang-kal*), each kingdom consisted of two classes of villages: aristocratic villages (*lo-kal*), whose members enjoyed rights to land by virtue of birth into the nobility, and commoner villages (*lo-bung*). Formally, a commoner's rights to land depended on the Rwot's permission, but, once allowed to settle, the commoner enjoyed inheritable rights to the land his household tilled. Whether members of aristocratic or commoner clans, all subjects paid *tyer* (tribute and *corvée*) to the Rwot. The Rwot regulated settlement and hunting rights through special officials, namely the father of the hoe (*won piny*) and the father of the hunt (*won dwar*), who normally enjoyed hereditary office. Whereas larger kingdoms had many such officials, smaller kingdoms combined the roles of Rwot and father of the hoe.[67] The extent of pre-colonial cultivation by communal work-groups (*awak*) as distinct from family labour is unknown, but it was sufficiently widespread to disconcert District Commissioner Postlethwaite, who employed Draconian measures between 1913 and 1915 to 'pacify' the Acholi, abolish the traditional political system and replace communal cultivation with individual household labour.[68] Cotton cultivation for export began in western Acholi in 1912 and eastern Acholi in 1916, but Acholi's incorporation into the world economy was initially hampered by the conflicting labour requirements of finger millet and cotton and by transportation bottlenecks.[69] Only 4,700 acres of cotton were cultivated in 1923. With the extension of the road network and the introduction of motor lorries, cotton acreage increased rapidly to 38,500 acres in 1931. Under threats of fines and imprisonment, all able-bodied adult males were required by successive District Commissioners to cultivate at least two acres of cotton. Yet, aside from seasonal fluctuations and a sharp drop caused by the shift to food production during the Second World War, cotton acreage remained fairly constant between 1938 and 1948, after which it rose to 130,000 acres in 1963. At the end of the colonial period, Acholi land tenure contained a mixture of hierarchical and egalitarian elements, some old and some new. The traditional father of the hoe could frequently be found occupying the lowest level of the colonial chiefly hierarchy: the village chief (*won paco*). Poorer households often combined to elect their own chief of the hoe and chieftess of the women, each complemented by the requisite bureaucracy, to organise the *awak* for men and communal weeding for women. On the other hand, by 1950 Girling noted the emergence of a new class of capitalist farmers, many of commoner origin and sometimes 'strangers', who were carefully staking out claims to land in anticipation of legitimation of marketable individual land titles. These upstarts employed agricultural workers either for cash or, more commonly, by the subterfuge of communal work-parties for beer and food.[70] In 1963 inequality in land-holdings was significantly higher in Acholi than in Teso and Lango.[71]

Despite superficial similarities, the Langi socio-political system was more egalitarian than its Acholi counterpart. There was no aristocratic-commoner distinction among the 150 or more Langi clans (*ateker*). Combining hereditary and democratic succession, clan members elected their leader (*adit*) from the sons of the deceased leader. Land was communally owned by the clan, which also regulated inheritance of cattle and personal property. Clans were linked by ritual groupings (*etogo*), age grades and family ties arising from clan exogamy. Dominant clan leaders forged clan alliances to become the *Jago* over several neighbouring clans. A militarily proficient *Jago* would be recognised as Rwot by neighbouring *Jagi* who acknowledged his leadership. The Rwot and *Jagi* regulated clan disputes and exercised military leadership in internal Langi raids. Periodically, a commander-in-chief (*twon lwak*) emerged among the Rwodi to lead the Langi people in external raids. The hierarchical features of the Langi political system were offset by its ephemeral nature. Moreover, the Rwot and *Jagi* could not demand *corvée* from subjects. At the village level, the work-group (*wang tic*) provided co-operative labour for clearing fallow ground, ploughing and weeding on a reciprocal basis among its 20 to 40 members. Four types of officials supervised agricultural and hunting activities. The *wang tic* elected a leader to oversee the work and subsequent beer party and to negotiate alliances with other work-groups for larger projects. The person in charge of communal cattle-herding was not elected but was the owner of the kraal (*won awi dyang*). As in Acholi, regulation of hunting was the task of hereditary guardians of hunting areas (*won arum*). The office of rain-maker (*won kot*) was also hereditary.[72]

Already in the nineteenth century Langi cultivators produced planned surpluses of sesame (sim-sim) for export to Bunyoro and Palwo in exchange for iron hoes which were used locally and traded to Teso for cattle. Tosh has discussed why the transition to cotton production for export proved more difficult. First, with the hoe, cotton required two-thirds more man-days per acre than sesame, an increase not always offset by the price differential between cotton and sesame during the first decade after the 1909 introduction of non-indigenous cotton varieties. Second, more cotton meant less food or the same food with more effort. Whereas sesame doubled as a local food crop and export crop, cotton (without local seed-oil extraction) added nothing to the local food supply and famine reserves. The three- to four-month growth-period for sesame readily fitted into the finger millet and sorghum cycle, but, as shown in Table 2.2, the long cotton season

Table 2.2: Annual Agricultural Cycle of the Interior Plateau

Month	J F M A M J J A S O N D	Growth-period	Comments
Dry season	* * 0 0 *		
Labour requirements			
Finger millet	0 * * 0 * * 0	4 months	Cycle begins earlier in Teso, later in Acholi
Cotton	0 0 * * * 0 * * *	5 months	Sorting requires as much labour as picking
Sesame	0 * 0 * 0	3-4 months	Mainly northern plateau
Groundnuts	0 * * 0 * *	4-5 months	Mainly southern plateau
Sorghum I	0 * * 0 *	Varies by variety, 3-5 months	Interplanted with millet to coincide with with first rains
Sorghum II	0 * * 0 *	"	Planted alone to coincide with second rains

Symbols:
(blank)   minimal or non-existent
0   moderate
*   peak

Note:
Because the grower can plant, weed and harvest only small areas at a time using hand-tools,. the labour cycle is longer than the growth-period for each crop.

Sources:
David N. McMaster, *A Subsistence Crop Geography of Uganda* (Cornwall, England: Geographical Publications, 1962), pp. 49, 51, 57-8 and 77-8; David N. McMaster, 'Cotton Cultivation', *Atlas of Uganda*, 2nd edn (Kampala: Uganda Department of Lands and Surveys, 1967), p. 52; David J. Vail, *A History of Agricultural Innovation and Development in Teso District, Uganda* (Syracuse, N.Y.: Maxwell School of Citizenship and Public Affairs, Syracuse University, 1972), p. 104; and Joan Vincent, *African Elite; The Big Men of a Small Town* (New York: Columbia University Press, 1971), p. 40.

interfered with peak labour requirements for food crops. Third, by planting cotton in June to allow adequate time for March sowing and early weeding of finger millet, the grower had to pick and sort cotton from late October to January, disrupting the traditional dry-season activities: ceremonies, rest, hunting and raiding. Fourth, the colonial state's cotton promotion was hardly designed to endear Langi to its large-scale cultivation. For the first time Langi males had to perform *corvée*, initially on the official estates of 'Ganda agents' sent to administer Lango, then on the estates of very untraditional Langi chiefs appointed to replace the agents after 1911.[73]

After slowly increasing to 6,300 acres in 1915, Lango cotton production rose to 27,700 acres in 1919 and 71,500 acres in 1928, spurred by construction of local ginneries and improvements in the road network which reduced the need to headload seed cotton over long distances. The colonial state abolished *corvée* for chiefs in 1934. The cash economy enabled some rain-makers, notably Won Kot Lingo, to amass wealth, even though the construction of modern granaries and transportation networks lessened the severe effects of local crop failure.[74] With an average output of 5,500 metric tons of cotton lint in the late 1950s, cotton production in the Lango cotton zone was only 13 per cent higher than in 1937-8.[75] On the whole, the egalitarian values embodied in the *wang tic* proved sufficiently strong to prevent the emergence of capitalist farmers in Lango, notwithstanding the wealth of certain colonial chiefs and rain-makers and long-standing inequality in cattle ownership. Anyone who tried to hire wage-labourers discovered that Langi were loath to hire themselves out to fellow Langi and that non-Langi labourers preferred the greater opportunities in Buganda. And, in contrast to Acholi, the Langi preserved the element of reciprocity in the *wang tic*, preventing it from being used as a disguised form of hired labour. No doubt maintenance of equality worked against the introduction of ox-drawn ploughs, which enabled the Iteso to increase cotton production and the cost of increased inequality between those who owned ploughs and those who did not.[76] In 1963 the distribution of land-holdings in Lango was more egalitarian, and the proportion of Langi cultivators participating in communal work-groups higher than in any other district in Uganda.[77]

Although the Langi language ultimately became 'Lwo-ised', the Langi, Iteso and Karimojong peoples shared a common language and origin. The close linguistic similarity between modern Ateso and Nga-karimojong (closer than that between Runyoro and Luganda or between the Moyo and Ogoko dialects of Madi) and some shared clan names and customs support the theory that the Iteso were pastoralists who, over the period 1600-1830, broke away from the Karimojong to undertake a more sedentary agricultural life in what became the Teso District. But Lamphear cites evidence from oral history that the fore-runners of the Iteso (and Langi) were agriculturalists and the fore-runners of the Karimojong (and Jie, Dodoth and Napore) were hunters and gatherers, not pastoralists, when they parted company as early as 1500, not in Karamoja, but near the Didinga Hills of south-eastern Sudan. In their separate southern migrations each group evolved a cattle and grain culture, and their paths sometimes crossed, but sedentary agriculture remained the primary activity of the proto-Iteso, and transhumant pastoralism became the primary economic activity of the proto-Karimojong.[78]

Iteso social groups were based on three different components: kinship (family, lineage and clan); territory (*etem* and *einere*); and the age-set system (*asapam* or *eigworone*). Within the nuclear, if sometimes polygamous, family (*ere*), cattle and personal property were inherited through and by men, but women retained rights to their granaries and to plots they tilled. Led by the *loepolokit* elected by male members, the lineage or extended family (*ekek*) regulated inheritance, land alloca-tion and organisation of communal herding and work-groups. The clan (*ateker*) exercised limited communal rights over the disposal of cattle, as evidenced by the pre-colonial use of *ateker* cattle brands. The functions of the clan leader, *apolon ka ateker*, and his mode of selection are not clear. Another official, the *apolon ka eriga*, regulated hunting on the clan's communal hunting ground. The basic territorial unit was the *etem* (settlement or hearth), roughly corresponding to a hamlet. The *etem*, together with the age-set (*aturi*), formed the basis for organising warfare and raids. Military leaders were chosen by popular consent. The *apolon ka ajore* was the military leader of one or more hamlets, and the *apolon ka ebuku* (leader of the shield), the commander of a large expedition. In addition, the *emuron*, as sorcerer and rain-maker, often wielded political and economic power over wide areas. The Iteso were divided into larger dialect groups, each known as an *einere*, which functioned as territorial sections. There were three major *einere* sections of the Iteso, plus the Kumam (Ikokolemu), who regarded them-selves as a separate ethnic group.[79]

The whole of what later became the Teso District experienced substantial demographic flux throughout the nineteenth century, stirred by the flood of Iworopom refugees from the Karimojong-Iworopom War of circa 1830, the trickle of settlers from Bunyoro,

Palwo, Lango, Busoga and Kenyi into land along Lake Kyoga, the spillover of Iteso into the future Bukedi and Busoga districts and the eddies of people moving within Teso in response to localised population pressure. Imports of iron hoes from Bunyoro via Lango in the nineteenth century reduced the labour required for soil preparation, compared to cultivation with the narrow wooden hoe or digging stick. With the same amount of labour it became possible to plant more finger millet, sorghum, sesame, groundnuts, cow peas, beans and that other innovation from Bunyoro, the sweet potato. The iron hoe raised the optimal land-to-labour ratio, while a greater and more varied food output contributed to a higher rate of population growth. Hence, because the eldest son normally inherited the major share of land, the introduction of iron hoes made it increasingly necessary for younger sons to leave the settlement when land within the extended family was reapportioned. Even so, land remained relatively plentiful on a district-wide basis.[80]

Kakungulu conquered much of Teso between 1899 and 1904 and introduced Buganda-style administration, *corvée* labour for chiefs and *corvée*-built roads. The northern *einere* of Usuku fell to Ganda-British overrule in 1907-8 following Ganda agent intervention on the southern side in the Usuku civil war that had erupted after the rinderpest epidemic and the great drought of 1894-6. The first Teso cotton crop was harvested in 1908-9, and the first ploughing school opened at Kumi in 1910. With a road network already in place, supplemented by waterways, cotton acreage expanded rapidly from 5,000 acres in 1910 to 33,500 acres in 1913 and 68,000 acres in 1923. However, as Vail observed, the bulk of pre-1920 production was not on peasant plots but on the estates of chiefs, cultivated by *corvée* labour, and headloaded to boats by *corvée* porters – 38,000 porters for the 1913-14 crop. Despite an unusually favourable cotton-price/poll-tax ratio between 1915 and 1919, small-holders produced little cotton beyond the mandatory half acre. The need to headload seed cotton great distances because of insufficient ox carts and motor lorries, the demands of chiefs for *corvée* labour for their own estates, military call-ups for the Carrier Corps, *kasanvu* labour, and the competing labour demands of the peasant's own finger millet and groundnut crops in the ideal months for cotton planting were factors restricting cotton production. After the war and disastrous cotton prices in the 1920-1 and 1921-2 crop years, the situation improved. The cotton-price/poll-tax ratio rose to almost pre-war levels. Britain ordered the colonial state to abolish *kasanvu*, and, as part of the transition from the dyarchy to salaried chiefs, the colonial state began to frown on the chief's commercial exploitation of *corvée* on his own estate. The number of motor lorries increased; instead of headloading the cotton to market, the growers and their cotton were now transported to the ginnery by lorry. Iteso small-holders worked out ways to fit cotton's labour requirements into the annual cycle of food production and to fit cotton's land requirements into the three or more field system in which each field or plot was planted in successive annual crops on a rotating basis for three to four years followed by three to seven years of rest.[81]

The small-holder's solution involved postponing cotton planting to late May, June or July to complete early weeding of finger millet, a compromise which minimised risk by ensuring adequate food production rather than maximum cash-crop output, and the adoption of the ox-drawn imported plough.

Compared to a metal hoe, a ploughing team of three persons and two to four oxen reduced labour requirements for soil preparation by more than 40 per cent on land cultivated the previous year and by more than 60 per cent on fallow grassland. Ignoring losses due to breakage and wear, the number of ploughs in Teso increased from 240 in 1922 to 8,280 in 1932 and 19,894 in 1939, or nominally one plough for every four taxpayers. Cotton production rose less dramatically from 10,700 metric tons of seed cotton in 1922 to 16,700 metric tons in 1937. By 1939 virtually all cropland in Teso was prepared by ploughing. A holder without a plough hired a ploughing team from a wealthier neighbour at Shs. 2 per day. If the field had been planted in crops the previous year, the ploughing team could prepare two-thirds of an acre per day. This meant an expenditure of Shs. 10 to prepare the average 2.1 acres for grain crops plus 1.3 acres for cotton, but a higher expenditure if the land had lain fallow for several years or if the holder had the field ploughed twice for a finer tilth. Given the low cotton prices between 1930 and 1947, a holder without a plough would find almost his entire cotton income going to his poll tax and ploughing expenses. The plough eliminated the labour constraint in soil preparation, but enabled the holder to plough more than he and his family could weed and thin, thereby creating a new labour bottleneck later in the season when the thinning and weeding of cotton conflicted with the weeding and harvesting of millet and groundnuts. Furthermore, whereas cotton accelerated soil exhaustion, ploughing without conservation measures accelerated soil erosion. And the pressure to produce more cotton to pay for taxes, school fees and consumer goods, combined with population growth, reduced the resting time for fallow land in more populous areas below the minimum required to restore fertility.[82]

By adopting contour ploughing and planting grass strips on slopes, growers temporarily averted disaster in the 1940s. Higher crop prices after 1948 led to a marked expansion in the total area under cultivation and a further increase in the number of ploughs to 60,000 in 1963, a nominal ratio of one plough for every two taxpayers, once again ignoring breakage and wear. By 1963 agricultural holdings, including fallow land, occupied 55 per cent of the land area of Teso, a percentage surpassed only in Bukedi and Busoga. Annual production of seed cotton averaged 21,600 metric tons in Teso from 1950 through 1959, more than before the Second World War, but less than in Buganda or Busoga. On a per capita basis, however, Teso produced more cotton than Buganda, but less than Busoga. The average size of a holding in Teso was 20.6 acres (median size: 13.8 acres), far larger than average holdings in other districts. The ratio of cattle to people was exceptionally high in Teso, 6.6 cattle per household in 1963, a figure second only to that for Karamoja District, with 21.6 cattle per household. Indeed, since the 1930s cattle sales to Kampala have provided the Iteso with their second most important 'cash crop'. Statistics on the distribution of plough ownership and cattle ownership are scarce, but most households were unable or unwilling to save the amount of money required for a pair of bullocks and a plough: 150 shillings in 1938 or 450 shillings in 1966. Cattle were also important in the bride-price, with 10 to 15 cattle as the average bride-price in the 1950s, notwithstanding a colonial law limiting the bride-price to 5 cattle. A plough owner with a marriageable son might find it necessary to part with his oxen as part of the bride-price, forcing him to borrow oxen in the ploughing season. Generally, possession of a plough was a sign of entrepreneurship; possession of a plough and the required oxen, a sign of wealth and power in the community. In the ethnically diverse Gondo parish on the Serere peninsula in southwest Teso, Vincent found a ratio of one plough for every 6.1 users in 1966.[83]

By the end of the colonial period, adoption of the plough had transformed traditional land tenure in Teso. As in Lango, a majority of the population in the late 1950s still resisted the concept of marketable individual ownership of land, despite the tradition of individual male ownership of cattle, the traditional use of contracts for herding and cattle exchange, the growing importance of the nuclear family since the introduction of iron hoes and the changes wrought by the commercialisation of agriculture. The buying and selling of land was rare, but the purchase of an improvement such as a house or an unharvested crop could form the basis for a valid claim to land in the immediate vicinity. Even so, inheritance and the opening of virgin land continued to be far more important than land purchase as a means of acquiring land. In contrast to Lango, the ownership of ploughs and oxen in Teso provided a few with the means to cultivate more land than others. From the ranks of the plough and oxen owners emerged the 'Big Men', the capitalist farmers who overcame labour constraints by hiring wage-labourers, usually unmarried Iteso men and immigrants, to weed and pick cotton. When hiring out their ploughing teams, the capitalist farmers and aspiring capitalist farmers collected professional fees, not wages, from the 'plough-less'. For in a capitalist division of labour, those at the top receive 'fees' for their work, while those at the bottom receive 'wages'. The 'Big Men' were also able to manipulate the traditional reciprocal work-parties (*eitai*) to obtain needed labour power from neighbours by payment of beer rather than wages.[84] Teso fell somewhere between Lango and Acholi on measures of equality in land distribution and the prevalence of communal labour, but qualitative differences — the scale of cultivation and the form of communal labour — placed Teso in an altogether different category.[85]

We have compared changes in land tenure under colonial rule in Buganda, Busoga, Bunyoro, southwest Sebei, Bwamba, Acholi, Lango and Teso, in short, the major cash crop areas. The analysis of the impact of ox-drawn ploughs in Teso can be extended, with few changes, to the cotton-growers in northern Bukedi and the commercial cattle and grain farmers in southeastern Sebei. Detailed agricultural histories have yet to be written for Ankole, Kigezi, West Nile, Madi, Bugisu and southern Bukedi, and for the Batoro and Bakonjo of Toro District. As for the peoples of Karamoja District, they were too poor in rainfall and too rich in cattle to be willingly drawn into the commercialisation of agriculture. To a surprising extent, they succeeded in remaining aloof from the colonial state which nominally encapsulated them and which periodically raided their cattle.[86] But, in some areas of Uganda, notably West Nile, Kigezi and even parts of Acholi, Ankole and Toro, transportation barriers and colonial economic policies combined to preclude both cash-crop cultivation and Karamoja-style 'opting out'. Here, in the periphery of the periphery, production of migratory labour became the major 'commercial' activity.

Migrant Wage-labour

Whether wage-labour would have emerged in Uganda without state intervention is an interesting but moot question. The fact is that the state did intervene to create the class of wage-labourers required to service and maintain the staple-producing economy. In few areas of economic policy was intervention by the colonial state so beset by contradictions, contradictions both between conflicting policy goals and between goals and actual outcomes.

The colonial state abolished slavery only to discover that 'free labour' did not step forward to sell labour-power at wage levels deemed appropriate by the colonial state and other employers. The 'labour problem' was exacerbated by the basic fact that the indigenous population had not (and has not) been 'freed' from possession of the means of production required to maintain and reproduce its labour power. Even after the 1900 agreement in Buganda and the demarcation of Crown Land elsewhere 'freed' the peasantry from ownership of land, peasants retained usufructuary rights to the land they occupied and tilled.

From the viewpoint of the buyer of labour-power, the problem was not just that the African could maintain his or her existence without selling labour-power as a commodity, but that the African had finite, limited needs. The acquisitive society based on possessive individualism had yet to become dominant in East Africa. The 'dearth of native labour' was aggravated by the sharp decline in African population caused by the diseases and wars which coincided with the penetration of East Africa by the external world economy.

Until the completion of the Mombasa-Kisumu railway, the colonial state resorted to the temporary expedient of rent-a-slave caravans for trade with the coast and imported indentured Indian labourers for construction of the railway.

Initially, the imposition of taxes and the introduction of imported consumer goods were the means by which the colonial state increased the necessities of the African population, both forcing and encouraging Africans to cultivate cash crops or sell labour-power in order to obtain money for the new necessities. In the words of a European missionary, 'The introduction of hut tax by Sir Harry Johnston with the full agreement of the Baganda Chiefs made labour easy'[87] — easily available.

The initial small surplus of cheap labour had evaporated by 1908. Africans living within 30 miles of the existing road and lake transportation network discovered that to obtain money for taxes and imported goods, cultivation of a half-acre or more of cotton was a more dignified, if hardly less strenuous, method than leaving one's family for several months to work for an alien employer.[88] Simultaneously, expanding cotton cultivation greatly increased the demand for labour. Growers themselves were initially required to headload seed cotton to the nearest market or ginnery. Porters were needed to pull *hamali* carts loaded with ginned cotton lint and other goods over rough roads and labourers were required to build and maintain trunk roads and the network of roads radiating from newly-established ginneries. Labourers were also needed to construct administrative centres. Although *luwalo* (unpaid communal labour) recruited by chiefs provided labour for local roads and local administrative headquarters, the supply of voluntary wage-labour and *luwalo* proved inadequate to meet the growing demands. Accordingly, between 1909 and 1922, the colonial state imposed *kasanvu* (paid compulsory labour) on able-bodied African males to bridge the gap between labour demand and labour supply.

The brief post-war boom brought renewed pressure for continuation and expansion of the system of compulsory labour. Most *kasanvu* labourers were employed on public works projects, notably road-building, but the temptation to use cheap *kasanvu* labour elsewhere proved difficult to resist. In 1920 the Department of Agriculture employed 80 labourers at the Entebbe Botanic Gardens. Although half of these employees were forced labourers, paid 38 per cent less than the going wage (Rs. 5 vs. Rs. 8 per month), the department cheerfully reported an ample supply of labour.[89] Furthermore, as Powesland notes, the going wage was itself depressed by the existence of *kasanvu*. The prospect of exemption from *kasanvu* artificially increased the supply of 'voluntary' wage-labour and thereby lowered wages.[90]

Planters and other expatriate commercial interests came to regard *kasanvu* as essential to the economy and, in 1920, proposed even more Draconian state intervention to ensure a plentiful supply of cheap labour. Their demands included the introduction of a passbook system for Africans; the creation of central registers of *luwalo, kasanvu* and contract labour performed by each adult African male; the stimulation of intertribal rivalry to promote labour recruitment and productivity; the prohibition of labourers leaving Uganda to work elsewhere; the introduction of differential poll taxes to penalise African males who had not engaged in sufficient wage-labour during the year; the levy of higher taxes on those, such as hawkers, who avoided *kasanvu* by claiming to be self-employed; the doubling of the *kasanvu* required from single males from one to two months; the imposition of enforced share-cropping on squatters on large European and African estates; the forfeiture of pay by labourers who failed to complete a 30-day work ticket within 45 days; the introduction of salaries for chiefs in lieu of tax rebates (rebates allegedly made the chiefs discourage migration of subjects); and the European supervision of *luwalo* labour.[91] To be sure, labour was not particularly productive in this early period, if European reports of four hours being the standard work-day are to be believed. Yet the short work-day was a necessary aspect of a system in which unskilled labourers were often paid less than subsistence rates. Most workers in Buganda had to combine work for Europeans with work for food on African estates to supplement their cash wages.[92] The subsidy to European planters afforded by *kasanvu* ceased in 1922 with the abolition of the system. *Kasanvu* proved to be essential for the viability of plantations rather than the economy as a whole. The subsequent increase in wages combined with unfavourable currency fluctuations to drive many European planters out of business.[93]

Other problems arose with the abolition of *kasanvu*. Recognising as early as 1919 that the Colonial Office would outlaw forced labour, Governor Robert Coryndon appointed L.H.C. Rayne 'to create and maintain a regular adequate flow of voluntary labour from populated areas to all employers both Government and private'.[94]

There were two central problems to be avoided: the creation of a genuine proletariat and the undermining of cash-crop cultivation. A European-style proletariat seemed morally repugnant to colonial administrators, who naively sought to preserve an idealised rural 'tribal order' from the urban horrors and vice of slums. More to the point, a proletariat freed from the constraints of rural society posed a political threat to the colonial order. Detribalisation and urbanisation, it was feared, would lead to social anomie in which agitators and mal-contents flourished.[95] But if the stable labour-force were to be grounded in rural society, how could one balance the conflicting labour demands of cash-crop production and of employers? Too high a wage would attract peasants away from cash-crop cultivation; too low a wage would fail to attract workers from the ranks of cotton growers.

Partly by design and partly by accident, the solution emerged: uneven development within Uganda and between Uganda and neigh-bouring territories generated sufficient migratory labour from the periphery to replace seasonal forced labour in the economic centre of the Protectorate. Migrant labour is semi-proletarianised labour in that the worker has not yet been 'freed' entirely from possession of land as a

means of production and subsistence. Migrant labour is paid at a level
below the subsistence level required for the maintenance and reproduction of labour-power (the cost of raising a family and providing for
old age), and hence remains tied to the soil to make up the difference
between wages and the subsistence level.[96]

As early as 1906, migrant workers from Toro, Bunyoro and Ankole
were to be found in Buganda, attracted by the availability of imported
cloth. The colonial state's imposition of poll taxes in outlying districts,
where lack of transportation depressed the prices fetched by cash
crops, further stimulated the flow of migratory labour to Buganda.[97]
The imposition of the poll tax in West Nile in 1917 brought forth a
stream of migrant labour into Bunyoro and Buganda. European and
Asian planters in Bunyoro thereupon campaigned to have West Nile
set aside as an exclusive labour reserve for Bunyoro employers. Labour
recruiters from Buganda were barred from West Nile in 1922 and 1923.
The government argued that reduced competition for West Nile labour
would help all employers keep wages low.[98]

From the idea that local people in cash-crop areas should be left
alone to grow crops whereas local people (or at least the adult males) in
less favoured areas should migrate to cash-crop areas to provide
ancillary labour in cultivation, processing, transport and construction,
it was a short but highly significant step to the view put forward in
1924 that the less favoured areas should remain underdeveloped in
order to ensure the continued flow of labour to the cash-crop areas. In
the following year the colonial state ordered the Department of Agriculture to cease promoting cotton in West Nile and other outlying
districts which provided labour for essential services in the 'producing'
districts. Ankole and Kigezi were designated labour reserves for
Buganda; West Nile and Acholi were designated for Bunyoro and the
eastern districts.[99] The proportion of adult males absent from West
Nile due to labour migration in 1926 was estimated to be 16 per cent.
This drain posed a threat to food cultivation in the area. In 1923 poll
taxes collected in Toro and Ankole could not cover the salaries of
chiefs. Those who left the 'labour reserves' tended to pay poll taxes in
the area in which they found work, which further enriched the 'producing' area and underdeveloped the 'labour reserve' area.[100]

Officially, the colonial state ended its policy of discouraging cash
crops in labour-producing areas in 1926.[101] But the world-wide
depression intervened before any major infrastructural projects could be
started in the labour-producing areas. Within the cash-crop core, the
Tororo-Soroti line was opened in 1929, and the Kampala-Jinja rail link

was opened in 1931, completing the line from Mombasa to Kampala.
The Kampala-Kasese line to the west was delayed until 1956; the
Soroti-Gulu link to the north was not opened until 1963; and the Gulu-
Pakwach link to the northwest opened the following year.[102] These late
extensions, when completed, had already been superseded by the development of lorry transport and road networks. None the less, in the
1920s and 1930s the availability of cheap rail transport was a key deter-
minant in the price paid by ginneries to growers for seed cotton.[103]
Even though the colonial state eventually encouraged cotton production in outlying districts, lack of transport combined with the low prices
of the 1930s to make the sale of labour-power (via migrant labour) a
more viable alternative.

A District Commissioner (DC) described the 1931 situation
succinctly before the British Joint Select Committee on Closer Union
in East Africa:

> Q: Would you say that there are any labour problems, that is to say,
> difficulty in obtaining labour for public works in Uganda now?
> DC: Not at the present time at all.
> Q: Is that due to the fact that they are more ready to come and
> work for wages owing to the economic slump in crops? Does it
> vary? When the crops are paying well, is it more difficult to get
> labour than when they are not?
> DC: Yes, I think that is so, undoubtedly. That applies definitely to
> the Nile where they cannot get such large sums for their cotton as
> they can down country.
> Q: When the price is very low, they go out for wages?
> DC: Yes.
> Q: And when it is a good price, they stay at home?
> DC; Yes. I do not think that the Nilotics, if they got a very good
> price for their cotton, would go out as frequently as they do now. I
> think they would probably be more inclined to stay at home and get
> their money by cultivating cotton.[104]

Even so, some members of the expatriate commercial community
continued to press the colonial state to discourage commodity production in labour reserve areas. In the words of a European member of the
Uganda Chamber of Commerce in 1937:

> It seemed a time had come to halt production for a time and consoli-
> date the position. In fact a return to the policy of Sir Robert

Coryndon would seem to be necessary whereby the backward areas
were not encouraged to produce but to form a regular supply of
labour on which the employers could rely.[105]

As Powesland has documented, the major employers of migrant labour
in Uganda were neither the colonial state nor the Indian and European
commercial community but the Baganda capitalist farmers, both large
and small.[106] By drawing a distinction between full-time workers and
jobbing labour, Richards unintentionally makes it appear that only
rich peasants could afford to employ migrant labour in Buganda.[107]
Powesland points out that the normal agricultural work-day was short
enough to enable labourers to work 'full-time' for two or more
growers, or to work in jobbing for many. The 1962/63 survey of coffee
growers in Buddu, Busiro, Kyagwe and Bulemezi counties found
that almost every household employed some seasonal paid help.
Farmers with only 1½ acres under coffee had average farming expenses
of Shs. 67 per annum, most of it for casual labour. These ordinary
households consisted of both employers and employees. The contribution of wages to household income by all working family members
totalled Shs. 200 per annum per household.[108]

The major source of migrant labour for Baganda cotton and coffee
farmers turned out to be Rwanda-Burundi (Belgian Ruanda-Urundi)
rather than outlying districts in Uganda. An estimated 46,000 migrants
came from Rwanda-Burundi in 1927, versus 6,400 from West Nile
(1926).[109] Between 1938 and 1951, the stream of migrants from the
southwest (Rwanda, Burundi, Tanganyika and the Belgian Congo)
averaged 80,000 per year. The flow from Rwanda-Burundi fluctuated
in response to famines, tax rates and opportunities at home versus
wage-rates and opportunities in Uganda and the exchange rate between
the Belgian franc and the British pound.[110]

Migrants made important contributions in other areas of the
economy, accounting for nearly three-fifths of the 14,400 workers in
the ginneries in 1934. West Nile supplied one-third of the labour force
in the ginneries and estates visited by J.F. Elliot in 1936.[111] Thirty
years later, the Madhvani sugar plantation at Kakira depended on
Rwanda-Burundi for 56 per cent of its 6,500 field workers, on Zaire for
19 per cent, and on the Sudan for a further 18 per cent. Migrants from
Kigezi and from Rwanda-Burundi provided 42 and 8 per cent respectively of the copper miners at Kilembe. Migrants accounted for most of
the 2,500 workers in the Kakira sugar refinery: Kenya, 22 per cent;
the Sudan, 17 per cent; West Nile, 9 per cent; Teso, 9 per cent; Zaire

and Rwanda-Burundi, 6 per cent each.[112]

Migrants faced terrible hardships: the long journey (on foot in the 1930s and 1940s) with little food or shelter, disease, low wages, inadequate rations, overcrowded and inadequate housing, long hours of work (usually for several employers), and the threat of lay-offs when seed cotton prices fell, as in 1926, 1931-4, 1938-9, 1942 and 1959.[113] Travel, health facilities and rations improved slightly in the 1950s, but even into the 1970s housing for workers remained 'substandard and unhygienic'. Employers succeeded in lengthening the working day from the 4 hours reported in 1920 to the Western standard of 8 to 9 hours, or a 48-hour week, in the post Second World War period. Working conditions often continued to be unsafe. In the 1970s asbestos workers were afforded little or no protection from asbestosis, and textile workers suffered from byssinosis ('brown-lung' disease).[114] Wages in rural areas lagged far behind minimum wages in the towns. Whereas urban workers obtained a minimum of Shs. 150 per month, plantation workers in Bunyoro received Shs. 3.25 per day, Shs. 3.40 at Kinyala, in 1971. In West Buganda, workers in the District Administration went on strike to win an increase from Shs. 53 to Shs. 73 per month.[115]

If migrant labourers faced hardships, so too did their families left behind in the 'labour reserves'. Whereas the colonial state in the 1920s had set 10 per cent as the maximum proportion of adult males which could leave 'labour reserves' without endangering local food supplies, far higher levels of emigration of adult males were reported in labour-exporting areas in 1952: 28 per cent in West Nile, 46 per cent in Kigezi, 16 per cent in Toro and at least as many in western Ankole.[116] The absence of male workers forced a switch in food crops in the West Nile, from finger millet to the less labour-intensive but much less nutritious cassava. This adversely affected the health of those who remained at home.[117]

Table 2.3 presents a basic outline of wage rates for selected years. The difference between the wage paid by the principal employer and the level required for subsistence had to be made up by taking a second job as part-time porter for a Muganda farmer or by growing the food and building the shelter one required on land belonging to a Muganda farmer. The hope of becoming permanent settlers kept many migrants going. By 1937 an estimated 28,000 non-Baganda had settled as tenants or landowners in Buganda, of whom 27 per cent hailed from Rwanda-Burundi.[118]

Some of the major contradictions engendered by the migrant labour system can be deduced from the suggestions of Baganda capitalist

Table 2.3: Monthly Cash Wages for Africans, 1897-1980

Year	Shs.	Remarks	Source
1897	6.00	Buganda	Powesland, p. 3
	9.33	Sudanese troops (Rs. 7)	Furley, p. 326
1900	24.00	K.A.R. soldiers (Rs. 18)	Furley, p. 326
	13.33	Uganda Police (Rs. 10)	Furley, p. 327
1907	6.25	Buganda (3 d./day). Shs. 4 tax	Powesland, p. 17
1908	6.00	Buganda (Rs. 4.50). Shs. 4 tax	Powesland, p. 21
1909	4.33	Labourers in Buganda	Blue Book, 1908-9
1912	5.00	Porter in Buganda	Blue Book, 1911-12
1913	6.00-8.00	Labourers for Baganda farmers	Powesland, p. 21
	5.33	Labourers on expatriate-owned plantations	
	6.67	Labourers for Public Works Department (PWD)	
1917	5.21	Agricultural labourer. Day rate of 2½ to 4d./day x 25	Blue Book, 1916-17
1920	4.67-8.00	Shillings value of plantation rate of Rs. 3.50-6.00 before currency crisis	
	7.00-12.00	Rs. 3.50-6.00 after currency crisis	Powesland, p.33
	10.67	Voluntary labour at Entebbe gardens (Rs. 8)	
	6.67	*Kasanvu* (forced) labour at Entebbe (Rs. 5)	Agr. Dept. 1920
1922	11.00-14.00	PWD rate in Buganda	Powesland, p. 35
	6.00-8.00	PWD rate in outlying districts	
1924	11.00-12.00	Labourers on plantations in Kampala area	Agr. Dept. 124
1925	18.00-22.00	Labourers on plantations in Kampala area	Powesland, p. 43
	14.00	PWD rate in Buganda	
1926	12.00	PWD rate in Buganda for migrant labourers	Powesland, p. 45
	18.00	PWD rate in Buganda for 'local' labourers	
1927	16.00	Maximum PWD rate in Buganda	Powesland, p. 48
	12.50	Agricultural labour. 43½ hour week	Blue Book, 1927
1928	13.54	Agricultural labour. 6½ d./day	Blue Book, 1928
1929	9.38	Agricultural labour	Blue Book, 1929
1932	8.33	Agricultural labour	Blue Book, 1932
	6.00-8.00	Bottom rate for labour in Kampala	Powesland, p. 53
	12.00	Government rate for labour in Kampala	

1934	6.00-12.00	Buganda, and no food rations	Powesland, p. 55
	7.00-15.00	Eastern and Northern Provinces, plus food rations	
	2.00- 9.00	Western Province mines, and no food	
	2.00- 7.00	Western Province mines, with inadequate food rations	
1935	8.00	With rations	Blue Book, 1935
	10.00	Without rations.	
1936	3.50- 5.00	Plantations paid Shs. 7 to 10 for a 30-day ticket which required 2 to 3 months to complete	Powesland, p. 58
1938	4.00-14.00	Agricultural labour	Blue Book, 1938
	7.00-15.00	PWD rate	
1942	7.00- 9.00	Rate paid by Baganda farmers, no food	Powesland, p. 70
1943	12.00	Sugar plantations, plus food and bonus of 0.50 per completed week	Powesland, p. 70
1944	6.00-28.00	Agricultural labour	Blue Book, 1944
	7.00-21.00	PWD rate	
1946	14.00	Agricultural labour	Annual Report on Uganda, 1946
1950	33.00	First minimum wage set for Kampala and Jinja	Labour Dept. 1952
	34.00	Estimated average Kampala wage for unskilled labour	Commission on Rents, 1964
1952	15.00-33.33	Agricultural labour on plantations Shs. 18 to 40 for a 30-day ticket plus Shs. 1 to 5 bonus per completed week and sometimes food and/or housing	Labour Dept., 1952
	30.00-40.00	Unskilled labour, construction, Kampala	
	43.60	Government labour, Kampala, plus housing	
	18.50	Government labour, Arua, plus housing	
	53.00-80.00	Unskilled labour, railways, Mengo, housing	
	18.33-25.00	Unskilled labour, underground miners, Toro and Ankole, plus food, attendance bonus and sometimes housing	
1952	39.62	Average agricultural wage, all Uganda	1957 Stat. Abstr
	25.96	Average mining wage, all Uganda	
1955	38.94	Agricultural wage (average)	1957 Stat. Abstr
	44.23	Mining wage (average)	
1956	41.91	Agricultural wage (average)	1957 Stat. Abstr
	49.61	Mining wage (average)	
	64. 16	Local government wage (average)	
1957	71.00	Estimated average wage for unskilled labourer in Kampala	Commission on Rents, 1964

1959	54.90	Agricultural wage (average)	1965 Stat. Abstr
	107.41	Mining wage (average)	
	84.58	Local government wage (average)	
1962	81.48	Agricultural wage (average)	1965 Stat. Abstr
	159.31	Mining wage (average)	
	129.04	Local government wage (average)	
1964	104.33	Agricultural wage (average)	1965 Stat. Abstr
	183.23	Mining wage (average)	
	154.54	Local government wage (average)	
1968	127.39	Agricultural wage (average)	1970 Stat. Abstr
	243.44	Mining wage (average)	
	224.08	Local government wage (average)	
1970	146.04	Agricultural wage (average)	1973 Stat. Abstr
	305.34	Mining wage (average)	
	259.41	Local government wage (average)	
	270.89	Average manufacturing wage, excluding cotton and coffee processing	
1971	156.00	Unskilled labour, central government	Min. Labour, 1971
	73.00	Unskilled labour, West Buganda District Administration	
	85.00	Unskilled labour, Kinyala Sugar Plantation, Bunyoro. Shs. 3.40/day	
	270.00-600.00	Semi-skilled workers, E.A. Steel Products	
1974	170.00	Minimum wage	
1977	240.00	Minimum wage	
1979	253.00	Sugar plantation wage for unskilled labour	Rehabilitation, pp. 77, 84-5, 165
	350.00	Sugar cane out-grower rate for unskilled labour	
	450.00	Minimum demanded by miners	
1980	400.00	Urban minimum wage	*Africa* 109 (Sept. 1980)

Notes:
Except where noted, average wage figures (1952-70) are national averages which include wages for skilled, semi-skilled and unskilled workers. The wages of unskilled workers in rural areas are generally far lower (see 1971 examples).
Key to sources:
P.G. Powesland, *Economic Policy and Labour* (Kampala: EAISR, 1957);
O.W. Furley, 'The Sudanese Troops in Uganda', *African Affairs*, vol. 58, no. 233 (October 1959), pp. 311-28;
Uganda, *Blue Books* and *Statistical Abstracts*, selected years;
Uganda, *Annual Report of the Department of Agriculture*, 1922 and 1924;
Uganda, *Annual Report of the Labour Department*, 1952;
Uganda, *Annual Report of the Ministry of Labour*, 1970 and 1971;
Colonial Office, *Annual Report on Uganda*, 1946;
Uganda, *Report of the Commission of Inquiry into the Structure and Level of Rents in the City of Kampala . . . , 1964*; and
Commonwealth Team of Experts, *The Rehabilitation of the Economy of Uganda* (London: Commonwealth Secretariat, 1979), vol. II.

farmers, cited by Richards from interviews in the early 1950s:

(a) that there must be a law that porters should scatter evenly over the country;
(b) that porters should be forced to work, or that they be 'made' to come from Ruanda-Urundi;
(c) that a law be passed to send immigrants back to the land they came from;
(d) that there should be a law that the immigrants must be porters and not tenants;
(e) that a law be passed to stop landowners leasing plots to foreigners; [and] . . .
(f) [that] the landlord . . . not be permitted to sell land to anyone other than a Muganda.[119]

No less than the European planters of 1920, the Baganda capitalist farmers felt the need for state intervention to secure cheap labour in the desired quantities and to prevent labourers from opting out by becoming squatters and future landowners. From the point of view of the migrant labourer, work in Buganda was made more tolerable at low wages offered by the Baganda farmers precisely because of the possibility of eventually becoming a *bupangisa* tenant or even a landowner within the 'producing' region served by transportation. The sixth suggestion on the list above, reveals the contradiction between capitalist tenant-farmers, who wished to keep migrants available as a reserve army of seasonal labour, and landowners, who profited from providing immigrants with secure access to land via *bupangisa* tenancy or outright purchase. Landlords could charge 'foreigners' more for land than it was socially acceptable to charge fellow Baganda. Baganda farmers were angered by the consequent 'loss' of labour (and land) entailed by such land sales and rentals.

Both the employer (whether Muganda, Indian or European) and the migrant labourer viewed the employer-employee relationship as necessarily short term − short term from the viewpoint of the employer because lifetime employment would have entailed paying a subsistence wage which covered not only food but the cost of supporting a family and providing for retirement; short term from the viewpoint of the labourer because employment at such low wages was hopefully only a short-run necessity on the road to permanent settlement. The short-run nature of the relationship prevented employers from improving the productivity of labour through the introduction of

new methods which required training the labourer. The cost of labour
per unit of output tended to be reduced by depressing wages rather
than by improving productivity.

Low productivity and low wages reduced the size of the domestic
market, as did the fact that a wide range of subsistence goods had yet
to become commodities. The scope for manufacturing based on
import substitution was thereby narrowed to mass consumption goods
of the lowest common denominator (cloth, soap, matches, sugar, edible
oil, hoes and simple enamelled cookware) plus a few 'luxury' items
for mainly urban consumption (bottled beer, cigarettes and shoes). The
Uganda Labour Department described in 1952 how the migrant labour
system blocked further industrialisation by reducing demand and
productivity:

> The question is how to change from a low-wage, low-output
> economy based on unstable immigrant labour to a high-wage, high-
> output economy dependent on a stabilised labouring class receiving
> a wage on which a worker can support his family without recourse
> to the hidden subsidy of his tribal land which at present so often
> produces both his food and his housing.[120]

When the state finally set a statutory minimum wage for workers in
Kampala and Jinja in 1950, it was a wage (Shs. 33 per month) based on
the cost of living (excluding retirement) of a single male worker rather
than a family.[121] Far from acting as a safety net, the minimum wage
'acted as a magnet to pull down wages' in a period of strong demand
for labour.[122] Nevertheless, the modest industrialisation strategy
implemented by the colonial state in the 1950s did require a small but
stable labour-force for the import-substitution sector and for capital-
intensive infrastructure projects. This stable labour-force was still a
migrant labour-force in that it continued to rely on the rural sector for
its retirement income, but it was sufficiently stable to be amenable to
trade unionism.

Accordingly, the metropolitan state had sent British trade union
advisers to ensure that trade unions in Uganda would emphasise economic rather than political issues and that there would be no repetition of
events such as the general strike of 1945. Mamdani dates such attempts
to guide the trade union movement to 1942, when Britain first sent
labour officers to the colonies to ensure 'that the growth of trade
unions among Africans took the right line'.[123] There was even resistance
to trade unions along the mildest social democratic lines. The East

Africa Royal Commission claimed that workers' interests could best be represented on 'trade boards, works councils, and joint staff committees' by appointed representatives of 'workpeople'. Furthermore, these non-elected representatives were not to be drawn from the ranks of the workers, or even Africans, though there should be 'a strong African element'. To ensure that these 'representatives' be knowledgeable and authoritative (in effect, deferential and petty bourgeoise), they were to be drawn from the ranks of African clerks and professionals.[124] Rejecting the Royal Commission's view that it was a waste of resources to encourage the development of British-style trade unions, Governor Cohen argued that, since trade unions would develop whether encouraged or not, the Labour Department had to ensure that they received the 'right guidance' during their development.[125] The prejudice against political activity by trade unionists continued into the post-colonial era. In 1970, the UPC regime passed a law barring members of the National Assembly from holding office in the Uganda Labour Congress (the only legal trade union) or any of its constituent branches.[126]

The Migrant Labourer as Soldier and Police

We end this brief survey of migrant labour by noting that two of the pivotal fields of employment in the colonial and post-colonial period were the military and the police. Whether due to height requirements, British stereotypes of martial races, a colonial reluctance to man the coercive apparatus with more educated southerners, or simply the difficulty of recruiting labourers from the major commodity-producing areas, the military and the police (to a lesser extent) tended to be drawn from the labour reserves. Lugard's small IBEA force grew considerably in 1891, when he persuaded Selim Bey to join the IBEA cause with 2,085 men (and some 6,000 dependants). Selim's soldiers at Kavalli's on the western shore of Lake Albert constituted the ragged remnants of Emin Pasha's Sudanese troops, augmented by new recruits from the Lendu. Lugard deployed these 'Sudanese' or 'Nubian' troops in a string of forts throughout western and southern Uganda. These troops formed the core of the Uganda Rifles, upon its establishment in 1895.[127] Several contingents of 'Nubian' soldiers were transferred eastward to form what became the Third Battalion of the King's African Rifles (KAR) in Kenya. Following the 1897 Mutiny, the Uganda Rifles were reorganised, and Baganda recruits and Indian troops added.

Commissioner Harry Johnston established the Uganda police in 1899 and, for reasons of economy, transferred many 'Nubians' from the Uganda Rifles (Rs. 18 per month) to the police (Rs. 10 per month), although Baganda probably constituted the largest part of the 1,060-strong police force.[128] With the initial 'pacification' of the Protectorate complete, the troop strength (of what was now the 4th Battalion of the KAR) declined to 1,075, of whom 671 were 'Nubians', 185 'Swahilis' (mainly Baganda), and 200 Sikhs.[129]

During the First World War, the conscription of some 200,000 men for the Carrier Corps and the KAR fell heavily upon the 'secondary' crop-producing regions: Lango, Teso and Bukedi. In the 1920s the number of 'Nubians' and Baganda declined in the 4th Battalion, although the remaining 'Nubians' were more likely to be promoted. A photograph taken in 1925 of the surviving 'native officers' of the 4th Battalion included the following:

2/Lt. Abdul Feraq Bakhit	2/Lt. Sakhair Ali
Lt. Ashe Mukasa	Lt. Mohamed Fadalla
2/Lt. Mulah Sadallah	Capt. Ali Owari
2/Lt. Salim Mustafa	Capt. Murjan Bakhit
Major Ali Mombur	Capt. Suar Karar
Lt. Said Jubara	Lt. Sabun Ibrahim.[130]

From the list it is apparent that a majority of the African officers were Muslim.

The reorganisation of the KAR in 1931 embodied two regressive features. First, the Ugandan practice of appointing African officers was terminated to bring the 4th Battalion into line with the rest of the KAR.[131] Re-Africanisation of the officer corps was reintroduced only in the 1950s, culminating in the 1959 promotions of Shaban Opolot, Pierino Okoya and Idi Amin to the rank of Major. Second, the six KAR battalions were organised into two brigades along tribal lines. The Northern Brigade, including the 4th Battalion, was to be recruited primarily from Nilotic tribes, whereas the Southern Brigade was to consist primarily of Bantu tribes. Tribal segregation was to be extended to the company and sub-unit levels as well.[132]

What of the 'Nubians' who had left the military or police? They settled in their own Muslim communities throughout Uganda: Bombo, Hoima, Arua, Entebbe, Jinja, Kumi, Lira, Masindi, Gulu, Kitgum and Aringa County. They became petty-traders, butchers, and, later, taxi-drivers.[133] The definition of who was a 'Nubian' became a matter of concern to the colonial state because the Native Courts were organised on tribal lines. As a 'detribalised', essentially urban group, the Nubi were classified as African and could be tried by Native Courts, yet they also enjoyed special access to the District Commissioner and British courts. The 1941 *Handbook on Native Courts* defined the 'Nubians' as follows:

> The term 'Nubi' is applicable only to persons who can prove they are descendents of the armed forces of Emin Pasha and his predecessors or that from association with the Nubi community extending over a period of many years they have lost all connexion with the tribes from which they originally sprang.[134]

Yet on the following page, the definition was restricted to 'those Nubi who joined the K.A.R. or Police or Prisons before 1933'. The handbook warned colonial administrative officers, 'a number of people may claim to be Nubis who are in fact not true Nubis but will be found on enquiry to be Lugbara, Acholi, or Madi, etc. it is the policy of the Government to give no special treatment to such as these'.[135]

During the Second World War, 55,000 Ugandans served as soldiers in Kenya, Ethiopia, Somalia, Madagascar, the Middle East and Burma.[136] Many more were conscripted into the East African Military Labour Service and the East African Pioneer Corps.

The war created manpower allocation problems which threatened food supplies. Military recruits were once again drawn primarily from 'the less productive areas', especially West Nile. Conscription was introduced in 1942 to fill the ranks of the EAMLS and the EAPC. As Powesland observed, 'The problem of balance arose at every turn.'[137] The manpower needs of the miltary had to be balanced against those of expatriate-owned firms engaged in 'essential production' (sugar, sisal, timber) and against the need to avoid draining the labour reserve districts of the bare minimum manpower needed to produce food for the families of the soldiers and migrant labourers. To lessen the severe burden on the West Nile, forced labour was reintroduced in Busoga in 1943, but this jeopardised the food supplies for the labour-force on the sugar plantations. At the same time, the colonial state's weapon of withholding labour supplies to force employers to improve working conditions (on plantations) was undermined by the need to maintain production.[138]

The end of the war generated concern among colonial administrators, who recognised that the existing structure of the economy could not absorb so many skilled and semi-skilled workers. There were, for example, 6,000 truck and car drivers among the returnees, yet openings existed in the civilian economy for only 600 drivers.[139] Although many returnees used their gratuities to become traders, the colonial state encouraged most to re-enter farming.

By the close of the colonial period the bulk of the army consisted of Acholi, West Nilers, Iteso and Langi. In 1950, Girling examined the occupations of Acholi migrants (based on information from kinfolk at home) and found that in a sample of 194 employees, half were engaged as unskilled labourers, 15 per cent as soldiers, and 15 per cent as policemen, prison guards or game wardens.[140] Fairly accurate figures are available for the ethnic composition of the Uganda police: 15.5 per cent Acholi, 15.2 per cent Iteso, 7.5 per cent Langi, 6.1 per cent Alur, 4.5 per cent Lugbara, 4.2 per cent Basoga, 4.0 per cent Bagisu, 3.8 per cent Madi, 3.8 per cent Baganda, and 3.7 per cent Kumam. Only 0.5 per cent were 'Nubian'.[141] The southern kingdoms (the core) were underrepresented, and the secondary cash-crop are as (the semi-periphery) were overrepresented, as were the labour-producing areas in the northwest (but not the southwest).

Notes

1. Uganda, *Blue Book, 1901/02*. The troops of the 4th Battalion consisted of Sudanese, Swahilis, Baganda and 'Wakavirondo' (Abaluyia), while the 5th Battalion was composed entirely of Sikhs from India.
2. H.R. Wallis, *The Handbook of Uganda*, 2nd edn (London: Crown Agents for the Colonies, 1920), passim.
3. See the list of duties of the *saza* chief in Buganda in Article 9 of the 1900 agreement, 'Uganda Agreement', in Donald Anthony Low and R. Cranford Pratt, *Buganda and British Overrule, 1900-1955* (London: Oxford University Press, 1960), Appendix II.
4. Between the capture of Kabaka Mwanga in 1899 and the investiture of Kabaka Daudi Chwa in 1914, the Kabaka's government was headed by the Regency composed of Apolo Kagwa, Zakaria Kizito Kisingiri and Stanislaus Mugwanya. Katikiro Kagwa in effect dominated the Kabaka's government from Mwanga's rebellion in 1897 until his forcible retirement in 1926.
5. Calculations based on population estimates for 1923 and annual cotton acreage estimates in Uganda, *Blue Books, 1911/12* through *1920*.
6. Calculations based on the population estimates for 1927 and annual cotton acreage estimates in Uganda, *Blue Books, 1921* through *1931*.
7. Philip Geoffrey Powesland, *Economic Policy and Labour*, ed. by Walter Elkan (Kampala: East African Institute of Social Research, 1957), pp. 23-8.
8. Anthony Clayton and Donald C. Savage, *Government and Labour in Kenya, 1895-1963* (London: Frank Cass, 1974), pp. 108-46; and Powesland, *Economic Policy and Labour*, p. 32.

9. Dan Mudoola, 'The Politics of Higher Education in a Colonial Situation: Uganda, 1920-1941', University of Dar es Salaam, unpublished paper, 1978.

10. Nizer A. Motani, *On His Majesty's Service in Uganda: The Origins of Uganda's African Civil Service, 1912-1940* (Syracuse: Maxwell School of Citizenship and Public Affairs, Syracuse University, 1977), p. 5.

11. Motani, *On His Majesty's Service*, p. 6.

12. Lloyd A. Fallers, *Bantu Bureaucracy*, 2nd edn (Chicago: University of Chicago Press, 1965), p. 149; and Uganda, *Blue Book, 1924*, pp. 65-71.

13. Dan Mudoola, 'Colonial Chief-Making: Busoga, A Case Study 1900-1940', paper presented to the Universities of East African Social Science Conference, Dar es Salaam, December 1970, p. 28.

14. As Governor Mitchell caustically observed,

These 'chiefs' of our creation were invested with many of the traditional attributes attaching to tribal authority — tribute and services in particular. A probable explanation is, in part at any rate, that in earlier days Governments were willing enough for these convenient administrative arrangements to be made, but loath to find the money to pay for them, and it seemed a reasonable expedient to put the burden on the peasantry in a form not at that time involving money payment nor any very onerous obligations.

Uganda, *Native Administration* (Mitchell's Address on 12 May 1939) (Entebbe: Government Printer, 1939), p. 9.

15. Information compiled from the following sources: Donald A. Low, 'Uganda: The Establishment of the Protectorate, 1894-1919', *History of East Africa*, ed. Vincent Harlow, E.M. Chilver and Alison Smith (Oxford: Clarendon Press, 1965), vol. II, pp. 104-9; John Gray, 'Kakunguru in Bukedi', *Uganda Journal*, vol. 27, no. 1 (1963), p. 52; G.N. Uzoigwe, *Revolution and Revolt in Bunyoro-Kitara*, Makerere History Paper No. 5 (Kampala: Longman Uganda, 1970), p. 54; Fallers, *Bantu Bureaucracy*, p. 149; J.S. La Fontaine, *The Gisu of Uganda* (London: International African Institute, 1959), p. 12; D.J.W. Denoon, 'Agents of Colonial Rule; Kigezi, 1908-1930', Universities of East Africa Social Sciences Conference Paper, Kampala, 1968, pp. 10, 19; H.F. Morris, *A History of Ankole* (Nairobi: East African Literature Bureau, 1962), p. 43; Kenneth Ingham, *The Kingdom of Toro in Uganda* (London: Methuen, 1975), pp. 112-21; J.C.D. Lawrance, *The Iteso* (London: Oxford University Press, 1957), p. 35; Edward H. Winter, *Bwamba; A Structural-Functional Analysis of a Patrilineal Society* (Cambridge: W. Heffer and Sons, 1955), pp. 227-31; and Audrey I. Richards (ed.), *East African Chiefs* (London: Faber and Faber, 1959), p. 84 (L.A. Fallers, 'The Soga'), p. 157 (D.J. Stenning, 'The Nyankole'), pp. 317-18 (A.W. Southall, 'The Alur'), and pp. 330, 337 (John Middleton, 'The Lugbara').

16. L.A. Fallers, 'The Soga', *East African Chiefs*, pp. 84-6; A.W. Southall, 'The Alur', *East African Chiefs*, pp. 318-19; and Cherry Gertzel, *Party and Locality in Northern Uganda, 1945-1962* (London: The Athlone Press, 1974), p. 57. Stages two through four of the four-part model are adapted from Southall.

17. Low, 'Uganda: The Establishment of the Protectorate', p. 93; R. Cranford Pratt, 'Administration and Politics in Uganda, 1919-1945', *History of East Africa*, vol. II, p. 494; and Uganda Protectorate, *Native Administration, 1939*, p. 24.

18. Most of these tasks were set out in the Native Authority Ordinance of 1919. See Lord Hailey, *Native Administration in the British African Territories; Part I. East Africa* (London: HMSO, 1950), p. 29; Pratt, 'Administration and Politics in Uganda', p. 489; and David N. McMaster, *A Subsistence Crop Geography of Uganda* (Bude, Cornwall: Geographical Publications Ltd, 1962), p. 66.

19. J.V. Wild, 'Note on the Busuulu and Envujjo Law', 10 March 1948, in *The Transformation of Land Tenure in Buganda Since 1896*, ed. Henry W. West (Leiden: Afrika-Studiecentrum, 1971), pp. 79-86; R. Cranford Pratt, 'The Politics of Indirect Rule', in Donald Anthony Low and Pratt, *Buganda and British Overrule, 1900-1955* (London: Oxford University Press, 1960), pp. 237-8.

20. Michael Twaddle, 'The *Bakungu* Chiefs of Buganda under British Colonial Rule, 1900-1930', *Journal of African History*, vol. 10, no. 2 (1969), pp. 316-19.

21. David E. Apter, *The Political Kingdom in Uganda*, 2nd edn (Princeton: Princeton University Press, 1967), pp. 134-49; Pratt, 'The Politics of Indirect Rule', pp. 233-4; and West, *The Transformation of Land Tenure in Buganda*, p. 4.

22. Henry W. West, *Land Policy in Buganda* (Cambridge: Cambridge University Press, 1972), pp. 139-50; and Apter, *The Political Kingdom*, pp. 141-6.

23. Apter, *The Political Kingdom*, p. 146; and Pratt, 'The Politics of Indirect Rule', pp. 234-5.

24. Pratt, 'The Politics of Indirect Rule', p. 236.

25. Peter C.W. Gutkind, *The Royal Capital of Buganda* (The Hague: Mouton, 1963), pp. 62-74; and Apter, *The Political Kingdom*, pp. 149-58.

26. West, *Land Policy in Buganda*, pp. 69-79; and Wild, 'Note on the Busuulu and Envujjo Law'. *Bibanja* is the plural of *kibanja*. Wrigley maintains that *envujo* was waived on the first quarter-acre plot of cotton, C.C. Wrigley, *Crops and Wealth in Uganda; A Short Agrarian History* (Kampala: East African Institute of Social Research, 1959), p. 53.

27. Kabaka to Governor, 25 June 1926; and Kabaka and Ministers to Governor, 6 July 1926; as summarised in Wild, 'Note on the Busuulu and Envujjo Law', pp. 82-3. In owning 350 square miles (90, 653 hectares) of official *mailo* estates and up to 150 square miles (38,852 hectares) of private *mailo* estates, the Kabaka had a very personal stake in preventing the abolition of *envujo*. West, *Land Policy in Buganda*, pp. 44, 48.

28. West, *Land Policy in Buganda*, p. 70; and Governor William Gowers, Minute dated 15 July 1925, as cited in Wild, 'Note on the Busuulu and Envujjo Law', 80.

29. Colonial officials denounced *envujo* on cash crops as 'repugnant to justice and morality' and a source of 'oppression and extortion'. Yet the initial remedy proposed by Governor Gowers – payment of *envujo* to the colonial state rather than to African landlords – demonstrated that colonial officials were more eager to reduce landlords' incomes than to raise tenants' incomes. William Gowers, Minute on Envujo, 15 July 1925, and Report of the Postlethwaite Committee, 31 December 1925, as cited in Wild, 'Note on the Busuulu and Envujjo Law', pp. 80-2.

30. Uganda Protectorate, *Report on the Commission of Enquiry into the Cotton Industry of Uganda, 1929* (Entebbe: Government Printer, 1929), p. 17.

31. A.B. Mukwaya, *Land Tenure in Buganda; Present Day Tendencies* (Kampala: East African Institute of Social Research, 1953), pp. 10 and 37.

32. Twaddle, 'The Bakungu Chiefs of Buganda', pp. 319-21.

33. Nizar A. Motani, *On His Majesty's Service in Uganda: The Origins of Uganda's African Civil Service, 1912-1940* (Syracuse: Maxwell School of Citizenship and Public Affairs, 1977), pp. 11-25. Among the many grievances of the BGNEA were the following: the exclusion of African government employees from the war bonus after the First World War; the denial of free housing and housing allowances to African employees; more favourable treatment for Goan clerks who were not even British subjects than for African clerks who were; and regulations forcing African employees to wear a Khanzu robe rather than a Western suit and tie. The Uganda Protectorate Land Office at Entebbe even ordered its inside African staff to go barefoot!

34. Mahmood Mamdani, *Politics and Class Formation in Uganda* (New York: Monthly Review Press, 1976), p. 127.

35. First, under the 1900 agreement, African *mailo* land in Buganda totalled 9,000 square miles, compared with 377 square miles of *mailo* in the Toro Agreement of 1900, 217 square miles of *mailo* in the Ankole Agreement of 1901 as amended in 1921, and no *mailo* land in the Bunyoro Agreement of 1933. Elsewhere there were neither agreements nor *mailo* estates. Apart from *mailo* land in Buganda, Toro and Ankole, virtually all land in Uganda was legally Crown Land. Second, whereas the agreement with Buganda stipulated that, in the event of conflict, the agreement took precedence over the laws of the Protectorate (Section 5), in the other three Agreement territories (Ankole, Toro and Bunyoro) the laws of the Protectorate took precedence over the agreements. See for example the Ankole Agreement, section 7, paragraph 6, as printed in Morris, *A History of Ankole*, Appendix C. The colonial state could therefore unilaterally abrogate any or all provisions of such an agreement by simply using its official majority in the Legislative Council to pass a law stating so. Third, aside from written legal niceties, the colonial state and the Colonial Office accorded the Buganda agreement of 1900 an unusual degree of respect and deference until 1953.

36. See footnote 35, and the following sources: M.L. Perlman, 'Land Tenure in Toro', East African Institute of Social Research Conference Paper, Limuru, Kenya, January 1962, p. 1; Lord Hailey, *Native Administration in the British African Territories, Part I*, p. 48; and J.H.M. Beattie, 'The Kibanja System of Land Tenure in Bunyoro', *Journal of African Administration*, vol. 6, no. 1 (January 1954), pp. 18-28. In Toro, 255 of 377 square miles of *mailo* were private estates; in Ankole only 62 of 217 square miles of *mailo* were inheritable private estates. Despite official non-recognition and even prohibition, *marketable* private rights to land existed to a greater or lesser degree in Sebei, Kigezi, Toro, Bunyoro and southern Busoga by 1950, in addition to Buganda.

37. Serwano Kulubya, *Omuwanika* (Minister of Finance) of Buganda, Testimony before the Joint Select Committee on Closer Union in East Africa, 12 May 1931, Great Britain, Parliament, *Parliamentary Papers* (Lords) *1931* (VII 85), 'Joint Select Committee on Closer Union in East Africa', II: 'Minutes of Evidence', p. 570, paragraphs 5847-9.

38. Mukwaya, *Land Tenure in Buganda*, p. 36; and West, *Land Policy in Buganda*, pp. 155-6.

39. Uganda Protectorate, Land Transfer Ordinance of 1906; Buganda Land Law of 1908; Secretary of State for the Colonies, decision barring further leases and sales to non-Africans, 1916; resolution of the Lukiko, 1921, requesting that non-Africans be barred from seizing African land for non-payment of debt; and 1922 resolution of the Provincial Commissioner opposing mortgaging of African land to non-Africans. West, *Land Policy in Buganda*, pp. 132-9.

40. West, *Land Policy in Buganda*, pp. 83-4, 89-91, 136 and 154; and Audrey I. Richards, 'Methods of Settlement in Buganda', *Economic Development and Tribal Change; A Study of Immigrant Labour in Buganda* (Cambridge: W. Heffer and Sons for EAISR, 1954), pp. 130-1.

41. Uganda, *Annual Report of the Department of Agriculture*, 1922-48. Following the financial collapse of many European-owned plantations in the early 1920s, the Department of Agriculture began distributing arabica seedlings to African growers in Bugisu and robusta seedlings to growers in Buganda in 1925. Already in 1922, the Department of Agriculture observed that African coffee planters were able to obtain unusually high yields from robusta coffee trees by spacing the trees widely and training the branches rather than pruning them. Uganda, *Annual Report of the Department of Agriculture*, 1922, p. 11.

42. Uganda, *The Patterns of Income and Expenditure of Coffee Growers in*

Buganda, 1962-63 (Entebbe: Statistics Division, Ministry of Planning and Economic Development, 1967), pp. 1-2, 9-11, 15 and 21; Uganda, *Report on Uganda Census of Agriculture* (Entebbe: Government Printer), vol. I (1965), pp. 56-63; vol. II (1966), pp. 14, 18, 36 and 39; and West, *Land Policy in Buganda*, pp. 79-82. On the basis of data in the census of agriculture, the Gini index of inequality for land-holdings (area cultivated by the household, as distinct from area owned or rented) in Masaka District was 0.55 in 1962-3. See also footnote 48, below.

43. Eric R. Wolf, *Peasants* (Englewood Cliffs, New Jersey: Prentice-Hall, 1966), p. 16.

44. Barrington Moore, Jr., *Social Origins of Dictatorship and Democracy; Lord and Peasant in the Making of the Modern World* (Boston: Beacon Press, 1967), p. 11.

45. Uganda, *Report of the Agricultural Productivity Committee*) Entebbe: Government Printer, 1954), p. 32, as cited in West, *Land Policy in Buganda*, p. 91.

46. Estimate of total number of landowners in 1967 from West, *Land Policy in Buganda*, p. 196.

47. Mukwaya, *Land Tenure in Buganda*, pp. 24-9. Between 1920 and 1950 the number of female landowners in the sample rose from 9 to 70, and the proportion of land held by women from 3.5 to 15.3 per cent of the sample area.

48. Calculations based on Mukwaya's data, including 1950 figure of 6,606 taxpayers in the sample area, plus my own estimate of 3,573 taxpayers in the sample area in 1920. The Gini index of inequality is based on the Lorenz curve, which is a plot of the cumulative proportion of a good (such as land) obtained by the cumulative proportion of the population. The line of equality would be a line drawn at a 45° angle, bisecting the angle between the X and Y axes, so that 20 per cent of the population received 20 per cent of the good, 50 per cent of the population received 50 per cent of the good, etc. The Gini index of inequality can be calculated as twice the area between the empirical Lorenz curve and the line of

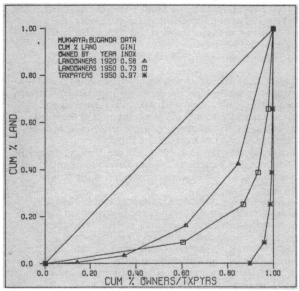

equality. Therefore, a Gini index of 0.0 represents absolute equality, and 1.0 represents absolute inequality. The illustration accompanying this footnote shows three Lorenz curves based on Mukwaya's data. The curve traced by triangular symbols is the cumulative percentage of land owned by the cumulative percentage of all landowners in 1920 (N = 135). The curve traced by square symbols is the cumulative percentage of land owned by the cumulative percentage of all landowners in 1950 (N = 687). And the curve traced by stars is the cumulative percentage of land owned by the cumulative percentage of all taxpayers in 1950 (N = 6606). In all cases the amount of land in the sample is 20,893 hectares (51,626 acres). See Mukwaya, *Land Tenure in Buganda*, pp. 25, 29-30; and Tord Høivik, 'The Lorenz Curve as a Peace Research Tool', *Journal of Peace Research*, vol. 14, no. 4 (1977), pp. 275-85.

49. Excluding the surviving original *mailo* owners, who comprised 4.8 per cent of the owners and owned 16.1 per cent of the land in the sample, the new owners and the transferred land they acquired were distributed as follows according to the method of transfer:

	Purchase	Inheritance	Gift	Total
Percent of new owners	60.7	20.2	19.1	100.0
Percent of transferred land:	28.4	62.5	9.1	100.0

Calculated from data in Mukwaya, *Land Tenure in Buganda*, pp. 29-37.

50. West, *Land Policy in Buganda*, pp. 119-22, 161-2 and 224.

51. See footnotes 35 and 36.

52. It was the *Land Tenure Proposals*, a 1955 White Paper, that first called for adjudication and registration of individual titles on Crown Land. For Governor Andrew Cohen's proposals for encouraging progressive farmers and for establishing District Land Boards to facilitate individualisation of landownership throughout Uganda, see Uganda, *Despatch from the Governor of Uganda . . . on the . . . Report of the East Africa Royal Commission, 1953-1955* (Entebbe: Government Printer, 1956), pp. 41, 49, 51, 54-7. On the 'creation of a class of yeoman farmer[s]', see Uganda, *Annual Report of the Department of Agriculture, 1960*, pp. 24-5. See also J.C.D. Lawrance, 'A Pilot Scheme for Grant of Land Titles in Uganda', *Journal of African Administration*, vol. 12, no. 3 (July 1960), pp. 135-43.

53. Compare Walter Goldschmidt, *Culture and Behavior of the Sebei; A Study in Continuity and Adaptation* (Berkeley: University of California Press, 1976), pp. 147-9; and John Locke, 'Of Property', *Two Treatises of Government* (1960), ed. Peter Laslett (Cambridge: Cambridge University Press, 1963), Book Two, Ch. 5. For the Sebei hens-to-riches story, see Goldschmidt, *Culture and Behavior of the Sebei*, p. 134; for the Bugisu rats-to-riches story, see La Fontaine, *The Gisu of Uganda*, p. 20. On the varieties of Sebei cattle contracts see Goldschmidt, *Culture and Behavior of the Sebei*, pp. 127-36.

54. Goldschmidt, *Culture and Behavior of the Sebei*, pp. 151-3; and Locke, 'Of Property', paragraph 28, lines 20-30, p. 330 in Cambridge edition.

55. Goldschmidt, *Culture and Behavior of the Sebei*, pp. 147-79, 193-202.

56. Government-registered titles to land did not exist in Sebei in 1962, making statistical information difficult to obtain. In a very small sample of 17 parcels totalling 12.7 acres, acquired between 1949 and 1962, Goldschmidt found the price had varied between Shs. 285 and Shs. 1,235 per acre, and averaged Shs. 750. In Buganda, the price per acre in prime coffee-growing areas ranged from Shs. 53 in 1950 (Mukwaya) to sub-county averages of Shs. 125 to Shs. 400 in 1964-5 (West). Goldschmidt, *Culture and Behavior of the Sebei*, p. 171; Mukwaya, *Land Tenure in Buganda*, Figure 2, p. 39; and West, *Land*

Policy in Buganda, Map L, pp. 208-9. These differences in land prices between southwestern Sebei (Sasur) and coffee-growing areas in Buganda might well be due to the fact that the Sebei grew the more valuable arabica coffee, suited to high altitudes, whereas the Baganda, with few exceptions, grew robusta. Between 1955/6 and 1959/60, the ratio of arabica to robusta prices for growers averaged 1.6 to 1. Uganda, *Annual Report of the Department of Agriculture*, 1960, pp. 6-10, 42; and Uganda, *1965 Statistical Abstract*, pp. 40-1.

57. Goldschmidt, *Culture and Behavior of the Sebei*, pp. 152-60, 196-9.

58. E.H. Winter, *Bwamba Economy* (Kampala: East African Institute of Social Research, 1955), pp. 1-11.

59. Winter, ibid., pp. 11-16, 25, 32, 36, 38 and 40. Winter estimated the working day of an Amba woman to be seven hours, whereas the Amba man's work-day averaged only three hours, illustrating the great inequality in the sexual division of labour. In 1950 average family cash income was only Shs. 133, of which Shs. 24 had to be paid by the adult male in taxes to the central and Toro governments. The value of subsistence product was estimated at an average Shs. 380 per family. Harmsworth reported that the Bagwere in Bukedi District also refused to work as wage-labourers for members of their own ethnic group. In both cases the refusal was grounded in the conviction that wage-labour enriched the employer, whose previous status had been no better than that of the employee. Josephine Harmsworth, 'Cows for Christmas', paper presented to the Universities of East Africa Social Science Conference, Dar es Salaam, January 1963, p. 3; and Winter, *Bwamba Economy*, p. 40.

60. Fallers, *Bantu Bureaucracy*, pp. 148-54, 164-74; C.C. Wrigley, *Crops and Wealth in Uganda* (Kampala: East African Institute of Social Research, 1959), p. 49; and Josephine Harmsworth, 'Dynamics of Kisoga Land Tenure', paper presented to the Universities of East African Social Science Conference, Limuru, Kenya, January 1962, p. 2.

61. Fallers, *Bantu Bureaucracy*, pp. 165-77; Harmsworth, 'Dynamics of Kisoga Land Tenure', pp. 3 and 5.

62. On feudalism as a precondition for autonomous capitalism, see Perry Anderson, *Lineages of the Absolutist State* (London: New Left Books, 1974), pp. 20-1, 28-9, 49-51, 397-431. See also note 6, Ch. 1.

63. Fallers, *Bantu Bureaucracy*, pp. 178, 219-20; and Harmsworth, 'Dynamics of Kisoga Land Tenure', p. 7.

64. H.B. Thomas and J.G. Rubie, *Enquiry into Land Tenure and the Kibanja System in Bunyoro, 1931* (Entebbe: Government Printer, 1932), as cited in A.R. Dunbar, *A History of Bunyoro-Kitara* (Nairobi: Oxford University Press, 1965), pp. 143-9; and J.M. Beattie, 'The Kibanja System of Land Tenure in Bunyoro', *Journal of African Administration*, vol. 6, no. 1 (January 1954), pp. 21-3. Only in the 'lost counties' of Bunyoro occupied by Buganda at the end of the nineteenth century were there *mailo* estates, but these were of course owned by Baganda landlords.

65. Beattie, 'The Kibanja System of Land Tenure in Bunyoro', pp. 24-8.

66. The first commercial African tobacco was marketed in 1927. In 1932 growers received Shs. 0.16 per pound for tobacco leaves, while the colonial state levied an excise tax of Shs. 0.50 per pound on buyers. By 1953 the excise duty on tobacco had risen to at least Shs. 7 per pound, but growers received only Shs. 0.67 per pound. When the price to growers rose to over Shs. 1.00 in the late 1950s the excise duty rose to Shs. 11.00 per pound. Colonial Office, *Annual Report on the Social and Economic Progress of the People of Uganda, 1933*, Colonial Annual Report No. 1670 (London: HMSO, 1934), pp. 24, 60; Colonial Office, *Report on Uganda for the Year 1951* (London: HMSO, 1952), p. 28; and Dunbar, *A History of Bunyoro-Kitara*, 141-2, 151-2, 164, 171-3, 195-7.

67. R.M. Bere, 'Traditional System of Land Tenure Amongst the Acholi', as found in F.K. Girling, *The Acholi of Uganda* (London: HMSO, 1960), Appendix D, pp. 230-3.

68. Girling, *The Acholi*, pp. 8, 95-6, 171-5.

69. J.D. Tothill and the Staff of the Department of Agriculture, Uganda, *Agriculture in Uganda* (London: Humphrey Milford, Oxford University Press, 1940), p. 202. Acholi had previously cultivated local cotton for knitted decoration.

70. Girling, *The Acholi*, pp. 61, 189-202, 233; Uganda, *Blue Book, 1931*; and Uganda, *Report on Uganda Census of Agriculture*, vol. III (1966), p. 49.

71. The Gini index of inequality in land-holdings was 0.57 in Acholi (N = 51,000 households), 0.44 in Teso (N = 100,000), and 0.39 in Lango (N = 71,000), using data from Uganda, *Report on Uganda Census of Agriculture*, vol. III (1966), pp. 14, 18 and 19. In the absence of legal title to land, a land-holding was defined as land actually tilled, plus fallow land and non-communal grazing land. See also footnote 48. Only 31.9 per cent of Acholi holders reported participating in communal work-groups in 1963. Although higher than Buganda (6.1 per cent), the figure was lower than either Teso (57.2 per cent) or Lango (72.7 per cent). Uganda, *Report on Uganda Census of Agriculture*, vol. I. (1965), p. 63.

72. T.T.S. Hayley, *The Anatomy of Lango Religion and Groups* (Cambridge: Cambridge University Press, 1947), pp. 23, 40-8, 56-60, 71, 74-5, 104, 115, 145 and 148-52; and J.H Driberg, 'The Lango District, Uganda Protectorate', *Geographical Journal*, vol. 58, no. 2 (August 1921), p. 126.

73. John Tosh, 'Lango Agriculture During the Early Colonial Period; Land and Labour in a Cash-Crop Economy', *Journal of African History*, vol. 19, no. 3 (1978), pp. 415-39. Labour requirements for cotton amounted to 122 man-days, per acre; sesame 75 man-days; sorghum 27 man-days; and finger millet 72 man-days; according to G.B. Masefield, 'Agricultural Change in Uganda, 1945-1960', *Stanford University Food Research Institute Studies*, vol. 3, no. 2 (May 1962), p. 103. Assuming equivalent yields per acre for sesame and seed cotton, the price differential for cotton and sesame was inadequate to compensate for additional labour in three years out of eight between 1912/13 and 1919/20, according to Lango price data in Uganda, *Blue Books*, 1913 through 1920; and Driberg, 'The Lango District', p. 130. Planting dates and yields are taken from David N. McMaster *A Subsistence Crop Geography of Uganda* (Cornwall, England: Geographical Publications, 1962), pp. 49, 51, 57-8 and 77-8; and David McMaster, 'Cotton Cultivation', *Atlas of Uganda*, 2nd edn (Kampala: Uganda Department of Lands and Surveys, 1967), p. 52. In explaining the decline of Langi age-set ceremonies, Hayley may have overestimated the role of Ganda agents and missionaries and neglected the impact of the dry-season labour demands of cotton harvesting and sorting.

74. Uganda, *Blue Books*, 1916, 1920 and 1929; Tosh, 'Lango Agriculture', pp. 429, 431 and 437; and Hayley, *Anatomy of Lango Religion and Groups*, pp. 74-5.

75. Uganda, *Report of the Uganda Cotton Commission, 1938* (Entebbe: Government Printer, 1939), p. 119; and Uganda, *Annual Report of the Department of Agriculture, 1960*, p. 32. The Lango Cotton Zone includes all of Lango District plus Kaberamaido (Kumam) county in Teso District. Including Kaberamaido county inflates the acreage statistics for Lango by roughly 6 per cent.

76. Tosh, 'Lango Agriculture', pp. 435-8. Tosh weakens an otherwise excellent analysis of labour constraints as barriers to Langi adoption of the ox-drawn plough by dwelling too long on the labour needed to clear tree stumps from land left fallow for several years. Labour for tree stump removal proved a problem but hardly an insurmountable barrier in Teso, whose terrain, climate and vegetation resembled that of Lango.

77. See footnote 71.

78. J.C.D. Lawrance, *The Iteso* (London: Oxford University Press, 1957), pp. 1-16, 51-71; J.B. Webster, 'Pioneers of Teso', *Tarikh*, vol. 3, no. 2: *Peoples of Uganda in the 19th Century*, ed. G.N. Uzoigwe (London: Longman for the Historical Society of Nigeria, 1970), pp. 47-58; and John Lamphear, *The Traditional History of the Jie of Uganda* (Oxford: Clarendon Press, 1976), pp. 61-105. Using a list of approximately 95 meanings, linguists found the percentage of words in common to be 73 per cent for Ateso and Ngakarimojong, 65 per cent for Luganda and Runyoro, and 67 per cent for Moyo and Ogoko dialects of Madi. Peter Ladefoged, Ruth Glick and Clive Criper, *Language in Uganda* (London: Oxford University Press, 1972), pp. 53-84.

79. Lawrance, *The Iteso*, pp. 51-83 and 126-47; Pamela Gulliver and P.H. Gulliver, *The Central Nilo-Hamites* (London: International African Institute, 1953), pp. 15-22; and David Jeremiah Vail, *A History of Agricultural Innovation and Development in Teso District, Uganda* (Syracuse, N.Y.: Maxwell School of Citizenship and Public Affairs, Syracuse University, 1972), pp. 20-32.

80. Webster, 'Pioneers of Teso'; Vail, *History of Agricultural Innovation*, pp. 32-42; Lawrance, *The Iteso*, pp. 15, 134-41; Joan Vincent, *African Elite: The Big Men of a Small Town* (New York and London: Columbia University Press, 1971), pp. 25-32, 111-12 and 117-25; and Margaret Trowell and K.P. Wachsmann, *Tribal Crafts of Uganda* (London: Oxford University Press, 1953), pp. 90-103. Vail presents data on the labour requirements for soil preparation with a wooden hoe, but the source he cites compares the labour required for soil preparation with a plough and with a *jembe*, a metal hoe. Cf. Vail, *History of Agricultural Innovation*, p. 36; and T.J. Kennedy, 'Study of Economic Motivation Involved in Peasant Cultivation of Cotton', *East African Economics Review*, vol. 10, no. 2 (December 1963), pp. 88-95.

81. Lawrance, *The Iteso*, pp. 17-30; J.B. Webster, 'The Civil War in Usuku', *War and Society in Africa*, ed. Bethwell A. Ogot (London: Frank Cass, 1972), pp. 35-64; Vail, *History of Agricultural Innovation*, pp. 44-50, 64-91, 146; Vincent, *African Elite*, pp. 41-3; and Tothill (ed.), *Agriculture in Uganda*, pp. 43-4. The ratio of cotton prices to poll taxes was as follows:

Cotton season	Seed cotton price (Shs./100 lbs)	Poll tax (Shs.)	Ratio Cotton price/poll tax
1915-16	9.33	5.00	1.87
1916-17	11.00	5.00	2.20
1917-18	13.33	5.00	2.67
1918-19	14.00	5.00	2.80
1919-20	20.00	5.00	4.00
1920-21	8.00	7.50	1.07
1921-22	3.00	15.00	0.20
1922-23	30.00	15.00	2.00
1923-24	29.00	15.00	1.93
1924-25	25.00	15.00	1.67
1925-26	21.00	15.00	1.40

Sources: Uganda, *Blue Books*, 1915-1920; and Vail, *History of Agricultural Innovation*, p. 146. Cotton yields varied greatly, between 200 and 400 lbs/acre.

82. Tothill (ed.), *Agriculture in Uganda*, pp. 56-7, 77-84; Kennedy, 'Study of Economic Motivation Involved in Peasant Cultivation of Cotton', p. 91; J.M. Watson, 'Some Aspects of Teso Agriculture', *East African Agricultural Journal*, vol. 6, no. 4 (April 1940), p. 210; and Vail, *History of Agricultural Innovation*, pp. 91-118, 127-35, 146. On the rhythm of human activity over the annual crop

cycle, see the useful charts in Vail, *History of Agricultural Innovation*, p. 104; and Vincent, *African Elite*, pp. 40 and 214. Although the soil exhaustion problem was very real, even acute in some densely populated parishes, there was a tendency to overdramatise its effects on cotton yields. The picture of declining cotton yields that emerges from official statistics is very much the product of highly inflated estimates of cotton acreage made by chiefs and validated by district officials, both eager to demonstrate progress beyond the previous year's (inflated) estimates. In the 1963-4 season Teso produced 30,570 metric tons of seed cotton. Using data from the chiefs, Teso had 143,900 hectares planted in cotton, yielding a disastrously low 212 kilograms of seed cotton per ha. Using data from trained and impartial enumerators employed in the 1963 census of agriculture, Teso had only 88,200 hectares planted in cotton, for a yield of 347 kg/ha, not a very good yield, but hardly disastrous. Seed cotton output from Vail, *History of Agricultural Innovation*, p. 175; conflicting acreage statistics from Uganda, *Report on Uganda Census of Agriculture*, vol. III (1966), p. 63.

83. Tothill (ed.), *Agriculture in Uganda*, p. 81; McMaster, *A Subsistence Crop Geography of Uganda*, pp. 96-8; Vail, *History of Agricultural Innovation*, pp. 127-42, 171, 175; Uganda, *Annual Report of the Department of Agriculture, 1960*, p. 32; Uganda, *Report on Uganda Census of Agriculture*, vol. III (1966), pp. 14-22; Uganda, *1965 Statistical Abstract*, p. 7; Watson, 'Some Aspects of Teso Agriculture', p. 209; Lawrance, *The Iteso*, pp. 93, 143, 202-7; Uganda, *Report on Uganda Census of Agriculture*, vol. I (1965), pp. 64-6; and Vincent, *African Elite*, pp. 119-25, 198-203.

84. Fred G. Burke, *Local Government and Politics in Uganda* (Syracuse: Syracuse University Press, 1964), pp. 165-6; Lawrance, *The Iteso*, pp. 228, 234, 244-6, 256; Gulliver and Gulliver, *The Central Nilo-Hamites*, pp. 19-21; and Vincent, *African Elite*, pp. 187-208, 231-55.

85. See footnote 71. On the other hand, a higher proportion of holders in Teso (51.8 per cent) had access to communal grazing land than did holders in either Lango (41.1 per cent) or Acholi (20.2 per cent). Uganda, *Report on Uganda Census of Agriculture*, vol. I (1965), pp. 72-3. Attempts by 'progressive' farmers to enclose the grazing commons in Teso usually resulted in retaliatory violence from angry neighbours. Vail, *History of Agricultural Innovation*, p. 125.

86. On Bukedi, see Burke, *Local Government and Politics in Uganda*, pp. 178-222; Harmsworth, 'Dynamics of Kisoga Land Tenure'; and Harmsworth, 'Cows for Christmas'. On southeastern Sebei, see Goldschmidt, *Culture and Behaviour of the Sebei*, pp. 179-83, 194-5. On the Karimojong of Karamoja, see Neville Dyson-Hudson, *Karimojong Politics* (Oxford: Clarendon Press, 1966), pp. 22-80, 236-9.

87. Albert C. Cook, 'Further Memories of Uganda', *Uganda Journal*, vol. 2, no. 2 (October 1934), p. 103.

88. The attraction of cotton-growing versus the attraction of wage-labour may be expressed as the ratio of grower prices for seed cotton (Shs. per 100 kg) to the monthly wage of an unskilled labourer. The ratio was 3.94 (19.69/5.00) in 1911 and 4.32 (23.04/5.33) in 1913 versus, say, 1.14 (273.27/240) in 1978. With iron hoe cultivation, an acre of cotton requires about 122 man-days of labour (ftn 73) and yields between 200 and 400 pounds of seed cotton (ftn 81). If we make three highly artificial assumptions, namely: (a) the adult male performs all the labour on the cotton plot (in fact, women and children do most of the weeding and picking); (b) the worker has no extra outlays compared to the grower (in fact, the worker must buy both food and shelter); (c) the grower/worker seeks only to maximise income for 122 days of effort (in fact, many other factors enter into the picture: the availability of land, the comfort of remaining at home versus the lure of adventure), then a ratio below 4.4 should attract a low-yield (200 lb/acre) grower

into wage-labour, whereas the ratio would have to drop below 2.2 to attract a high-yield (400 lb/acre) grower into wage-labour, which it did after 1958.

89. Uganda, *Annual Report of the Department of Agriculture, 1920*, p. 23. Normally, the exchange rate was Rs. 15 per £1.

90. Powesland, *Economic Policy and Labour*, p. 31.

91. Uganda, *Report of the Uganda Development Commission, 1920* (Entebbe: Government Printer, 1920), pp. 13-19.

92. Powesland, *Economic Policy and Labour*, pp. 25, 39 and 55.

93. Powesland, *Economic Policy and Labour*, pp. 31-7.

94. Powesland, *Economic Policy and Labour*, p. 25.

95. Frederick Lugard, *The Dual Mandate in Tropical Africa*, 4th edn (Edinburgh and London: William Blackwood and Sons, 1929), p. 515.

96. Immanuel Wallerstein, 'The Rural Economy in Modern World Society', *The Capitalist World Economy* (Cambridge: Cambridge University Press, 1979), pp. 126-7.

97. Powesland, *Economic Policy and Labour*, pp. 15, 21.

98. Ibid., pp. 36, 37.

99. Ibid., pp. 40-1.

100. Ibid., pp. 40, 46.

101. Ibid., p. 44.

102. A.M. O'Connor, *Railways and Development in Uganda*, (Nairobi: Oxford University Press on behalf of EAISR, 1965), pp. 21-4, 50-5, and 92-7.

103. O'Connor, *Railways and Development in Uganda*, p. 7; and Powesland, *Economic Policy and Labour*, pp. 40-1, 45, and 67.

104. C.L. Bruton, District Officer, testimony in Great Britain, Parliament, *Parliamentary Papers* (Lords) *1931* (VII 85), 'Joint Select Committee on Closer Union in East Africa', II: paragraphs 6021-4, p. 586 (13 May 1931).

105. D.N. Stafford, Minutes of the Uganda Chamber of Commerce, 29 January 1937, Uganda Chamber of Commerce Archives, Makerere University Library, Kampala.

106. Powesland, *Economic Policy and Labour*, pp. 38-9.

107. Audrey I. Richards, 'Methods of Settlement in Buganda', *Economic Development and Tribal Change: A Study of Immigrant Labour in Buganda*, ed. Richards (Cambridge: W. Heffer and Sons for EAISR, 1954), pp. 123-4.

108. Uganda, *The Patterns of Income and Expenditure of Coffee Growers in Buganda, 1962-63* (Entebbe: Statistics Division, Ministry of Planning and Economic Development, 1967), pp. 1, 9 and Appendices II and III.

109. Powesland, *Economic Policy and Labour*, pp. 46 and 49.

110. Ibid., pp. 58, 67 and 81.

111. Ibid., pp. 55 and 57.

112. Azarias Baryaruha, *Factors Affecting Industrial Employment; A Study of the Ugandan Experience, 1954 to 1964* (Nairobi: Oxford University Press for EAISR, 1967), pp. 56 and 69.

113. Powesland, *Economic Policy and Labour*, passim.

114. Uganda, *Annual Report of the Ministry of Labour, 1970*, pp. 20, 25-8.

115. Uganda, *Annual Report of the Ministry of Labour, 1971*, pp. 7, 26-7.

116. Powesland, *Economic Policy and Labour*, p. 46; and Uganda, *Annual Report of the Department of Labour, 1952*, p. 34.

117. Uganda, *Annual Report of the Department of Labour, 1952*, p. 35.

118. Powesland, *Economic Policy and Labour*, p. 62.

119. Audrey I. Richards, 'The Problem for Buganda', *Economic Development and Tribal Change*, p. 198.

120. Uganda, *Annual Report of the Labour Department, 1952*, p. 6, as cited in Powesland, *Economic Policy and Labour*, p. 80.

121. Uganda, *Annual Report of the Labour Department, 1952*, pp. 19 and 44. Although there were 59 strikes and disputes involving 6,004 workers for a total of 8,618 lost man-days in 1952, the Labour Department blandly stated that in 'only a few cases did genuine grievances exist'. When demand for labour had been slack in 1938-9 and 1942, the Labour Department had argued that wages had to be linked to the laws of supply and demand. In 1952, by contrast, when demand for labour was unusually strong, the Labour Department argued that the workers' claims for higher wages were not justified by movements in retail prices (p. 19). The Labour Department's attitude towards workers' grievances did improve in the post-colonial period. In 1971, the department investigated 7,841 complaints and settled 6,259 in favour of the employees, and it even complained in 1970 about the asymmetry of the conflict between 'a well-organised group of employers on the one hand and disorganised and poorly financed workers' organisations on the other'. Uganda, *Annual Report of the Ministry of Labour, 1970*, p. 5, *1971*, p. 27.

122. Great Britain, *East Africa Royal Commission 1953-55 Report*, Cmd. 9475 (London: HMSO, 1955), p. 156.

123. Colonial Office, *The British Territories in East and Central Africa, 1945-1950*, Cmd. 7987, pp. 141-2, as cited in Mahmood Mamdani, *Politics and Class Formation in Uganda* (New York: Monthly Review, 1976), p. 190.

124. Great Britain, *East Africa Royal Commission 1953-55 Report*, pp. 160-2.

125. Uganda, *Sessional Paper No. 4 of 1956/57; Despatch from the Governor of Uganda*, p. 32.

126. Uganda, Trade Unions Act (1970), section 22 (5).

127. H. Moyse-Bartlett, *The King's African Rifles* (Aldershot: Gale and Polden, 1956), pp. 49-53; and O.W. Furley, 'The Sudanese Troops in Uganda', *African Affairs* (London), vol. 58, no. 233 (October 1959), pp. 311-28.

128. Moyse-Bartlett, *The King's African Rifles*, p. 131; and Furley, 'The Sudanese Troops in Uganda', pp. 326-7.

129. Moyse-Bartlett, *The King's African Rifles*, p. 132.

130. E.F. Twining, 'Uganda Medals and Decorations', *Uganda Journal*, vol. 2, no. 3 (January 1935), pp. 208-9.

131. Twining, ibid., p. 209.

132. Moyse-Bartlett, *The King's African Rifles*, p. 463.

133. Dennis Pain, 'The Nubians', *Expulsion of a Minority: Essays on Ugandan Asians*, ed. Michael Twaddle (London: University of London, Athlone Press, 1975), pp. 182-6. Pain's article is one of the few excellent pieces on the Uganda 'Nubians'.

134. Uganda, *Handbook on Native Courts, 1941*, p. 5.

135. Ibid., p. 6.

136. Colonial Office, *Annual Report on Uganda, 1946*, pp. 3, 91; and E.F. Whitehead, 'A Short History of Uganda Military Units Formed During World War II', *Uganda Journal*, vol. 14, no. 1 (March 1950), pp. 1-14. Whitehead lists 26 Ugandan Africans who were awarded medals for service in the Second World War.

137. Powesland, *Economic Policy and Labour*, p. 74.

138. Ibid., pp. 70, 74.

139. Uganda, *Report of the Civil Reabsorption and Rehabilitation Committee* (Entebbe: Government Printer, 1945), pp. 4, 10.

140. F.K. Girling, *The Acholi of Uganda* (London: HMSO, 1960), p. 218.

141. Nelson Kasfir, 'Cultural Sub-Nationalism in Uganda', *The Politics of Cultural Sub-Nationalism in Africa*, ed. Victor A. Olorunsola (New York: Anchor Books, Doubleday, 1972), pp. 82-3. I have combined the figures for Alur and Jonam.

3 THE COLONIAL STATE IN THE WIDER ECONOMY: CHANGING CONSTRAINTS AND PRIORITIES

The case of the colonial state in a colonial society presents a complex variation of the state/society *problématique*. First and foremost, the colonial state was an alien administrative-coercive apparatus, imposed by the metropolitan state over a more or less arbitrarily defined territory for the economic and strategic ends of the metropole. The colonial state established institutions and mechanisms to expropriate surplus from domestic producers both for its own maintenance and for the benefit of metropolitan interests in industry, commerce, banking and shipping. Whereas the modern European state emerged amidst domestic struggles among the monarch, the landed nobility and the bourgeoisie, the colonial state was created as the bureaucratic-military apparatus through which the metropolitan bourgeoisie exercised dominion over all indigenous social strata.[1] Although the colonial state enjoyed considerable autonomy over indigenous strata, its autonomy in relation to the metropolitan state was more limited. Even so, the colonial state's responsibility for day-to-day decisions gave rise to a measure of autonomy.

Second, notwithstanding its alien origin and its forcible installation, the colonial state was the state, or governing class, *vis-à-vis* social strata and ethnic groups in the colony. It intervened in domestic class structures, encouraging or forcibly creating new social classes and retarding the formation of other social classes.[2] Having embedded itself in the social formation of the colony, the colonial state emerged as the focus and arbiter of domestic political conflict. In the process, it became somewhat less alien and less illegitimate.

Third, the colonial state's dominion over all indigenous social strata and ethnic groups was itself both partial and relative. Shifts in the world economy and changes in world prices affected both the resources of the colonial state and the matrix of domestic, regional and global socio-economic forces in which it operated. Maintenance of colonial overrule with an economy of coercion necessitated the formation of political alliances with domestic strata and ethnic groups which placed additional constraints on the colonial state's domestic autonomy. The colonial state's intermediary role in domestic class, ethnic and regional

134

antagonisms was very much a balancing act in which its interventions had unforeseen consequences. At times it foundered in its intermediary role and failed to achieve the goals desired by the metropolitan state. At all times the goals of the metropolitan state in any one colony had to be co-ordinated with the overall aims of the Empire. The colonial state was therefore more overdetermined than overdeveloped.[3] It was overdetermined in that the economic structure which gave rise to the superstructure of the colonial state consisted of the entire world economy while the colonial state's domain encompassed only a small part of that world economy. Although the colonial state was authoritarian, being neither omniscient nor omnipotent, it was also weak.

None the less, the colonial state did have the power to regulate land and labour policy to ensure that the colonial export-import trade took precedence over production for domestic human needs. The colonial state and expatriate firms determined the overall orientation of the domestic economy through control of general economic policy and transport policy and through control of monetary, financial and marketing structures. Social services were provided primarily to the expatriate community in urban centres and were initially extended to the indigenous population only in so far as these services appeared to aid the production of export commodities or the maintenance of colonial rule.

The Arena and the Environment of the Colonial State

The outlining of the pre-colonial arena of the entire interlacustrine region — its common structures, networks and processes — must await the completion of research by David Cohen and others.[4] Hansen has outlined the colonial creation of the Uganda political arena as embodying the establishment and deepening of five structures: (1) the pyramidal administrative and centralised legal system; (2) trade and (unequal) economic development; (3) the cobweb-like infrastructure; (4) the network of Catholic and Protestant missions and schools; (5) the vertical ethnic differentiation arising from Buganda's central location and the use of the Buganda administrative system as a model elsewhere. These structures gradually unified the territory, created a political centre as the focus of conflict and differentiated Uganda from surrounding territories.[5]

Is it possible to sketch the corresponding structures which shaped the international and regional environment of the colonial state?

Gartrell has warned of the travesty of reducing the international environment to the metropole-colony dyad.[6] The metropole-colony dyad was itself embedded in and crosscut by other structures. At the global level there was the capitalist world system with its periodic expansion and contraction, its fluctuating world market prices, and its changing vertical international division of labour among the core, semi-periphery and periphery. Next there was the British Empire which had its own hierarchy: its own core (England), semi-periphery (Canada, South Africa, Australia, New Zealand and India), and periphery Through a common language, hierarchial administrative structures, legal system, trading patterns, financial flows and monetary structures the Empire integrated its colonies and differentiated them from the French, Portuguese and other empires. The ability of the colonial state to divert trade to the benefit of the metropolitan state was enhanced by the importance of purchases by the colonial state and its British staff in the overall imports of, say, Uganda. But the reciprocal obligations with other powers under the Congo Basin treaties placed some limits on distorting the market to benefit the metropolis. Britain's decline within the core of the world capitalist system in the 1930s and 1940s led to increased intervention in colonial export marketing to obtain benefits formerly provided by the operation of the 'free' market. The movement of resources was also shaped by the network of expatriate banks, trading firms, mines, processing plants and shipping lines whose boundaries first crosscut, later overlapped and then once again crosscut the boundaries between competing empires.[7] International migration by Europeans and Asians into East Africa further complicated regional structures by introducing the international status group category of race.[8] Surplus flowing to the core of the Empire was reduced by the demands of colonial administrators and other expatriates for social amenities (housing, pensions, leaves, children's education, servants, cars) befitting their international status group, demands which resulted in what I have termed structural corruption. Similarly, to maintain living standards compatible with their international status group, the much larger group of commercially marginal European farmers in Kenya had to create the East African common market in which surplus flowed to Kenya from Uganda and Tanganyika. Finally, structures created consciously or unconsciously by humans were influenced by physical factors (Uganda's land-locked position, climate, the terrain and distance) and technical factors (the bulkiness of seed cotton, the foreign demand for agricultural products of uniform quality, and the versatility of cotton and its by-products). The colonial state therefore operated within a complex matrix of structures in which the metropolis-colony dyad was an important part, but only a part of the whole.

The Sub-imperialism of Expatriate Firms

Banking institutions and monetary structures were required as a lubricant to integrate Uganda into the world capitalist system. The Indian rupee circulated as the official currency in Uganda between the 1901 demonetisation of cowrie shells and the 1919 establishment of the East African Currency Board.[9] Recognising that the shortage of specie (coins) and the lack of credit and banking facilities fettered the production and circulation of commodities, the colonial state in 1903 invited the National Bank of India (now the National and Grindlays Bank) to establish a branch at Entebbe. There was a remarkably modern tone to the negotiations which followed. The wary foreign investor asked the host government (the colonial state) to conduct a pre-investment survey of business conditions (which evidently took 30 months to complete) and demanded guarantees from the state ('suitable accommodation' and 'protection from the natives').[10] After more negotiations, the colonial state agreed to deposit with the bank all surplus state funds and the salaries of European government employees. It also supplied the branch with a guard for five years, free use of the Treasury's 'strong room', a vault door, real estate services and a plot with a 99-year lease at £10 per acre.[11]

The National Bank of India opened its office at Entebbe in 1906 and expanded to Kampala and Jinja in 1911. Faced with the prospect of competition from the Standard Bank of South Africa, which opened its Kampala branch in 1912, the National Bank of India pressed the colonial state for formal recognition of its monopoly as official bankers to the state. The resulting agreement of 1913 remained in force until 1966.[12] By 1920 the colonial state had Rs. 1.7 million (£170,000 at the temporarily inflated rate of Rs. 1 to Shs. 2) on deposit with the National Bank of India. While in London, the General Manager of the Standard Bank and Viscount Alfred Milner lobbied Governor R.T. Coryndon to transfer some of the Uganda government accounts to the Standard Bank. Colonial state officials threatened termination of the 1913 agreement to force NBI to give the European salariat the same favourable exchange rate that the bank accorded the colonial state. The colonial state made one arbitrary exception to the 1913 agreement by transferring the Uganda Railway account from NBI to Standard Bank.[13]

At one level, the above story illustrates two familiar themes: that officials in peripheral states can extract personal concessions from expatriate firms and that expatriate firms can extract concessions from peripheral states. But, more importantly, the story is about the competition for Uganda between India-based British capital (NBI) and South Africa-based British capital (Standard Bank). The opening round in the competition had, of course, been fired by India-based British capital: the Mackinnon-Mackay group (IBEA, British and India Steam Navigation Co., Peninsular & Oriental Steamship Co., Smith-Mackenzie, and Mackinnon, Mackenzie & Co.).

There were three major colonial partitions of Africa, the first two launched by outside forces, the third by the interaction of outside forces with internal structures and conditions. The political 'scramble' for Africa by European powers between 1880 and 1900 constituted the familiar first partition. What Hopkins terms 'the second partition' occurred between 1890 and 1930 as European-owned firms launched offensives from three initially competing bases — Europe, South Africa and India — to carve out commercial empires in Africa.[14] The third partition consisted of the regional variations in the form of incorporation into the capitalist world system, described by Samir Amin: in west Africa, the classical colonial trade economy in which the production of commodity exports was carried out primarily by peasant producers; in central Africa, the economy of concession companies in which foreign firms simply plundered natural resources; and in eastern and southern Africa the economy of labour reserves in which European settlers directed the labour of Africans in mines and on plantations.[15]

In the second partition, West Africa became the domain of European-based firms, and southern Africa the domain of South Africa-based firms.[16] Central Africa was dominated initially by European-based firms, then jointly by these and by South Africa-based firms. East Africa became the joint preserve of India-based European capital and South Africa-based European capital.[17] In 1924, for example, the ships of the British and India Steam Navigation Company called at Mombasa 53 times on the Mombasa-Bombay run versus 15 on the Mombasa-Europe run. The South Africa-centred Union Castle line called at Mombasa 22 times. There were, of course, other European lines serving Mombasa: France, 52 calls; Italy, 36, etc.[18] Except for shipping, European-based firms rarely gained prominence in East Africa, and South Africa-based firms did not enter West Africa in accord with the spheres of influence agreement signed between Unilever and Anglo-American in 1931.[19] This partition gradually broke down after the Second World War. Sometimes the old pattern prevailed, as when

Lonrho (southern Africa) and Steel Brothers (India) bought firms from European settlers in East Africa who were pessimistic about their future under African majority rule. Increasingly the partition failed to hold, as when Lonrho and Unilever expanded into West Africa and East Africa, respectively. The banks, which formerly operated in only one or two zones, now extended branches into all zones. National and Grindlays Bank (ex-NBI) opened merchant bank subsidiaries in West Africa and was itself partially taken over (40 per cent) by the First National City Bank of New York.

Commerce in East Africa, as in West Africa, was firmly dominated by expatriates throughout the colonial period. But commerce in East Africa did not give rise to huge vertically and horizontally integrated trading firms such as those found in West Africa: United Africa Company (Unilever), G.B. Ollivant (now part of Unilever), John Holt (now part of Lonrho), Société Commerciale de l'Ouest Africain (SCOA), Compagnie Française d'Afrique Occidentale (CFAO), Maurel et Prom, G.L. Gaiser and Cadbury. By contrast, the Uganda Company, Smith-Mackenzie, British East Africa Corporation, Dalgety, Mitchell Cotts, A. Baumann, Twentsche Overseas, and Leslie and Anderson – the few large trading firms operating in East Africa – were mere shadows of their West African counterparts.

Several factors might explain the smaller size of the expatriate trading firms in East Africa. The smaller size of the East African market might not support giant firms. The East African firms tended to be more specialised along product lines. None spanned the entire range from industrial to basic consumer goods; indeed, except for automobiles, European firms were virtually absent from retail trade, in sharp contrast to the West African pattern. The absence of European firms from East African retail trade might be explained by the ability of Asian competitors to undercut them. But if Indians could undercut Europeans in East Africa, why could the Syrians and Lebanese not do the same in West Africa? Was distance a factor?

But these explanations approach the problem from the wrong angle. It was the European settlers in Kenya who retarded the emergence of large-scale European expatriate firms in East Africa.[20] Through their economic nationalism and protectionist policies, the settlers restricted the 'open economy' which was essential for the emergence of UAC, SCOA and CFAO in West Africa. Conversely, the emergence of the Madhvani and Mehta manufacturing groups in Uganda and the Chandaria group in Kenya could not have occurred in a more open economy, such as in West Africa.

The Partial Closure of the East African Market

Two seemingly contradictory events occurred in 1923. On the one hand, the creation of a protected East African market for foodstuffs produced by European settlers appeared to mark the ascendancy of their interests over the free trade interests of large-scale merchant capital (based in East Africa, India, South Africa and Europe). On the other hand, the 'Indians in Kenya' White Paper, which declared the paramountcy of African interests in Kenya,[21] was certainly a victory for large-scale ('metropolitan') capital over settler interests. The position of settlers on both issues is unambiguous; the position of large-scale capital on the economic issue is less clear.

Using the infant industry argument, the settlers had pressed for high tariffs on imported foodstuffs: wheat, maize, flour, butter, cheese, bacon, etc. The establishment of a common external tariff and the elimination of internal tariffs among the East African territories provided settlers with a wider protected market. On the political front Kenya's settlers pressed unsuccessfully for internal self-rule or responsible (white-minority) government, like that granted to Rhodesia's settlers the same year.[22]

The interests of large-scale capital were equally clear on the political issue: responsible government was opposed by 'metropolitan' capital, which viewed settlers as an expensive and economically unviable nuisance.

The common external tariff had divided support among large-scale merchant capital. As might be expected, the Uganda Chamber of Commerce opposed the tariff, as did the Tanganyika government, which unilaterally slapped a tariff on Kenya butter and cheese in 1925.[23] Yet the London and Manchester Chambers of Commerce supported the customs union. Why? Brett offers the explanation that, by enabling the expatriate firms to operate within the region as a single unit, the customs union lowered overhead costs by eliminating the need for separate establishments in each territory.[24] But surely the expatriate firms would have achieved the same ends by opposing tariffs altogether. The customs union was clearly a second-best alternative.

The metropolitan state's acquiescence in the East African customs union requires further explanation. We can find that explanation in Tanganyika, which became a British mandated territory under the League of Nations after the First World War. Just as the establishment of the East African Currency Board in 1919 had among its aims the reassurance of British investors that Tanganyika would remain within the Empire, so too did the East African customs union offer British investors reassurance about Tanganyika.[25] The fact that the hoped-for British investment spurned the reassurance and gravitated toward Kenya rather than Tanganyika, helps explain the Tanganyika government's exasperation with the common tariff.

Previously, rice, wheat, wheat flour and sugar had attracted an *ad valorem* duty of 15 per cent. The new specific duties were equivalent to an *ad valorem* duty of at least 30 per cent on the 1923 import prices: rice and wheat, Shs. 5 per 100 lb (effectively 32 and 35 per cent of the import value); wheat flour, Shs. 6 per 100 lb (40 per cent); and sugar, Shs. 12 per 100 lb (39 per cent). In addition, butter, cheese and ghee (clarified butter) drew an import duty of one shilling per pound (38 to 40 per cent); bacon Shs. 0.80 per lb (31 per cent); and soap, Shs. 5 per 100 lb (13 per cent). Tobacco and timber carried an *ad valorem* duty of 50 per cent. When the 1929 slump lowered world prices, it raised the effective percentage value of the specific duties. Protests from Tanganyika, Uganda and non-settlers in Kenya forced a lowering of the common tariff in 1930 to 20 per cent plus a 10 per cent suspended *ad valorem* duty on most items.[26]

One effect of the tariff was to tax East African food-buyers to subsidise Kenyan settlers. Another effect was to accelerate the uneven development within East Africa in which Kenya became the core, Uganda the semi-periphery, and Tanganyika the periphery.

The common tariff was not a total loss for Uganda. It spurred the peasant cultivation of tobacco and the plantation cultivation of sugar. Nanji Kalidas Mehta, already prominent in cotton ginneries, started the first large-scale sugar plantation in 1922 at Lugazi between Kampala and Jinja. Seven years later Muljibhai Madhvani founded what was to become an even larger sugar plantation and the basis for an industrial empire at Kakira, northeast of Jinja.[27]

The Lugazi sugar factory began operating in October 1924, and was producing 3,600 metric tons by 1926. Sugar production surpassed local consumption in the early 1930s, and the total area devoted to sugar cane increased to 6,000 hectares by the late 1930s. In addition to supplying the Ugandan and Kenyan markets, Uganda exported 33,800 metric tons of unrefined sugar and jaggery, worth Shs. 15.3 million, to the Sudan, Tanganyika and the United Kingdom in 1948.[28] The industrial ventures of the Madhvani and Mehta groups were largely financed by their successful exploitation of the protected East African market for agricultural products. Aranow estimates that in the 1950s the sugar works received Shs. 800 per ton in the East African market, double the prevailing world sugar price of Shs. 400 per ton.[29]

Uneven Development Within East Africa

While the sugar planters' exploitation of the East African market escaped much comment (save criticism of the poor living conditions of the field-hands), the Kenya settlers attracted anger and criticism from all quarters. Temperate-zone farming was simply commercially unviable in East Africa, at least up to 1937, when the cultivation of coffee and pyrethrum as exclusive European crops finally saved the farmers.[30] Until then, the settlers who survived did so by taxing other sectors to subsidise their marginal farming operations. To make matters worse, the quality of their produce was generally quite low until the early 1930s.[31] The most stinging attack on the settlers came from Sir Humphrey Leggett, chairman of the British East Africa Corporation. An offshoot of the British Cotton Growing Association, the BEA Co. had diversified from cotton ginneries in Uganda into plantations in Kenya.[32] In his 1931 memorandum to the Joint Select Committee on Closer Union in East Africa, Leggett laid bare the economic props which the settlers had won from the colonial state and proceeded to make the case for the replacement of the 'colonists' by plantations owned by large-scale firms and by peasant agriculture in which expatriate firms controlled the processing and marketing. His exposé of the fundamental economic weakness of the settlers revealed the deep antagonism between large-scale European capital and the settlers.

Among the props cited by Leggett, were the following:

(1)   the initial construction of the railway without charge to the Kenya community;

(2)   the exceptionally favourable freight rates for export commodities produced by settlers: for example, a freight rate of ¼d per ton-mile for maize, compared to rail operating costs of ¾d per ton-mile;

(3)   the protection afforded to farmer-settlers by the 1923 import duties and freight rates on imported foodstuffs many times the export freight rate for the same item;

(4)   the allocation of all operating profits (£1.75 million) from the railway to the Kenya Treasury between 1901 and 1922, despite the fact that the major profits were derived from shipping cotton produced by Uganda peasants;

(5)   the allocation of all customs revenue to Kenya between 1903 and
       1909, of which £800,000 should have gone to Uganda;
(6)   the allocation of most Kenya government expenditures to the
       European settlers, with too little allocated to African health and
       education despite the fact that the major part of government
       revenues were derived from rail revenues in adjacent territories
       and from poll taxes and customs duties falling on Africans;
(7)   the 1930 allocation of £100,000 by the Kenya Treasury to aid
       settlers who had exhausted their credit with banks and other
       financial intermediaries;
(8)   land grants totalling 1¼ million acres for the Soldier Settlement
       Scheme (1,500 families) and 26,000 choice acres for the Disabled
       Officers Colony (80 families) in 1919-20, of which only half the
       soldier-settlers and none of the officers survived financially.

Leggett concluded that high freight rates, high taxes, high labour
costs (because of high food costs), and misallocation of expenditures
had forced plantations, the Kenya government and the entire African
population of East Africa to subsidise the 1,500 or so settlers and their
families. Aside from suggestions for turning agriculture over to
European-owned plantations and African peasants, Leggett made the
novel proposal that Mombasa be declared a joint territory of Kenya and
Uganda, since its growth was built on the trade from both.[33]

Opposition to Kenya's artificially enhanced economic status and
resistance to Kenya settlers' proposals for an East African political
federation were among the few issues which united Africans and non-
Africans in Uganda. Fearing alienation of their land to settlers, Africans
strongly objected to 'closer union' in the 1920s and early 1930s. Fear
of the planned East African Federation helped precipitate the 1949
riots in Buganda. Kabaka Edward Mutesa's opposition to the proposed
East African Federation was a central issue in his standoff with the
colonial state which culminated in his being deported in 1953.[34]

Europeans and Asians in Uganda criticised subsidies to Kenya
settlers and objected to the subordination of Uganda's development to
Kenya's. In 1920 the planters opposed the construction of the rail
extension into Uasin Gishu Plateau to serve settlers, arguing that it
could only be financed by further increases in already high freight
rates on non-settler produce. Paradoxically settler representatives in the
Kenya Legislative Assembly complained about the extension of the
railway to Kampala, ignoring that revenue from Uganda links was
essential to subsidise the low freight rates and rail feeder lines enjoyed

by settlers.[35] Representing the Uganda Chamber of Commerce, Dr
H.H. Hunter's 1931 hastily compiled catalogue of grievances included
the 1902 transfer of the Highlands from Uganda to Kenya, a complaint
to be echoed by Amin 44 years later.[36] In 1943 members of the
Uganda Chamber of Commerce (R.G. Vedd, A.S. Folkes and R.J.
Mehta) objected to the undue preference shown Kenya in siting new
industries in East Africa. Folkes complained that Ugandan trading
firms were not permitted to import goods directly but had to do business through Kenyan firms which charged a 7½ per cent commission.[37]

Increasingly the debate was not only about the division of the
existing East African 'pie' – between British and East Africa, among
Kenya, Uganda and Tanganyika, between large firms and settlers within
Kenya, and among African, expatriate firms, Africans and the colonial
state within Uganda – but also about the direction and location of
future growth in the pie.

The amenities which settlers had wrested for themselves in Kenya
proved irresistible for European firms in general; they chose to locate
East African headquarters in Nairobi and branches elsewhere. Common
services of the East African territories, as they developed, established
headquarters in Kenya. The influx of foreign investment and the head-
quartering of private (insurance, shipping, banking) and public
(railways, customs, harbours) services in Kenya rather than Uganda
allowed Kenya to finance a sizeable visible trade deficit throughout its
modern history whereas Uganda had to show a sizeable visible trade
surplus to balance the outflow on the services account.

The colonial banking system, in which expatriate banks were
incorporated overseas and had their regional headquarters in Nairobi,
operated to pool savings from rural areas and make them available to
borrowers in urban areas. Within East Africa banks pooled savings from
all three territories to lend to borrowers in Nairobi and Mombasa.
Within the colonial system as a whole, banks pooled savings from agricultural colonies to lend in the metropole. None the less, as shown by
the advances/deposits ratio of commercial banks in Uganda, there was
(up to the Asian expulsion) an increased tendency over time to lend
within Uganda the deposits pooled in Uganda: 1938, 0.33; 1948, 0.45;
1958, 0.66; 1968, 0.76; 1971, 0.79; and 1973, 0.61.[38]

The colonial currency system also served to channel resources from
colony to metropole. Niculescu notes that currency issues represent
interest-free loans by the currency-absorbing population to the
currency-issuing authority.[39] In the case of the East African Currency
Board (1919-66), sterling served as backing for EA Shilling. However, in

contrast to the West Africa Currency Board, the EA Shilling was never 100 per cent backed by sterling; the proportion of backing hovered around 49 per cent.[40] Even so, the sterling reserves of the EACB represented a largely interest-free loan by East Africa to Britain, which could otherwise have been used to purchase the equivalent amount of British goods for East Africa. By the end of 1948, the total sterling assets of East Africa stood at £105 million, representing a loan of that amount by East Africa to Britain through the intermediary of the EACB.[41]

Conflicts Within Uganda over Marketing and Processing

Critics of the colonial state's intervention in crop marketing and processing have focused on two issues: first, whether elimination of restrictions on free-market forces would have resulted in more efficient marketing, better use of facilities and higher prices for growers; second, whether the measures taken to maintain export quality reflected a genuine concern or merely served as a smokescreen for the promotion of monopolies that excluded Africans from trade and processing.[42]

Bauer's classic well-argued critique of colonial marketing structures in West Africa[43] could be extended *mutatis mutandis* to their Ugandan equivalents: the 1909 destruction of hand-gins, the 1918 Cotton Rules, the Cotton Control Board (1924), the Native Produce Marketing Ordinance (1932), the Coffee Grading Ordinance (1932), the Cotton Zone Ordinance of 1933, the Cotton Exporters' Group (1943), the cotton and hard coffee price assistance funds (1944), the Lint Marketing Board (1949), and the Coffee Marketing Board (1953). In Uganda, as in Nigeria and the Gold Coast, regardless of original intent, such measures served to protect monopolies, increase inefficiencies in marketing and processing and lower the prices paid to growers.

Nevertheless, the debate between the proponents of the self-regulating market and the defenders of the colonial state's intervention in the market is a red herring. The colonial state's restrictions on the market in Uganda worked to the benefit of non-African interests in marketing and processing and to the detriment of African growers simply because growers had no control over the establishment and implementation of these measures. The unequal structure of representation was the problem, not state intervention in itself. In a footnote to his case for the self-regulating competitive market, Bauer does note that *producer-controlled* selling monopolies may improve the producers' position, though at the expense of consumers.[44]

Therefore, for growers the best of all possible worlds is not the self-regulating market but a producer-controlled selling monopoly. This is what the European settlers had achieved with the Kenya Farmers' Association (1919), the Kenya Co-operative Creameries (1925), the Wheat Board, Maize and Produce Board, Kenya Meat Commission and other settler-controlled marketing and processing agencies.[45] Within the capitalist world system, the self-imposed restraint required for the maintenance of the competitive market is negated by the axiomatic quest for wealth and power. Individuals therefore enter into combinations (corporations, trade unions, monopolies, cartels, professional associations) to distort the market in their favour and to protect themselves from others who would do the same — a classic prisoners' dilemma. As van Zwanenberg and King observed, Uganda and Kenya each had marketing boards which served the interests of those who had won a majority of the unofficial seats within the respective colonial legislative councils. The only difference, the crucial difference, was that this political influence was exercised in Kenya by the (European) settler-farmers and in Uganda by the (non-African) processors and merchants.[46]

Apter noted that the Uganda Legislative Council was not an independent legislative body but rather an advisory institution 'to represent the commercial interests of the European and Asian communities'.[47] The analysis of the backgrounds of the unofficial members of the Legislative Council from 1921 to 1952 (Table 3.1) demonstrates the prominence of cotton and coffee marketing and processing interests on the Council. The racial breakdown shows that until after the Second World War there was an inverse relationship between the racial share of population and the share of unofficial seats.

Buying pools or cartels were allegedly formed among cotton ginneries as early as 1908. According to one source, the ginneries appealed to Governor Bell to have hand-gins banned, which he did ostensibly to protect the uniformity of exports by controlling the availability of cotton seeds.[48] Under the 1918 Cotton Rules, middlemen were prohibited from buying seed cotton within a five-mile radius of an established ginnery. The Cotton Control Board protected established ginneries by ceasing to license new ones after 1926. Faced with high overheads due to the proliferation of ginneries faster than the growth of cotton production, the ginneries avoided rationalisation of the industry through competition by appealing to the state for assistance in setting prices and in establishing buying pools. The state responded with a

Table 3.1: Backgrounds of Unofficial Members of the Legislative Council, 1921-52

| Background | 1921-44 (no African members) | | | | 1945-52 | | |
	Europeans Permanent	Europeans Temporary	Asians Permanent	Asians Temporary	Africans	Europeans	Asians
Cotton industry							
BEA Co.	3	—	—	—	—	—	—
Uganda Co.	1	3	—	—	—	3	2
Other	1	2	1	4	—	—	—
Coffee industry							
A. Baumann	—	1	—	—	—	1	—
Other	—	1	—	—	—	—	—
Bankers	6	1	—	—	—	—	—
Lawyers	7	1	5	—	—	—	1
Planters	1	5	—	—	—	—	—
Insurance	—	2	1	—	—	—	1
Doctors	—	—	3	2	—	2	1
Businessmen not elsewhere specified	1	2	4	4	—	—	—
Senior officials of Kingdoms and Native Administration	—	—	—	—	14	—	—
District Council member	—	—	—	—	1	—	—
School masters	—	—	—	—	2	—	—
Vacant or unknown	—	—	1	—	—	2	—

The racial composition of the unofficial members of the Legislative Council was as follows:

	1921-31	1932-44	1945-6	1946-7	1947-8	1949-52	1959
Africans	0	0	3	3	4	8	18
Asians	1	2	2	3	3	4	7
Europeans	2	2	2	3	3	4	7

Sources: David Apter, *The Political Kingdom in Uganda*, pp. 168-9; Beverly Gartrell, 'The Ruling Ideas of a Ruling Elite', p. 268; and Tarsis B. Kabwegyere, *The Politics of State Formation*, p. 142.

pricing formula which allowed even the most inefficient ginneries to show a profit on a modest out-turn by shifting market risks onto the growers. Moreover, once again citing the need to protect export quality, the colonial state promulgated the Cotton Zone Ordinance in 1933, which divided Uganda into 14 zones and forbade movement of seed cotton from one zone to another. The Zone Ordinance greatly facilitated the formation of buying pools within each zone.[49]

Throughout the depression, ginneries enjoyed a minimum fixed return per pound of ginned cotton, whereas growers bore the brunt of the drop in world prices. Declining prices in the absence of alternative sources of income forced cotton growers to increase production throughout the 1930s simply to maintain previous levels of cash income, which went to pay for taxes, school fees and those imported items which had become necessities.

Despite doubled cotton production, the total amount received by growers for seed cotton was slightly lower in 1938 (Shs. 46 million) than 1929 (Shs. 48 million), and the annual average for 1929-38 was only Shs. 38 million.[50] Wrigley attempts to demonstrate that falling export prices for cotton may have been more than offset by the fall in import prices for cloth, kerosene, hoes, etc., so that the barter value of a given quantity of cotton was higher after 1935 than it had been in 1929.[51] Wrigley acknowledges that the use of external trade statistics ignores transport charges, import duties and traders' margins. He notes that these were not reduced proportionately to the reduced price of landed imports. Indeed, while the external terms of trade may not have declined the internal terms of trade faced by the grower declined precipitously. Between 1928 and 1938 the price growers received for seed cotton declined by 61 per cent from Shs. 21.36 to Shs. 8.24 per 100 pounds. In the same period the Kampala retail price for Americani (grey unbleached cloth) declined by only 29 per cent, kerosene -33 per cent, soap -17 per cent, and hoes actually increased in price by 40 per cent. The grower gained only on sugar, whose retail price fell by 72 per cent. African wages fell as sharply as grower prices: -70 per cent in agriculture, -61 per cent in the Public Works Department. Moreover, a similar story emerges if we compare internal prices for 1928 and 1944 (Table 3.2). It may be argued that by growing more cotton, the total purchasing power of growers improved (rising income terms of trade) despite the declining ratio between grower prices for cotton and retail prices for imports (declining barter terms of trade). There is some evidence for this. Between 1928 and 1938 imports of cotton piece-goods rose by 30.1 per cent, from 23.9 million to 31.1 million yards.

Most of the increase was in printed cloth rather than the cheaper unbleached grey cloth (Americani).[52]

Table 3.2: Retail Prices in Kampala, 1928, 1938 and 1944

Item and quantity	1928	1938	1944	% change 1928-38	% change 1928-44
		Price in Shs.			
Americani grey cloth (yd)	0.70	0.50	2.00	−28.6	+185.7
Kerosene lamp oil (4 gal.)	10.50	7.00	7.65	−33.3	−27.1
Hoes (each)	1.25	1.75	3.03	−40.0	+142.4
Sugar (1b)	0.40	0.11	0.18	−72.5	− 55.0
Soap (1b)	0.60	0.50	0.55	−16.7	− 8.3
Sources of income					
Grower price for seed					
cotton (100 lb)	21.36	8.24	14.00	−61.4	−34.5
Monthly wage (low end of range)					
Agricultural labour	13.50	4.00	6.00	−70.4	−55.6
Public Works Dept	18.00	7.00	7.00	−61.1	−61.1

Sources: Uganda, *Blue Book, 1928, 1938,* and *1944,* sections on prices and wages.

Throughout the 1930s, ginneries enjoyed increasing returns on investment since the increase in cotton output was shared by a fixed number of ginneries. The average output per working ginnery rose from 1,351 bales to 2,967 bales between 1929 and 1938. For the ginneries, the slump was a boom period.[53]

Ehrlich tends to discount the impact of buying pools on the reduced price paid to cotton growers, citing the well-known fact that such pools are inherently unstable. Using a three-year series of prices before and after the introduction of buying pools, he shows that the ratio of Liverpool prices for lint cotton to Uganda prices to growers for seed cotton did not alter significantly in the seasons 1934/35-1936/37 compared to 1924/25-1926/27.[54] A more dramatic shift can be detected if the comparison is made over a longer time period using the Mombasa f.o.b. price rather than the Liverpool c.i.f. price (most Uganda cotton in this period was shipped to Bombay before being trans-shipped to Liverpool, Japan or Bombay's own textile mills). Using the ratio of lint export prices to seed cotton grower prices, we find that the ratio averaged 4.13 in the seven years before the introduction of the Cotton Zone Ordinance (1926/27-1932/33) and 5.10 in the following seven years (1933/34-1939/40). The reduction in the standard deviation of the ratio from 0.43 to 0.26 in the two periods

demonstrates the stabilising effect of the Cotton Zone Ordinance.[55]
The fact that some ginnery owners opposed the formation of buying
pools is natural. The colonial state's intervention reduced the need for
competition and thereby removed the cotton ginnery owners from a
'prisoners' dilemma' in which each ginnery's efforts to maximise its
individual share of the market had reduced the total surplus accruing
to ginners.[56] By enforcing class hegemony among the ginnery owners,
the colonial state rescued them from internal competition.

With the establishment of the Cotton Exporters' Group in 1943, the
colonial state openly intervened in cotton marketing to aid the metropolitan state through bulk buying, which guaranteed Britain wartime
supplies of the longer than $1\frac{1}{8}$ inch cotton staple at prices as little as
half the going world price.[57] Simultaneously the colonial state established price assistance funds to skim off the marketing surplus into
reserve funds which were lent to Britain at little or no interest. Continuation of the bulk-buying practice after the war eventually backfired,
because low grower prices discouraged production and thereby reduced
ginnery output and profits. This led to an unusual three-way squabble
among the colonial state, ginneries and growers which culminated in
the 1948-9 cotton hold-up and the birth of the nationalist political
parties.

Arguing the need for price stabilisation in the face of shipping
problems caused by the war, the colonial state assumed control of
cotton and coffee export marketing, though it paid established marketing firms a 2½ per cent commission for arranging exports. Bulk sales at
below world market prices to the British Ministry of Supply determined the price used in the formulas which set ginnery margins and
grower prices. That which was not sold to the Ministry of Supply was
sold on the world market, and the difference between the bulk price
and world price went into the cotton and hard coffee price funds.[58] In
effect, the surplus became a loan to the metropolitan state. By 1948
these 'price assistance' funds totalled £10 million. In the post-Second
World War commodity boom, which peaked during the Korean War, the
colonial state's cotton and coffee funds appropriated a further £44.5
million from African growers (1948-53), in addition to poll taxes,
export taxes and import duties. The East African Royal Commission
criticised the price assistance funds as a 'forced saving technique'.[59]
But it was a loan extracted from growers by the colonial state to the
metropolitan state, which made repayment to the colonial state rather
than growers.

The period 1943-52 was one in which cotton growers in Uganda received less for their seed cotton in proportion to the export price than any other period in Uganda's history. The average ratio of the export price of lint cotton to the grower price for seed cotton was 8.85 in this ten-year period. Only in 1949 did the price to growers first surpass the price paid 25 years earlier, in 1925. The low prices the cotton growers received in relation to high world prices and grower demands for entry into crop processing and marketing were specifically excluded from the terms of reference of the 1948 cotton commis-. sion.[60] The colonial state attempted to divert attention from these issues, especially the first, by focusing on the malpractices of the ginneries: the poor quality of ginning standards and the methods used to cheat growers.

Mettrick has calculated that over the entire period 1945-60 payments to growers for seed cotton and for coffee totalled £231,872,000 after £118,950,000 had been appropriated by the colonial state as export taxes, contributions to development funds, and contributions to price assistance funds. Hence, even before taking into account poll taxes, excise taxes and import duties, 'cotton growers had 38 per cent and coffee growers 25 per cent of their revenue deducted before receipt'.[61]

The 'forced loan' to Britain in the price assistance funds was eventually reinvested in Uganda, as capital goods from the United Kingdom, which built the physical and social infrastructure deemed necessary to attract foreign investment. The rationale for this infrastructure expenditure and other concessions to attract foreign investment was the unequal bargaining situation between East Africa and the industrialised nations. In the oft-repeated phrase of the 1955 commission, ' . . . East Africa needs the skill and capital of the non-African more than the non-African needs East Africa'.[62] Hence the surplus extracted from Africans had to be lavished on non-African interests rather than on Africans. Expenditure on infrastructure to attract foreign investment was deemed productive expenditure; expenditure on African social services, an unproductive luxury.[63]

Wrigley argues that the heavy levies on cotton and coffee growers could be justified as a tax on monopoly rent. Growers, particularly coffee growers, possess land which is globally scarce. Hence revenues from coffee 'bear no relation to the incomes which their recipients could have earned by applying their land and labour any other way'.[64] Wrigley makes the point that land suitable for coffee constitutes a national asset which should be taxed. But the tax was levied by the colonial state as a loan to the metropole, which was repatriated to

Uganda primarily as the infrastructure to attract foreign investors and only secondarily to finance social services for growers. Furthermore, the argument that the growers could not have earned comparable income in other ways neglects the intimate link between the minimum wage for unskilled labour and the grower price for cash crops. Had the price to growers been higher, had the growers been allowed to keep more of their so-called 'monopoly rent', the price of wage-labour would also have risen. The colonial state recognised the intimate interdependence of grower prices, wage levels, labour supply, food costs and construction costs:

> In Uganda, the prices paid to producers of cotton and, to a lesser extent, for coffee, are the yardstick which governs the whole internal price structure of the Protectorate and these prices have repercussions not only on food prices but on such related factors as wage rates and building costs.[65]

By depressing grower prices, the colonial state depressed African wage-rates and income from alternate sources.

In the debate over the colonial state's intervention to ensure the quality of export crops, Bauer views mandatory grading schemes and other measures as costly and unnecessary; the market, according to Bauer, provides its own quality control. Ehrlich views the quality control issue as an irrational obsession; Brett sees it as a smokescreen for other motives. Both agree that the quality control measures served to reduce grower incomes and delay African entry into marketing and processing. Mamdani and Gartrell, on the other hand, perceive the quality control as a necessary feature of colonial marketing. For Mamdani it is a service by the colonial state to the metropolitan bourgeoisie, to provide, say, cotton of the needed technical quality. For Gartrell, quality control was essential to keep and expand Uganda's share of the world market for medium-long cotton fibres.[66]

Mamdani and Gartrell are correct that quality control is needed to obtain the highest prices in the long run for staples. The corrective provided by market forces is slower and more costly to producers in the long run than some form of internal quality control, whether provided by the producers or the state. Even so, the means used by the colonial state to ensure the needed quality revealed an ideological bias which, as Brett notes, led to the use of quality arguments as a rationale to protect the monopsony of non-African interests.

When complaints arose about the quality of Uganda's cotton in

1908, the state banned hand-gins and ordered growers to burn plants at
the end of the season. Compulsion was the instrument chosen to ensure
that growers produced high quality cotton. The Cotton Zone Ordinance
of 1933 was ostensibly introduced to protect quality, yet there is no
evidence of complaints by buyers about cotton quality in that period,
though declining world demand and prices may have accentuated the
need for quality.

By contrast, when overseas buyers complained about the quality of
cotton in the 1940s due to poor ginning and storage practices by
ginneries,[67] the colonial state relied on exposure, persuasion and incentives rather than compulsion to improve the 'shocking' standards and
practices of the ginneries. The 1948 cotton commission found that
ginneries undermined the quality of both seed stocks and exported lint
by mixing seed cotton of various types. Although the policy of bulk
sales was admitted to be a factor in lowering quality, the commission
lamely argued that controlled export marketing was essential for
stability. While agreeing that the ginning industry required rationalisation to improve quality, the commission urged that the ginning price
formula be sufficiently generous to allow the majority of the dilapi-
dated and inefficient ginneries to break even and proposed that buying
pools (which protected the weak ginneries) be made statutory for a five-
year period. The commission urged adoption of saw-ginning (with
British equipment, naturally) to save labour costs and to increase the
optimal size of ginneries, despite reports that overseas buyers considered saw-ginned cotton to be of lower quality than roller-ginned
cotton.[68]

The colonial state's concern for export quality was thus highly
selective, as were its methods to improve quality. Whereas persuasion
and incentives were used to improve the output of non-African processing and marketing firms, compulsion was the primary method to
improve the output of African growers.

Recasting the Division of Labour

At the level of economic structure, Lugard's dual mandate thesis set
forth the responsibility of the metropole for its colonies in terms of
trusteeship 'on the one hand, for the advancement of subject races, and
on the other hand, for the development of its material resources for the
benefit of mankind'.[69] The development of local natural resources for
the benefit of mankind entailed externally-oriented rather than auto-

nomous development. 'Advancement of subject races' initially entailed
no more than the imposition of law and order and the organisation of
the local labour-force required for the extraction and export of local
resources.

While not totally barred, local industry was to be fostered under
foreign ownership, and to be concentrated in processing raw materials
for export rather than for local needs, or in production of consumer
goods which were in declining branches of industry in the metropole.
Lugard presents a very sophisticated argument for official encouragement and toleration of certain forms of industry in colonial territories.
However, throughout the argument, he makes it abundantly clear that
local industry must be subordinate to the production of primary
products for export and the general benefit of British trade.[70]

As early as 1893 Lugard noted with some displeasure the fact that a
Muganda blacksmith, trained by the CMS missionary Mackay, could
produce the equivalent of an entire year's imports of guns from
Britain: 'He could repair a lock, make temper a spring, and detect a
cause of error with marvelous skill; but it was regretable that the only
trained workman should be a gunsmith, whose talent was equivalent to
an annual import of arms.'[71] Similarly, an attempt by Kabaka Mwanga
in the 1890s to purchase a sawmill was blocked by the colonial state,
allegedly because the machinery was not in good order and that there
was a shortage of skilled labour.[72] The colonial state reserved skilled
labour for itself in this period.

African attempts to enter the processing side of the cotton industry
were hampered by the colonial state's intervention on behalf of established European and Indian cotton ginnery owners. The destruction of
hand-gins in 1908-9 removed Africans from control of processing.[73]
Yet the quality of the Uganda cotton crop and the price it could
command in the world market was threatened not by the fact that it
was hand-ginned but by the fact that growers used the seed by-product
of hand-ginning for new planting thereby threatening the uniformity of
the crop. It would have been sufficient to require growers to use only
government-issued seeds. Two decades later, in 1926, a Muganda landowner, Sepiriya Kadumukasa, applied for permission to erect a cotton
ginnery on his own land, but his application was refused by the Cotton
Control Board on the grounds of overcapacity in the ginning
industry.[74]

In 1930, aspiring African capitalists formed the Baganda Cotton
Company which made two attempts to enter the industry. The first was
an agreement under which the Uganda Company would gin cotton

purchased by the Baganda Cotton Company for a fixed fee, with the long-term goal of eventually buying out one ginnery. The Uganda Company advanced the BCC money for the purchase of the crop, but the BCC, despite its buying efforts at 47 marketing centres and ginneries, was able to purchase less than 2,000 bales, and subsequently wound up in the High Court owing the Uganda Company £5,000 for money advanced. Its effort in the 1931 season was even more disastrous. It leased a ginnery from the Imperial Cotton Company. Short of working capital, the BCC proceeded to buy seed cotton from growers in return for chits, which it was subsequently unable to redeem for cash.[75]

By the late 1930s the colonial state appeared to be on the verge of allowing the formation of growers' co-operatives which might take over existing cotton ginneries, as long as this represented African co-optation into the existing monopsonistic marketing structure. This time, the Uganda Company opposed the colonial state's recognition of co-operative societies precisely because, under the proposed regulations, there would be 'no way out of granting ginneries to cooperative societies'.[76] The whole issue was shelved by the onset of the Second World War, and African co-operative societies were brought into the ginning industry only after the rebellion and cotton hold-up of 1949.

Throughout the colonial occupation, colonial policy regarding the control of productive forces and the domestic division of labour was subordinate to the requirements of expanding export commodity production under metropolitan hegemony. In the domestic division of labour, colonial policy was quite explicit in the 1920s and 1930s: Africans were to be directed into one of two activities: production of cash crops for export or the sale of labour-power to employers. This was clearly spelled out in a telegram from the Chief Secretary at Entebbe to a Provincial Commissioner:

I understand from Postlethwaite differences of opinion exists [sic] between him and D.C. Mbarara as to policy with reference to labour and cotton. I am directed by the Governor to state that the line to be adopted is not one of definite pressure towards cotton production. Natives to be informed that three courses are open, cotton, labour for Government, labour for planters, but no attempt is to be made to induce them to choose any one in preference to the others. Only one thing to be made clear is they cannot be permitted to do nothing, and be of no use to themselves or the country . . . [77]

In other words, Africans had to reallocate labour time from production for for their own use to production to service the external economy. A hybrid alternative emerged to become increasingly important: the sale of labour-power to capitalist African farmers producing cash crops for sale in the world market.

African entry into trade upset the colonial ideal of the proper cultural division of labour in Uganda just as the entry of Africans into cash-crop production upset the settler ideal in Kenya. The acquisitive spirit was to be instilled in Africans to encourage increased export production and increased labour.[78] Paradoxically, African entry into marketing and money-lending was viewed as an improper manifestation of this acquisitive spirit. However, Africans in Uganda were not faced with legal restrictions on borrowing as were Africans in Kenya and Tanganyika, although debts of £10 or more incurred by an African to a non-African had to be recorded in written form.[79]

Ironically, the victory of the nascent African bourgeoisie in preventing wholesale alienation of land to non-Africans also prevented African traders and farmers from using land as collateral for bank loans. Outside Buganda there was little freehold land which could be used as collateral.[80] Within Buganda *mailo* land could not be mortgaged to non-Africans because land transfers from Africans to non-Africans faced the insurmountable barrier of having to be approved by both the *Lukiko* and the Governor. After passage of the Busulu and Envujo Law of 1927, *mailo* land encumbered with tenants lost its attraction as collateral between African borrowers and lenders. The Ghanaian practice of circumventing restrictions on land alienation by pawning one's house failed to develop in Uganda, where, aside from the official homes for chiefs, there were few African houses worth pawning. There were, however, some instances of Ugandans mortgaging crops to obtain money from money-lenders. Although the inability to mortgage land undoubtedly retarded the emergence of African traders, colonial administrators viewed the restriction as essential to keep peasant growers out of peonage to money-lenders.

The colonial state's establishment of the Uganda Treasury Savings Bank for Africans in 1907 provides further evidence of the colonial view of the proper role for Africans.

> [The bank] ... would ... enable the native population to 'store' their money which at present they are quite unable to do with any safety. In giving them this power it would in due course lead to thrift amongst them by instigating a healthy competition to possess

as much money as their friends and neighbours and from this would naturally follow an incentive to greater exertions to obtain money by planting saleable produce and hiring themselves to employers of labour.[81]

However, the African customers failed to come forward in the anticipated numbers to deposit savings in the bank at 2½ per cent interest. Moreover, the savings bank did not lend out its deposits to Africans or even non-Africans in Uganda, but rather invested them in Transvaal 3 per cent Guaranteed Stock.[82] The Treasurer of the Uganda Protectorate tried to explain the lack of depositors as due to African naïveté:

> The idea of the Bank is new to the natives and they have not yet grasped the object of its formation. They look upon any money they may deposit as a loan to the Government and state that they can get a larger interest for their money by trading or investing it in cattle.[83]

It would appear that Africans grasped only too well the object of the savings bank's formation. The minority who had any savings after paying taxes and purchasing necessities shunned the bank in order to use their savings to enter trade or to lend to fellow African traders via the formation of small commercial syndicates.[84] By early 1911 the number of customers in the savings bank's branches at Entebbe, Kampala and Jinja stood at 322 with total deposits of £3,500. The majority of depositors appear to have been African police and Indian artisans.[85]

At times the colonial state's intervention to protect the vertical ethnic division of labour was more direct. When the president of the Young Busoga Association protested against the formation of a cotton-buying pool in his district in 1929, the colonial state ordered him to resign from the YBA or from his position as *gombolola* chief.[86] The principle was certainly not the need for an impartial colonial bureaucracy; European members of the colonial salariat were free to make political comments. The cotton-buying rules which prohibited middlemen from operating within a five-mile radius of established ginneries in 1918 were followed by the native Produce Marketing Ordinance of 1932 which established stiff entry requirements for wholesale traders in a wide range of agricultural products: groundnuts, leaf tobacco, sesame, coffee and beeswax. Traders were required to have permanent buildings. Those who failed to meet these requirements, i.e., African petty traders, were banned from buying or selling agricultural produce within a given radius of several miles of 'established trading centres'. Once again the argument for the trade restriction was the need to protect quality in order to promote diversification of exports. The measure appears to have been designed to protect established European and Asian firms from competition by Asian middlemen. It was strongly opposed by Asian merchants in general. According to Yoshida and Belshaw, the net effect was to bar Africans (' the latecomers') from entry into wholesale trade.[87]

Africans finally entered processing in the late 1940s and early 1950s through grower co-operative societies. The original intent of the Labour government in the metropole had been to nationalise all ginneries.[88] Nationalisation was anathema to ginnery owners and other expatriate firms. In defiance of previous experience, the Uganda Chamber of Commerce argued that African participation in processing was best fostered by private industry and that nationalisation would reduce African participation to the status of employee rather than owner. According to H.R. Fraser of A. Baumann & Co. (which handled 40 per cent of the robusta coffee crop[89]), the process of African entry into processing would take a long time:

> How and when can the African be fitted to play his part in the free participation of industry? Only after he had obtained the basic education, development of character and subsequent training necessary to enjoy the full scope of responsibility and ownership. It may therefore be stated that the development of any industry must have as its three main, and equally important, aims – African participation, efficiency and economy. In order to permit of the African enjoying participation to the fullest possible extent, he must be taken into industry gradually, coached and trained to undertake responsibilities which, at the moment, are far beyond his capabilities. All these can be achieved under commercial enterprise, but can they under Nationalisation? . . . African participation is both necessary and possible under commercial enterprise more so than under Nationalisation where, in fact, African participation cannot exist in any other form than that of employed persons.[90]

When sufficiently pressed by the threat of nationalisation, the expatriate firms ceased opposing and instead embraced the gradual entry of growers' co-operative societies into the ginning industry.[91] Their change of heart was made all the less painful by the fact that the state used Shs. 25.5 million of the surplus extracted from growers to buy out owners of the 35 'silent' ginneries with pool shares.[92] By the 1960-1 season, co-operative societies handled 31 per cent of the cotton crop, buying 60,800 metric tons of seed cotton, of which three-fifths could be ginned in the 15 ginneries owned by the societies.[93]

Turning from the internal division of labour to the economic structure, one finds that, apart from crop-processing, manufacturing was slow to develop, notwithstanding the fears expressed by Bell in 1909 that the Indian capitalists would quickly set up textile mills in Uganda to compete with Lancashire.[94] The Bombay textile magnates were then preoccupied with the home industry.

Industry in Uganda received its first impetus from crop-processing. The bulkiness of cotton necessitated establishment of ginneries throughout the cotton-growing areas. Similar considerations about weight, value and transportation costs encouraged the establishment of the first import-substitution industries by 1919: brick and tile kilns, soda water, distilleries and machinery repair.

Second, Uganda's landlocked position 1,300 kilometres from the ocean proved to be both a help and a hindrance in the development of manufacturing. In the short run it made imports of machinery and spare parts difficult. In the medium run, it provided some additional natural protection for local manufacturing firms. In the long run, it may prove to be a liability in the emergence of export-oriented manufacturing.

The third impetus came from the common East African agricultural tariffs erected by Kenyan European settlers in 1923, in which the inclusion of sugar as a protected commodity led to the rise of the Indian sugar barons. The tobacco and soap industries also benefited from the protective tariff.

The fourth impetus for industrialisation came during the Second World War, when shipping problems and the shift in European industry from consumer goods to war material provided natural protection for infant industries producing goods for domestic consumption.

The fifth impetus came from changes in the international division of labour. Between 1890 and 1950 textiles had constituted the major class of imports into Uganda, accounting for one-fifth to over one-third of all imports in any given year. From the Industrial Revolution to 1920, textiles had been a leading core-state industry, but between 1920 and 1950 they became a leading industry of the semi-periphery, and an industry of the periphery after 1950.[95] To the extent that Lancashire resisted the inevitable as textiles became a standard industry in the product cycle between 1920 and 1950, it found itself competing – not with Europe and the United States — but with Japan and India. Japan's success in East Africa was impeded by distance and the absence of a Japanese immigrant community. Japanese capital did gain entry into the Uganda cotton-ginning industry between the wars.[96] By the end of the Second World War cotton textiles were no longer a major export of Britain. Cotton yarns and fabrics had accounted for about one-fourth of British exports between 1912 and 1925. Between 1930 and 1945 manufactured cotton goods seldom accounted for more than 15 per cent or less than 11 per cent of all British exports. But by 1946 cotton textiles had fallen to 7 per cent of all exports, and below 4 per cent by 1955. What had replaced cotton? Machinery, electrical goods, motor vehicles and chemicals. Machinery and electrical goods accounted for roughly 9 per cent of British exports between 1922 and 1930, over 20 per cent in 1947 and later. Exports of motor vehicles (and aircraft) surpassed cotton textiles in 1946, as did chemicals.[97]

In 1909 textile mills in Uganda, had they existed, would have posed a threat to a vital British export industry. In 1945 textile mills in Uganda offered an opportunity for British exports of machinery and dyes.

Gartrell remarks that the metropolitan state shifted from a somewhat negative to a permissive stance regarding import-substitution industries in the colonies.[98] It mattered little to Britain where such industries were located: for example, Uganda as opposed to Kenya. Strangely enough, the sixth impetus for the growth of manufacturing in Uganda was the economic nationalism of the colonial state and of the Asians. Governor John Hall launched new infrastructure projects to compete with Kenya in attracting foreign investment.[99] When the foreign investment failed to materialise, the colonial state stepped in to use the Uganda Development Corporation as the vehicle of industrialisation. Asians already in manufacturing took advantage of the new infrastructure investments, notably the hydroelectric scheme at Jinja, whereas many Asian merchants foresaw the coming Africanisation of trade and moved upstream in the domestic division of labour, into manufacturing.[100]

Hence, at the end of the colonial period Africans prepared to move up in the domestic division of labour, and Uganda moved up a small notch in the international division of labour. But the spirit of Lugard's 'dual mandate' survived, as could be seen in Colin Legum's *Must We Lose Africa?*:

Any restatement of colonial policy made to reflect Britain's new relationship with its dependent territories must focus attention chiefly on the importance of providing for the maintenance and extension of British *influence* at the same time as political *control* is relinquished.

What is meant by British influence? It is the continuation of Britain's mission of helping advance African society towards those social, economic and political standards which, generally speaking, characterize Western society. It would not be true to say that in maintaining its influence, Britain is 'entirely disinterested': it is enormously interested for three clearly-defined reasons: it believes in Western values; it is naturally anxious to ensure that the task of Westernizing African society, which it has already done so much to achieve, should be successfully accomplished; it is interested to see created in Africa a stable political system that will serve the good of Africans and non-Africans and promote Western security; it is interested in the opportunities for expanding mutually-beneficial trade relations; and it has interests (both 'selfish' and 'unselfish') vested in the idea of the Commonwealth of Nations.

If the present signs are correctly judged, African leaders are willing to accept British influence thus defined. And so long as this willingness exists, so long will Britain be a profoundly effective directing force in Africa.[101]

Guns and Butter: Expenditures of the Colonial State

One must view sceptically the claims that the shift in state expenditures from preponderant emphasis on coercion to social services in the 1920s was motivated by a sense of altruism. Pratt, for example, argues that sincerely held altruism motivated this shift in state expenditure:

> The trusteeship concern for the security, the development, and the welfare of Africans was no mere rationalization of an economic necessity. It was a strongly held conviction that was itself an important determinant of policy in Uganda.[102]

What is not at issue is the genuineness of the colonial officials' concern for Africans. Nor is there any question that there was a shift from guns to butter in colonial state expenditure after 1920 (see Figures 3.1 and 3.3). What is at issue is whether altruism can explain the shift.

The colonial archives are replete with expressions of officials'

Figure 3.1: Guns (Coercion) and Butter (Services), Uganda, 1901-80

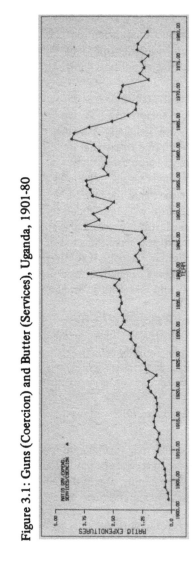

Figure 3.2: Ratio of Export Price to Grower Price, Uganda, 1911-78

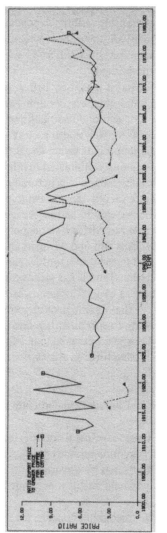

Figure 3.3: Uganda State Budget for Coercion, Agriculture, Education and Health, 1901-80

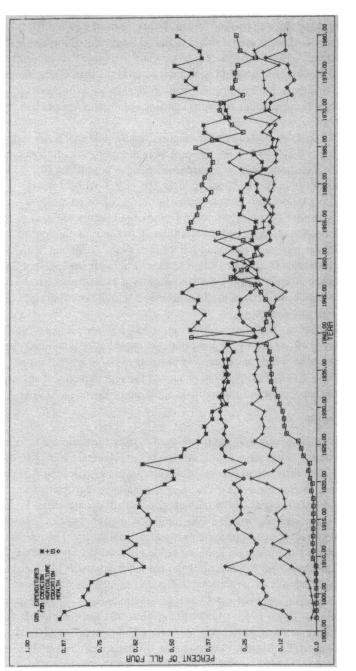

concern for the welfare of Africans. Expressions of concern for the welfare of Africans even abound in the statements of European settlers in Kenya.[103] None the less, it is empirically verifiable that in terms of social services, Africans in Uganda were better off than their counterparts in Kenya, even though Africans in Uganda paid for these social services through higher taxes, which they could afford as peasant producers.

Of a total estimated African population of 3,802,900 in Uganda in 1938, some 309,387 or 8.1 per cent were attending school. By comparison in Kenya, out of a total estimated African population of 3,253,700 (probably an underestimate), only 82,105 or 2.5 per cent were attending school. But even if proportionately 3.2 times as many Africans were attending school in Uganda as in Kenya, the fact remained that even in Uganda less than 30 per cent of children of school age were able to attend school each year.[104] Coming from Tanganyika to Uganda in 1935, Governor Philip Mitchell viewed the incidence of taxation on Ugandan peasants as excessively high, but found that both African local governments and the colonial state firmly opposed any reduction.[105]

Services for Africans — education, roads, water supplies and so forth — may not have been very good but they were better than in Kenya and Tanganyika.[106] But were they better because of the greater altruism of Uganda's colonial officials or because of the requirements of the colonial economy and the political agitation of Uganda's Africans?

Education

Initially, it appears that the interests of non-African employers were paramount in education. As Pratt points out, Makerere was established in 1922 in response to pressure from employers who needed African artisans.[107] Subsequent expansion of the Makerere curriculum was guided 'by the needs of the relevant government departments'.[108] The 1925-35 period was marked by a running conflict between Christian missions and the colonial state over educational policy. The missions pursued a curriculum emphasising academic subjects. The colonial state tried to reduce aid to academic-oriented mission schools in order to promote schools which stressed 'technical, manual, or agricultural education' to 'meet the career needs of their students'.[109] Then as now, the phrase 'career needs of students' is both that and a euphemism for the labour needs of employers. Africans allied themselves with the missions in the dispute. In response to the suggestion that there should be a special kind of education for Africans consisting mainly of technical education, Serwano Kulubya, Omuwanika (Finance Minister) of Buganda, declared: 'That I do not agree with because we require leaders for our people; I say that the principal system of education as it is known in this country [i.e. Britain] should be extended to us.'[110]

For the colonial state, too little technical education contributed to a shortage of artisans, whereas 'too much' academic education contributed to a politically dangerous situation.[111] Not altruism, but economic and political concerns guided the colonial state's education policy. In the end, though, the colonial state yielded to political pressure from missions and African leaders for continued aid to academic-oriented schools.

The question of academic versus technical education raises broader issues with regard to the maintenance of structural dependence. Lugard argued that the colonial system of education in India, by stressing academic subjects rather than technical ones, not only created a surplus of white-collar workers but also quite probably retarded industrial development.[112] Lugard has a valid point. Structural transformation of a dependent economy into an economy geared more to local resources and human needs requires engineers, technicians and agronomists as much as (if not more than) bureaucrats and clerks. But it is equally obvious that under state capitalism the state administrative salariat is a privileged stratum compared to technicians, workers and peasants. It is in the interest of the local bourgeoisie, in terms of individual advance-ment, to press for academic rather than technical education in the colonial period. The key question is the following: who controls the state apparatus? In India technical education would advance the indus-trial development of India primarily for the benefit of British rather than Indian capital. In a socialist state technical education *should* ideally advance the interests of workers and peasants. Whether it in fact does so depends on who controls the state apparatus and for whom.

In Uganda, emphasis on academic education undermined colonial rule but also tended to preserve structural dependence by creating an educated African bourgeoisie which benefited from the maintenance of structural dependence and which despised manual labour and looked down on wage-labourers. In passing, it should be noted that access to education rather than ownership of land became the passport to administrative cadres in Uganda from the 1930s onward, although it was agricultural surpluses which were the key to obtaining school fees for one's children.

Health

In health, the major concern of the medical department prior to 1920 was the health of the European salariat of the colonial state, with some additional funds being appropriated for controlling the worst ravages of famines, sleeping sickness and other diseases among Africans. When it became clear in the 1920s and 1930s that the influx of migrant labourers seriously threatened existing health standards in Buganda, economic considerations reinforced altruistic concern for the welfare of Africans. In the words of Powesland, 'migration from Belgian territory was now accepted as a net advantage to Uganda, even if it entailed extra costs in defence of public health'.[113] Both African and non-African employers demanded cheap migrant labour and shoved the cost of keeping them in minimal health and in preventing epidemics onto the state. The state did establish dispensaries, hospitals and rest camps along the labour migration routes. For the most part, the altruism of the colonial state apparatus yielded little more than expressions of concern about poor working conditions existing in cotton ginneries, the unhealthy housing conditions among migrant workers, the appalling conditions on sugar plantations, and the reliance of ginneries on child labour working 12-hour shifts.[114]

Agriculture

The planter-dominated 1920 Development Commission noted with satisfaction that the research efforts of the Department of Agriculture were devoted almost entirely to plantation crops rather than the cotton and food crops grown by Africans.[115] But, in 1920, the Agriculture Department began directing more resources towards African cash crops. In that year the cotton research stations opened at Serere and Bukalasa.[116] The Bugisu Coffee Scheme was geared to African growers. Yet in 1931, a Busoga *saza* chief could still complain about the absence of research on food crops. When asked if the Department of Agriculture did 'good work', Yekoniya Zirabamuzale replied, 'Yes, they are doing that, but I do not think it would be of great use to the natives because the natives live on bananas.'[117] By the late 1930s there was more research on food crops, but most research continued to concentrate on export crops.[118]

African education in agronomy lagged badly. There was only one African enrolled in agriculture at Makerere in 1946,[119] plus an undetermined number at the agricultural school at Bukalasa.

Vail has described the agricultural extension services for African growers as a two-tier system throughout the colonial period in which services were reserved for the elite and compulsion for the masses.[120] The elite group of farmers, consisting of collaborative chiefs in the early colonial period and 'progressive farmers' in the post-Second World War period, received adequate extension help from European agricultural officers and African assistants. Some of this technical knowledge (assuming it was correct, which it often was not in the early years) was supposed to 'trickle down' to ordinary growers. But realising the trickle-down effects to be slow and inadequate, the colonial state employed coercive rules and laws to ensure proper cultivation by ordinary African growers. There were rules about when to plant cotton, how much to plant, when to uproot and burn plants, how much cassava had to be planted as a reserve crop, and so forth. Disobedience of the rules constituted disobedience of the 'traditional authority' of the chiefs.

Conclusion

In a confidential briefing to European colonial officials, Governor Mitchell described the real world of East Africa in 1939:

> If, resolutely shutting our minds to the effects of habit or the perhaps still lingering romance of the primitive and picturesque, we look at modern East Africa as it really is, the picture is disturbing.
>
> Poverty is widespread and the people suffer from a great number of diseases, and generally from malnutrition as well. A great part of the soil is poor and becoming poorer through bad methods of cultivation. Water supplies are inadequate and nearly always impure. Housing for the majority is bad, and it even seems to some of us as if to-day less trouble is taken in plastering and finishing off the hut than was the case twenty-five years ago.
>
> Employment for wages often means worse housing and food, while the wages themselves are low, and the level of effort and efficiency poor. There are enlightened employers who house, feed and pay their workmen well but they are to-day exceptional, and it is the merest humbug to pretend otherwise.
>
> Education is still rudimentary and inefficient except for the favoured few, and although this is at least improving rapidly, there is a terribly long way to go and in the meantime less than 5 per cent of the population attain the standard which is compulsory for every child in the United Kingdom.[121]

The reality of the condition of Africans in Uganda was harsh in 1939, and deteriorated further during the war. Only after the war and after the rebellions of 1945 and 1949 did conditions begin to improve.

Notes

1. Hamza Alavi, 'The State in Post-Colonial Societies: Pakistan and Bangladesh', Bangladesh', *New Left Review*, no. 74 (July-August 1972), pp. 60-2; and Perry Anderson, *Lineages of the Absolutist State* (London: New Left Books, 1974), pp. 397-431.
2. Mahmood Mamdani, review of *Colonialism and Underdevelopment in East Africa*, by E.A. Brett, *The African Review* (Dar es Salaam), vol. 3, no. 4 (1973), pp. 635-44.
3. See the critique of the Alavi-Saul concept of the overdeveloped colonial state in W. Ziemann and M. Lanzendörfer, 'The State in Peripheral Societies', *The Socialist Register, 1977*, ed. Ralph Miliband and John Saville (London: Merlin Press, 1977), pp. 143-77.
4. David Cohen, 'Misango's Song: Adventure and Structure in the Precolonial African Past', paper presented to Centre of African Studies Workshop, Dalhousie University, Halifax, Nova Scotia, 29 February 1980, pp. 10-11, 20-7.
5. Holger Bernt Hansen, *Ethnicity and Military Rule in Uganda*, Research Report no. 43 (Uppsala: Scandinavian Institute of African Studies, 1977), p. 36.
6. Beverley Gartrell, 'The Ruling Ideas of a Ruling Elite: British Colonial Officials in Uganda, 1944-52', PhD thesis, City University of New York, 1979, pp. 397-8 and 489-90.
7. Anthony G. Hopkins, 'Imperial Business in Africa; Part II. Interpretations', *Journal of African History*, vol. 17, no. 2 (1976), pp. 276, 279.
8. Immanuel Wallerstein, 'Social Conflict in Post-Independence Black Africa: The Concepts of Race and Status Group Reconsidered', *The Capitalist World Economy* (Cambridge: Cambridge University Press, 1979), pp. 179-80.
9. A.S. Njala and S.A. Obura, 'Evolution of the East African Currencies', Bank of Uganda, *Quarterly Bulletin*, vol. 3, no. 2 (March 1971), pp. 51-4.
10. A.J. Turnbull, Assistant Manager, National Bank of India Ltd, Mombasa, to Lt. Col. J. Hayes Sadler, Commissioner, Uganda Protectorate, 19 September 1903, File 197/06, item 1, Secretariat Minute Papers (SMP), National Archives, Entebbe; and George W. Wilson, Acting Commissioner, Uganda Protectorate, to A.J. Turnbull, NBI, Mombasa, 5 March 1906, File 197/06, item 2, SMP, National Archives, Entebbe.
11. File 197/06, items 2, 10, 14, 17, 19; File 2024-I, items 19, 21, 33, 55, 113, 210, and 234, SMP, National Archives, Entebbe.
12. 'Commercial Banking in Uganda Prior to the Establishment of the Bank of Uganda', Bank of Uganda, *Banking in Uganda*, 6 March 1970, p. 10. The agreement itself may be found in File 2024-I, item 55, SMP, National Archives, Entebbe. Even after the termination of the agreement, National and Grindlays Bank (NBI's successor) continued to cultivate a special relationship with the Uganda government.
13. File 2024-I, item 210, SMP; R.T. Coryndon to Chief Secretary, Uganda Protectorate, 22 July 1920, File 2534, SMP; and File 2024-I, item 234, SMP.
14. Hopkins, 'Imperial Business', pp. 275-6.
15. Samir Amin, 'Underdevelopment and Dependence in Black Africa: Historical Origin', *Journal of Peace Research*, vol. 9, no. 2 (1972), pp. 105-19.

16. West Africa: Bank of British West Africa, Banque de l'Afrique, Royal Niger Co., African and Eastern Trading Co., Société Commerciale de l'Ouest Africain, Compagnie Française d'Afrique Occidentale, G.L. Gaiser, John Holt, Elder Dempster, Woermann, and Ashanti Goldfields. Southern Africa: Standard Bank, Dominion and Colonial, Union Steamship, Castle Mail, Anglo-American, British South Africa Co., and De Beers.

17. National Bank of India, Standard Bank, Smith-Mackenzie, A. Baumann, Leslie & Anderson, British and India Steam Navigation and Union Castle.

18. *Annual Trade Report of Kenya and Uganda, 1924*, p. 37.

19. Hopkins, 'Imperial Business', p. 276.

20. On the economic nationalism of the white settlers, see E.A. Brett, *Colonialism and Underdevelopment in East Africa; The Politics of Economic Change, 1919-39* (London: Heinemann, 1973), pp. 77-8, 205; and Arghiri Emmanuel, 'White-Settler Colonialism and the Myth of Investment Imperialism', *New Left Review*, no. 73 (May-June 1972), pp. 35-57.

21. Great Britain, *Parliamentary Papers* (Commons) *1923* (XVIII 141), 23 July 1923, Cmd. 1922, 'Indians in Kenya', p. 10. In 1931, the paramountcy of African interests was restated as meaning 'no more than that the interests of the indigenous population should not be subordinated to those of a minority belonging to another race, however important itself'. Great Britain, *Parliamentary Papers* (Lords) *1931* (VII 1), 'Joint Select Committee on Closer Union in East Africa', I: 31. In essence, by reserving for itself the trusteeship of African interests, the metropolitan state declared its own paramountcy over the immigrant communities.

22. Mahmood Mamdani, 'Review of *Colonialism and Underdevelopment in East Africa* by E.A. Brett', *African Review* (Dar es Salaam), vol. 3, no. 4 (1973), p. 642.

23. Brett, *Colonialism and Underdevelopment*, p. 100.

24. Ibid., p. 99.

25. The 'desire to put a definite end to the uncertainty regarding the future of the [Tanganyika] mandate which, however unwarranted, still appears to exist in some quarters' was one of the motives behind the move for closer union. Great Britain, 'Joint Select Committee on Closer Union in East Africa', I: 7. The representative of the Uganda Chamber of Commerce, Dr H.H. Hunter, stated that 'the only reason' Uganda supported closer union with Kenya and Tanganyika was that 'Uganda was informed that if such a Union came about Tanganyika would become part of the Empire and could never be separated from it'. Great Britain, 'Joint Select Committee on Closer Union in East Africa: Appendices', (VII 1095) III: 30. The desire to put 'a definite end to the uncertainty' on the part of British capital regarding the future of Tanganyika also explains why it was Tanganyika which received the larger part (55.5 per cent) of the £1.5 million allocated to East Africa under the Colonial Development Fund between 1929/30 and 1939/40. Brett, *Colonialism and Underdevelopment*, p. 137.

26. Uganda, *Blue Book, 1922*, and *1930*; and Brett, *Colonialism and Underdevelopment*, p. 101.

27. Uganda, *Annual Report of the Department of Agriculture, 1922*, p. 8; and City Council of Kampala, *Kampala: Official Handbook* (Kampala: University Press of Africa, 1970), p. 134.

28. Uganda, *Annual Report of the Department of Agriculture, 1924, 1926* and *1938*; Cyril Ehrlich, 'The Uganda Economy, 1903-1945', *History of East Africa*, ed. Vincent Harlow, E.M. Chilver and Alison Smith (Oxford: Clarendon Press, 1965), vol. II, p. 434; and *Annual Trade Report of Kenya and Uganda, 1948*.

29. Philip Thompson Aranow, 'Alien Entrepreneurs; The Indians in Uganda,

1958-68', BA Honours Thesis, Harvard College, 1969, p. 36.

30. Paul Van Zwanenberg, 'Kenya's Primitive Colonial Capitalism; The Economic Weakness of Kenya's Settlers up to 1940', *Canadian Journal of African Studies*, vol. 9, no. 2 (1975), pp. 287-91; Brett, *Colonialism and Underdevelopment*, p. 184; and C.C. Wrigley, 'Kenya: The Patterns of Economic Life, 1902-45', *Oxford History of East Africa*, vol. II, p. 249.

31. Brett, *Colonialism and Underdevelopment*, p. 99.

32. Wrigley, 'Kenya: The Patterns of Economic Life', pp. 221-2.

33. Great Britain, 'Joint Select Committee on Closer Union in East Africa', III: 44-60.

34. See the submissions of African leaders in Great Britain, Colonial Office, *Papers Relating to the Question of the Closer Union of Kenya, Uganda, and the Tanganyika Territory*, Colonial No. 57, 1931; Uganda, *Report of the Commission of Inquiry into the Disturbances in Uganda during April 1949* (Entebbe: Government Printer, 1950), pp. 101-2, 113-15; and David Apter, *The Political Kingdom in Uganda*, 2nd edn (Princeton: Princeton University Press, 1967), pp. 276-300.

35. Cf. Uganda, *Report of the Uganda Development Commission. 1920*, p. 11; and Kenya, *Minutes of the Proceedings of the Legislative Council*, 30 May 1924, p. 165, and 17 December 1924, pp. 390 ff.

36. Great Britain, 'Joint Select Committee on Closer Union', III: 31.

37. Uganda Chamber of Commerce, Minutes of Monthly Meetings, 12 October 1943 and 9 November 1943, Makerere University Library, Kampala.

38. R.M.A. van Zwanenberg and Anne King, *An Economic History of Kenya and Uganda, 1800-1970* (Atlantic Highlands, N.J.: Humanities Press, 1975), p. 291; and Uganda, *1973 Statistical Abstract*, p. 76. Financing the marketing cycle of cash crops was the major lending activity of the commercial banks, accounting for about half of all loans and advances in any given year, with the peak activity between January and July. In addition, the banks provided credit facilities to Asian and European trading firms to discount bills of exchange and lent funds to the government. Only after the Second World War did the British banks establish subsidiaries with authority to lend funds for periods longer than a year: Barclays Overseas Development Corporation, National and Grindlays Finance and Development Corporation, and Standard Bank Development Finance Corporation. The type of development fostered by these subsidiaries in Uganda can be illustrated by loans granted up to 1970. On the positive side (in terms of expanding production for local consumption), there were loans to local textile mills and sugar refineries. On the mixed side (loans for export-oriented development), there were loans for tea plantations, ranches, the ill-fated Soroti meat canning plant, and a horticultural export project. On the more dubious side there were loans with little or no direct benefit for the majority of the population in rural areas: the construction of government buildings, petrol stations for major international petroleum companies, tourist lodges, an exclusive club for the elite, jets for the East African Airways, urban public works, and government real estate ventures. Source: interviews with bank representatives, Kampala, 1971.

39. B.M. Niculescu, 'Sterling Balances and the Colonial Currency System: A Comment', *Economic Journal*, vol. 64 (September 1954), pp. 618-19.

40. van Zwanenberg and King, *An Economic History of Kenya and Uganda*, pp. 286-7.

41. W.T. Newlyn, 'The Colonial Empire', *Banking in the British Commonwealth*, ed. R.S. Sayers (Oxford: Clarendon Press, 1952), p. 441.

42. P.T. Bauer, *West African Trade* (London: Routledge & Kegan Paul, 1954); Cyril Ehrlich, 'The Marketing of Cotton in Uganda, 1900-1950', PhD Thesis, University of London, 1958; M. Yoshida and D.G.R. Belshaw, 'The Introduction of the Trade Licensing System for Primary Products in East Africa, 1900-1939',

EAISR Conference Paper, Kampala, January 1965; Brett, *Colonialism and Under-development*, pp. 237-62; Mamdani, 'Review of *Colonialism and Underdevelopment*', pp. 635-44; and Gartrell, 'The Ruling Ideas of a Ruling Elite', pp. 378-433.

43. *West African Trade*, passim.

44. Bauer, *West African Trade*, p. 376 (1964 edn). The concept of 'unequal structure of representation' is borrowed from Rianne Mahon.

45. National Christian Council of Kenya, *Who Controls Industry in Kenya?; Report of a Working Party* (Nairobi: East African Publishing House, 1968), pp. 9-10.

46. Cf. Apter, *The Political Kingdom*, pp. 221-2.

47. Ibid., p. 43.

48. Letter from L.R Ramsingh, 14 December 1909 [1908?], SMP File 115/1908, National Archives, Entebbe, as cited in Ehrlich, 'The Marketing of Cotton in Uganda', pp. 80-1.

49. Ehrlich, 'The Marketing of Cotton in Uganda', pp. 137-229.

50. The total output of lint cotton was 36,760 metric tons in 1929 and 76,970 in 1938. Uganda, *Report of the Uganda Cotton Commission, 1938* (Entebbe: Government Printer, 1939), pp. 118-24.

51. C.C. Wrigley, *Crops and Wealth in Uganda* (Kampala: EAISR, 1959), p. 61. Cf. Ehrlich, 'The Marketing of Cotton in Uganda', p. 289, for a more realistic view of the growers' barter terms of trade.

52. *Annual Trade Report of Kenya and Uganda, 1928* and *1938*.

53. Uganda, *Report of the Uganda Cotton Commission, 1938*, p. 122.

54. Ehrlich, 'The Marketing of Cotton in Uganda', p. 254.

55. Data found in Appendix A.3. For a given set of observations, the standard deviation is a measure of the dispersion of the observations about their mean.

56. The 'prisoners' dilemma' story may be found in Anatol Rapoport, *Fights, Games and Debates* (Ann Arbor: University of Michigan Press, 1960).

57. In 1943, the export price for Uganda cotton lint (B.P. 52 variety, f.o.b. Mombasa) was Shs. 142 per 100 lb, whereas the UK bulk-buying price was only Shs. 71 per 100 lb. Ehrlich, 'The Marketing of Cotton in Uganda', p. 286. In that year, approximately half the cotton went to India, half to the UK. Gartrell notes that the initial colonial official acceptance of the bulk-buying arrangement quickly waned, especially after the war ended. Yet the colonial officials made no attempt to campaign openly against the system, which ended only in 1952. Gartrell, 'The Ruling Ideas of a Ruling Elite', pp. 398-404.

58. Gartrell, 'The Ruling Ideas of a Ruling Elite', p. 400.

59. Great Britain, *East Africa Royal Commission 1953-1955 Report*, Cmd. 9475 (London: HMSO, 1955), pp. 80-2.

60. Uganda, *Report of the Uganda Cotton Industry Commission, 1948* (Entebbe: Government Printer, 1948), p. 5.

61. Hal Mettrick, *Aid in Uganda: Agriculture* (London: Overseas Development Institute, 1967), p. 43. Lury comes up with somewhat different figures: 31 per cent for cotton and 21 per cent for coffee. Both agree that coffee growers were taxed less than cotton growers, a tax policy which subverted the stated aim of favouring cotton over coffee as the export crop. The levies on growers were especially high in the period up to 1952. In 1951, payments to growers totalled less than Shs. 280 million whereas the price assistance funds took in more than Shs. 500 million. D.A. Lury, 'Dayspring Mishandled? The Uganda Economy 1945-60', *History of East Africa*, ed. D.A. Low and Alison Smith (Oxford: Clarendon Press, 1976), vol. III, pp. 226-7.

62. Great Britain, *East Africa Royal Commission 1953-55 Report*, p. 386.

63. Against a background of rapidly mounting price assistance funds, Governor J. Hathorn Hall insisted that Uganda could not afford greater per capita

expenditures on health and education until financial resources expanded through increased production. Uganda, *A Development Plan for Uganda* (by E.B. Worthington) *and the 1948 Revision* (by Douglas Harris) (Entebbe: Government Printer, 1949), pp. xi-xii, 45. Many of Hall's cost-cutting suggestions were, none the less, worthwhile, such as the proposal that preventative medicine be given priority over curative medicine or that public buildings be less elaborate than their European counterparts. But the real thrust of the Hall recommendations was to hold back on social service spending in order to build infrastructure to attract foreign investment in secondary industry. Gartrell, 'Ruling Ideas of a Ruling Elite', pp. 365-8.

64. Wrigley, *Crops and Wealth in Uganda*, pp. 71-2.

65. Uganda, *Report of the Commission of Inquiry into the Disturbances . . . During April 1949* (Entebbe: Government Printer, 1950), paragraph 39 of the accompanying 'Memorandum'.

66. See footnote 41.

67. J. Littlewood, Chairman of the Empire Cotton Growing Association, *Uganda Herald*, 4 October 1949, as cited by Lury, 'Dayspring Mishandled? The Uganda Economy', p. 232.

68. Uganda, *Report of the Uganda Cotton Industry Commission, 1948*, paragraphs 93-106, 113, 115-16.

69. Frederick D. Lugard, *The Dual Mandate in British Tropical Africa*, 4th edn. (Edinburgh and London: William Blackwood and Sons, 1929), p. 606.

70. Lugard, ibid., pp. 510-15.

71. Frederick D. Lugard, *The Rise of Our East African Empire; Early Efforts in Nyasaland and Uganda* (Edinburgh and London: William Blackwood and Sons, 1893), vol. I, p. 478.

72. E.J.L. Berkeley to Marquis of Salisbury, 'Report on the Trade and Industry of Uganda', 2 November 1896, in Great Britain, *Parliamentary Papers* (Commons), Foreign Office Diplomatic and Consular Reports on Trade and Finances No. 1844, *1897*, C. 8277, p. 6.

73. Cyril Ehrlich, 'Cotton and the Uganda Economy, 1903-1909', *Uganda Journal*, vol. 21, no. 2 (1957), pp. 169-72.

74. Minutes of the Cotton Control Board, 13 September 1926, Agricultural Department, Entebbe, as cited in Ehrlich, 'The Marketing of Cotton in Uganda', p. 233.

75. Ehrlich, 'The Marketing of Cotton in Uganda', pp. 260-2.

76. J.M. Cameron, Managing Director, Uganda Company, as quoted in letter from the Uganda Chamber of Commerce to the Chief Secretary, Entebbe, 2 March 1937, 'Objecting to "An Ordinance Relating to the Constitution and Regulation of Co-operative Societies"', Uganda Chamber of Commerce Archives, Makerere University Library, Kampala.

77. As cited in the Ormsby-Gore Report. Great Britain, *Parliamentary Papers* (Commons) *1925* (IX 855), Cmd. 2387, 'Report of the East Africa Commission', pp. 142-3.

78. On the misunderstandings and conflicting rationalities arising from contact between capitalist and pre-capitalist producers, see, *inter alia*, E.E. Rich, 'Trade Habits and Economic Motivation Among the Indians of North America', *Canadian Journal of Economics and Political Science*, vol. 26, no. 1 (February 1960), pp. 35-53; and Abraham Rotstein, 'Innis: The Alchemy of Fur and Wheat', *Journal of Canadian Studies*, vol. 12, no. 5 (Winter 1977), pp. 6-31.

79. Great Britain, *East Africa Royal Commission 1953-55 Report*, pp. 72, 97; and Jan Jørgensen, 'Multinational Corporations and the Indigenization of the Kenyan Economy', *Multinational Firms in Africa*, ed. Carl Widstrand (Uppsala: Scandinavian Institute of African Studies, 1975), pp. 150, 173.

80. It is only necessary to cite three 'neutral' rules of procedure governing bank loans to understand why ordinary African growers never qualified for loans:
(a) Small farmers (those with less than 100 acres under crops) are considered poor risks due to under-capitalisation and the vagaries of weather, disease and insects;
(b) Loans of less than Shs. 1,000 are too costly to administer (high administrative costs were partly due to the fact that loan officers were, almost without exception, well-paid Europeans);
(c) Banks require realisable security for bank loans. Land which cannot be alienated to non-Africans cannot be presented as security to a European bank. Land encumbered by tenants with inheritable rights is of low market value except to tenants themselves.

81. Sub-Commissioner, Jinja, Busoga, to Deputy Commissioner, Entebbe, 18 May 1906, File 9501-I, SMP, National Archives, Entebbe.

82. Uganda Treasury Savings Bank, Annual Report 1911-12, File 1936-A; and File 2056, SMP, National Archives, Entebbe.

83. G.D. Smith, Treasurer of Uganda Protectorate, to Deputy Commissioner, Entebbe, 19 October 1907, File 9501-I, SMP, National Archives, Entebbe.

84. Ibid.

85. Uganda Treasury Savings Bank, Annual Report, 1911-12.

86. Ehrlich, 'The Marketing of Cotton in Uganda', pp. 198-9.

87. Yoshida and Belshaw, 'The Introduction of the Trade Licensing System for Primary Products in East Africa, 1900-1939', passim.

88. Gartrell, 'The Ruling Ideas of a Ruling Elite', pp. 404-23.

89. Ibid., p. 251.

90. 'Nationalisation of Uganda's Industries', 11 May 1951, Uganda Chamber of Commerce Archives, Makerere University Library, Kampala.

91. Gartrell, 'The Ruling Ideas of a Ruling Elite', pp. 414-15.

92. Lury, 'Dayspring Mishandled? The Uganda Economy', p. 232; and Gartrell, 'The Ruling Ideas of a Ruling Elite', p. 420. As for the ginneries which remained in operation, Lury calculates that the cost-plus formula gave ginnery owners a return on investment of almost 40 per cent in 1962 and probably even more in earlier years.

93. Lury, 'Dayspring Mishandled? The Uganda Economy', pp. 232-3. Under the continuing pool agreements, the growers' co-operative societies could only gin up to the limit of their pool share; the rest of the seed cotton they bought had to go to other ginneries in the pool.

94. Governor H. Hesketh Bell to Secretary of State, 14 September 1909, in Great Britain, *Parliamentary Papers* (Commons) *1909*, Cd. 4910, 'Report on the Introduction and Establishment of the Cotton Industry in the Uganda Protectorate', p. 11.

95. For a classification of industries by national income per capita in the 1970s, see Seev Hirsch, *Rich Man's, Poor Man's and Every Man's Goods; Aspects of Industrialization* (Tübingen, West Germany: Kiel University, Institut für Weltwirtschaft, Studien No. 148, 1977). The role of the product-cycle in the spread of industries to the periphery is discussed in Stephen Hymer, 'Multinational Corporations and the Law of Uneven Development', *Economics and World Order*, ed. J.N. Bhagwati (New York: Free Press, 1972), pp. 113-40.

96. Ehrlich, 'The Marketing of Cotton in Uganda', p. 232; and Mahmood Mamdani, *Politics and Class Formation in Uganda* (New York: Monthly Review, 1976), pp. 92-3.

97. Calculations based on data in Board of Trade, *Statistical Abstract for the United Kingdom*, no. 69 (1910-1924), no. 78 (1913 and 1920-1933), and no. 81 (1913 and 1923-1936); and Central Statistical Office, *Annual Abstract of*

Statistics for the United Kingdom, no. 84 (1935-1946), no. 91 (1954), and no. 100 (1963).

98. Gartrell, 'The Ruling Ideas of a Ruling Elite', p. 373.

99. Ibid., p. 373.

100. Hall's strategy was more successful than Gartrell, using van Zwanenberg's statistics, would have us believe. Van Zwanenberg states that Kenya's manufacturing sector was 50 per cent larger than Uganda's in 1954 and 350 per cent larger in 1968. But it appears that the Uganda figures used in the comparison omit agricultural processing and food manufactures in the 1960s, whereas the Kenya figures include them. Moreover, the figures for the 1950s apparently include mining for each nation, whereas the 1960s figures exclude mining. A more accurate comparison can be made using the following data:

Value-added in mining and manufacturing combined

Year	Uganda	Kenya	Ratio K/U
1954	10.0 £ million	15.0 £ million	1.50
1958	11.9 £ million	21.7 £ million	1.82
1962	12.5 £ million	23.9 £ million	1.91
1964	24.75 £ million	35.63 £ million	1.44
1969	43.55 £ million	58.86 £ million	1.35

Sources: 1954-62, *Oxford History of East Africa*, vol. III, p. 613; 1964-8, Uganda, *1973 Statistical Abstract*, p. 91; and Kenya, *Statistical Abstract 1972*, p. 37.

Clearly the growth shown in the table between 1962 and 1964 for both countries is misleading. What actually happened was an improvement in the method of measuring and surveying manufacturing activity. Cf. van Zwanenberg and King, *An Economic History of Kenya and Uganda*, p. 132.

101. ©Colin Legum, *Must We Lose Africa?* (London: W.H. Allen, 1954), pp. 231-2. Reprinted by permission.

102. R. Cranford Pratt, 'Administration and Politics in Uganda, 1919-1945', *History of East Africa*, vol. II, p. 483. Pratt himself notes that the colonial officials' desire for European style accommodations took precedence over the needs of Africans:

> The housing, the offices, and the public buildings which the Protectorate Government felt necessary absorbed a much higher share of public revenues than in wealthier countries, leaving less for other more productive works expenditures . . . In the years 1927-29, for example, £394,213 was spent on public buildings and £103,713 on roads . . . (p. 484).

Once again we find an example of the structural corruption caused by the life-style expectations of Europeans as an international status group.

103. See the testimony by representatives of European settlers in Kenya before the Joint Select Committee for copious examples of solicitude for the welfare of Africans, Great Britain, 'Joint Select Committee on Closer Union in East Africa', II: 'Minutes of Evidence', and III: 'Appendices', nos. 19 and 20.

104. Kenya, *Blue Book, 1937*; and Uganda, *Blue Book, 1938*, sections on population and education. Calculations based on the assumption that about 27 per cent of the African population is of school age.

105. Philip Mitchell, *African Afterthoughts* (London: Hutchinson, 1954), p. 165.

106. Gartrell, 'Ruling Ideas of a Ruling Elite', p. 458. Mukherjee's work

contains a well-documented condemnation of the absolute inadequacy of social conditions in Uganda in the early 1950s. Ramkrishna Mukherjee, *The Problem of Uganda: A Study in Acculturation* (Berlin: Akademie-Verlag, 1956), passim.

107. Pratt, 'Administration and Politics in Uganda', p. 521.

108. Ibid., p. 526.

109. Ibid., pp. 521-6.

110. Great Britain, 'Joint Select Committee on Closer Union in East Africa', II: 565.

111. Pratt, 'Administration and Politics in Uganda', pp. 526-7.

112. Lugard, *The Dual Mandate*, p. 427.

113. Powesland, *Economic Policy and Labour*, p. 49.

114. Ibid., pp. 68-74.

115. Uganda, *Report of the Uganda Development Commission, 1920*, p. 36.

116. Smaller experimental farms were started at Ngetta, Bugusege, Kawanda, Mbale, Mukono, Bubulu, Wanyange, Kamuge, Kyembogo and elsewhere. J.D. Tothill (ed.), *Agriculture in Uganda* (London: Oxford University Press, 1940), pp. 101-10.

117. Great Britain, 'Joint Select Committee on Closer Union in East Africa', II: 564. In fairness to the Department of Agriculture, it did undertake some research on African food crops in 1922. It found 37 varieties of *matoke* and discovered that, since *matoke* was very low in protein content, it should be supplemented by beans and peas. Nevertheless, there is no record that the Department made any attempt to communicate these findings to Africans. Uganda, *Annual Report of the Department of Agriculture*, 1922, pp. 15, 34.

118. Even Tothill's classic study devoted 198 pages to general information, 268 pages to export cash crops, and only 72 pages to African food crops, Tothill, *Agriculture in Uganda*. David N. McMaster began the task of rectifying matters in 1962 with the publication of *A Subsistence Crop Geography of Uganda* (Cornwall, England: Geographical Publications, 1962).

119. Uganda, *A Development Plan for Uganda*, p. 31.

120. David Jeremiah Vail, *A History of Agricultural Innovation and Development in Teso District, Uganda* (Syracuse, N.Y.: Maxwell School of Citizenship and Public Affairs, Syracuse University, 1972), p. 155.

121. Uganda, *Native Administration* (Entebbe: Government Printer, 1939), p. 29.

4 THE STRUGGLE FOR CONTROL OF THE POST-COLONIAL STATE: POLITICAL MOVEMENTS AND PARTIES, 1938-62

Economic and political nationalism can be analysed from two perspectives: first, the populist, trans-class struggle against domination by external forces; second, the domestic struggle among classes and strata competing for control or influence over state power. The strength of each nationalist movement and party in Uganda depended on the horizontal and vertical dimensions of its composition.

The horizontal dimension was the extent to which a movement or party was able to forge elite alliances across Uganda among members of emerging privileged strata: capitalist farmers, traders, white-collar workers, teachers and other professionals. The vertical dimension was the extent to which each movement or party was able to forge populist trans-class bonds between its leadership and the mass of less privileged followers, using appeals based on region, religion, ethnicity or upward mobility to smooth differences arising from class antagonisms.

Regional antagonisms and contradictions presented opportunities as well as obstacles to any given movement or party, especially since there were multiple levels of regional conflict. First, there was a political contradiction between the encapsulated Kingdom of Buganda and the colonial state of the Uganda Protectorate. Second, there was an economic contradiction between the export-commodity producing areas of southern and central Uganda and the labour-exporting regions of the north, the northwest and the southwest. Third, there was an economic and political contradiction between regions with *de jure* or *de facto* systems of private ownership of land (Buganda, southwest Sebei, southern Busoga and parts of Kigezi, Toro, Ankole and Bunyoro) and the rest of Uganda, where, aside from official estates granted to chiefs, African cultivators were technically tenants on Crown (Public) Land. Fourth, there was the contradiction between the peasant-based economy of Uganda and the settler-dominated economy of Kenya. Finally, there was the widening gap between urban and rural areas within Uganda, a regional and class problem temporarily obscured by ethnicity, by European and Asian monopolisation of urban administrative and commercial roles.

Outside Buganda, in the period between the end of primary

176

resistance and the founding of modern nationalist movements, political struggles centred on four issues: first, opposition to sub-imperialism by non-indigenous chiefs, usually Baganda, but sometimes Batoro, Banyoro, Bagisu and 'Sudanese'; second, campaigns by chiefs and traditional elites for Buganda-style land settlements; third, popular opposition to oppression by appointed chiefs; fourth, struggles against the European and Indian monopolisation of crop-processing and trade. Except for the outstanding issue of the 'lost counties' captured from Bunyoro by Buganda in 1894 and the cultural imperialism of Baganda teachers and clergymen outside Buganda, Buganda's sub-imperialism was rolled back, though at the cost of acknowledging domination by the colonial state. Despite repeated efforts extending from 1900 to the mid-1930s, elites in districts and kingdoms outside Buganda failed to win land settlements similar to Buganda. The struggle against appointed chiefs and against non-African monopolisation of trade had less of a regional bias, being vital issues within and outside Buganda. By 1937 the colonial state had conceded in principle the right of growers to form co-operatives as a basis for entry into cotton ginning. Nevertheless, implementation of African entry into ginning was delayed by rearguard action by Asian and European ginnery owners until 1949, when a cotton hold-up by growers forced the issue. Even so, controversy continued into the nationalist period over the pace of Africanisation of trade and over state control of growers' co-operative societies.

Over time, social stratification among Africans became markedly more differentiated. With the spread of commodity production, the spread of education and transportation, and the growth of state machinery at both national and district levels, there arose new strata.

Wage-labourers were not a homogeneous class. There were differences between agricultural labourers primarily employed by European-owned plantations and those primarily employed by capitalist African farmers. There were differences between full-time wage-labourers and part-time employees with individual land-holdings, between rural agricultural labourers and those employed in crop-processing or, increasingly in the 1940s and 1950s, in factories in Jinja and Kampala. Within factories, there were divisions between white-collar or skilled workers, who tended to be Baganda or Kenyan, and unskilled workers, who tended to be migrant labourers with high turnover.[1] Also politically important were transport workers and relatively high status domestic servants in urban areas.

By the end of the Second World War, peasants were stratified by the size of land-holding, security of tenure, type of cash crop and access to transportation. On the downward side, they were stratified by the extent to which a grower was also a tenant, part-time wage-labourer or migrant labourer, and, on the upward side, by the extent to which a grower was a landlord or capitalist farmer employing wage-labourers, or by the extent to which a grower diversified into trade, transport and politics as independent trader, lorry-owner, co-operative society official, petty chief or political party cadre. The more successful and ambitious growers invested their surplus in one or more of the following: purchase or rental of land, hiring of wage-labour, children's education, purchase of a lorry, bus or taxi, investment in trade, or even money-lending.[2]

As the colonial state began promoting African clerks and began hiring African agronomists, medical officers, lawyers, surveyors and teachers, education became a new mechanism for social mobility and stratification, in addition to land-holding and scale of commodity production. Intermediate-level chiefs tended to be recruited from the ranks of educated clerks in the colonial state apparatus. In time, an urban-oriented African bourgeoisie came into existence alongside rural capitalist farmers, an urban strata based not so much on commerce as on the professions: teaching, religious work, medicine, law and public administration. This urban stratum was well suited for mobility within the structurally dependent framework of the Ugandan economy, but lacked the vision, expertise and experience required to transform the economy into one that was more integrated and less dependent. For this urban stratum, the question of what was to be done centred almost exclusively on Africanisation of the state bureaucracy and Africanisation of trade rather than on transformation of the economic structure.

Furthermore, within urban areas there emerged after the Second World War a lumpenproletariat of marginal artisans, hawkers, thieves, prostitutes and police informers of negligible political importance.[3]

Finally, in addition to all the above 'new' strata, there remained the traditional aristocracies and the appointed colonial chiefs in the kingdom and district administrations who continued to control local institutions of state power in close collaboration with the colonial state itself. These collaborative strata could view only with misgivings the rise of nationalist movements and parties as competing centres of power and legitimacy.

In forging trans-class alliances, nationalist movements and parties therefore operated within an increasingly diversified and increasingly vertically stratified social structure. None the less, given the social mobility of some in the 1940s and 1950s, even narrow economic interests could command broad appeal among the rural population.

Many peasants and migrant labourers aspired to become capitalist farmers. Large sections of the rural population engaged in a bit of trade and were thus prepared to support more affluent African traders in struggles against Asian monopolisation of commerce. Finally, most rural families attempted to send at least one child to school in order that a member of the family might someday become a teacher, professional or white-collar worker. We turn then to the nationalist movements and parties.

The Nationalist Movements

The populist nationalism of the *bataka* movement in the 1920s was embodied in the trans-class alliance between Baganda clan heads and tenant farmers against the landlord-chiefs. However, the colonial state split the alliance by siding with the emerging capitalist tenant-farmers in hopes that security of tenure would create a stable class of yeoman proprietors (which it did) and would stimulate cotton production (on the contrary, it stimulated coffee production).

The founding of the Native Civil Servants' Association in 1922 marked the start of white-collar trade unionism among Africans in Uganda.[4] This nationalist association waged a lengthy uphill battle for African equality with other state employees and for Africanisation of the civil service. It was bitterly ironic that the colonial state's refusal to improve the salaries and working conditions of its African clerks should transform this non-tribal association into a major recruiting ground for state-appointed 'tribal' chiefs. Even more ironic was the fact that, by the time the association won its battle for Africanisation in the 1950s and 1960s, the gap between a civil servant's salary and the ordinary Ugandan's income had widened to the extent that what had begun as a struggle for equality with Asian and European civil servants ended as a struggle for inequality among Africans.

Early ethnic political movements included the Mubende Banyoro Committee, the Young Busoga Association, the Young Baganda Association, the Young Lango Association, the Young Acholi Association, the Young Bagwere Association and the Bugisu Welfare Association. The history of the last five groups is, at best, sketchy, though all were led by emerging traders, farmers and professionals pressing for changes in the *status quo*.[5]

One of the first modern political movements in Uganda, the Mubende Banyoro Committee (MBC) was founded in 1921 and revived in 1931 by Erisa Kalisa to press for the return to Bunyoro of the five and a half 'lost counties' seized by Buganda in the late nineteenth century. With its membership concentrated in Buyaga and Bugangazi counties of Mubende District, Buganda, the MBC's political activity consisted of organising Banyoro in the 'lost counties' to petition both the Buganda and Uganda governments for 'Banyoro-isation' of administrative posts, landownership and education in the 'lost counties' and for the return of the counties to Bunyoro.[6]

The Young Busoga Association in the 1920s was both a populist class alliance between chiefs and peasant growers against the monopsony of cotton ginneries and a vehicle of protest in the unsuccessful struggle by African and even Indian petty traders against the takeover of all cotton buying by the ginneries,[7] hence a part of the struggle of petty traders to maintain their economic existence in Busoga. In this instance the colonial state deprived the movement of its leading cadres, the chiefs, by threatening those chiefs who took part in the movement with removal from office. It virtually eliminated middlemen in the buying of cotton throughout Uganda by establishing cotton zones and encouraging ginneries to form oligopolistic buying pools which controlled cotton buying via the *kyalo* transport system that eliminated independent lorry drivers.[8]

Blue-collar trade unionism in Uganda began in 1938 with the founding of the Uganda Motor Drivers' Association by Joseph Kivu and Fenekasi Musoke. The association of lorry, bus and taxi drivers was populist rather than class-oriented because it included independent owner-drivers as well as transport employees of ginneries and bus companies and because of its close links with the populist Sons of Kintu, also founded in 1938.[9]

The Buganda-based Sons of Kintu was named for Kintu, the semi-legendary founder of Buganda. The Sons of Kintu pressed for the retirement of older chiefs and ministers such as Nsibirwa and Kulubya, who were regarded as overly subservient to the colonial state and who had failed to forge links with the emerging capitalist farmers who had risen from tenant status. The Sons of Kintu attracted not only capitalist farmers and traders who opposed alienation of more *mailo* land to the colonial state for cotton research and Makerere College and the leasing of land outside Kampala township by Baganda landowners to non-African traders, but even chiefs, clanheads and higher Buganda functionaries who had allied themselves with emerging capitalist farmers and traders: S. Bazongere, S.K. Njuki, A. Sanya, S. Kitala Kisingiri, J. Kamulegeya, Y.S. Bamuta, Paulo

Kavuma, Shem Spire Mukasa, Paulo Robert Mukasa, Prince Suna, D.M. Mukubira, and Samwiri Wamala.[10] The Sons of Kintu was led by Ignatius Kangaye Musazi, who later played a leading role in the founding of the Uganda General Transport and Workers (Trade) Union, the Uganda African Farmers Union, the Federation of African Farmers, the Bataka Party, the Uganda National Congress, the Uganda National Movement, and the Uganda-Soviet Friendship and Cultural Society.[11] The Sons of Kintu was populist in that it marked an attempt by wealthier capitalist farmers and traders to forge a class alliance with poorer peasants and urban workers against the *rentier* landlords, Indian and European merchants, and the Baganda political compradors of the colonial state. Furthermore, its monarchial and neo-traditional rhetoric were but instrumental tactics of its trans-class populism which concealed the ultimate aim of taking over control of the state for the benefit of the emerging African bourgeoisie of traders, capitalist farmers and professionals.

Political Agitation in 1944-5 and the 1945 General Strike

Following the 1939 death of Daudi Chwa II, the populist alliance in Buganda failed to get its nominee, Prince Mwanda, selected Kabaka.[12] However, it did succeed in ousting M.L. Nsibirwa from the post of Katikiro (Prime Minister of Buganda) and replacing him with the populist Samwiri Wamala. The alliance then directed its efforts towards ousting S.W. Kulubya, the Omuwanika (Treasurer), and towards agitation against further alienation of *mailo* land around Kampala for the township and for Makerere College. An anonymous pamphlet, *Buganda Nyaffe* (Buganda Our Mother), published in 1944, alleged that this was the first stage of wholesale European expropriation of *mailo* land.[13] The new Kabaka, Edward Mutesa II, sided with Kulubya in supporting the expropriation of land for Makerere.

The agitation by farmers and traders over the land issue coincided with agitation in 1944-5 by the Kampala municipal workers for higher wages. Troops were called in; one worker was killed. Thereupon, a general strike was called, and acts of sabotage were carried out throughout Uganda. The Second World War period had exacerbated the grievances of almost all African strata — farmers angry over artificially low commodity prices set by the colonial state, workers angry over low wages tied to low commodity prices, and everyone angry over high consumer goods prices caused by war shortages and the cutting off of

cheap Japanese textile imports. Moreover, the war had introduced a
new element, the return of some 55,000 ex-soldiers from service in
Ethiopia, Somalia, Madagascar, Palestine, Ceylon, India and Burma.
Musazi credited the ex-servicemen's political consciousness and
organisational ability as indispensable to the general strike of January
1945.[14]

The colonial state responded to the 1945 general strike and rebellion
by imprisoning or sending into rural exile the alleged leaders (including
Samwiri Wamala, I.K. Musazi, Prince Suna, D.K. Makubira,
S. Bazongere and F. Musoke), and restoring Martin Luther Nsibirwa to
the post of Katikiro. It also expanded police political intelligence,
banned *Buganda Nyaffe* as seditious, published a counter-pamphlet
designed to 'appeal to native mentality', increased state control of
trade unions, and encouraged ex-servicemen to return to rural areas and
take up farming. On a more positive note, the colonial state forced an
increase in the number of elected members in the *Lukiko* and raised
wages throughout the Protectorate for both Africans and non-
Africans.[15]

The colonial state instructed the Kabaka to introduce a new land
expropriation law to the Lukiko, entitled 'The Law to Empower the
Kabaka to Acquire Land for Purposes Beneficial to the Nation'.[16]
Having sacked most chiefs suspected of populist leanings, Nsibirwa
dutifully pushed the bill through the Lukiko, but was assassinated
immediately after the bill passed. Thereupon, the colonial state intervened to appoint the son of Apolo Kagwa, E.M. Kawalya Kagwa, as the
new Katikiro.

Political Agitation in 1947-9 and the 1949 Cotton Hold-up

Except for achieving token representation in the Lukiko through an
elaborate system of indirect elections, the populist alliance led by
capitalist farmers and traders could point to few gains from the 1944-5
agitation. With considerable justification, they could now argue that the
Buganda government had lost its legitimacy, being newly staffed with
appointees whose primary qualification was unquestioning loyalty to
the colonial state; the Kabaka, the ministers and most *saza* chiefs were
viewed as little more than British lackeys. In the 1947/48 cotton
season the disparity between prices to growers and world prices was
mockingly large as was the surplus in the colonial state's Price Assistance Funds for cotton and coffee. A decade of inaction had passed

since the colonial state first promised growers' co-operative societies
that they would be allowed to buy cotton ginneries. Against this background, the Bataka Party, formed in 1946 to press for the removal of
Kulubya and for the democratic election of *saza* chiefs, renewed its
efforts. Drawing crowds of 1,000 to 8,000 for its meetings throughout
Buganda, the Bataka Party voiced popular grievances over prices to
growers, the surplus appropriated by the colonial state, the indirect
election of chiefs, the current regime in Buganda, the increase in
Luwalo tax from Shs. 10 to Shs. 14, the Land Acquisition Law of 1945
and the Town Planning Law of 1947, the rumoured surrender of
mineral rights on *mailo* land to the colonial state, and, last but not
least, Colonial Office Papers No. 191 of 1945 and No. 210 of 1947
which appeared to revive the prospect of federation with Kenya and
Tanganyika.[17]

The Bataka Party was founded by James Miti who had been active in
the 1920s *bataka* movement. Other prominent leaders included Spartas
Mukasa, Semakula Mulumba, Yoswa (Joseph) Kivu, Erifazi Semberege,
Paulo Robert Mukasa, Shem Spire Mukasa, Nasanaeri Mayanja, and
numerous traders who linked local *miruka* Bataka Party groups led by
capitalist farmers.[18]

In order to control growers' co-operative societies, the colonial
state's Co-operative Societies Ordinance of 1946 gave the Registrar of
Co-operative Societies wide-ranging powers including the power to
appoint a supervisor for each registered society. Furthermore, by
banning societies from giving remuneration to its officers, the ordinance effectively prevented societies from having full-time officers.
Finally, societies were barred from making loans or giving credit to
members except with the approval and supervision of the Registrar.[19]
When appeals to the Governor to change these provisions failed, a
number of farmers, led by I.K. Musazi, formed the Uganda African
Farmers' Union in 1947 to mobilise all farmers in Uganda to take
control of the marketing of cash crops.[20] By registering as a
partnership in April 1948 under the Business Names Ordinance rather
than as a co-operative society, the UAFU circumvented the restrictions
of the Co-operative Societies Ordinance.

The year 1948 marked a low point in relations between the colonial
state and the cotton ginnery owners, a factor which the Uganda African
Farmers' Union was able to exploit to its advantage. Since the colonial
state takeover of cotton exports in 1943, cotton ginneries had been
paid a fixed margin per unit of output regardless of world prices, which
were soaring. Although the margin was generous, ginneries could

increase their revenue only by increasing output or by cheating growers. Since total output was dependent on growers who responded in acreage to prices set by the state, the ginneries were upset that the low grower prices had resulted in only 170,000 bales of lint cotton being produced in the 1947/48 season – a 26 per cent decline from the previous year.[21] The ginnery owners urged the colonial state to increase the grower price from Shs. 22 to Shs. 30 per 100 pounds of seed cotton, and joined growers in criticising the colonial state's mounting Price Assistance Fund surplus.[22] The colonial state responded to this criticism with a devastating exposure of wholesale cheating practices employed by ginneries in buying cotton from growers, as detailed in the 1948 cotton commission report.[23] The African vernacular press supporting the Uganda African Farmers' Union, notably *Gambuze* and *Mugobansonga*, gleefully exploited this opportunity to document growers' grievances using ammunition provided by the colonial state against ginneries and by the merchant-oriented *Uganda Herald* against the colonial state.

Furthermore, it is only in the context of this dispute between ginneries and the colonial state that it is possible to explain Governor J.H. Hall's extraordinary response to I.K. Musazi's request for permission for the UAFU to build seed cotton storage sheds and to collect seed cotton for ginning by a negotiated processing fee:

> His Excellency wishes you to be informed that the activities described in your letter in connection with the collection of seed cotton do not appear to be in conflict with the regulations as they now stand, provided it is collection from your members and not the purchase of seed cotton that is contemplated. You would also have to conform with the provisions of the Cotton Zone Ordinance. It is considered, however, that you would experience certain difficulties in arranging for the ginning of the cotton collected by you and, if these difficulties were overcome, the resultant lint cotton would have to be sold to the Cotton Exporters' Group at the same price as that paid to ginners of equivalent quantity lint. It should also be borne in mind that the Cotton Exporters' Group do not deal in lots of less than fifty bales of lint.[24]

Armed with the Governor's implied blessing, the Uganda African Farmers' Union proceeded to build and rent sheds for cotton storage throughout Buganda and to encourage farmers to store seed cotton on their own premises or those controlled by the UAFU following the

December 1948 harvest. When negotiations with ginneries broke down, the cotton storage scheme transformed itself into a cotton hold-up, and Musazi left for England to seek the support of Fenner Brockway and others in lobbying for higher prices to growers.[25]

Faced with the cotton hold-up, the colonial state and ginneries closed ranks. On 12 March 1949, the colonial state outlawed the storage of cotton anywhere in Buganda except on licensed premises, the only licensed premises being those belonging to cotton ginneries.[26]

For its part, the Buganda government, led by the Regents and 16 of the 20 county chiefs, had already, in August 1948, requested that the colonial state outlaw the Bataka Party. Well ahead of the colonial state, Katikiro Kawalya Kagwa had, in January 1949, instructed county chiefs to discourage growers from storing cotton or turning it over to the UAFU. By these actions the Buganda government merely deflected the full fury of the Bataka Party and the UAFU from the colonial state and non-African merchants to itself. Following the colonial state's ban on storage of cotton in unlicensed premises, the Kabäka, Edward Mutesa II, granted an audience to delegates of the UAFU only to urge them to comply. The colonial state extended the buying season deadline in Buganda to 14 April 1949.[27]

On the day following the expiry of this deadline, a crowd of 500 people gathered at the Kabaka's Lake and agreed to mobilise to present their grievances to the Kabaka on 25 April. Of the nearly 4,000 people who assembled on 25 April, the Kabaka received eight delegates, who presented him with five written demands:

(1) Your Highness should open the rule of democracy to start giving people power to choose their own chiefs.
(2) We want the number of sixty unofficial representatives (i.e. in the Lukiko) to be completed.
(3) We demand the abolition of the present Government.
(4) We want to gin our own cotton.
(5) We want to sell our produce in outside countries, *that is free trade.*

The oral presentation by the delegates included additional demands: revision of the Co-operative Societies Ordinance; state assistance for growers to obtain tractors and coffee-hulling machinery; and establishment of a bank for African farmers and traders. One of the delegates, Eryeza Bwete, claimed the UAFU had spent Shs. 20,000 on its propaganda campaign in the countryside to teach people 'a sense of ownership'.[28]

Hence liberal democracy, free trade and a sense of ownership formed the core of the 'radical' values of the populist alliance. None the less, the movement and its demands threatened the ruling coalition of the colonial state, the Buganda government and the non-African commercial interests. Rejecting the first three demands, the Kabaka agreed to investigate the fourth and fifth demands, over which he had no power. He then ordered the assembled people to disperse. When the police attempted to use the Riot Act to disperse the 800 or so people who remained the following day, a genuine riot erupted and spread to all parts of Buganda as mobs burned the homes and offices of unpopular chiefs appointed by the late Nsibirwa.[29] The colonial state declared a state of emergency in Buganda, arrested 1,724 persons, instituted press censorship and outlawed the Bataka Party and the Uganda African Farmers' Union, seizing the assets of both. The cotton season was re-opened for eleven days.

The official inquiry into the cotton hold-up and the 'disturbance' made much of the fact that only 500,000 pounds of seed cotton (400 bales of lint equivalent) were seized from the UAFU, which had claimed to possess 3.5 million pounds (2,800 bales of lint, itself less than 1 per cent of Uganda's output). The official estimate may have been low for political reasons; some seized cotton was burned by officials. Moreover, as the boycott continued, many growers were undoubtedly forced by economic circumstance to sell to ginneries what they had earlier pledged to the UAFU. The size of the 1948-9 crop, 391,000 bales of lint, or more than any year from 1938-9 until 1953-4, is evidence that farmers planted more cotton in anticipation of UAFU's success in raising grower prices.[30]

Although the relative gap between world prices and grower prices did not narrow to pre-war levels until 1952-3, growers enjoyed an increase in *absolute* prices during and following the boycott. The five original demands of the populist alliance met with some success. The demand for 60 elected representatives in the Buganda Lukiko was met in two stages: 50 by 1950 and 60 by 1953. The top three ministers in the Buganda government were quietly replaced by the end of 1950, with Paulo Kavuma, a *saza* chief linked to the populist alliance and Sons of Kintu, emerging as the new Katikiro. Progress in Africanising agricultural processing was far slower. By 1953 African co-operative societies controlled 5 cotton ginneries and were about to take over 3 more plus 6 new coffee-curing works. By 1960 growers' co-operative societies controlled 12 of Uganda's 130 ginneries: 3 in Buganda, 6 in

Busoga and Mbale cotton zones, 1 in Bunyoro and 2 in Lango. Growers' co-operatives owned 6 coffee-hulling works and 29 estate coffee factories, which together handled 29.4 per cent of robusta coffee exports. The colonial state established the Uganda Credit and Savings Bank in 1950 and the African Loans Fund in 1954 to provide loans to African farmers and traders who were unable to obtain credit from the foreign-owned commercial banks, but this new credit was limited in its magnitude and effects. In response to pressure from I.K. Musazi's new organisation, the Federation of Partnerships of Uganda African Farmers, Governor Cohen had the Legislative Council modify some restrictions on co-operative societies. On the other hand the demand for elected chiefs was not fulfilled in Buganda until 1973. The demand for 'free trade' was not met, but the colonial state and the statutory marketing boards which controlled exports were gradually Africanised.[31]

The Problem of Africanising Trade 1949-62

The period between the 1949 cotton hold-up and formal political independence in 1962 demonstrates that removal of barriers to African entry into commerce was not sufficient to ensure Africanisation of commerce.

There was slow but virtually uninterrupted progress in the elimination of barriers to African entry into commerce and crop-processing. Indeed, there was tangible state encouragement of Africanisation of commerce: the Uganda Credit and Savings Bank, the African Loans Fund, development projects to build urban premises for African traders, the 1955 report on *The Advancement of Africans in Trade*, state-assisted entry of co-operative societies into crop-processing and the raising of grower prices closer to world prices. Within Uganda, the populist alliance led by African traders and farmers appeared to be in the ascendant politically: witness Governor Cohen's willingness to listen to the grievances of I.K. Musazi's newly-formed Federation of Partnerships of Uganda African Farmers and the sudden growth in membership and influence of the Uganda National Congress from 1952 onward. The violent 1959 trade boycott was not simply a demonstration against the slow pace of Africanisation of commerce but evidence that the very process of Africanisation, so vital to both African populists and the British neo-colonial strategy, had been blocked and undermined by structural changes in the economy during the 1950s.

To begin with, the colonial state's commitment of resources to

Africanisation of trade was minimal compared to resources allocated to joint ventures in import substitution and to infrastructure required to attract foreign capital: Shs. 12 million for the initial capital of the Credit and Savings Bank and Shs. 3 million for the African Loans Fund versus Shs. 100 million transferred from Price Assistance Funds to start the Uganda Development Corporation in 1952, and a total Shs. 464 million transferred from the Cotton Price Assistance Fund to the African Development Fund (later the Capital Development Fund) between 1952 and 1957 for infrastructure projects such as roads and the Owens Falls hydro-electric installation.[32]

The colonial state strategy of neo-dependence − joint state and British ventures in import substitution and British-supplied, Uganda-financed infrastructure investment − involved bringing into Uganda literally thousands of British and other non-African experts to supervise the building of the Owen Falls hydro-electric dam, roads, bridges, and Uganda Development Corporation joint venture industries controlled by a combination of the colonial state, the metropolitan state and foreign capital, while Africanisation of the growing state bureaucracy necessitated importing British teachers to staff schools to train African administrative cadres. The industrial expansion and the higher producer prices for Africans, in the period beginning in 1953, in turn attracted additional immigrants into trade to service the high income consumption emerging in rural areas in the relative prosperity of the 1950s. Between 1949 and 1959, the number of Europeans in Uganda increased from 3,448 to 10,866 (an increase of 215 per cent); and the number of Indians and Pakistanis, from 35,215 to 71,933 (an increase of 104 per cent).[33]

To service the credit needs of Indian traders, both the Bank of India and the Bank of Baroda entered Uganda in the 1950s, opening one branch apiece in Kampala and Jinja. The 1950s also marked the expansion of the 'big three' British banks (Grindlays, Barclays and Standard) into 'up-country' districts, partly as camp followers of the Indian traders, partly to mop up whatever savings remained in rural areas after the colonial state allowed producer prices to rise to levels more closely approximating world prices. New Indian traders could count on relatives or communal counterparts to guarantee bank loans. African traders and farmers faced problems in finding co-signers and in mortgaging crops or land. Thus most of the African savings channelled into British or Indian banks were lent, as in the past, to Indian and European merchants and manufacturers, to multinational corporations, and to the state.[34]

Although members of the Uganda Chamber of Commerce shed crocodile tears over the 'exploitation' of the African growers by the state's price assistance funds[35] and objected strenuously to both co-operative society entry into crop-processing and the colonial state's entry into import substitution, the more dynamic elements in the non-African merchant class seized the opportunities of the 1950s to move upstream in the domestic vertical division of labour, from the politically exposed retail trade into wholesale trade, and from wholesale trade into import-substitution manufacturing.

The concessions granted to African traders by Cohen's administration in the early 1950s were more than offset by these immigration factors. It is also necessary to point out the limited magnitude of state aid to African traders in comparison to the large number of African traders desiring to use these services. Only a few could benefit. For example, had the entire initial capital of the African Loans Fund been lent equally among African traders, each would have received an average loan of Shs. 100. The colonial state was not willing to engage in reverse discrimination to offset the advantages accumulated by non-African traders and merchants in the 1930s and 1940s under state protection. To do so would have meant undermining British banks who had committed themselves to lending large sums of credit to European firms and to Asian traders to finance imports under the indenting system.[36] Although the number of African traders increased in absolute terms in the 1950s, the relative share of retail trade controlled by African traders declined during this period of rapid growth.[37] Asian traders entered areas previously reserved for African traders, rural areas and the *Kibuga* (the African area of Mengo bordering Kampala). To be sure, the entry of Indian traders into African suburbs could not have succeeded were it not for African landlords more interested in higher rents than in solidarity with African traders.[38] Africans producing milk and eggs for sale in urban areas lost these markets after 1957 to Kenyan imports, which boasted superior packaging and the racial distinction of having been produced by Africans under European supervision, which appealed to the expanding European and Indian population in Uganda's urban areas.[39] Had the colonial state been seriously interested in strengthening the comprador class of African traders in the 1950s, it would have restricted Asian immigration and assisted Ugandan producers of dairy products.

The Buganda Lukiko viewed the influx of non-African immigrants with suspicion and noted that the colonial state had embarked on its industrialisation strategy without consulting the government of

Buganda:

> . . . when the British Government started the industrialization of Uganda, we were not consulted. And the opinion of the Great Lukiko is not sought as regards immigration control, with the result that hundreds of immigrants flock into the country monthly without His Highness' Government knowing the purpose.[40]

All these factors, most notable of which was the entry of Indian traders into exclusively African trading areas, served as a backdrop to the explosive trade boycott organised by the Uganda National Movement. The UNM was founded in 1959 by Augustine Kamya, a leading Muganda trader and staunch monarchist, with the aid of I.K. Musazi and E.M.K. Mulira. The UNM launched a boycott of Asian traders throughout Buganda, which was initially supported by the entire African community, if for no other reason than the fact that no African wished to be accused of defending Asian traders. Through violence and intimidation the UNM boycott succeeded in driving Indian traders out of many rural areas. However, the very violence and length of the boycott led to its loss of support. The colonial state brought pressure on the Buganda government to denounce the boycott by threatening to cut off financial support. Under this colonial pressure, the Kabaka issued a statement condemning both the violence and boycott. Similar statements appeared in vernacular newspapers such as *Munno*. Another factor contributing to the end of the boycott was the fact that not only were African landlords threatened with loss of rent, but all African traders were eventually tied to an Asian retailer or wholesaler as supplier. The colonial state finally outlawed the Uganda National Movement in the same year.[41]

The Class Basis of Buganda Separatism

With the delimiting of Buganda from the Uganda Protectorate in 1908,[42] the quasi-autonomous Kingdom of Buganda became encapsulated within an altogether dependent colonial state. It was ironic that the Kingdom of Buganda, having earlier conquered the rest of the Uganda Protectorate for British imperialism through the sub-imperialism of Ganda agents and *bakungu* chiefs should, from 1953 onward, give rise to a separatist movement that advocated Buganda's secession from the very entity it had helped to create — an entity which functioned as a labour reserve for Buganda-based capitalist farmers.

Apter's claim that the Protectorate government did 'everything in its power to promote unity in Uganda', whereas the Baganda pursued a policy of 'divide and rule', holds true only for the 1950s.[43] Before the Second World War, it was the colonial state that barred other districts from obtaining Buganda-style land tenure. It was the colonial state that initially divided Uganda into commodity-producing areas and non-producing labour reserves; it was the colonial state that vetoed the 1925 attempt by African rulers of kingdoms and districts to hold regular joint meetings; it was the colonial state that encouraged inter-tribal rivalry in the First World War carrier corps; and it was the colonial state that nurtured Buganda's sense of supremacy throughout much of the colonial period.[44]

As elsewhere in Africa, Britain had pursued a policy of divide and rule, the main beneficiaries within Uganda being the non-African merchants, the Baganda aristocracy, the *rentier* landlords and the capitalist farmers; the main external beneficiaries were the bourgeoisie in the metropole (Great Britain) and in sub-imperialist centres (Kenya, India and South Africa). It was for the benefit of the metropolitan bourgeoisie that Britain amalgamated Buganda with Uganda and advocated the amalgamation of Uganda with the rest of East Africa.

What was the class basis of Buganda's resistance to a unitary government in Uganda? For the 'Mengo hierarchy', the struggle against amalgamation with Uganda was a struggle for political survival and the perpetuation of privilege. This hierarchy consisted of the royal family, the higher functionaries of the state apparatus of the Kingdom of Buganda, and the appointed *saza* chiefs, whose control of the Buganda Lukiko was threatened by the election of Lukiko members by capitalist farmers, traders, teachers, professionals and state employees. Through its power to appoint *gombolola, miruka* and *batongole* chiefs (subject to the advice and approval of the colonial state) the hierarchy could use patron-client relationships to mobilise popular support throughout Buganda, aided by emotional appeals to Buganda patriotism and to the traditional legitimacy of the Kabakaship itself. Such was the case in the controversy over the colonial state's withdrawal of recognition from, and deportation of, the Kabaka in 1953 over the issues of East African federation and the place of Buganda within Uganda.[45]

For a second stratum, *rentier* landlords, amalgamation of Buganda with the rest of Uganda in a unitary state with uniform laws would appear to threaten the *mailo* system of land tenure which was unique to Buganda. For these landlords, an independent Buganda, or at least a federal relationship between Buganda and Uganda, would be preferable to the unitary state advocated by Governor Cohen.

For a third stratum, African traders, the situation was more complex. Baganda-based traders comprised approximately half the African traders in Uganda;[46] whereas the Baganda comprised only one-sixth of the total African population of Uganda. On the one hand, a unitary or federal Uganda would offer Buganda-based traders a larger market which they could hope to dominate, given their location and longer commercial experience, but only if they could successfully compete with or eliminate their Indian competitors and Indian and European merchant houses. On the other hand, an independent Buganda, while offering a smaller market, offered a greater political opportunity for using control of state power to restrict and eliminate non-African competition in retail and wholesale trade.

A fourth stratum, the Baganda professionals, faced a similar situation, but once the colonial state committed itself to Africanisation of the salariat in the 1950s, the majority of this stratum saw larger gains to be obtained in a unitary or federal post-colonial state than in an independent Buganda.[47]

For a fifth stratum, non-Baganda migrant labourers, the preferable form of the post-colonial state was clearly a unitary Uganda or at least a federal Uganda in which non-Baganda working in Buganda for capitalist African farmers or non-African employers could have a moral claim as co-citizens to Uganda-wide economic and social expenditures of tax revenues from the producing areas located primarily in the south. An independent Buganda would reduce migrant labourers, who comprised as much as 45 per cent of the African population of Buganda,[48] to the status of foreign 'guest-workers' who, like their counterparts in South Africa or in the European Economic Community, would have no claim to the transfer of state resources from the producing area to the 'home country', which bore the costs of reproduction of labour.

Finally, for the largest stratum in Buganda, the farmers who used migrant labour to produce commodities for sale in the world market, the struggle against amalgamation with the rest of Uganda was not simply a struggle for existing land-tenure rights, even less so an atavistic struggle based on 'tribalism', but a struggle for economic hegemony. The economic basis of the patriotism of the capitalist farmers lay in the identification of the *mailo-kibanja* land-tenure system with Buganda autonomy, and Buganda autonomy in turn with the institution of the Kabakaship. Independence for Buganda or even continued protectorate status for Buganda while the remainder of Uganda became independent offered capitalist farmers in Buganda distinct economic advantages. It would enable them to restrict or deny citizenship, landownership and social services to both non-Africans (Asian and European merchants and administrators) and the 45 per cent of the African population in Buganda which was non-Baganda. An independent Buganda would further reduce northwest and southwest Uganda to labour reserves or bantustans, economically dependent on commodity-producing areas in Buganda, Busoga, Lango, Teso, Bunyoro and Bugisu-Sebei. Migrant labourers could then exercise no claim on the Buganda national product beyond the basic wage for single adults.

Hence the economic interests of capitalist farmers and traders of Buganda reinforced tradition-based ethnicity to allow Baganda farmers and traders to unite with the Mengo hierarchy and a few professionals under the banner of Buganda's independence. Uniting the contradictory goals of neo-traditional subservience to the Kabaka and the modern economic nationalism of the populist alliance, the movement's demands for an independent Buganda shook Uganda first in 1953-5, then in 1960, and most recently in 1966.[49]

Class and Regional Basis of Nationalist Political Parties, 1952-62

The major political parties in Uganda were the Uganda National Congress, the Democratic Party and the Progressive Party in the 1950s, and the Uganda People's Congress, the Democratic Party and the Kabaka Yekka in the 1960s. Three of these parties, the Uganda National Congress (UNC), the Uganda People's Party (UPC), and the Kabaka Yekka (KY), were inextricably linked to the populist alliance led by African traders and farmers.

The Progressive Party, despite its name, was dominated by an elitist conservative faction of the populist alliance: the intelligentsia of teachers, professionals, educated businessmen and landlords, and part of the salariat of the Buganda government. Founded in 1955 by E.M.K. Mulira, the party failed to achieve a popular base and folded permanently in 1959, when Mulira joined the Uganda National Movement in search of the masses which had eluded him in the Progressive Party. Thanks to the indirect method of electing representatives to the Lukiko, lack of a popular base did not prevent the Progressive Party from winning 12 seats in the Buganda Lukiko and the support of another 20 elected representatives. For a number of reasons, not least of which was Mulira's principled opposition to Sempa's land deal, the Progressive Party became branded as the immediate enemy by the Buganda aristocracy and higher Buganda functionaries. Although a Buganda party, the Progressive Party envisaged a federal post-colonial state to be called the United States of Uganda,[50] as might be expected, given its professional base.

By contrast, the UNC was an all-Uganda party, the first to have branches in both Buganda and the rest of Uganda. Founded by I.K. Musazi and Abu Mayanja in 1952, the UNC started out as the political arm of Musazi's Federation of Partnerships of Uganda African Farmers. Its strength lay in the export-commodity producing areas of Uganda. As Bowles points out, within Buganda the UNC concentrated on coffee and cotton growers and on opponents of the Mengo hierarchy; outside Buganda the UNC appealed to cotton growers. The UNC had limited support where little cotton was grown (West Nile, Toro and Bugisu) and virtually no support where no cotton was grown (Ankole, Kigezi and Karamoja).[51]

In the abbreviated platform on the back of its membership cards, the UNC advocated a federal state, universal suffrage under a common roll for *citizens*, early self-government, African control of the economy and 'Education, Health and Justice for all'.[52] By stressing citizenship, the UNC reminded the metropolitan and colonial states of the uncertain status of resident Europeans and Asians. By demanding a common roll, the UNC rejected multi-racialism, the one-race-one-vote formula of reserved legislative seats for Europeans and Asians, in favour of the non-racial one-person-one-vote system of electing representatives. The slogan 'African control of the economy of Uganda' was sufficiently populist to appeal to Africans of every stratum and region without raising potentially divisive questions about the pace, form and direction of African control of the economy.

Despite its claims to represent trans-class and trans-regional interests, the class origins of the UNC leadership mirrored the party's disproportionate support in commodity-producing regions. According to Apter, 34 per cent of UNC branch chairmen were traders; 29 per cent were farmers; and 16 per cent described themselves as full-time politicians. In the UNC central committee, 10 of 19 members were professionals or aspiring professionals (lawyers, clerks, journalists, school masters and a student at Cambridge) and another 5 were traders. Significantly all important branch members tended to be farmer-traders, persons who pursued both occupations. Within Buganda, branch meetings were usually held at the homes of *batongole* chiefs.[53] Outside Buganda, the occupational and class background of the UNC leaders varied from district to district.

The former chairman of the Lango UAFU, Yokosafati Engur, founded the first Lango branch of the party in 1952. Its active leadership consisted of small shopkeepers, traders, cultivators and a few teachers. The Lango UNC branch campaigned for an African National Assembly to replace the Uganda Legislative Council, for direct election of Legislative Council representatives throughout Uganda rather than in Buganda alone, for the abolition of hawker licences, for an end to Indian domination of commerce, for a less arbitrary (and less progressive?) system of graduated poll tax assessment and for an end to unpaid forced labour (*ber lobo*) for the chiefs. But it was its 1955-7 campaign against the extension of marketable private ownership of land into rural Lango that won the UNC its greatest popular support. The Lango UNC even opposed co-operative farms as a back door to the introduction of private ownership of land.[54]

Though sprinkled with farmers and traders, the UNC leadership in Acholi consisted primarily of government employees and teachers with past experience in the military and police. Peter Oola, who founded the first Acholi branch in 1953, worked in the Public Works Department and had served in the King's African Rifles, while his rival, Otema Allimadi, worked in a medical dispensary and had served in the Army Medical Corps. The Acholi party operated under several handicaps: the remoteness of party branches from national party headquarters in Kampala; the rigorous ban on political meetings (except in Gulu and Kitgum) imposed by chiefs between 1954 and 1958; and the traditional rivalry between kingdoms in western Acholi, led by Payera, and eastern Acholi, led by Padibe (and Pajule), which ensnared the party. The Acholi UNC campaigned for direct election of representatives to the district council, for more medical dispensaries and for a new system of allocating education bursary awards. It objected to forced labour for chiefs, oppressive manipulation by chiefs, the provisions of food at below market price for officials on tour, and the alienation of land for game reserves. It opposed the appointment of Amar Maini, an Asian, as government minister and campaigned against the 1955 land tenure proposals.[55] In Acholi, Lango and Teso, opposition to the land tenure proposals stemmed from fears that private landownership would enable Europeans, Asians and Baganda to buy large tracts of land, but there appeared to be less opposition to the principle of private landownership in Acholi than in Lango.

Support for the UNC was limited in Bunyoro, not because the district lagged behind others in cotton production – Bunyoro's cotton output per capita was in fact slightly above the national average – but because the national party appeared to be dominated by politicians from Buganda, Bunyoro's old rival. Although Dr I.K. Majugo organised the first UNC branch in Bunyoro in 1953, George Magezi, the party's candidate in the first direct election of Legislative Council representatives (1958), discreetly avoided the UNC label in the campaign to retain the seat he had held as a nominated member since 1953. As elsewhere, the party became embroiled in internal rivalries; in Bunyoro the conflict was between Hoima-side, where the political capital was located, and Masindi-side, where much of the agricultural processing was located. There was also a conflict within the Bunyoro UNC between the progressive, populist faction led by Majugo, royal nephew of the Omukama, and the conservative faction led by Magezi, a substantial farmer and landowner who was also son-in-law of the Omukama. This important conflict carried over into the Uganda People's Congress, UNC's successor.[56]

At the national level, despite its antipathy to the chiefly hierarchy and traditional rulers, one of the first tasks which befell the UNC was mobilising support for the return and restoration of Kabaka Edward Mutesa of Buganda, following his deportation by Governor Cohen in 1953. Deportation transformed the Kabaka into a symbol of African nationalism and resistance to domination by European settlers in the proposed East African Federation. The UNC campaigned energetically for the Kabaka's return, linking that issue to demands for African self-government, staging demonstrations, sending petitions to Britain, organising a boycott of European and Asians products, and sending a delegation to the 1955 London conference that hammered out final details arising from the Namirembe agreement for the return of the Kabaka.[57] By including delegates from outside Buganda, such as Engur from Lango, the UNC stressed the unity of the party on the deportation issue.

Mindful of the violence of the 1945 general strike and the 1949 cotton hold-up and militarily preoccupied with the ongoing 'Mau Mau' Emergency in Kenya, the British government yielded to the unified Uganda opposition. Yet the Kabaka's return proved self-defeating for the political aims of the UNC. Britain's continued insistence on special legislative representation for European and Asian 'tribes' reinforced tribalism within the UNC: many Baganda members now viewed separate independence for Buganda as a means to escape multi-racialism. The deportation affair revealed deep divisions within the

UNC over the future framework of Uganda. UNC members outside Buganda tended to favour a unitary post-colonial state, although members in the Agreement Districts (Bunyoro, Toro, Ankole) and Busoga were partial to a federal structure, as were moderates within Buganda. However, an increasing number of members in Buganda shifted from a pro-federal to a pro-separatist stance.

In 1958 the five UNC members in the Legislative Council split, when Magezi and Nadiope formed the Uganda People's Union (UPU), a coalition of seven non-Baganda Legislative Council members. Outside the Legislative Council, the UPU had no formal organisation, but the national UNC itself split into at least two factions in 1959-60: one led by Milton Obote and Abu Mayanja, and the other by I.K. Musazi.

Within Buganda, the anti-populist Mengo hierarchy emerged in full control of the Buganda government after the return of the Kabaka in 1955. Thanks to the Namirembe and London Agreements, the Buganda government assumed more control over social services within Buganda. Although formally reduced to a constitutional monarch, the Kabaka exercised more real power after 1955 than any Kabaka since 1888. The Buganda traditional hierarchy thwarted the UNC's anticipated gains in the 60 elected Lukiko seats by refusing to hold direct elections for Lukiko representatives. Led by Michael Kintu, Amos Sempa and the Kabaka, the Buganda hierarchy succeeded in blocking the emergence of political parties in the Lukiko as alternate centres of political power.[58]

The Lango UNC fared better, winning greater control of the district council in direct elections from 1955 onward. By 1960 the party controlled the Lango Appointments Board which selected chiefs and other district officials. The Lango UNC's opposition to the chiefly hierarchy lessened as it gained increasing control over recruitments to that hierarchy. From 1957 the party even championed the creation of the post of *won nyaci*, a ceremonial constitutional head of the district, to be elected by the district council. The UNC-dominated district council elected Engur as *won nyaci* in 1960, a *fait accompli* reluctantly accepted by the colonial state the following year.[59]

In Acholi, the UNC's quest for control of the district council faced stiff competition from several sources: first, the incumbent chiefly hierarchy appointed by the colonial state; second, the traditional aristocracy which was itself divided into regional factions based on the old kingdoms; and third, the Democratic Party (DP) which was quite strong in Acholi. In efforts to gain support from the traditional aristocracy, both the UNC and DP took positions which undermined their democratic aspirations. The Acholi UNC from 1955 onward found itself favouring recruitment of chiefs neither by election nor by an elected council, but by the traditional aristocracy. Moreover, the UNC became identified with Payera's claim to Acholi paramountcy, as did the DP with Padibe's claim. Despite misgivings, both parties supported creation of the post of *layola*, a ceremonial constitutional head of the district, to be selected from the 'leading families'.[60]

Throughout Uganda, the economic grievances which fuelled farmer support for the UNC lessened somewhat in the period 1953-9. The colonial state narrowed the gap between prices to growers and world prices; ended the blatant discrimination in prices between coffee grown on non-African estates and coffee grown by Africans; and allocated some of the surplus in price assistance funds to African education, loans to farmers and traders, and other projects of relevance to the populist alliance.[61] Dissatisfaction continued to mount over the slow pace of Africanisation of ownership of cotton ginneries and coffee-processing plants and over the influx of Indian traders into rural areas. This dissatisfaction culminated in the 1959 trade boycott. Yet, on the whole, the period 1955-9 was a period of reduced political activity on the part of the populist alliance; it was a period of economic rather than political consolidation, as capitalist farmers took advantage of better prices, as African traders attempted to take advantage of the African Loans Fund, as African teachers won pensions and salary increases, and as African professionals gained entry into the upper levels of the state bureaucracy.[62] Certainly this was a period of increasing economic stratification among Africans in both rural and urban areas.

The third major party was the Democratic Party (DP). Founded in 1956 by Matayo Mugwanya in Buganda, branches opened in Lango and Acholi that same year, and in Bunyoro and elsewhere by 1958 when Benedicto Kiwanuka assumed leadership of the DP. The DP was founded by Catholics who objected to Protestant domination of appointed offices and nationalist Catholics who viewed the UNC as yet another vehicle of Protestant hegemony. Although allocation of chiefs' posts to Catholics in proportion to the Catholic share in the population was a major goal of the DP, it was not in any sense a party of chiefs.[63] The party leadership was largely in the hands of teachers and other professionals rather than chiefs. Never a separatist party, it favoured a unitary post-colonial state in expectation that this would enable the Catholic plurality in Uganda to take control under the leadership of Catholic professionals who had been denied power by the Protestant minority; the latter had controlled internal appointments in alliance with the smaller Muslim factions through collaboration with the British since the late nineteenth century. Hence the DP platform advocated rapid Africanisation of the civil service rather than immediate self-government.[64] The DP was strongly anti-Communist and feared that more radical elements in the UNC (later UPC) would nationalise church property such as schools or hospitals after independence. In its efforts to save Catholic Church property from this 'Communist' threat, the DP received solid, often too open, support from European Catholics in Uganda. According to Welbourn, the Democratic Party was actively disliked by some British officials who viewed it as a party that was politically and economically anti-British.[65]

The grievances of Catholics over appointments could easily be documented. In Buganda the population was 35 per cent Catholic, 28 per cent Protestant, and 14 per cent Muslim; yet *saza* chiefs were 40 per cent Catholic, 50 per cent Protestant and 10 per cent Muslim, while in the late 1950s, four of the six ministers of the Buganda government were Protestant and one each Catholic and Muslim.[66] In Toro, where 28 per cent of the population were Catholic, 21 Protestant and 2 per cent Muslim, 70 per cent of the chiefs were Protestant, only 30 per cent Catholic and none Muslim. Although Catholics slightly outnumbered Protestants in Ankole (27 versus 24 per cent), Protestant chiefs outnumbered Catholic chiefs by more than 2 to 1.[67] In Acholi, where 30 per cent of the population were Catholic and 22 per cent Protestant, the DP charged that the early lead of Protestants in mission education had resulted in Protestant domination of appointed offices. In the predominantly Catholic Padhola area of West Budama in Bukedi District, only 9 of 31 nominated county council members were Catholic in 1956.[68]

After failing to forge an alliance with the Progressive Party, its Protestant counterpart, the DP embarked upon the task of building a mass base, recruiting in predominantly Catholic areas, also among Catholic Banyaruanda migrant labourers in Buganda and the Bunyoro in the 'lost counties'. In Kigezi, Ankole and West Nile, areas with limited export-commodity production, it did well. In regions with specific local grievances, it was even able to win Protestant support, as in Bunyoro where the UNC was linked to Buganda's control of the 'lost counties' and in eastern Acholi where the UNC was linked to Payera's claims to Acholi supremacy. But in some predominantly Catholic cotton-growing areas, the DP fought an uphill battle with the UNC's claim to represent the farmer. For example in Teso, a Catholic, C.J. Obwangor, led the UNC (later UPC) to victory in most areas, leaving the DP in power only in southern Teso.[69]

At the national level, both the Democratic Party's success in 1961 and its fall from power in 1962 hinged on animosity between the party and the Protestant-dominated Mengo hierarchy. When the Buganda government called for a boycott of the March 1961 parliamentary elections to press its claim for special constitutional status for Buganda, the Buganda DP ignored the boycott. In a Buganda turnout of less than 2 per cent of eligible voters, the DP swept 20 of 21 seats. Elsewhere the DP won 23 seats for a total 43 seats nationally, or a majority of the 82 seats.[70] Hence the first Prime Minister of Uganda, Benedicto Kiwanuka, was reviled by the Buganda government both for ignoring the boycott and for daring to place himself, a Catholic Muganda commoner, in a position superior to the Kabaka of Buganda. To remove the DP from power, the Buganda government entered party politics in collaboration with the populist alliance within and outside Buganda.

Whereas the Democratic Party maintained a continuous existence from 1956 through 1969, the Uganda National Congress dissolved into several factions in 1959, only to re-emerge as the alliance between the Uganda People's Congress and the Kabaka Yekka. The geneology of both these 'new' parties is outlined in Figure 4.1. Uganda People's Congress (UPC) was formed by a merger of Milton Obote's faction of the UNC and the Uganda People's Union in 1960. The origins of Kabaka Yekka (KY) are more complex. Having failed to obtain the political separation of Buganda from the rest of Uganda in 1960, and outraged at having been outmanoeuvred by the DP in the 1961 election, the Buganda government founded its party of the state – Kabaka Yekka ('the King alone') – controlled by the Kabaka through the chiefs.[71] It was immediately infiltrated by farmers and traders from the Uganda National Movement and from I.K. Musazi's faction of the UNC and professionals from the short-lived United National Party set up in 1960 as a Buganda counterpart of the UPC, controlled by professionals in consultation with the Kabaka.[72]

From the outset, and indeed prior to its formal founding by S.K. Masembe-Kabali, Kabaka Yekka was allied with Obote's UPC. According to Mutesa, the negotiations between himself and Milton Obote were arranged by Abu Mayanja and Daudi Ocheng soon after the 1961 election victory by the DP.[73] The UPC agreed to support Buganda's demands at the 1961 and 1962 constitutional negotiations in London for a federal post-colonial state with strongly entrenched powers for Buganda, postponement of settlement of the 'lost counties' dispute between Bunyoro and Buganda, allocation of key cabinet port-

Figure 4.1: Genealogy of Uganda People's Congress (UPC) and Kabaka Yekka (KY)

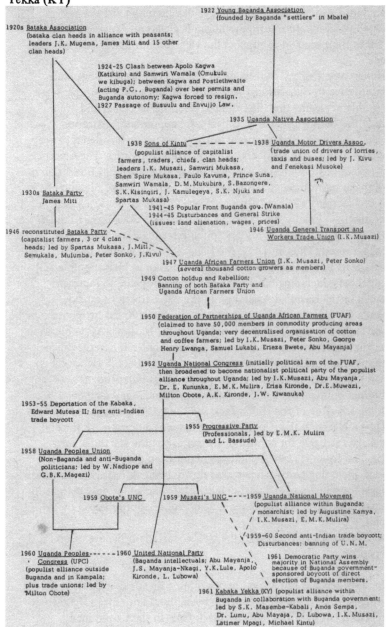

1922 Young Baganda Association
(founded by Baganda "settlers" in Mbale)

1920s Bataka Association
(bataka clan heads in alliance with peasants;
leaders J.K. Mugema, James Miti and 15 other
clan heads)

1924-25 Clash between Apolo Kagwa
(Katikiro) and Samwiri Wamala (Omukulu
we kibuga); between Kagwa and Postlethwaite
(acting P.C., Buganda) over beer permits and
Buganda autonomy; Kagwa forced to resign.
1927 Passage of Busuulu and Envujjo Law.

1935 Uganda Native Association

1938 Sons of Kintu — — — — — — 1938 Uganda Motor Drivers Assoc.
(populist alliance of capitalist   (trade union of drivers of lorries,
farmers, traders, chiefs, clan heads;   taxis and buses; led by J. Kivu
leaders I.K. Musazi, Samwiri Mukasa,   and Fenekasi Musoke)
Shem Spire Mukasa, Paulo Kavuma, Prince Suna,
Samwiri Wamala, D.M. Mukubira, S. Bazongere,
S.K. Kisingiri, J. Kamulegeya, S.K. Njuki and
Spartas Mukasa)

1930s Bataka Party
James Miti

1941-45 Popular Front Buganda gov. (Wamala)
1944-45 Disturbances and General Strike
(issues: land alienation, wages, prices)

1946 reconstituted Bataka Party   1946 Uganda General Transport and
(capitalist farmers, 3 or 4 clan   Workers Trade Union (I.K. Musazi)
heads; led by Spartas Mukasa, J. Miti,
Semukala, Mulumba, Peter Sonko, J. Kivu)

1947 Uganda African Farmers Union (I.K. Musazi, Peter Sonko)
(several thousand cotton growers as members)

1949 Cotton holdup and Rebellion;
Banning of both Bataka Party and
Uganda African Farmers Union

1950 Federation of Partnerships of Uganda African Farmers (FUAF)
(claimed to have 50,000 members in commodity producing areas
throughout Uganda; very decentralised organisation of cotton
and coffee farmers; led by I.K. Musazi, Peter Sonko, George
Henry Lwanga, Samuel Lukabi, Erieza Bwete, Abu Mayanja)

1952 Uganda National Congress (initially political arm of the FUAF,
then broadened to become nationalist political party of the populist
alliance throughout Uganda; led by I.K. Musazi, Abu Mayanja,
Dr. E. Kununka, E.M.K. Mulira, Erisa Kironde, Dr. E. Muwazi,
Milton Obote, A.K. Kironde, J.W. Kiwanuka)

1953-55 Deportation of the Kabaka,
Edward Mutesa II; first anti-Indian
trade boycott

1955 Progressive Party
(Professionals, led by E.M.K. Mulira
and L. Bassude)

1958 Uganda Peoples Union
(Non-Baganda and anti-Buganda
politicians; led by W. Nadiope and
G.B.K. Magezi)

1959 Obote's UNC   1959 Musazi's UNC — — — 1959 Uganda National Movement
(populist alliance within Buganda;
monarchist; led by Augustine Kamya,
I.K. Musazi, E.M.K. Mulira)

1959-60 Second anti-Indian trade boycott;
Disturbances; banning of U.N.M.

1960 Uganda Peoples — — — — — 1960 United National Party
Congress (UPC)   (Baganda intellectuals; Abu Mayanja,
(populist alliance outside   J.S. Mayanja-Nkagi, Y.K. Lule, Apolo
Buganda and in Kampala;   Kironde, L. Lubowa)
plus trade unions; led by
Milton Obote)

1961 Democratic Party wins
majority in National Assembly
because of Buganda government-
sponsored boycott of direct
election of Buganda members.

1961 Kabaka Yekka (KY) (populist alliance within
Buganda in collaboration with Buganda government;
led by S.K. Masembe-Kabali, Amos Sempa,
Dr. Lumu, Abu Mayaja, D. Lubowa, I.K. Musazi,
Latimer Mpagi, Michael Kintu)

folios to Baganda in the post-colonial state, and indirect election of
Buganda's representatives to the National Assembly. The UPC also
entered into a semi-secret agreement to designate the Kabaka as head
of state in Uganda. In return, the Buganda government agreed to block
the DP in Buganda and to support the UPC in forming the post-colonial
regime.[74]

Having won the key concession of indirect election of Buganda's
representative to the National Assembly, the Buganda government had
few problems rigging the 1961 Lukiko elections to defeat and even
exclude the Democratic Party. Chiefs were appointed registration
officers for the election; electoral districts were gerrymandered to keep
religion – that is, the Democratic Party – out of politics. The Chairman
of the Elections Committee was Abu Mayanja, Minister of Education in
the Kabaka's government and treasurer of Kabaka Yekka; the Supervisor of Elections was Fred Mpanga, Legal Officer to the Kabaka's
government.[75] Finally the campaign by Kabaka Yekka against the DP
was fought on the issue of loyalty to the Buganda government and the
Kabaka himself. Thus, in 1962, the Kabaka Yekka won 63 of 66
elected seats in the Buganda Lukiko. The Lukiko in turn appointed 21
KY members, including one Indian and one European, to represent
Buganda in the National Assembly. In the 1962 elections outside
Buganda for seats in the National Assembly, the UPC led by Obote won
37 seats; the DP won 24. Final standings in the National Assembly were
somewhat different since the National Assembly itself had the power
to appoint nine additional 'specially elected' members.[76] Hence the
UPC-KY coalition won control of state power at independence.

Formal political independence came to Uganda on 9 October 1962
with the lowering of the Union Jack and the hoisting of the red, yellow
and black Ugandan flag. Political independence did not mark the end
of the class struggle for control of the state, but the start of a new
phase. The colonial state apparatus had not been dismantled, but its
salariat, including army officers, was slowly being Africanised. The class
struggle for control of the post-colonial state had so far only marginally
affected control of the economy and control of appropriation of
surplus.

As the Secretary-General of the UPC observed on the eve of political
independence:

Independence is not an end by itself but a means to a greater
struggle . . . To the UPC, Independence should not mean the mere
replacement of White faces by Black faces in the Government

machinery nor the acquisition of mansions and latest fashionable cars by a few top leaders, while everything in the country-side continues to be as it was under Imperialism.[77]

Political independence had not resolved the contradiction between producers and non-producers; between commodity-producing areas and labour-exporting areas; between Buganda and the rest of Uganda. It had changed the political parameters within which class contradictions would henceforth operate.

Analysis of Occupational Backgrounds in the 1962 National Assembly

Autobiographical information supplied by members of the National Assembly in *Who's Who in East Africa,*[78] was analysed to compare differences in occupational backgrounds of parliamentary members of the three political parties: UPC, KY and DP. Aside from problems of objectivity in the data source, such an analysis tells us little about ordinary party members and provides only a partial picture of the leadership since parliamentary members were only one element of the leadership. None the less, the lack of subsequent elections led to atrophy in the extra-parliamentary organisations of these political parties. Hence, an analysis of the occupational backgrounds of parliamentary members provides information about the class origins if not the class interests of individuals who in their own right were to become increasingly powerful patrons and dispensers of privilege in Uganda in the 1960s.

The major finding was that there were few significant differences among the occupational backgrounds of the parliamentary representatives of the three political parties. The overwhelming majority, 75.7 per cent of the 37 elected UPC members, 83.3 per cent of the 24 elected DP members, and 85.7 per cent of the 21 Lukiko nominated KY members, were drawn from the ranks of teachers, professionals and the administrative salariat.[79] None the less, using Fisher's exact test,[80] it was found that some differences between the UPC and the KY members and one difference between the KY and the DP members were statistically significant at the 0.05 level.

Surprisingly, none of the KY members identified themselves as having been associated with agricultural co-operatives or, less surprisingly, with trade unions, whereas almost one fourth of UPC members in the National Assembly reported either agricultural co-operative or trade union backgrounds.[81] Almost one half of the KY members were professionals in a capacity other than teachers, whereas only one fifth of UPC members were professionals in a capacity other than teachers.[82] Both these differences were statistically significant.

As might have been expected, there were noticeable differences among the three parties in the proportion of parliamentary representatives who identified themselves as businessmen: KY, 33.3 per cent; UPC, 24.3 per cent; and DP, only 8.3 per cent. But only the difference between the KY and the DP in the proportion of parliamentary members identifying themselves as businessmen was statistically significant at the 0.05 level.[83]

A breakdown of reported occupational backgrounds of members of the National Assembly is presented in Table 4.1. It should be noted that there is considerable overlap between categories since most members listed two or more occupations and since it proved impossible to determine a member's primary occupation. Furthermore, in a state whose leader verbally espoused socialism by 1964, parliamentary members might have been somewhat less than open in reporting their extra-parliamentary capitalist ventures, particularly those acquired through exercise of political power.[84] Parliamentary representatives who reported their business interests in the 1970 debate on the Prevention of Corruption Bill were subjected to interruptions and abuse by more powerful representatives who presumably had even more extensive business interests to conceal. Moreover, although capitalist farmers were not much in evidence among the reported occupations of KY representatives in the National Assembly (less than 10 per cent), capitalist farmers controlled well over a third of the elected seats in the Buganda Lukiko which had considerable autonomous power under the 1962 constitution.

To the extent that parliamentary representatives were leaders of their respective parties (the 'big men'), the commanding heights of all three political parties by 1962 were controlled by that portion of the populist alliance which by 1962, was also beginning to take effective control of the salariat of the post-colonial state. However, the salariat was not yet a conscious class, but rather a class in formation and even a class already divided not only by region but by the contradiction between the goal of state control of the economy through the salariat and the individualistic goal of having a private business outside state control. Outside Buganda populist alliance pressure for Africanisation of trade was tempered by knowledge that rapid Africanisation would primarily benefit Baganda traders who might then use commercial power in trade as a base for increased political control over the state.

Table 4.1: Occupational Backgrounds of Members of Uganda Parliament, 1962

Party	UPC		DP		KY	
N =	37		24		21	
Occupation	N	%	N	%	N	%
Public administration	13	35.1	8	33.3	8	38.1
Professional	7	18.9	5	20.8	10	47.6
Teacher, headmaster	13	35.1	12	50.0	8	38.1
Businessman	9	24.3	2	8.3	7	33.3
Farmer	2	5.4	1	4.2	2	9.5
Labour union, growers' co-operatives	9	24.3	3	12.5	0	0
Army, police, prisons	1	2.7	2	8.3	2	9.5
None of above or no information	7	18.9	3	12.5	3	14.3

Sources: List of members, Uganda, *Parliamentary Debates; Official Proceedings,* Second Series, 1 (1962). 1962 political party membership, F.W. Welbourn, *Religion and Politics in Uganda, 1952-1962* (Nairobi: East African Publishing House, 1965), pp. 67-9. Occupational backgrounds, E.G. Wilson (ed.), *Who's Who in East Africa, 1965-66* (Nairobi: Marco Publishers Ltd, 1966).
Notes: Most members listed two or more occupations, hence percentages do not total 100%. Comparison of percentages should be done cautiously because the number of cases is small. The category 'professional' includes the following: doctor, barrister-at-law, veterinarian, journalist, surveyor, health inspector and agronomist. The list of members includes those nominated by the Buganda Lukiko, but excludes the 9 'specially elected' members chosen by the National Assembly.

Notes

1. Walter Elkan, *An African Labour Force: Two Case Studies in East African Employment* (Kampala: East African Institute of Social Research, 1956), pp. 9, 11; and Azarias Baryaruha, *Factors Affecting Industrial Employment; A Study of Ugandan Experience 1954 to 1956* (Nairobi: Oxford University Press for the East African Institute of Social Research, 1967), pp. 38, 47, 56 and 69.

2. In 1949 Mukherjee described some members of the 'nascent bourgeoisie' in Gulu, Acholi. The founders of the Acholi Bus Company included the headmaster of a Church Missionary Society school and a former county chief who also lent money to smaller Indian shopkeepers. The children of the ex-chief included a Sub-Inspector of Police, a secondary school headmaster, a student at Makerere College and a secondary school teacher. The ex-chief's son-in-law was a doctor and close relative of a third partner in the bus company. Ramkrishna Mukherjee, *The Problem of Uganda* (Berlin:Akademie-Verlag, 1956), p. 206.

3. Aidan W. Southall and Peter C.W. Gutkind, *Townsmen in the Making; Kampala and Its Suburbs* (Kampala: East African Institute of Social Research, 1957), pp. 63-5, 84-8.

4. The NCSA was renamed the Government Native Employees' Association in 1923, the British Government African Employees' Association in 1934 and the Uganda African Civil Servants' Association in 1939. Nizar Motani, *On His*

Majesty's Service in Uganda (Syracuse: Maxwell School, 1978).

5. Mamdani dates the founding of the Young Baganda Association to 1915 as a forerunner of the NCSA, but Motani's history of the NCSA treats the Young Baganda Association as an entirely separate association founded in 1919. On the other hand, Apter dates the Young Baganda Association to 1922 as an organisation of Baganda 'settlers' in Mbale, Eastern Province. Finally, Clayton and Savage state that Harry Thuku's Young Kikuyu Association, founded in 1921, was modelled on the 'vocal effective' Young Baganda Association. Mahmood Mamdani, *Politics and Class Formation in Uganda* (New York and London: Monthly Review Press, 1976), p. 164; Nizar Motani, 'The Ugandan Civil Service and the Asian Problem, 1894-1972', *Expulsion of a Minority*, ed. Michael Twaddle (London: University of London, Athlone Press, 1975), p. 101; David . Apter, *The Political Kingdom in Uganda*, 2nd edn (Princeton: Princeton University Press, 1967), p. 213; and Anthony Clayton and Donald C. Savage, *Government and Labour in Kenya, 1895-1963* (London: Frank Cass, 1974), p. 120. Similarly, Lord Hailey dates the Young Lango Association to 1944 as a movement opposed to autocratic chiefs, whereas Gertzel dates its founding to 1937 as an association of teachers and county chiefs interested in getting council representation to push for improvements in education. Lord Hailey, *Native Administration in the British African Territories, Part I* (London: HMSO, 1950), p. 61; and Cherry Gertzel, *Party and Locality in Northern Uganda, 1945-1962* (London: University of London, Athlone Press, 1974), pp. 31 and 35, but see also p. 28. On the Toro, Bugwere, Bugisu and Acholi associations, see Mamdani, *Politics and Class Formation*, p. 171; Apter, *The Political Kingdom*, p. 218; and Gertzel, *Party and Locality*, p. 58.

6. Roger J. Southall, *Parties and Politics in Bunyoro* (Kampala: MISR, 1972), pp. 10-14; Andrew D. Roberts, 'The "Lost Counties" of Bunyoro', *Uganda Journal*, vol. 26, no. 2 (September 1962), pp. 194-9; and Great Britain, Parliament, *Parliamentary Papers* (Commons) *1961-62* (XI 1119), 'Report of a Commission of Privy Counsellors on a Dispute Between Buganda and Bunyoro', Cmnd. 1717.

7. Cyril Ehrlich, 'The Marketing of Cotton in Uganda, 1900-1950; A Case Study of Colonial Government Economic Policy', PhD Thesis, London University, 1958, pp. 193, 198-9.

8. The ginneries' control of cotton transportation may help explain why Uganda had only 1,813 registered motor lorries by 1934, whereas the Gold Coast (Ghana) with about the same size and population, yet a less bulky export crop, had 4,141 lorries in 1932. Great Britain, Colonial Office, *An Economic Survey of the Colonial Empire (1932)*, Colonial Office No. 95 (London: HMSO, 1934), p. 85; and Harold Beken Thomas and Robert Scott, *Uganda* (London: Humphrey Milford and Oxford University Press, 1935), p. 239.

9. Apter, *The Political Kingdom*, p. 204; and I.K. Musazi, 'Strikes and Disturbances in Uganda: Their Origins and Results', in Milton Obote Foundation, *Labour Problems in Uganda* (Kampala: Milton Obote Foundation, 1966), pp. 17-25.

10. Peter C.W. Gutkind, *The Royal Capital of Buganda* (The Hague: Mouton and Company, 1963), pp. 72-5 and Appendix, 'Administration of Kibuga 1909-1958'; and Apter, *The Political Kingdom*, pp. 202-14.

11. Biographical information as supplied by Musazi to E.G. Wilson (ed.), *Who's Who in East Africa, 1965-66* (Nairobi: Marco Publishers Ltd, 1966); and information gathered from *Voice of Uganda*, 1974.

12. Apter, *The Political Kingdom*, p. 213.

13. Daudi Musoke Mukubira was the author of *Buganda Nyaffe*. See Gutkind, *The Royal Capital of Buganda*, p. 38; and Uganda, *Report of the Commission of Inquiry into the Disturbances in Uganda during April 1949* (Entebbe: Government

Printer, 1950), p. 109.

14. Musazi, 'Strikes and Disturbances in Uganda', p. 19; and Colonial Office, *Annual Report on Uganda, 1946,* pp. 3, 91. Figures exclude the many forced labourers in the East African Military Labour Service. Acutely aware of the limited paid employment opportunities for returning servicemen (6,000 demobilised drivers, for example, versus only 300 to 600 openings for drivers) and alert to the political potential of soldiers who had fought 'for democracy' overseas, the colonial state set up programmes to persuade demobilised soldiers to return to the land and warned officials not to encourage the formation of ex-soldier associations. With their savings, many returned soldiers attempted to enter trade. That comparatively few were successful is indicated by the fact that there were only 11,600 African retailers in 1952. Uganda, *Report of the Civil Reabsorption and Rehabilitation Committee* (Entebbe: Government Printer, 1945), pp. 3-4, 10-12, 14-15; and Uganda, *Sessional Paper No. 4 of 1956/57; Despatch from the Governor of Uganda . . . on the Subject of the Report of the East Africa Royal Commission* (Entebbe: Government Printer 1956), p. 10.

15. Uganda, *Report of the Commission of Inquiry into the Disturbances which Occurred in Uganda during January 1945* (Entebbe: Government Printer, 1945); and Apter, *The Political Kingdom*, pp. 228-9.

16. Apter, *The Political Kingdom*, p. 230.

17. Uganda, *Report of the Commission of Inquiry into the Disturbances in Uganda during April 1949* (Entebbe: Government Printer, 1950), pp. 100-18.

18. Ibid., pp. 85-100; and Apter, *The Political Kingdom*, p. 241.

19. Uganda, Co-operative Societies Ordinance of 1946, sections 33.4, 41.1 and 56.1, as cited in A.B. Mukwaya, 'The Rise of the Uganda African Farmers' Union in Buganda, 1947-1949', Paper presented to East African Institute of Social Research Conference, Moshi, Tanganyika, June 1957, p. 5.

20. Mukwaya, 'The Rise of the Uganda African Farmers' Union', p. 2; George Shepherd, Jr., *They Wait in Darkness*, (New York: John Day Company, 1955), pp. 221-54; and Musazi, 'Strikes and Disturbances in Uganda'. An American, Shepherd served two years as General Manager of the Federation of Partnerships of Uganda African Farmers in the early 1950s, working closely with Musazi, Mayanja and Henry Lwanga. After turning his post over to John Stonehouse, Shepherd toured the United States to raise money for the co-operative movement in Uganda, but was unable to return to Uganda. In the darkness of the McCarthy era, the US government refused to renew Shepherd's passport.

21. Uganda, *Annual Report of the Department of Agriculture 1960,* Appendix II (d), p. 35.

22. Mukwaya, 'The Rise of the Uganda African Farmers' Union', pp. 3-4.

23. The terms of reference of the commission specifically *excluded* examining either the disparity between grower prices and world prices or the entry of growers into crop-processing and marketing. Uganda, *Report of the Uganda Cotton Industry Commission 1948* (Entebbe: Government Printer, 1948), p. 5 (terms of references) and pp. 13-22 (cheating of growers by ginneries).

24. Uganda, *Report of the Commission of Inquiry into the Disturbances in Uganda during April 1949*, p. 76.

25. Ibid., p. 78; and Shepherd, *They Wait in Darkness*, pp. 18-20.

26. Uganda, *Report of the Commission of Inquiry into the Disturbances in Uganda during April 1949*, p. 16. By barring the producer from possession of the product of his own labours, the colonial state reduced the 'independent' grower to a status little better than that of a piece-worker. Yet the state rejected the idea of compelling ginneries to gin other people's cotton as 'an unwarrantable interference with liberty'. Ibid., p. 69.

27. Ibid., pp. 16, 79-80.

28. Ibid., p. 23.

29. Ibid., pp. 25-65. In the *kibuga* itself (*kibuga*: the capital of Buganda which bordered Kampala), 115 buildings were burned.

30. Ibid., pp. 47-8, 78-81; and Uganda, *Annual Report of the Department of Agriculture 1960*, Appendix II (d), p. 35.

31. Great Britain, *Parliamentary Papers* (Commons) *1953/54* XXV 239), 'Withdrawal of Recognition from Kabaka Mutesa II of Buganda', Cmd. 9028; Great Britain, *Parliamentary Papers* (Commons) *1953/54* (XXV 285), 'Report of the Namirembe Conference', Cmd. 9320; Uganda, *Sessional Paper No. 4 of 1956/57; Despatch from the Governor of Uganda*, p. 17; and Uganda, *Annual Report of the Department of Agriculture, 1960*, pp. 5-6, 8-9.

32. Uganda, *Sessional Paper No. 4 of 1956/57*, p. 20; and Uganda, *1965 Statistical Abstract*, p. 72.

33. Henry Olivier, 'Some Aspects of the Owen Falls Scheme', *Uganda Journal*, vol. 17, no. 1 (March 1953), p. 30; and Uganda, *1965 Statistical Abstract*, p. 5.

34. Whereas the 1955 Committee on the Advancement of Africans in Trade called for more *loan* facilities for African traders, the colonial state responded with a call for more *savings* facilities for African traders. Uganda, *Government Statement on the Report of the Committee to Make Recommendations for the Advancement of Africans in Trade and Commerce* (Entebbe: Government Printer, 1955), p. 3. The three British banks were the only commercial banks in Uganda until 1950. Between 1906 and 1949, they established ten branches, all in four towns: Kampala (3), Jinja (3), Mbale (3) and Entebbe (1). Suddenly in the 1950s, the banks added 12 towns to the network, opening 20 branches and 5 agencies in the 'new' towns and a further 12 branches and one agency in the four 'old' towns. Whereas the British banks accounted for four-fifths of the 'up-country' expansion, two-thirds of the new branches in the 'old' towns were opened by 'new' banks: Uganda Credit and Savings Bank (Uganda Commercial Bank after 1965), Bank of India, Bank of Baroda, and the Nederlandsche Handel-Maatschappij (Algemene Bank after 1964). Irving Gershenberg, *Commercial Banking in Uganda* (Kampala: MISR, 1973), pp. 4-5, 28-9, and 44.

35. V.M. Clerk, representing the India-based cotton firm of Narandas Rajaram, referred to the £22 million in the Price Stabilisation Fund as 'exploitation of the African masses'. Uganda Chamber of Commerce (UCC), 'Notes of a Meeting Between Representatives of the UCC and the Right Honourable James Griffiths, Secretary of State for the Colonies', 16 May 1951, UCC Archives, Makerere University Library, Kampala. The UCC executive committee, headed by H.R. Fraser of the leading coffee firm of A. Baumann, objected to state ownership of industry on several grounds, including the allegation that in a state-owned industry, 'African participation cannot exist in any form other than that of employed persons.' For the moment, however, the Chamber felt African participation at any higher level was 'far beyond his capabilities', UCC, 'Nationalization of Uganda's Industries', 11 May 1951, UCC Archives, Makerere University Library.

36. After receiving the original indent (purchase order) from an Asian or European importer in Uganda, a British manufacturer or supplier presented the indent and copies of the invoice and bill of lading to a London factor for discounted payment. The London factor allowed the importer up to 180 days (technically, the United Kingdom to Uganda transportation time) in which to repay. The importer in turn sold the bill of lading for the shipped goods to a local wholesaler in exchange for a promissory note, which was discounted for cash at a bank branch in Uganda. With either the bill of lading or the actual landed goods, the wholesaler sold the imported goods to sub-wholesalers and/or retailers in exchange for promissory notes, which were discounted at local banks. Hence, a

single consignment of goods exchanged hands many times before its actual
arrival, and generated a pyramid of loans totalling several times its value because
of the 'float' created by the chain of promissory notes not yet due. Ultimately
the promissory notes were secured, not by the consignment, but by real estate:
the shop, store or go-down (warehouse) belonging to the merchant or trader. Even
so, a large chunk of the commercial banks' assets consisted of promissory notes
and other discounted receivables generated by the import trade. Interview with
Ismaili merchant, Kampala, September 1970; and John Stonehouse, *Prohibited
Immigrant* (London: Bodley Head, 1960), p. 91.

37. Although Cohen optimistically estimated a rise in both the number of
African retailers (from 11,600 to 14,000) and the African share of retail trade
(from one-third to one-half) between 1952 and 1956, Wrigley presents the more
sober estimate that, by 1962, Africans comprised 75 per cent of all retailers, but
carried only one-third of the retail trade volume. The 1966 Census of Distribution
estimated there were only 14,000 retailers of all races. The census was silent on
the racial distribution of either ownership of retail firms or trade volume. Of 111
large retail firms (10 or more employees), 45 had an annual turnover of Shs. 2
million or more; none were African owned. Uganda, *Sessional Paper No. 4 of
1956/57; Despatch from the Governor*, p. 10; Christopher Wrigley, 'The
Changing Economic Structure of Buganda', *The King's Men*, ed. Lloyd A. Fallers
(London: Oxford University Press, 1964), pp. 50-1; and Uganda, *Census of
Distribution*, vol. I (1967), p. 25, and vol. II (1969), p. 3.

38. Gutkind, *The Royal Capital of Buganda*, pp. 40-52.

39. Uganda, *The Geographical Income of Uganda, 1957* (Entebbe: Government Printer, 1958), p. 5.

40. 'Memorandum by the Great Lukiko', September 1953, as reprinted in
Great Britain, *Parliamentary Papers* (Commons) *1953/54* (XXV 239), Cmd.
9028, 'Withdrawal of Recognition from Kabaka Mutesa II of Buganda', Appendix
F, p. 30.

41. E.M.K. Mulira, 'Why I am in the Uganda National Movement', May 1959,
in *Mind of Buganda*, ed. Donald Anthony Low (Berkeley and Los Angeles:
University of California Press, 1971), pp. 196-9; Edward Mutesa, *Desecration of
My Kingdom* (London: Constable, 1967), pp. 153-5; and 'Buganda Has Sunk to
the Lowest Conditon', editorial, *Munno*, 18 July 1959, p. 5 (tr. by Gerald
Kibirige).

42. Great Britain, 'Withdrawl of Recognition from Kabaka Mutesa II of
Buganda', Cmd. 9028, p. 4.

43. Apter, *The Political Kingdom*, p. 294.

44. Grace S.K. Ibingira, *The Forging of an African Nation* (Kampala: Uganda
Publishing House and New York: Viking Press, 1973), p. 27, on the colonial
state's veto of the 1925 meeting; and Uganda, *Report of the Uganda Development Commission, 1920*, p. 16,on the need to stimulate inter-tribal rivalry among
workers.

45. Great Britain, 'Withdrawal of Recognition from Kabaka Mutesa II of
Buganda', Cmd. 9029; and 'Report of the Namirembe Conference', Cmd. 9320.

46. This is an estimate extrapolated from the proportion of African traders
resident in Buganda. In 1953, of 11,634 African traders in Uganda, 6,683 were
residents of Buganda. Uganda Protectorate, *Advancement of Africans in Trade*,
p. 15, as cited in Lloyd A. Fallers, S. Elkan, F.K. Kamoga, and S.B.K. Musoke, 'The
Modernization of Social Stratification', *The King's Men*, ed. L.A. Fallers
(London: Oxford University Press, 1964), p. 145.

47. Thus, the two political parties controlled largely by professionals, the
Democratic Party and the Progressive Party, opposed Buganda's separation.

48. According to the 1959 population census, 45.1 per cent (828,027) of the

1,834, 128 African inhabitants of Buganda were non-Baganda. The figure includes the 57,887 Banyoro in the 'lost counties'. Uganda, *1965 Statistical Abstract*, p. 10.

49. See the Lukiko's Memorandum on independent status for Buganda, September 1960, as found in Apter, *The Political Kingdom*, pp. 479-88.

50. 'Progressive Party Manifesto, 1955', in *Mind of Buganda*, ed. D.A. Low, pp. 183-90. Low attributes the party's lack of success outside Buganda to the manifesto's excessive use of Luganda terms and idioms. See also Apter, *The Political Kingdom*, pp. 337-40.

51. B.O. Bowles, 'Economic Anti-Colonialism and British Reaction in Uganda, 1936-1965', *Canadian Journal of African Studies*, vol. 9, no. 1 (1975), pp. 56-7. Support for the UNC's successor, the Uganda People's Party (UPC), in the 1962 election also varied in proportion to each district's level of cotton production. We exclude Buganda, which did not have direct elections for parliamentary representatives in that year. In the remaining 12 districts, the correlation coefficient between the UPC's share of the total vote and seed cotton output per capita was 0.579. Using an alternate measure, the dichotomous variable of *1* if cotton acreage per capita were above the Uganda mean and *0* if acreage were below the mean, the point biserial correlation between acreage and the UPC's share of the vote was 0.638.

52. Apter, *The Political Kingdom*, p. 320.

53. Ibid., pp. 316-22. Assuming traders to be socially superior to farmers, Apter was puzzled (p. 322) by the fact that some politician-traders hoped to become farmers. By drawing a distinction between small-scale cultivators and capitalist farmers, it is possible to resolve the ambiguity. A small-scale cultivator entered petty trade in order to accumulate sufficient savings to return to the land as a large-scale farmer, producing on the basis of wage-labour rather than just family labour.

54. Gertzel, *Party and Locality*, pp. 34-49.

55. Ibid., pp. 60-70.

56. Southall, *Parties and Politics in Bunyoro*.

57. Great Britain, 'Report of the Namirembe Conference', Cmd. 9320; Stonehouse, *Prohibited Immigrant*, pp. 107-10; Apter, *The Political Kingdom*, pp. 276-300; and Gertzel, *Party and Locality*, p. 37.

58. Donald Anthony Low, 'Political Parties in Uganda, 1949-1962', *Buganda in Modern History* (Berkeley and Los Angeles: University of California Press, 1971), pp. 190-2; and Apter, *The Political Kingdom*, pp. 372-89.

59. Gertzel, *Party and Locality*, pp. 44-6.

60. Ibid., pp. 70-6.

61. Bowles, 'Economic Anti-Colonialism', pp. 56-9; Great Britain, 'Withdrawal of Recognition from Kabaka Mutesa II of Buganda', Cmd. 9028, p. 6; and Uganda, *Sessional Paper No. 4 of 1956/57; Despatch from the Governor*.

62. Even so, there was slow progress in Africanising the higher civil service. By 1960, Africans held only 16.5 per cent (193) of the 1,171 posts in the A and B scale of the civil service. Uganda, *Report of the Public Service Commission 1960*, p. 10. African teachers became pensionable only in 1952, had their salaries raised in 1956, and won a non-contributory pension plan in 1958. Uganda, *Annual Report of the Education Department, 1960*.

63. Cf. Mamdani, *Politics and Class Formation*, pp. 216-20.

64. Apter, *The Political Kingdom*, pp. 340-4.

65. F.B. Welbourn, *Religion and Politics in Uganda, 1952-62* (Nairobi: East African Publishing House, 1965), pp. 37-8. On the other hand, some colonial officials, alarmed at the socialist rhetoric of the UNC (UPC), viewed the DP as a moderate alternative.

66. Ibid., p. 17.

67. Audrey I. Richards and B.K. Taylor, 'The Toro', and D.J. Stenning, 'The Nyankole', *East African Chiefs*, ed. Audrey Richards (New York: Frederick A. Praeger, 1959), pp. 143 and 171; and Welbourn, *Religion and Politics*, p. 68.

68. Gertzel, *Party and Locality*, p. 71; and Fred. G. Burke, *Local Government and Politics in Uganda* (Syracuse, N.Y.: Syracuse University Press, 1964), p. 200.

69. Welbourn, *Religion and Politics*, pp. 37-41, 68-9; and Burke, *Local Government and Politics*, pp. 152-4. See also footnote 51.

70. Welbourn, *Religion and Politics*, pp. 22-4; Terence J. Hopkins, 'Politics in Uganda: The Buganda Question', *Boston University Papers on Africa: Transition in African Politics*, ed. Jeffrey Butler and A.A. Castagno (New York: Praeger, 1967), pp. 256-7; and Mutesa, *Desecration of My Kingdom*, pp. 158-9.

71. Audrey I. Richards, 'Epilogue', *The King's Men*, ed. L.A. Fallers, pp. 356-94; Cherry Gertzel, 'How Kabaka Yekka Came to Be', *Africa Report*, vol. 9 (October 1964), pp. 9-13; and I.R. Hancock, 'Patriotism and Neo-Traditionalism in Buganda; The Kabaka Yekka Movement, 1961-62', *Journal of African History*, vol. 11, no. 3 (1970), pp. 419-34.

72. On the United National Party, see Apter, *The Political Kingdom*, p. 348.

73. Mutesa, *Desecration of My Kingdom*, p. 160. Ibingira's version of these events has B.K. Kirya and Ibingira persuading a recalcitrant Obote and evasive Baganda to forge the UPC-KY alliance. Grace Ibingira, *The Forging of an African Nation* (New York: Viking Press, 1973), p. 202.

74. Mutesa, *Desecration of My Kingdom*, p. 160.

75. Ibid., pp. 160-4.

76. Welbourn, *Religion and Politics*, p. 33.

77. Ibid., pp. 33-4; Hopkins, 'Politics in Uganda', p. 257 and 262. Six of the nine specially selected seats went to the UPC, three to Kabaka Yekka. Total standings in the National Assembly were therefore as follows: UPC 43; KY 24; and DP 24.

78. John Kakonge, then Secretary-General of the UPC, in UPC, *Second Annual Delegates' Conference, Mbale 4th, 5th and 6th August 1962* (Conference Programme), p. 5.

79. E.G. Wilson (ed.), *Who's Who in East Africa, 1965-66* (Nairobi: Marco Publishers Ltd, 1966).

80. Unlike Table 4.1, these figures control for overlap in members reporting two or more occupations.

81. The null-hypothesis, that differences in occupational background of members of the National Assembly from two different parties were due to chance, was tested using Fisher's exact probability test for a 2 by 2 table. This consists of calculating 'the total probability of the observed distribution and of all less likely ones in the same direction, that is, for all values of d from 0 up to the observed value' of d, where d is the smallest cell frequency. J.F. Kenney and E.S. Keeping, *Mathematics of Statistics*, Part Two, 2nd edn. (New York: D. Van Nostrand, 1951), p. 231. Hence for a given distribution

	X	not X
Y	a	b
not Y	c	d

where d is the smallest frequency, and X and Y are attributes or treatments,

$$p' = \frac{(a+b)! \ (c+d)! \ (a+c)! \ (b+d)!}{N! \ a! \ b! \ c! \ d!}$$

and $P = p'_0 + p'_1 + p'_2 + \ldots + p'_d.$

82. The contingency table was as follows:

Party vs. Occupation	Trade union or agric. co-op.	No trade union or agricultural co-op.
UPC	9	28
Kabaka Yekka	0	21

since the smallest cell frequency is zero, $P = p'_d$ or 0.01168.

83. The contingency table was as follows:

Party vs. Occupation	Professionals (excl. teachers)	Non professionals (incl. teachers)
UPC	7	30
Kabaka Yekka	10	11

The smallest cell frequency is 7. $P = 0.02325$, since $p'_7 = 0.01838$, $p'_6 = 0.00415$, $p'_5 = 0.00649$, etc.

84. The contingency table was as follows:

Party vs. Occupation	Businessmen (merchant, trader or manager)	Non-businessmen
Democratic Party	2	22
Kabaka Yekka	7	14

$P = 0.04206$.
($P = 0.03622 + 0.00551 + 0.00033$).

5 THE POLITICAL ECONOMY OF THE OBOTE REGIME, 1962-71

In 1962, the Secretary-General of the UPC declared the overriding economic goal of the Obote regime to be the transformation of political independence into economic independence.[1] Although this goal could command widespread popular support, the regime's strategy for achieving it revealed two faulty assumptions.

Map 2: Uganda, 1967 District Boundaries

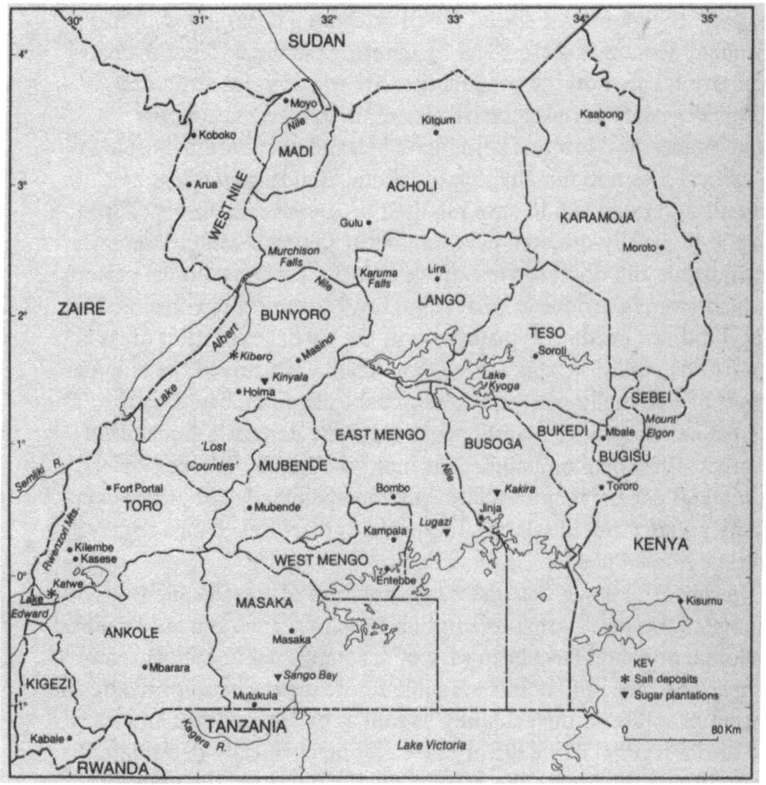

The first assumption was that the UPC was a party of the masses, 'the common man', and that the Africanised state bureaucracy could be transformed into an instrument to serve the needs of the people in 'fighting ignorance, disease and poverty' — to use the oft-heard UPC slogan. This assumption ignored the fact that the UPC's own base and that of the administrative salariat lay within the domestic coalition which had supported and benefited from the dependent pattern of development during the colonial occupation, particularly the post-war phase. The political and administrative cadres of the regime were part of the problem as elements in the 'infrastructure of dependence',[2] rather than instruments of progressive social change.

The second assumption was that the structure of the Ugandan economy could be redirected from a dependent to a more equal relationship with the external economy through the following reforms: diversified sources and types of foreign 'aid', diversified trade links, increased import substitution and expanded state control of the economy. By ignoring the need for an integrated economy with inter-dependent economic sectors and by ignoring the need to build a party organisation based on the producing strata to carry out structural reforms necessary for progressive economic transformation, the regime's piecemeal reforms perpetuated Uganda's subordinate role in the vertical international division of labour. Building an integrated domestic economy would have required progressive income redistribution and internally-oriented development planning based on domestic human needs and domestic resources, a shift from the colonial pattern in which Uganda produced what it did not consume and consumed what it did not produce.[3] Instead, with the partial exception of its import-substitution strategy, the Obote regime continued the colonial pattern of externally-oriented development planning, based on the external demands of the world market and the domestic demands of the urban elite. Economic independence was thereby reduced to multilateral dependence and nationalised dependency structures operated by an Africanised salariat, rather than structural change to serve domestic human needs.

This is not to argue that the transformation of the Ugandan economy from its external orientation to self-reliance and auto-centred development would have been easy or accomplished in a short span of time. The range of choices available to the regime was limited by the existing structure of the economy as well as by the political and social base of the regime. While history does not mechanically determine the future, it does determine the present, thereby limiting the range of future possibilities by closing off certain options. As a consequence of Uganda's incorporation into the capitalist world economy at the turn of the century,

the option facing the Obote regime was not a *tabula rasa* choice
between absolute economic dependence and absolute economic
independence *vis-à-vis* the international economic system, but rather
a choice between *continuing* to support the 'inherited' structure of
dependence and *beginning* to build an integrated economy thereby
creating the possibility for building socialism.[4]

At the outset, however, the *mode* of Uganda's incorporation into the
world economy — peasant production of agricultural commodities by
family and migratory labour — determined the economic and social
parameters of the problems and options facing the Obote regime.

The Politics of Buying Time: The Changing Alliances of the Obote Regime

Having neglected to build a political movement based on the organisation of the productive strata (agricultural labourers, peasants and
workers), or more accurately, having refrained from doing so by an
accurate assessment of what the colonial state expected of a
'responsible' nationalist movement, the UPC drew most of its active
support from professionals, teachers, the salariat, 'white-collar' trade
unionists, and political notables in Kampala and outside Buganda. In
order to attain control of the post-colonial state, and in order to remain
in power, the party was forced to make further compromises with the
other elements of the infrastructure of dependence.

Compromising alliances with elements of the infrastructure of
dependence could be justified as part of a strategy of buying time. An
alliance might be struck with one element or strata within the infrastructure of dependence at a given point in time in order to challenge
and defeat a second element or strata, thereby remaining in power to
challenge the first element or strata at a later point in time. This was
the essence of Obote's strategy.

The UPC regime consisted of the party itself, its current allies, plus
the state salariat. Between 1961 and 1971, the regime's primary
alliances shifted, first from the 1961-4 pact with Kabaka Yekka (itself
the uneasy union of populists and the traditional Mengo hierarchy) to
the volatile 1964-6 grand alliance of political notables in which the
bloated UPC absorbed and internalised conflicts among the nation's
elite, then to the temporarily more stable 1966-71 alliance between
Obote's centre faction of the UPC and Amin's faction of the army.

There were also secondary alliances with the trade unions, agricultural co-operative societies, traders' associations, youth groups, religious groups, and most importantly, with sections of the Asian community involved in manufacturing and wholesale trade.

The UPC-KY Alliance (1962-4)

The 'national' bourgeoisie of Buganda owed their relatively privileged position among Africans in Uganda to the colonial alliance between the Baganda and the British. While the bourgeoisie resented the racial restrictions and paternalism of the colonial period, at heart many Baganda were Anglophiles who viewed independence with mixed emotions: on the one hand, no longer would they be able to count on British support to remain first among equals in their relations with other Ugandans; on the other hand, the coming of political independence presented the prospect of replacing the British with Baganda in the Uganda civil service, since earlier and longer access to education and administrative posts ensured there would be larger numbers of qualified Baganda than qualified non-Baganda available to fill Africanised posts. More importantly, political independence presented the opportunity of using state power to remove the social and economic barriers which favoured non-Africans in commerce. In turn, Baganda commercial succcess could further the political power of the Baganda bourgeoisie *vis-à-vis* other Ugandans. Having failed in its attempt to achieve economic supremacy via separate independence for Buganda, the Baganda bourgeoisie made an alliance with the UPC to attain the best possible terms of entry into the post-colonial state.

From the perspective of the UPC, the alliance between it and the KY was necessary to bring the Buganda Kingdom into the post-colonial state, to gain electoral victory over the Democratic Party, and to ensure UPC dominance in the coalition government. Neither side had any illusions about the permanency of the alliance between republican 'socialists' and capitalist monarchists. If there were illusions, these were about the circumstances under which the alliance would ultimately be terminated and in whose favour.

The UPC made significant concessions to the traditional hierarchy and capitalist farmers in Buganda. Precisely because their UPC allies espoused socialism in the form of group farms and co-operatives, the Baganda delegates to the final London constitutional conference in the summer of 1962 fought for and won guarantees that the National

Assembly could make no laws altering land tenure in Buganda without consent of the Buganda Lukiko. The 1962 Constitution explicitly reserved the following matters to the Lukiko:

> ii) any provision for altering or replacing the Public Lands Ordinance 1962, so far as that Ordinance has effect in relation to the Kingdom of Buganda, or for altering or replacing any other law with respect to the tenure of land vested in the Land Board of the Kingdom of Buganda;
> iii) any provision for altering or replacing the system of mailo land tenure in the Kingdom of Buganda as in force immediately before 9th October 1962.[5]

Since entrenchment was contingent on maintaining the semi-autonomy of Buganda within the federal post-colonial state, the capitalist farmers acquired a vested interest in preserving the institutions of the Kingdom of Buganda, notably the Kabakaship and the Lukiko. The neo-traditionalism of Baganda farmers enjoyed a solid economic rationale.

The traditional hierarchy of Buganda acquired entrenched privileges in the 1962 constitution: control over the Kabakaship; control over Buganda's representatives in the National Assembly through election by the Lukiko; control over local administration including the appointment of chiefs; control over administering customary law by the Buganda courts (including enforced subservience of subjects to the Kabaka); control over a new local constabulary and palace guard; and control over many social services, notably education and the distribution of scholarships. The constitution further guaranteed federal funds for the cost of services run by the Buganda government, initially set at a minimum of Shs. 1. 5 million per month.[6]

Although the UPC-KY alliance was based more on expediency than political principle, it was not without harmony of class interests which transcended the contradiction between Buganda and Uganda. The leadership of the KY movement included not only reactionary Baganda traditionalists such as Amos Sempa, but progressive, that is to say bourgeois, professionals: Abu Mayanja, J.S. Luyimbazi-Zake, Apolo Kironde, Godfrey Binaisa, and other former members of the UNC who might have joined the UPC at the start, had it not appeared to be disrespectful to the Mengo hierarchy.[7]

For the African traders in Buganda, the main concern had been the desire to use control of the post-colonial state to supplant themselves in the place of the non-African commercial stratum. From 1959 onward Baganda farmers and traders not only opposed the granting of special seats to ethnic minorities in the National Assembly but also fought any implication that a common electoral roll might automatically confer the right of citizenship on non-Africans.[8] Though the 1962 Constitution provided that non-Africans would be given exactly two years to apply for automatic Uganda citizenship, the terror of the 1959-60 economic boycott in Buganda ensured that many Asians would hesitate to give up British passports. Thereafter, applications for citizenship would not be given automatic approval by the state.[9] In this respect, the 1962 Constitution hammered out by UPC and KY delegates met the demands of African traders both in Buganda and elsewhere.

For the would-be aristocratic stratum outside Buganda, the very success of the Mengo hierarchy in obtaining entrenched status within the federal system served as an incentive to emulate the Mengo hierarchy. If Buganda could not be absorbed within a unitary post-colonial state, then aspiring aristocrats elsewhere would do their best to emulate Buganda's status as a state within a state. Thus the 1962 federal constitution reserved autonomous powers for the kingdoms of Buganda, Ankole, Bunyoro and Toro, and created a virtual kingdom in the Territory of Busoga, which had not enjoyed such status under the colonial rule. The pro-republican UPC regime became ensnared in royalty — both formally allied with the Kabaka through KY and infiltrated by nobles such as Nadiope of Busoga and Ibingira of Ankole; moreover, the success of kingdoms led to a proliferation of would-be kings — the Kyabazinga of Busoga, the Umuinga of Bugisu, the Kingoo of Sebei, the Ruta Kirwa of Kigezi, the Ekaraban of Teso, the Laloya Maber of Acholi, and the Won Nyaci of Lango — all of whom posed obstacles to bourgeois politicians who were mere commoners.[10] For the bourgeois commoners the spread of monarchism in the form of constitutional heads beyond Buganda, Bunyoro, Ankole and Toro appeared to mark a resurgence of Buganda sub-imperialism in political structures.

The UPC-KY alliance was a victory for conservative forces both in Buganda and elsewhere in that KY members were awarded key portfolios in the 1962 cabinet: Finance and Economic Affairs, in addition to the more mundane Health, Education and Community Development. This alone restrained any incipient socialist tendencies on the part of the new regime. The five KY members of the 15-minister coalition cabinet demonstrated their ultimate allegiance by prostrating themselves before the Kabaka after taking national office.[11] The Economic Affairs portfolio went to J.T. Simpson, who had once served as general manager of the Uganda Company. As former chairman of the Uganda Development Corporation, he symbolised the alliance between state firms and foreign capital. The Finance portfolio went to Amos Sempa, the arch-conservative who thought it daring to quote John Stuart Mill.[12] However, any economic policy conflicts that might have arisen between the UPC and KY were overtaken by political conflicts over Buganda's status: the division of territory between UPC and KY branches, the funding of Buganda's social services, and the 'lost counties' dispute.

In 1963 contrary to its earlier tacit agreement with the KY, the UPC began to establish party branches in Buganda outside Kampala. Following Obote's 1964 pronouncement on the desirability of a one-party state,[13] the KY and its political front, the Uganda National Union, began to proselytise outside Buganda.

The financial dispute arose over interpretation of the 1962 Constitution's provision that the central government finance Buganda expenditures on social services which it had run autonomously since 1955. The Buganda government interpreted the constitution to require the central government to supply unlimited finances for these services. Rejecting this interpretation and impatient with Buganda's delays in submitting accounts for audit, the central government took legal action against the Buganda government and won a favourable interpretation of the financial clauses of the constitution in the Uganda High Court in May 1964.[14]

In the final analysis, the UPC-KY alliance foundered on the issue of the 'lost counties'. Although Buganda had won a postponement of the referendum in the 'lost counties' of Buyaga and Bugangazi at the 1962 constitutional conference, the 1962 Uganda (Independence) Order in Council clearly stated that a referendum should be held in those counties at some point after 9 October 1964 to determine whether the counties were to be transferred to Bunyoro to remain in Buganda, or to become a separate district.[15] In the interim the counties were to be administered by the central government. In a futile effort to improve its chance of winning the referendum, the Buganda government instituted a settlement scheme for Baganda ex-servicemen at Ndaiga in Buyaga county. The Kabaka exercised personal supervision over the Ndaiga scheme, forcing his ministers and petitioners to travel 200 miles from Mengo to Ndaiga to conduct government business. The costs of the settlement scheme grew beyond Shs. 2 million, and reports of graft, corruption and kick-backs escalated. The futility of the exercise became apparent when the central government ruled that only those already resident in the counties in 1962 would be eligible to vote. Even the Buganda Lukiko grew weary of the scheme and refused to approve the 1964 estimates for the continuation of the project.[16]

It was in this period that Uganda National Assembly amended the constitution to enable the National Assembly to elect a president as head of state to replace the British Governor-General. True to its secret commitment to Mengo in 1962, the UPC voted with the KY to elect the Kabaka as President for a five-year term, with the ceremonial post of Vice-President going to William Nadiope, the Kyabazinga of Busoga and powerful member of the UPC executive.[17] Presidential duties called Mutesa away from the growing Ndaiga scandal.

Meanwhile, the UPC-KY coalition in the National Assembly disintegrated through defections by members of the 'progressive' KY faction to the UPC. They were joined by a number of Democratic Party members who also crossed the floor to the UPC. By early June 1964, the number of UPC members in the National Assembly had risen from 43 to 58, three short of a two-thirds majority.[18] The alliance with KY had become dispensable, and the alliance formally ended in August 1964, the same month in which the UPC introduced the bill establishing a November referendum in the 'lost counties'.

As expected, the November referendum in Buyaga and Bugangazi counties resulted in an overwhelming mandate for the return of the counties to Bunyoro. The transfer of the counties struck a severe blow to the pride of the Baganda. The Kintu administration in Buganda fell on 9 November 1964 after failing to survive a Lukiko motion of no confidence.[19] Mayanja-Nkangi replaced Kintu as the new Katikiro of Buganda. For his part, Edward Mutesa II, as President of Uganda, refused to sign into law both the bill authorising the referendum and the subsequent bill effecting the transfer of the two counties to Bunyoro in January 1965. Equally futile attempts were made to overturn the referendum results in the courts. Aside from its symbolic significance, the transfer cut the number of *sazas* in Buganda from 20 to 18, and thereby reduced the number of patronage posts available for distribution by the Mengo hierarchy. In terms of revenue, the two counties' contribution to the finances of Buganda amounted to only 3 to 4 per cent of total revenue from the graduated poll tax, but even this reduction may have been painful coming on the heels of the central government's victory in interpreting the financial clauses of the constitution. The financial crisis was magnified in 1965 by a severe drought which reduced farmers' incomes and thus the tax base of the Buganda government.

An interesting side-effect of the return of the counties to Bunyoro
was that landlord-tenant relationships in those two counties remained
under the jurisdiction of the Busulu and Envujo Law despite the
territorial transfer, thus protecting the interests of capitalist farmers on
private *mailo* estates. Ownership of official estates did change hands
when Banyoro chiefs replaced Baganda chiefs.[20]

An ominous side-effect of the transfer was a series of incidents of
violence perpetrated by officials of the central government and
Buganda in the period 1964-5, which indicated that both sides were
prepared to use violence and extra-legal means to enforce their respective interpretations of the position of Buganda within the post-colonial
state. These incidents were the Uganda police massacre of six civilians
at Nakulabye, near Kampala; the deaths of twelve Baganda school
children in a suspicious road accident involving an army lorry; the
Kabaka's machine-gunning of Banyoro traders and bystanders in a
Buyaga market; and the shooting of a further seven Banyoro at the
Kabaka's lodge at Ndaiga.[21]

Alliances and Contradictions Within the UPC (1962-7)

From its founding in 1960 to its demise in 1971, the UPC was largely a
national confederation of locally powerful political notables competing
for control over allocation of state patronage to enhance their local
patron-client relationships and their personal business ventures in
farming, trading and transport. Given the UPC's origin as a merger
between one faction of the old UNC, itself the loosely structured
political arm of a non-hierarchical confederation of traders and leaders
of agricultural co-operative societies, and the Uganda People's Union, a
coalition of political notables in the pre-independence Legislative
Council, it is hardly surprising that the UPC failed to develop a centralised hierarchy.

While many of the political notables within the UPC favoured a
strong central *state* both as a counterweight to the Buganda traditional
hierarchy and as a weapon to Africanise commerce, they opposed
and subverted attempts to create a disciplined centralised political
party.

Even in Lango, Obote's home district, the UPC was not particularly
egalitarian or peasant-based. Although less Westernised in language,
symbols and values than the administrative cadres who represented the
state apparatus in the town of Lira, the Langi leaders of rural UPC

branches tended to be the 'big men' — political brokers who were often large farmers, traders or professionals. They were not 'common men', though through 'hospitality and generosity' they formed a patron-client link between the common man in the countryside and the party head-quarters in Kampala.[22]

For the 1962 elections, the UPC chose its candidates more on the basis of proven ability to mobilise electoral support, regardless of methods used, than on the basis of ideological harmony. Despite the UPC's reputation as a radical populist party, its elected representatives at the local and national level were often directly linked to 'traditional' chiefly hierarchies and aspirant capitalists in farming and trade.[23]

A radical UPC would have required a highly centralised national organisation with the power to by-pass party notables at the local level rather than a multi-centred coalition in which the focus of power remained entrenched at the district and constituency levels controlled by dispensers of patronage. These local political notables favoured Africanisation of control of the economy and the state salariat, but opposed any progressive restructuring of the economy which might diminish their own prerogatives.

At the national level, the UPC parliamentary group soon became the *de facto* if not the *de jure* central committee of the party, and Parliament, the forum for the parochial and class interests of the political notables. Already in 1963 one-third of the UPC members of Parliament also sat on the UPC central executive committee; only 4 of 20 executive committee members were not parliamentarians. Though still the largest bloc, the parliamentary notables' control of the UPC slipped slightly in 1970, when members of Parliament won only 46 of the 134 UPC branch chairmanships.[24]

As Uganda moved towards a dominant one-party state in the period 1963-5, the rise of the UPC within Parliament, district councils and kingdom legislatures was accompanied by growing conflict within the UPC and by the entropy of the party organisation outside Parliament.[25] The extra-parliamentary UPC came to life momentarily only when factional disputes among political notables within Parliament, district councils or kingdom legislatures required the mobilisation of local support to oust the members of an opposing faction.

By the end of 1964, the UPC controlled all district councils and kingdom legislatures outside Buganda.[26] Within the National Assembly, a steady stream of Democratic Party and KY members crossing over to the UPC, culminated in a two-thirds majority after the break-up of the UPC-KY alliance in August 1964. At the end of 1964,

the DP received a severe blow when the DP parliamentary leader Basil
Bataringaya and five other DP members crossed over to the UPC,
leaving the DP with only nine members on the opposition benches in
Parliament, in addition to those KY members who joined the opposition following the break-up of the UPC-KY alliance.[27]

Aware of its weak coercive power *vis-à-vis* the central state, the
Buganda government shifted to a strategy of undermining the Obote
regime from within. In both April and July 1965, the KY seriously
debated whether to disband and merge with the UPC. Despite official
denials by the Katikiro of Buganda, the Kabaka apparently urged
trusted KY members to infiltrate the UPC. Abu Mayanja led a group of
three KY members of Parliament and four Lukiko members who
crossed over to the UPC in July, along with 1,000 ordinary KY
members. Within a few days they were joined by Prince Alfred Joseph
Kigala of the Buganda royal family and three more KY members of
Parliament.[28] Significantly, these prominent crossings occurred during
Obote's visit to the People's Republic of China and presaged an orches-
trated anti-Communist campaign within the UPC. By the end of 1965,
party standings in Parliament were as follows: UPC 74; DP 9; KY 8;
independent 1.[29]

Conflict within the UPC escalated between 1964 and 1966 as three
factions fought for control in three major conflicts: the contest for
UPC Secretary-General in 1964; the February 1966 campaign for
control of the Buganda UPC; and the February-March 1966 struggle for
national control of both the party and the state. In these battles, the
conservative faction led by Ibingira, Ocheng and conservative KY
'defectors' represented traditional rulers and large-scale landlords. The
radical faction — Kakonge, the UPC Youth League (UPCYL) and left-
wing trade unionists — claimed to speak for the dispossessed: the
unemployed and the labouring poor in rural and urban areas. Obote,
Odaka, Onama and Binaisa, a progressive KY defector, led the centre
faction representing professionals, aspiring businessmen and trade
unionists.

The economic programme of the conservative faction began with
chauvinist demands for protection of privilege based on land and birth.
The conservatives viewed with suspicion the UPC slogan of 'African
socialism', and pinned their hopes on state recognition of traditional
rulers as a bulwark against socialism. They opposed group farms and
even co-operative societies as dangerous encroachments on private
property, and favoured channelling all state aid in agriculture to 'progressive' (capitalist) farmers. They themselves coveted parastatal

corporations such as the Uganda Development Corporation and the
Uganda Electricity Board:

> . . . as gradually . . . people get richer and richer, the Government
> should more or less push itself out of these Corporations. The
> Government should throw its shares to the public as time goes on,
> to be bought by ordinary citizens until such time that these com-
> panies are run by individuals themselves.[30]

The conservatives' vision of economic independence contented itself
with replacing white and brown faces with black faces among the
economically powerful. For Ibingira, it was the fact that the urban
wealthy were Asians that was the problem, not the existence of
inequality itself: 'It suddenly became humiliating that all the towns in
the Protectorate should be inhabited and owned by Indians; and that
they should be the people with the money, the big cars, and the
mansions.'[31]

By contrast, the economic programme of the UPC centre embodied
a 'commanding heights' strategy of expanding state control of the
economy through joint ventures with foreign firms and collaboration
with Asian capital in wholesale trade and manufacturing. Since the
uneven and unequal pattern of colonial development had created
north-south imbalances in opportunities for the aspiring African
bourgeoisie, the state would locate new manufacturing plants in areas
other than Jinja and Kampala and would assist African traders, progressive farmers, co-operative societies and group farms throughout Uganda.
Led by northern political notables and by northern and southern professionals and civil servants, the UPC centre saw a harmony of interests
between the commanding heights strategy and its own class interest as
managers of the state apparatus, parastatal industry and co-operative
societies.

The 'radical' faction established its base among school-leavers and
young urban migrants who left the rural areas to search for jobs. By
1963 the UPC Youth League (UPCYL), led by Raiti Omongi,
Katabarwa and P. Kamunanwire, had emerged as an organised political
force on the national scene in Uganda. Many of its activities proved to
be embarrassing to UPC notables: organising strikes in Kampala garages;
kidnapping the British editor of *Uganda Argus* and forcing him to
engage in manual labour; holding the Minister of Internal Affairs
(Onama) prisoner and demanding that the party spell out its socialist
goals; enforcing the display of portraits of the Prime Minister and

President in shops and factories; staging a sit-in at the elite Uganda Club in Kampala; and leading demonstrations against US intervention in the Congo and against Tshombe's bombing of villages in western Uganda.[32]

But it was UPC Secretary-General Kakonge's attempt to create an ideologically committed mass party controlled by an extra-parliamentary national organisation using youth leaguers as cadres that posed a real threat to party notables. Kakonge's espousal of scientific socialism was well known, while the Youth League called for the abolition of private property.[33]

Adoko Nekyon, Obote's cousin, spearheaded the establishment of the National Union of Youth Organisations (NUYO) in 1963-4 to undercut the UPCYL. Controlled by the state rather than the party, NUYO was designed to de-politicise school-leavers and unemployed youth by inculcating in them the values of work, culture and 'development' (undefined), and by avoiding analysis of the context in which work and development would take place. Its material attraction lay in the fact that the state paid NUYO members up to two shillings per day while actively engaged in 'development' training and rural projects. Total NUYO membership rose to 30,000 in a nation in which only 15 per cent of the annual output of 80,000 school-leavers could find employment.[34]

Ibingira and Nekyon mobilised conservative and centre factions to remove Kakonge from the post of Secretary-General at the 1964 delegates conference at Gulu. Nekyon made a strong anti-Communist speech which was interpreted as an attack on both Kakonge and the UPCYL, although neither could be said to be more than socialist. Joseph Kiwanuka, hardly a leftist, attacked the election irregularities that enabled Ibingira to replace Kakonge. Equal voting rights were granted to all delegates whether they represented the party at the *gombolola* or *saza* level. Ibingira's faction packed the conference with delegates drawn from the *gombolola* level. Even so the vote was close: Ibingira won by only 100 votes.[35]

The attempt by the UPCYL to encourage Kakonge to form a new progressive political party failed after Kakonge returned to the UPC fold as a specially elected member of Parliament and Director of Planning. Physical attacks on the national UPCYL members became more frequent following the establishment of rival UPC youth wing groups at the local level, controlled by the conservative and centre political notables. Following the 1966-7 crisis, progressive youth movements disappeared from the Uganda political scene; former leaders were absorbed into NUYO, the state salariat or the UPC-backed factions in the labour movement. Only in the late 1960s did progressive youth movements reappear in the form of the Uganda Vietnam Solidarity Party and the National Union of Students of Uganda (NUSU).[36]

The battle between UPC radical and centre factions for control of the trade union movement also led to co-optation of the radicals by the centre. Headquartered in Kampala, the Uganda Trade Unions Congress (UTUC) tended to focus its activities there. A rival organisation, the Uganda Federation of Labour (UFL), was founded in 1961 to champion the neglected interests of workers in the Jinja area. Founded by John Reich, the UFL was initially based on the Eastern Province Transport and General Workers Union (formerly the Busoga Motor Drivers Union), the Tobacco Workers Union, and the Uganda Sugar and Allied Workers Union (Kakira), but rapidly expanded to attract UTUC affiliates in the Jinja area. The UFL received implicit endorsement of the UPC at the Mbale delegates conference in 1962, which attacked the UTUC for imperialist links with the US-dominated ICFTU (the International Confederation of Free Trade Unions).[37] The UFL and UPCYL formed an active alliance, in which the UPCYL helped the UFL to extend its activities to Kampala in the motor trade strike of 1963.

Using the CIA-financed patronage of ICFTU overseas study leaves, UTUC temporarily won back the leaders of disaffected UTUC affiliates in Jinja. The next threat to UTUC's 'autonomy' came in August 1964, when 12 of its 28 affiliates were wooed away by former UFL and UPCYL organisers to establish the Federation of Uganda Trade Unions (FUTU), which immediately declared its support for the UPC.[38] Unlike the Jinja-centred UFL, FUTU's strength lay in the Uganda Public Employees Union, the Petroleum and Oil Workers Union and the Kilembe Mine Workers Union. To protest the UPC's dismemberment of the UTUC, the UTUC president, Humphrey Luande, resigned from the party and crossed the floor of the National Assembly to sit as an independent. In the wake of the 1966 crisis, the state forced UTUC and FUTU to merge into the Uganda Labour Congress (ULC). The ULC none the less elected Luande as president rather than the UPC-backed candidate. In April 1968, the state closed the ICFTU Labour College at Makerere and took control of the ULC, pending its reorganisation under tighter state control. This reorganisation was embodied in the Trade Unions Act of December 1970, which also barred members of the National Assembly from holding office in the ULC or any affiliate (Section 22 (5)). Although directed against Luande, the clause made it impossible for trade union officials to sit in Parliament.

Overall, the left leadership of the UFL/FUTU was not so much
expelled as absorbed by the UPC and by the personnel departments of
firms eager to put the radicals' organising talents into the service of
capital rather than labour.[39] Clerical worker domination of trade union
leadership within each industry greatly facilitated co-optation of trade
unionists. Clerks viewed the trade unions' political struggle primarily
in terms of demands for higher wages and Africanisation of white-
collar positions within capitalist and state capitalist firms, rather than a
struggle for control of the state and economy by producers.

UPC-Right versus UPC-Centre: the 1966 Crisis

The fact that a major leader of the so-called Nilotic or UPC centre
faction was Godfrey Binaisa, a Muganda, and that a major leader of the
so-called Bantu or conservative faction was Daudi Ocheng, an Acholi
who owned land in Buganda and served as Secretary-General of Kabaka
Yekka, should warn us that class interests could and did override
ethnic identity. The south-north ethnic cleavage had its economic basis
in the contradiction between the 'early' commodity-producing areas of
the south and the 'late' commodity-producing areas of the centre and
north. The African bourgeoisie and traditional rulers in each area used
ethnic or status group identity to mobilise support and to obscure
class antagonisms within each region.[40] For the UPC centre, the
ideology of tribalism was more than a threat to the unity of Uganda,
tribalism threatened the unity and hegemony of the central
bureaucracy.

It is not clear whether a formal alliance existed between the right
faction within the UPC led by Grace Ibingira, Secretary-General of the
UPC, and the conservative forces of landlords and traditional rulers
outside the UPC led by Edward Mutesa and Daudi Ocheng. There were
antagonisms between these two conservative factions. Ibingira
denounced the KY for setting up front organisations outside Buganda
and strongly supported the referendum in the 'lost counties'.

Nevertheless, the two groups worked in parallel in the period May
1965 to February 1966 to remove the centre-left factions led by
Obote from power within the UPC. Ibingira, for his part, hints that a
formal alliance existed:

When Obote later dissolved the [UPC-KY] alliance and began to
plot political death for Buganda, we chose, rather than betray our

allies and friends, to stand by them in what became a very costly undertaking for some of us.[41]

By mid-1965 former KY members were organising within the UPC in collaboration with Ibingira to take over the party in the Buganda region. Augustine Kamya, founder of the populist UNM and a staunch pro-monarchist trader, emerged as the vocal chairman of the Katwe branch of the UPC in Buganda, attracting KY supporters to the UPC. Another prominent Baganda businessman, Kezekia Segwanga Musisi, opened a Buganda UPC 'head office' to attempt to oust Attorney-General Godfrey Binaisa from chairmanship of the Buganda Region UPC.[42]

Meanwhile, Uganda was shaken by the spill-over from the second Congo crisis, which erupted during Moise Tshombe's tenure as Prime Minister (10 July 1964-13 October 1965). Obote viewed Tshombe as a traitor to the cause of African independence and an agent of American and Belgian imperialism. Because the OAU charter forbade interference in the internal affairs of member states and because there was sympathy within Buganda for Tshombe's strong pro-Western stance,[43] Obote's assistance to anti-Tshombe rebels led by Christopher Gbenye and General Nicholas Oleng in the period December 1964 to March 1965 was kept secret from both the public and the cabinet. Obote arranged for Gbenye to meet and brief the East African heads of state at a meeting in Mbale in January 1965. It was during this period that the rebels entrusted Col. Idi Amin with money, ivory and eleven bars of gold, each weighing 20 pounds, to purchase arms. From the sale of the gold, Amin deposited Shs. 480,000 in the bank towards weapons purchases.[44]

In May 1965, the Kenyan government seized 75 tons of Chinese weapons being transported secretly from Tanzania to Uganda via Kenya. Whether destined for remnants of the Congolese rebels, the Ugandan border forces or Army units defending Obote from potential internal opposition, the weapons sparked a crisis in Kenyan-Ugandan relations and triggered anti-Tanzanian and pro-Kenyan comments in the Buganda press. To secure the release of the arms and the accompanying Ugandan soldiers, Obote was forced to travel to Nairobi and make a personal apology to the Kenyan government.[45]

The period May 1965 to February 1966 marked the appearance of an anti-Communist scare campaign led by Ibingira and echoed by the press.[46] Obote's strong stand against American intervention in the Congo, the arms incident, the publication of Kakonge's Five-Year Plan, and Obote's July visits to Yugoslavia, China and the Soviet Union fuelled speculation that the Obote regime was moving towards increased state control of the economy and a left-of-centre foreign policy.

By February 1966 the UPC-right and KY members infiltrating the UPC had succeeded in replacing Binaisa with Dr E.B.S. Lumu as chairman of the Buganda Region UPC. However, a similar effort failed in Bunyoro where the pro-centre Katuramu survived the party putsch organised by Magezi and Ibingira.[47]

Having consolidated its position where it could among political notables at the district and kingdom level, the conservative faction shifted its attack to the national level. On 4 February 1966, Daudi Ocheng introduced a motion in Parliament calling for the suspension of Col. Idi Amin from military duties and an investigation into the alleged receipt of gold and ivory from Congolese rebels by Amin, Obote, Onama and Nekyon. The motion was introduced during Obote's absence from Kampala. With the exception of Kakonge, members of Parliament voted to support Ocheng's motion. During the following days there were rumours of mysterious troop movements in and out of the capital as the two opposing factions struggled to ensure the presence of units loyal to one faction and the absence of units loyal to the other.[48]

Returning to Kampala from his tour of northern districts, Obote counter-attacked, sending Amin on a two-week leave and appointing Judge de L'Estang of the Appeal Court to chair a commission of inquiry into Ocheng's allegations (the commission's findings, published in August 1971, cleared Obote and the others of any wrong-doing[49]). Obote arrested the core of the UPC right at a cabinet meeting on 22 February 1966: Grace Ibingira, Minister of State and Secretary-General of the UPC; Dr E.B.S. Lumu, Minister of Health and newly-elected chairman of the Buganda UPC; B.K. Kirya, Minister of Mineral and Water Resources; Mathias Mbalule Ngobi, Minister of Agriculture and Co-operatives; and George B.K. Magezi, Minister of Housing and Labour. Three of the arrested cabinet members – Kirya, Ngobi and Magezi – were substantial capitalist farmers and leaders of growers' co-operative societies in the 'old' commodity-producing regions of the south.[50] Obote simultaneously suspended the 1962 Constitution and assumed all state power. The coercive arm of the salariat, the police, led by Erenayo Wilson Oryema, and the Army, led by Deputy Chief of Staff Col. Idi Amin after Shaban Opolot's suspension, supported Obote's assumption of power. The 'southern' as well as 'northern' members of the state salariat backed Obote.

Support for Obote's takeover was voiced by the district councils or kingdom legislature in Lango, Kigezi, Bunyoro, Busisu, Teso, Karamoja, Acholi, West Nile and Madi. Obote accused both former President Edward Mutesa and former Vice-President William Nadiope of approaching foreign governments for military assistance to remove him.[51]

On 15 April 1966, Obote presented an interim constitution, without debate, to the National Assembly, sitting as citizens. The slogan of the new order was 'one country, one Parliament, one Government, one péople', led by an executive President: Milton Obote. The new constitution struck directly at the power of the traditional hierarchy in Buganda. Chiefs were henceforth barred from sitting in Kingdom legislatures and district councils to ensure control of these bodies by middle-class political parties rather than by chiefs allied with traditional ruling families. Second, abolition of the Buganda Civil Service Commission ensured central state control of the Buganda salariat. Third, the state undermined the economic power of chiefs by eliminating official (but not private) *mailo* estates. Fourth, the state undermined the coercive power of the Kabaka by eliminating the Buganda High Court and the separate Buganda court system which had formerly enforced submissive deference to the Kabaka's regime. Fifth, by seizing official (but not private) *mailo* estates, the central government undermined the economic base of chiefs, completing the process begun by the colonial state in the 1920s. Sixth, the federal division of legislative authority was virtually abolished by giving the National Assembly sovereign legislative powers in all matters, save laws of succession for traditional rulers. Finally, constitutional heads of kingdoms and districts were barred from holding other public office.[52]

For a brief moment, Obote's constitution appeared to succeed in reopening the pre-KY split between the populist alliance and the traditional Mengo hierarchy. Two UPC members of the Lukiko, Birudadi L.K. Muwonge, a Katwe trader, and Edward Kitayimbwa, a farmer, sent an open letter to the Katikiro urging acceptance of the new constitution.[53] But the chiefs allied with the hierarchy refused to ratify a document which ensured their political demise and embarked instead upon a campaign to tighten loyalty to the Kabakaship and chiefs. Defying the new constititution, the appointed chiefs remained in the Lukiko and won a 75 to 0 vote for a resolution in support of the Kabaka's appeal to the United Nations against the constitutional changes in Uganda.[54] Outside the Lukiko, the chiefs launched the third trade boycott since

1952, which was immediately banned by the central government.

Finally, in May, the Lukiko passed a resolution demanding that the central government remove itself from the soil of Buganda. Following the arrest of three *saza* chiefs by the central government, the Kabaka reiterated the Lukiko's demand for the central government's withdrawal from Buganda. The central government responded with a military take-over of the Kabaka's palace at Lubiri and the proclamation of a state of emergency in Buganda. Edward Mutesa escaped and, once again, went into exile in England. Buganda was divided into four admini-strative districts.[55]

The following year, after considerable discussion, a new republican constitution was introduced abolishing all traditional rulers and all local legislatures. By postponing National Assembly elections to 1971, the regime effectively disenfranchised the seven Buganda constituencies whose MPs had refused to swear allegiance to the 1966 constitution.

Although 1967 saw tightening of party discipline within the UPC, marked by the expulsion of members suspected of loyalties to Ibingira or the banned Kabaka Yekka, a new centre-conservative split emerged within the UPC between President Obote and Felix Onama, the new Secretary-General of the UPC. The new centre faction led by Obote consisted of 'new party' recruits and the salariat, which favoured the 'commanding heights' strategy (state capitalism). The new conservative faction led by Onama consisted of traders, farmers and 'old party' notables who favoured state aid to individual African capitalists in agri-culture and trade, exclusion of Asians from commerce, and privati-sation of state corporations.[56]

The Commanding Heights Strategy

The changes in government policy coinciding with the 1966 crisis, particularly the expansion of the government's role in the economy and the maintenance of the State of Emergency in Buganda, provided both the impetus and the means for the Obote regime to restructure its basis of power. Whether by design or necessity, the economic policy of the regime evolved into a 'commanding heights' strategy in which the state assumed control or direction of leading institutions in the (dependent) economy.

The obvious elements in the commanding heights strategy were three-fold: (1) the establishment of new state corporations and the expansion and reorganisation of existing 'parastatal' bodies inherited from the colonial period; (2) the setting forth of a more active state role in economic development in the Second Five-Year Plan; and (3) the ambitious nationalisation measures issued as part of the 1969-70 'Move to the Left'.

Less obvious, but no less important, was the fact that the commanding heights strategy lacked the conscious, programmatic commitment to socialism which guided the Tanzanian government in its Arusha Declaration (1967) and discipline code (*Mowongozo*) for party cadres and state salariat, nor did it have the expedient embrace of state-assisted capitalism which characterised the Kenyatta regime's revisionist approach to African socialism.

In Uganda, the State of Emergency and Obote's alliance with Amin's faction within the Army ensured the containment of the hegemonic political aspirations on the part of neo-traditionalists and certain middle-class elements in Buganda. So too, did the commanding heights strategy and the Obote regime's *de facto* alliance with the Asians and with the salariat constrain the scope for economic hegemony by the rising Baganda bourgeoisie.

When UPC supporters hailed the Move to the Left as the third step on the road to full independence, all agreed that formal political independence in 1962 had constituted the first step, but opinions differed on the second step. John Kakonge termed the Second Five-Year Plan, which he had helped draft while Director of Planning, as the second step, whereas Obote pointed to the 'Uganda Revolution' (the events leading from the 1966 crisis to the 1967 republican constitution) as the second step toward full independence. Ultimately, their difference was one of emphasis rather than substance; the commanding heights strategy and the 'Obote Revolution' formed the warp and the woof (weft) in the fabric of the First Republic.

The first facet in the commanding heights strategy was hardly new. It continued the colonial policy of using parastatal bodies to operate infrastructural services (the Uganda Electricity Board and the East African parastatal corporations for railways, harbours, air transport, posts and telecommunications, development finance, and shipping) and extended the post-war policy of launching parastatal corporations as multi-purpose vehicles for promoting economic diversification, import substitution, Africanisation of commerce, and joint ventures between the state and private, usually foreign, firms. The Obote regime established new parastatals in housing, insurance, banking, wholesale and retail trade, marketing of agricultural produce, external trade, tourism, dairy farming, cattle ranching and tea cultivation.[57]

Even with these new 'rivals', the flagship of the parastatal corporations remained the Uganda Development Corporation (UDC), which grew from net fixed assets of U. Shs. 153 million in 29 subsidiary and 11 associate companies employing 14,376 in 1963 to assets totalling U. Shs. 312 million in 37 subsidiary and 18 associate companies employing 23,981 in 1970.[58] By 1970 the operations of UDC subsidiary and associate firms extended into ten major areas: agriculture (tea plantations, cattle breeding), textiles (spinning and weaving cotton textiles, shirt making), construction materials (cement, asbestos cement), food and beverages (Waragi, spirits, meat packing, frozen fish, wheat flour milling, animal feeds, cassava starch), tourism (hotels, game lodges), banking (development finance), real estate (office blocks), chemicals (superphosphate fertilisers, sulphuric acid), mining (copper, tungsten), and metal products (steel ingots, hoes, enamelware, appliances).

Not all UDC ventures proved successful. The Soroti meat canning factory, for example, closed in 1970 after losing U. Shs. 27 million, while the Lira starch factory limped from one loss to the next because it was unable to pay the price farmers demanded for cassava. Subsidiaries with management agents sometimes encountered friction between UDC's goals and the goals of the managing agent. For example, Twiga Chemicals, managing agents for the Tororo fertiliser factory, required approval from its parent (ICI Ltd) for UDC fertiliser exports beyond the East African Community.[59]

Despite such problems, UDC enjoyed an enviable record compared with similar state corporations elsewhere in Africa. It also avoided the scandals which plagued the National Trading Corporation from its inception.

The second facet of the commanding heights strategy emerged after the failure of the 1963 attempt to transform the East African Common Services Organisation into a political federation. Fearing subordination within a strong East African Federation, the Kingdom of Buganda and, later, the UPC objected to the proposed union.[60] Although the common market was retained (subject to inter-member transfer taxes) along with now more decentralised common services in the revamped East African Community of 1967, the member states (Uganda, Kenya and Tanzania) had, by 1966, dismantled the East African Currency Board to create separate currencies and central banks. Both the establishment of the Bank of Uganda and the dissolution of the UPC-KY alliance enabled the Obote regime to pursue more *dirigiste* policies in the Second Five-Year Plan than it had in the First Plan.

The Second Plan, 1966/67-1970/71, contained four innovations. In addition to conventional economic indicator targets, it set comprehensive five-year targets for physical outputs. It provided sectoral estimates of private as well as public (government, parastatal and East African Community) development expenditures. It proposed a doubling of the total development expenditure levels achieved in the first plan, from U. Shs. 2,480 million to U. Shs. 4,800 million, and an increase in the government and parastatal share of this expenditure from 56.5 per cent to 62.5 per cent. Finally, it set forth an ambitious 15-year perspective plan for doubling per capita income by 1981. Although the plan hoped to increase the proportion of central government development spending financed by foreign sources from just over two-fifths in the First Plan to 56 per cent in the Second Plan, only half the expected foreign financing materialised, much of it high-interest contractor finance. The government filled the remaining gap through domestic borrowings from the Bank of Uganda. Domestic sources thereby financed 72 per cent of the central government's U. Shs. 2,110 million share of development expenditures during the Second Plan.[61]

Despite lip service to the importance of domestic savings, domestic investment and domestic effort — and indeed despite the high level of domestic surplus squeezed from the rural sector — the Obote regime had expected Uganda's economic salvation to come from abroad, through foreign investment, foreign aid (preferably without political 'strings'), and higher prices for export commodities.[62] Necessity rather than design forced the regime to turn from externally-oriented development financing to central bank borrowing.

The third facet in the commanding heights strategy, the partial nationalisation of major firms, emerged in the Move to the Left campaign of 1960-70. The Move to the Left consisted of five documents by Obote.[63]

First, the National Service proposal (October 1969) called for one to two years of compulsory national service by every able-bodied person in Uganda. Though the service period could consist of three months per year, the National Service scheme failed to recognise that the agricultural cycle in many regions did not allow for such three-month absences. Moreover, given widespread dacoity (*kondoism*) in Uganda, the proposal aroused fears that national service would be a boon to thieves preying on empty homesteads. Obote's opponents seized on the proposal as a plot to establish concentration camps, destroy family life and collectivise farming.

Second, The Common Man's Charter (December 1969) outlined the ideological framework of the Move to the Left. Twelve of its forty-four clauses attacked 'feudalism', Obote's term for Buganda hegemonism and neo-traditionalism. While it accorded a place to private firms and foreign investment in the economy, the charter suggested that some private firms and possibly even *mailo* land be nationalised in order to place control of the means of production into the hands of 'the people as a whole' (in effect, into the hands of the state salariat). Finally, echoing Disraeli, the charter warned that the growing gap between rich and poor might lead to the creation of two nations within Uganda. Without specifying the form of the remedy, the charter called for income redistribution to close the income gap and widen the market for mass consumer goods.

The third document, Communication from the Chair (April 1970), endorsed the unification of pay scales for employees in the state bureaucracy and parastatal bodies and ended several of the prerogatives of state employees.

The Nakivubo Pronouncement (May 1970) called for the 60 per cent nationalisation of 80 major firms and the abolition of strikes. The nationalisation measures are examined in more detail below. The attempt to end strikes by declaring them to be archaic after the 'common man's' entry into ownership of the means of production (through state nationalisation) failed to impress workers. They demanded a raise in the minimum wage from a migrant worker subsistence wage to the wage required to support a family. They called on labour inspectors to enforce existing minimum wage legislation. Strikes continued to occur, for example, at the Kampala rayon textile mill in November and in the cement industry in January 1971.[64]

Finally, the 'one plus three' election proposal (July and August 1970) tried to diminish sub-national ethnic rivalry by requiring each candidate for the National Assembly to stand for election in three regional constituencies in addition to the candidate's home constituency. While the proposal itself attacked the tendency of 'old party' members, notables still sitting in the National Assembly from the 1962 election, to regard the party, constituency and nation as private property, 'new party' members charged the one-plus-three proposal inadvertently favoured 'old party' members who had the financial means to campaign in all four regions of Uganda.

One critic has argued that the nationalisation policy in the Move to the Left was haphazard and ill-conceived: haphazard in that the 80 or so firms originally scheduled to be nationalised excluded some of the largest firms and included other firms on the verge of bankruptcy, and ill-conceived in that management rights continued to be vested in the former owners through management contracts.[65]

Within manufacturing, however, the choice of firms to be nationalised was more consistent than critics have allowed. Nine sub-sectors accounted for 82 per cent of the total value-added in manufacturing in 1967: sugar refining and tobacco manufacture; brewing and distilling; woven cloths, knits and cord; sawmills and woodmills; pulp and paper and printing; refining animal and vegetable fats and oils; cement and non-metallic minerals; basic metal industries; and transport repair and parts. There were 224 firms in the nine sub-sectors, whose gross output totalled U. Shs. 817.8 million, but 72 per cent of this output came from 17 per cent of the firms: the 38 with 100 or more employees.[66]

Had the Nakivubo nationalisation measures been implemented, the Uganda government and parastatal bodies would have held controlling interest in 30 of the 38 large firms. Despite omissions and errors, the list of manufacturing firms scheduled for partial nationalisation was largely consistent with a commanding heights strategy of controlling the largest firms in the most important sub-sector of manufacturing.

In other sectors, notably banking and petrol distribution, the regime's nationalisation measures appeared less logical. In contrast to Tanzania's bank nationalisation which was followed by amalgamation of banks into a single system, there were to be as many separate bank branch networks in Uganda after nationalisation as before. Similarly, there were no plans for rationalisation of petroleum distribution following partial nationalisation.

Whatever the internal logic of the nationalisation plan, intractable negotiations and escalating compensation costs threatened its implementation. The government had hoped to finance its 60 per cent of shares in nationalised firms from its share of profits over a 15-year span. The owners of the nationalised firms demanded more rapid compensation. Under the Foreign Investments Protection Act (1964), owners of 'approved' firms were guaranteed compensation within six months after forcible acquisition. Under a retroactive amendment to the constitution passed in May 1970, owners of other firms were no longer guaranteed 'prompt payment of adequate compensation', but simply 'payment of reasonable compensation'.

By the end of January 1971, nine months of negotiations, often involving Obote himself, had yielded agreements with only six firms: Shell, Agip, Total, Brooke Bond, Grindlays Bank and Uganda-American Insurance.[67] Shell asserted that the final terms of its agreement were essentially identical to the joint venture proposal that Shell had

submitted to the government one year *before* the Nakivubo Pronouncement.[68]

Expatriate bank officials deplored the fact that the nationalisation
came on the heels of the requirement that commercial banks incor-
porate in Uganda with a minimum paid-up capital of U. Shs. 20 million.
Moreover, the May announcement caught banks with considerable
funds in Uganda at the end of the crop-financing cycle in contrast to
the banks' more favourable position in the timing of the Tanzanian
nationalisation of banks in 1967. Nevertheless, London officials of
Grindlays expressed guarded optimism that the new joint venture
would provide the bank with political insurance against total nationalisation. The agreement split the bank's Ugandan operations into two
components: the very profitable merchant banking side, 60 per cent
owned by Grindlays; and the more visible, but higher overhead, retail
branches, 60 per cent owned by the government. Both components
would be managed by Grindlays under a management contract. The
agreement with Uganda later served as the model for National and
Grindlays' joint venture proposal to the Kenya government.[69]

To pay for its holding in the six firms, the Uganda government had
to borrow U. Shs. 42.9 million by 30 June 1971, and had to allocate a
further U. Shs. 150 million for shares in the six and for a minority
shareholding in eleven additional firms acquired in the first year of the
Amin regime.[70] Had the entire Nakivubo package of 80 firms been
implemented, the total compensation cost would probably have
equalled one-third to one-half of the government development expenditures in the Second Five-Year Plan.

Overall, the major defect in the nationalisation measures, as in the
commanding heights strategy as a whole, was neither cost nor internal
consistency but rather the failure to address the problem of the
dependent structure of the economy. Control of the commanding
heights of leading sectors in the economy could not, by itself, further
economic independence, much less socialism. By itself, the
commanding heights strategy amounted to nationalisation of
dependency by a well-paid state salariat. What was needed was a wider
strategy of structural transformation of the economy to meet basic
human needs using local resources.

The Africanization of the Salariat

The salariat of Uganda included employees of the central government bureaucracy and of the parastatal bodies. The Africanised salariat had its own class interests to protect and sought to emulate the life-style and bureaucratic standards of the departing European administrators. The standard operating procedures of the administrative bureaucracy, embodied in the cautious conservatism of the final three decades of the colonial occupation, though functional for the maintenance of the *status quo*, were markedly unsuited for the dramatic transformation of the structure of the Ugandan economy.

The Weberian ideal of a neutral state bureaucracy was a comparatively late development in Uganda. Far from being neutral *vis-à-vis* British imperialism, the Ugandan bureaucracy was the administrative agent of British imperialism. Its neutrality was only in relationship to party politics in Great Britain.

The establishment of the Public Service Commission in Uganda in 1955 shifted the reference point of political neutrality from British to Ugandan party politics. The imposition of Weberian norms within Uganda at this late date effectively froze the orientation, standards and operating procedures of the civil service in its colonial mould. A politicised European civil service had effected the transformation of Uganda into a structurally dependent economy. A 'neutral' Africanised civil service, suspicious of political parties and movements, would prove functional for the maintenance of Uganda's subordinate role within the capitalist world economy.

During the process of Ugandanisation, the 'maintenance of standards' included maintenance of colonial attitudes and standard operating procedures and retention of the life-style of colonial civil servants. At the higher levels, this life-style included the following amenities: free or subsidised housing, a government car and driver, servants, and a salary equal to or greater than the salary for a similar position in Great Britain. We may say that corruption in the colonial civil service was structural rather than personal. Dunbar recounts a minor but telling example of this structural corruption. In virtually every administrative township there was a golf course maintained by the colonial state for its (European) employees. The budgetary allocation for the golf courses fell under the heading of anti-malarial measures.[π]

Having won political independence, Ugandans were called upon to pay the pensions of their colonial occupiers. To obtain foreign exchange for the pensions of departing European administrators, Uganda had to borrow UK £2.7 million (US $7.5 million) from Great Britain in 1962-3. By June 1969, outstanding loans from Britain for the pensions had risen to U Shs. 111 million (US $15.5 million), or 13 per cent of the Uganda government's

long-term debt. The pension burden was partially lightened by the fact
.that 73 per cent of the total debt consisted of interest-free loans.[72]

Excluding teachers and the armed forces, employment in the public
service rose from 16,896 in 1962 to 27,066 in 1970, of which the proportion of Ugandan citizens increased from 81.4 to 90.6 per cent. Total
public sector employment, excluding parastatal corporations, declined
from 102,221 in 1959 to 88,480 in 1963 before rising to 128,815 in
1970.[73]

The number eligible for civil service prerogatives increased when the
public service expanded in 1967 to include teachers, district administration officials, and urban authorities. Some state agents remained
outside the ranks of the privileged: *miruka* chiefs, for example, earned
as little as U. Shs. 187 per month and were barred from joining trade
unions.[74]

Ugandisation posed two dilemmas, the one related to income distribution, the other to education.

On the one hand, paying the newly recruited Africans anything less
than the European rate would have smacked of racial discrimination.[75]
On the other hand, paying the European wage would have established
enormous income differentials between ordinary workers or peasants
and Africans in the higher civil service, with the latter being remuner-
ated at parity with salaries in the industrialised nations rather than in
terms of ordinary wages in the periphery of world economy. Faced
with this dilemma, both the British administrative elite and the Obote
regime opted for the latter alternative, justifying it on the basis of equal
pay for equal work.

In the 1960s higher civil servants received annual incomes of
Shs. 36,000 or more, *plus* free or subsidised housing, *plus* the use of a
government car or a state-subsidised car loan. The higher and intermediate level administrative echelons, earning at least Shs. 12,000 per
annum, grew from 4 per cent (600) of the central government salariat
in 1964 to 12 per cent (2,400) in 1970, with their share of the central
government wage bill increasing from 13 per cent of the total to 36 per
cent.[76]

By comparison, in the same period, three-fifths of the enumerated
labour force earned no more than the minimum wage of Shs. 1,800 per
annum. In rural areas where 95 per cent of the population lived, only 7
per cent of the graduated taxpayers reported annual cash incomes of
Shs. 2,000 or more in 1969. Even in the relatively prosperous coffee
areas of Buganda, 50 to 70 per cent of rural family units in 1962-3
earned an average of Shs. 1,730 per year, including the value of sub-

sistence product.[77] Therefore, even excluding the value of fringe benefits, intermediate echelon civil servants earned salaries seven times, and higher civil servants earned salaries twenty times the income of the majority of peasants and workers in Uganda.

Within an overwhelmingly rural district such as Acholi, the earnings of the salariat comprised 55 per cent of total earnings from paid employment and was equivalent to 42.6 per cent of growers' income from the sale of cotton. Total earnings of all 7,000 employees in the public and private sector in Acholi equalled 77 per cent of growers' income from cotton even though the 7,000 were only 2 per cent of Acholi's 340,000 population.[78]

Pointing to the common cultural and social origins of elites and masses and the income-levelling effects of extended families in East Africa, some scholars have argued that the gap between elites and masses is much narrower in East Africa than in industrial societies.[79] The validity of this argument is undermined by three facts. First, socio-cultural commonality of elites and masses in East Africa is more a function of the parvenu mobility of the elites than the result of any enduring egalitarian values. Second, the income-levelling effects of extended families are partially offset by the enhanced social power within the family of the family patron. Third, the income gap between elites and masses in East Africa is not only wider than in industrial societies but has rapidly widened. In Uganda the income gap between the urban elites and rural masses widened appreciably under the Obote regime.

In education, Ugandanisation posed a different dilemma. Should resources be allocated to expansion of the existing colonial educational system or to overhaul of the structure and curriculum? In the end, rapid expansion of the educational system to meet the adminstrative manpower requirements of Ugandanisation took priority over changing the curriculum to meet the changing needs of politically independent Uganda. Helped by loans, grants and teachers from the industrialised nations, the number of senior secondary schools admitting Africans rose from 19 schools with 3,153 students in 1958 to 73 schools serving 40,697 students in 1970. But this quantitative expansion was not matched by qualitative changes in the curriculum, which retained its British colonial orientation, producing paternalistic administrative cadres who lacked technical skills and scorned manual labour.[80]

Obote admitted in 1969 that Uganda had 'not moved very far from the results of the educational investments which the British wanted' when formal education was first introduced to Uganda.[81] He argued that the alternative – delaying Ugandanisation until the curriculum could be made more responsive to Uganda's needs – was even more unacceptable: Uganda could not afford to entrust the implementation of nationalist policies to a civil service composed largely of expatriates. Yet, in implementing nationalist policies, the Africanised salariat demanded the protection of its corporate prerogatives.

The Obote regime attempted to reduce the prerogative of members of the public service in April 1970. The austerity measures abolished acting allowances for most state employees temporarily filling higher positions, ended overtime payments to civil servants, reduced the frequency of salary increases from once a year to once every two years, and eliminated government guaranteed loans for the purchase of motor cars by parastatal and government employees. The curtailment of guaranteed car loans, which totalled U. Shs. 22 million by 1969, had a dramatic effect on motor car sales in Kampala: by October dealers reported sales down by one-third to one-half.[82]

Income Distribution Under the UPC Regime

Despite its 1962 electoral strength in cash-crop areas, and despite a lineage that could be traced, via the UNC, to the Uganda African Farmers' Union, the UPC governed in a period of stagnating rural incomes. This was partially due to lower world prices for coffee and cotton. For both crops the average Mombasa f.o.b. value was 13 per cent lower in the 1962-70 period than in 1953-61. Although the regime had no control over world prices, it was the government's and marketing board's activities which determined what portion of the world price would accrue to growers and what portion to central and local government coffers, crop processors, the marketing boards and various costs (transportation, insurance and other marketing expenses). Rather than cutting marketing costs, reducing crop-processors' margins or laying off their own employees, the marketing boards responded to declining world prices by cutting the price to growers. Significantly, robusta coffee growers, concentrated in Buganda, suffered greater price drops than cotton growers, mainly concentrated in the Eastern and Northern Regions. On average, growers received 4 per cent less for cotton and 41 per cent less for robusta coffee in the 1962-70 period, compared with 1953-61.[83]

Notwithstanding Buganda growers' suspicions, the government's cotton preference sprang more from economic than political factors.

The long-run world demand for cotton appeared better than that for coffee, especially robusta. Moreover, cotton lint and seeds were important domestic manufacturing inputs, while coffee offered little scope for increased manufacturing employment. But despite blandishments by the government and chiefs and despite pricing to reduce the attraction of coffee, growers continued to shift from cotton to coffee wherever land tenure, climate and soil allowed. Coffee still offered the grower a higher return than cotton for a given amount of effort.

Except for the mildly progressive graduated tax introduced in all areas except Busoga, the rural tax burden was both regressive and hidden, consisting of export taxes on coffee and cotton, and the tobacco levy, import duties, and surpluses appropriated by the marketing boards. School fees for children constituted an additional, though voluntary, burden. In hopes that their children might escape from farming into white-collar employment, poor and middle-income growers made severe sacrifices to send at least some children to school. School fees, marketing board surpluses and taxes resulted in a 'tax' burden equal to more than half of peasants' cash incomes.

Capitalist African farmers, on the other hand, not only enjoyed the advantages of economies of scale, but by serving as leaders of growers' co-operative societies, were able to enrich themselves by dipping into the till, juggling books, and granting themselves extremely soft loans. Thus the growers' co-operative societies, financed by a levy on all members and aided by state-guaranteed loans,[84] mainly benefitted the wealthier farmers.

Furthermore, under the Obote regime, national income was redistributed from rural areas to urban centres, from peasant growers, agricultural labourers, and rural traders to the urban salariat, the professionals, urban merchants, and the full-time proletariat (defined as those workers who had moved up from migrant labourer status, by earning at least three times the minimum wage).[85]

Rural income per capita increased from an average U. Shs. 305 in 1960-2 to U. Shs. 355 in 1967-9, or an annual increase of 2.2 per cent which was slightly less than the annual inflation rate of 4.2 per cent between 1961 and 1968. In the same period the average annual wage for employees rose from U. Shs. 1,505 to U. Shs. 2,978, or 10.2 per cent per annum, well ahead of the inflation rate. This reflected a change in the composition of the labour-force rather than an across-the-board wage increase. The full-time proletariat, those earning at least U. Shs. 6,000 annually, increased from 8,000 to 23,000, growing from 4 to 9 per cent of the labour-force between 1964 and 1969. At least three-fifths of all workers continued earning a bare minimum wage, which ranged in 1969 from U. Shs. 60 to 90 per month in crop-processing, U. Shs. 100 to 145 on plantations, U. Shs. 160 in construction, U. Shs. 150 to 200 in manufacturing, to over U. Shs. 200 per month in mining, formerly one of the poorest-paid jobs. Even in mining the average wage remained below the level required for the transition from a single migrant labourer to a full-time worker financially capable of supporting a family.[86]

The foregoing income analysis has excluded self-employed professionals, directors of firms, and self-employed entrepreneurs, many of whom, though by no means a majority, fared much better than the salariat and labour aristocracy.

In the manufacturing sector proper, remuneration for directors totalled U. Shs. 14.8 million in 1968, or U. Shs. 30,958 per firm; in crop-processing (cotton, coffee, tea), directors received U. Shs. 5.2 million, or U. Shs. 20,618 per firm, in part reflecting the difference between the two sectors in value-added per firm (U. Shs. 757,000 per manufacturing firm versus U. Shs. 240,000 per crop-processing firm).[87]

In commerce, over 40 per cent of both the 549 wholesale firms and the 111 large retail firms (10 or more employees) reported an annual turnover of U. Shs. 2 million or more in 1966. In urban areas three-fifths of small retail firms (less than 10 employees) reported a turnover of U. Shs. 100,000 or more. But half the 14,000 small retail firms throughout Uganda and three-fifths of the 10,500 small rural retail firms had annual sales below U. Shs. 10,000.[88] Given the fact that the bulk of small-scale retail trade consisted of low-margin staples (sugar, salt, matches, soap, kerosene), the majority of rural traders eked out an existence little better than that of the average rural household.

Among Africans, few fared better than the UPC politicians, especially the so-called 'old-party' members who had held seats in the National Assembly since 1962. The 1970 debate on the Prevention of Corruption Bill revealed much about this group.

Adoko Nekyon warned,

> ... there is a behaviour, there is an attitude we have adopted which is an offence to the public we lead and that is a tendency to all over night grow like mushrooms into wealthy individuals which we were not five or seven years ago ... [T]here seems to be an apparent race for getting rich quicker, mushrooming into wealth over five years; the root of this race must be faced, and this bill cannot rectify that

attitude.[89]

Nekyon went on to accuse unnamed members who praised the Common Man's Charter of being reactionaries who placed their private economic interests above loyalty to either party or nation.

Humphrey Luande accused ministers of having monopolised bus transport companies and of attempting to monopolise trading licences. He observed that some government ministers avoided publicity by registering businesses in their wives' names.[90]

The object of much of this criticism was Felix Onama, Minister of Defence and Secretary-General of the UPC. A leader of the new right-wing faction within the UPC, he was a director of the Guy Transport Company, general manager of the West Nile Co-operative Union and a large-scale farmer. It was Onama who once boasted that the public would be surprised to learn how many members of the National Assembly were also agents of the National Trading Corporation. According to Onama's cunning interpretation of the Common Man's Charter, peasants should work harder to raise their standard of living and everyone should save more in order to invest. He declared that he drove a Mercedes-Benz as part of his effort to implement the Charter, as a servant rather than a master of the public.[91]

Other members were more frank in their self-assessment. As Bileni Gaspare Oda declared, 'For one to say that there is no corruption in this country is only trying to deceive the world that there is no corruption, because, after all, all of us here [in Parliament] are corrupted.' To emphasise his point, he noted his ownership of houses on Tank Hill in Kampala and his transportation interests:

> . . . I, Oda, am a well-to-do man with seventeen buses along Arua, Moyo and Kampala routes but here is Dr. Sembeguya who is a poor man with two buses which he wants to run along the same routes; how can this man compete with Oda who is a Member of Parliament having seventeen buses on [the] Arua to Kampala route? How do you expect this man to compete with me? Because I do not allow this man to do business. It is corruption because how did I get these buses? Where did I get the money? . . . [92]

The sharp discontinuity between the politicians' self-enrichment and the UPC's sudden verbal conversion to socialism undermined both elite and mass support for the regime. On the one hand, the 'have-nots' disbelieved the sincerity of the conversion or the capacity of the regime to make good its promises. The rural population was not inclined to rush to the support of a regime which had already promised much but delivered little beyond a few rural schools, dispensaries and water bore-holes, amid declining grower prices and, since mid-1968, rapidly rising consumer prices. On the other hand, the 'haves' were either convinced that godless Communists had seized power or, more realistically, were aware that some income redistribution was in store. State employees, from bureaucrats to teachers, lamented their own loss of prerogatives while grumbling about the politicians' noticeable lack of austerity. Landlords and prosperous tenant-farmers in Buganda feared land reform. Merchants of all races feared further state takeovers. Only NUSU members flocked *en masse* to the banner of the Common Man's Charter. Their support and zeal proved of dubious value in rural areas, where proselytising students clashed with traditional respect for the elders.

Inequality and Violence

The growing income inequalities under the Obote regime intensified structural violence in terms of the growing gap between the actual con-ditions of rural life and what was technically feasible. There was also an increase in personal or direct violence under the Obote regime.

Personal violence can be grouped into five categories: authoritative violence by the state against groups or individuals; unauthorised violence by state officials against groups or individuals; violence within the state or between levels of the state apparatus; violence by individuals against the state or state officials; and violence by individuals against other individuals or groups not directly connected with the state. The violence accompanying the attempted secession by Buganda in 1966 involved all five categories of personal violence. The 1969 assassination attempt against Obote belonged to the fourth category; the regime's response of extending the State of Emergency from Buganda to all Uganda, banning of opposition parties and detention of suspected oppo-nents belonged to the first category; and the activities of soldiers at road-blocks often belonged to the second category.

Kondoism, violent robbery by bands of armed individuals, belongs to the fifth category. Kondoism or brigandage is common in most peripheral capitalist countries because of the weakness of the state apparatus. The Ugandan state was itself implicated in kondoism, first, by its failure to cope with the phenomenon, and, second, by the fact that kondos were often dressed as soldiers and armed with sub-machine guns that could only be obtained by the complicity of individuals within the army.

Interviews at the village level near Kampala in 1970 and 1971 revealed that local rivalries were a prominent factor in kondoism. Though frequently involving loss of life, kondoism at the village level was not particularly remunerative since the spoils involved transistor radios, blankets, second-hand automobiles, bags of coffee and the much sought after, but usually insignificant, hidden life savings of the victim. Villages established vigilante groups to patrol at night. A village member who was lax in volunteering for such duty might easily find himself the victim of a kondo raid perpetrated by real kondos or by a neighbouring vigilante committee hired by the local committee. Rival villages engaged in kondo raids against each other, and kondoism became a convenient means for redressing old scores.

The prevalence of kondoism, particularly the rise of kondoism after 1966, suggests that kondoism served as a cover for political activity, for acts of rebellion against state authority, for acts of political revenge and for acts of intimidation against Asian businessmen. Between 1966 and 1969, murders rose by 39.9 per cent, aggravated assault by 74.4 per cent and robbery by 28.6 per cent.[93] To the extent that kondoism was directed against Asians and Europeans, it might be viewed as a manifestation of economic nationalism that had few avenues of expression during Obote's tacit alliance with the Asian bourgeoisie. Kondoism might also be an apolitical protest against inequalities engendered by structural dependence. But there was a vast gulf between the rural kondo bands armed with crude *pangas* (harvesting knives) raiding villages for vengeance or simple loot and the urban gangs who staged payroll robberies with automatic rifles purchased on the black market. The former may have been Hobsbawm's pre-political primitive rebels, but the latter were armed entrepreneurs, not Robin Hood.

Ethnicity and Economic Structure: The UPC Alliance With Asians Against Buganda

At the time of independence, 73,000 Asians, (Indians, Pakistanis, Goans and Arabs) lived in Uganda. Approximately one-third had obtained citizenship by 1969, most of them during the period 1962-4 and most of these Ismailis. There was a tendency for male breadwinners to become citizens, and for females to retain other citizenship as a form of insurance in case of expulsion. Whereas 35.2 per cent of Asian males aged 15 to 49 were Ugandan citizens, only 28.7 per cent of Asian females in the same age group were Ugandan citizens.[94]

Within the Asian 'community', Goans were prominent in government service, but not in commerce and industry. Members of the Catholic Goan community (who were officially Portuguese subjects until India reclaimed Goa in 1961) comprised half the Asian clerks recruited into the colonial civil service. Of 4,588 trading licences held by Asians (in 1954), 31 per cent were held by Patidar Hindus, 28 per cent by Lohana Hindus, 25 per cent by Ismaili Muslims, and 16 per cent by others (Vania, Brahmin, Ithnasheri, Bohora, Sunni, Sikh, Goan, etc.). In manufacturing, the Patidars, Ismailis and Lohanas owned 36 per cent of 600 factories in 1954. But two family conglomerates founded in the 1920s, Madhvani and Mehta, towered above the rest. Industrial Promotion Services, a newcomer founded in 1961 by the Aga Khan and the Ismaili community, showed rapid growth.[95]

The Obote regime recognised that an economic policy which sought to shift economic control simply from non-citizens to citizens would tend to favour the Baganda bourgeoisie, which possessed a head start in terms of skills, experience, resources and location. The UPC sought to redress the regional-ethnic imbalance of the colonial period by regulating the commercial and political expansion of the Baganda bourgeoisie. The UPC's 'socialism' emphasised horizontal or geographical equality of opportunity for African professionals and traders throughout Uganda more than vertical or class antagonisms.

The Obote regime checked Baganda commercial expansion by two methods. First, the state, rather than individuals, was to control the commanding heights of the economy. The contradiction inherent in this tactic was that, while the non-Baganda had a preponderant influence within the UPC, Baganda professionals and clerks were better equipped to fill the administrative posts in a state-controlled economy. They had experience in the Buganda government and education from Makerere College, where Baganda students comprised 79 per cent of Uganda African students in 1922 and still 47 per cent in 1960.[96] Therefore, even a commanding heights strategy might aggrandise the power of the Baganda elite.

Second, the UPC regime checked Baganda commercial expansion by striking an alliance with the Asian commercial and administrative strata, allowing members of this politically vulnerable ethnic group to fill positions which would otherwise be taken over by the Baganda middle class. The contradiction inherent in this tactic was that it eventually aroused the opposition of even non-Baganda traders and allowed the

Baganda bourgeoisie to wave the flag of economic nationalism against the UPC centre.[97]

As Kasfir has shown, ethnic rivalry among Africans within the higher civil service was defused by the very pace of Ugandanisation and by the strategy of increasing the proportion of Asians in the salariat. First, the number of Baganda in the higher civil service increased from 23 to 105 between 1961 and 1967, but their share of Africanised posts decreased from 46.9 per cent to 35.6 per cent. This was still twice the proportion of Baganda in the African population, yet the trend indicated that the administrative salariat was becoming more regionally and ethnically representative. Second, although Asians comprised only 0.8 per cent of the Ugandan population, the percentage of Asians in the higher civil service rose from 5.7 per cent in 1959 to 13.4 per cent in 1967.[98]

The Obote regime instituted a number of measures which adversely affected the interests of Asian businessmen in Uganda: (a) the general freeze on processing citizenship applications after October 1964: (b) the take-over of coffee exports by the Coffee Marketing Board; (c) the enlarged role of African growers' co-operative societies in processing both cotton and coffee; (d) continued restrictions on Asians trading in rural areas; (e) restrictions on non-citizens engaged in trade imposed by the Trade Licensing Act of 1969; (f) the take-over of wholesale distribution of certain commodities by the agents and outlets of the National Trading Corporation; (g) the take-over of buying of agricultural produce by agents of the Produce Marketing Board; (h) the imposition of foreign exchange control and gradual tightening of foreign exchange regulations; and (i) the take-over of external trade by designated agents of the Export and Import Corporation.

Despite vocal pressure by African traders for Africanisation of retail and wholesale trade, the Obote regime's measures to effect Africanisation of commerce were enforced more slowly and more loosely than similar measures adopted by the Kenyatta regime in Kenya.[99] The regime preferred to leave large-scale commerce in the hands of Asians or the state. As ethnic outsiders, Asians could not aspire to control the state. Any unwanted attempt by non-citizen Asians to enhance their political role could be countered by the threat of expulsion. From 1967 onward, the Obote regime did apply pressure on Asian, European and parastatal firms to Africanise management and technical positions, but Africanisation of high-level positions within these firms did not affect management control.[100]

Within the culturally and economically divided Asian community two groups, for very different reasons, were able to maintain their status in commerce. Having opted for Ugandan citizenship, the Ismailis could claim that they had identified with African aspirations and should therefore be treated as ordinary Ugandan citizens.[101] Large Asian firms in wholesale trade and manufacturing, whether owned by citizens or non-citizens, were able to continue operation as before. Large Asian firms were named as agents of the Coffee Marketing Board, the Produce Marketing Board and the Export and Import Corporation.[102] In implementing the Trade Licensing Act, the Obote regime drew a distinction between large non-citizen firms, which were allowed to continue operations, and small non-citizen firms which were ordered to wind up their affairs or to sell to Africans.[103]

The UPC was largely financed by contributions from Asian firms.[104] The representation of Asian commercial interests in Parliament was guaranteed by malapportionment. Whereas the average parliamentary constituency contained a population of 79,000, Asian-populated constituencies averaged only 15,000.[105] In addition, the Obote regime awarded three of the nine specially elected seats in Parliament to prominent Asian businessmen. Postponement of the 1967 elections preserved Asian overrepresentation in Parliament.

At a UPC conference in December 1970, Obote hinted that most of the 12,000 stalled applications by Asians for citizenship would be approved shortly. In response to this announcement, the UPC delegates 'groaned disapprovingly'.[106] By 1970, both Baganda and non-Baganda traders had united in opposition to further concessions to Asian traders. They were joined by ambitious members of the salariat who wished to abandon the commanding heights strategy in favour of state aid to individual African traders and would-be traders such as themselves.

From the perspective of structural dependence, the Obote regime's collaboration with large Asian firms had two positive effects: first, it temporarily retarded the emergence of a conservative African mercantile class tied to the colonial pattern of trade; second, it encouraged Asian firms to shift from trade to manufacturing.

Together, the UDC, Madhvani and Mehta groups formed the big three, the core of industrial capital in Uganda.

Few figures are available for the Mehta Group, the oldest but smallest of the big three. Its main activities included the Lugazi sugar plantation and refinery, sugar machinery and agricultural tools (Ugma Steel and Engineering), tea-processing, cotton-ginning, electrical cables, paper sacks (joint venture with Madhvani), motor vehicle sales, and sugar plantation development (the Kinyala project for the government).[107]

The Madhvani Group was large enough to rival the UDC. Between 1966 and 1970 Madhvani's *net* turnover rose from 427.8 million shillings to 467.3 million shillings and the number of employees from 16,479 to 20,077. In the same period the UDC's *gross* turnover rose from 449.0 million shillings to 614.5 million shillings and the number of employees from 20,777 to 23,981. Whereas the UDC's activities were largely confined to Uganda, 35 per cent of the Madhvani Group's turnover was derived from its subsidiary and associate firms in Kenya and Tanzania. In Uganda, its fixed assets, totalling over 640 million shillings in 1970, were deployed in the following areas: the Kakira sugar plantation and refinery, cotton textiles, steel ingots (joint venture with UDC), beer, glass bottles, edible oils and fats, tin cans, soap, confectionery, matches (joint venture with UDC and Sikh Saw Mills), corrugated cardboard boxes, cotton seed cake and tea-processing.[108]

Admittedly, the industrial sector in Uganda had severe shortcomings. First, it was small; its contribution to the gross domestic product ranged from 6 to 7 per cent (8 to 9 per cent if one included cotton-ginning, coffee-curing and sugar-refining). Second, most manufacturing was of the import-substitution variety, based on existing patterns of consumption, imported technology and often imported raw materials. Third, industrial capital in Uganda was dependent on multinational firms, who used joint ventures, management contracts and technology licensing to integrate Ugandan manufacturing into the global marketing strategy of the multinational firms. Fourth, as noted earlier, the emergence of industrial capital in Uganda was initially the product of a defensive strategy of foreign (mainly British) capital and Asian merchant capital which shifted from trade to manufacturing in the 1950s and 1960s in order to move up within the domestic vertical division of labour, leaving smaller African and Asian retailers to fight over control of trade.

None the less, even a dependent, defensive manufacturing sector based on import substitution is better than no manufacturing sector at all. Once in place, the interests of Asian and state industrial capital were structurally different from the interests of the merchant bourgeoisie. The manufacturing sector was geared to import substitution within the framework of the East African market rather than the more narrow Ugandan market.

It was Semei Nyanzi, chairman of the UDC, who energetically lobbied for *reduced* restrictions on inter-East African trade in 1967, in order to have the largest possible protected market to exploit. It was Jayant Madhvani, managing director of the Madhvani Group, who spearheaded the formation of the Federation of Uganda Industries in 1968 in recognition of the fact that the interests of industrial capital could not be adequately served by the merchant-dominated Uganda Chamber of Commerce.[109] It is significant that Obote named the industrialist Jayant Madhvani, rather than a politician or a merchant, to be the first chairman of the Export and Import Corporation in 1970.

Uganda's manufacturing sector produced a growing range of mass-consumption goods (cotton piece-goods, rayon fabrics, blankets, clothing, shoes, vegetable oil products, soap, sugar, matches, enamel-ware and bicycle tyres), basic intermediate and producer goods (corrugated iron roofing, hoes, fish-nets, cement, paint, tiles, bricks, cattle feed, superphosphate fertiliser, paper products, food tins and glass-ware), as well as simple luxury goods (beer, spirits, soft drinks, cigarettes, candy and luggage).

There was a fair degree of intersectoral linkages between manufacturing and agriculture. The two largest cotton textile mills required 9,500 metric tons of cotton lint annually. Cotton seed was used in making margarine, vegetable ghee, soap and cattle feed. The sugar industry had, in turn, spawned an engineering works and steel industry (based on scrap metal) which produced spare parts for sugar and other machinery, construction materials, pipes and flat bars, which another firm used to produce 1.6 million hoes each year for farmers.

Although average value-added per industrial worker remained fairly constant under Obote, total African employment in manufacturing (excluding crop processing) rose steadily from 24,695 in 1962 to 39,455 in 1970, while by contrast, total African employment in the government administration (central and local) dipped from 44,012 in 1962 to 32,988 in 1967 before rising to 44,412 in 1970.[110]

The significance of the UPC-Asian alliance for economic structure can be illustrated using the Galtung-Hungrø trade composition index. Kenya in 1964 had an index score of –0.400, whereas Uganda had an index score of –0.809,[111] indicating that Uganda was more structurally dependent than Kenya. Thanks to European settler opposition to the imperialist pattern of colonial trade and thanks to the forcible creation of a larger working class in Kenya, Kenya entered the post-colonial era with an economic structure that was less dependent than Uganda's. Since the ethnic group that controlled the post-colonial state in Kenya was also the one which stood to benefit the most from Africanisation of commerce, the Kenyan state pursued a policy of rapid Africanisation, creating a Kikuyu mercantile class. In Uganda, however, the post-colonial state was controlled by ethnic groups that wished to check the rise of the Baganda traders who were first in line to benefit from Africanisation of trade.

Although the commanding heights strategy and the alliance between the UPC and Asian manufacturers and wholesalers were motivated more by exigencies of ethnic rivalry than by a conscious strategy to reduce structural dependence, in blocking temporarily the emergence of an African mercantile class and in forcing portions of the Asian mercantile class to enter manufacturing, the Obote regime caused a slight shift towards less dependence. The trade composition index for Kenya declined from -0.400 to -0.449 vetween 1964 and 1970, whereas Uganda's index improved from -0.809 to -0.736. Kenya's economy became slightly more dependent; Uganda's, slightly less dependent. Both the small magnitude of these shifts and Kenya's continued lead over Uganda signal the need for caution in interpreting these indices. Nevertheless, further support comes from comparison of trends in manufacturing employment in the two countries. Between 1962 and 1970, Kenya's employment in manufacturing grew at an annual rate of 4.2 per cent, whereas Uganda's manufacturing employment grew at an annual rate of 7.0 per cent, albeit from a smaller base.[112]

Conclusion: Legitimation Problems and the Rise of the Military

Both the 1966 revolution and the tacit alliance with Asian civil servants, manufacturers and wholesalers were part of the regime's strategy to counter Buganda hegemony in domestic affairs. Both were progressive, in so far as the first helped to dismantle the colonial infrastructure of dependence and the second, to promote a semi-autonomous manufacturing sector. But the regime chose to ignore its own role in the infrastructure of dependence.

The regime's support for income redistribution was at best half-hearted; its support for radical popular control of party, state and economy was non-existent. Beginning with his 1964 defence of the private acquisition of a coffee factory by two cabinet ministers, Obote condoned the possessive individualism of government members.[113] Moreover, the commitment to regional equality of opportunity spawned a stratum of African businessmen outside Buganda, especially in Arua, and 'Nubian' traders in the north and east, who joined Baganda businessmen in demanding more rapid Africanisation of trade.[114]

The commitment to more equal distribution of development projects and manufacturing plants sparked intense squabbling among districts, especially in the north. That home areas of migrant labourers tended to be Catholic and therefore DP only compounded the problem. Martin Abee Okelo (DP – West Nile and Madi Central) accused the government of regarding West Nile as a human zoo and source of cheap labour. He charged that the government feared 'if one, two, three or more industries are started in West Nile, the flow of labour from that district to other districts will be stopped'.[115] Accusations of government bias in locating the cassava starch factory and cotton-spinning mill in Lango rather than Acholi led to the sacking of the UPC district administration in Acholi and expulsion of Acholi party leaders in February 1968.[116]

After the 1966 revolution, the regime made few efforts at reconciliation in Buganda. It did reject Bunyoro petitions for further transfers of land from Buganda. Five former KY members of the Kabaka's government were allowed to join the UPC in August and September of 1967. Though it specifically excluded Edward Mutesa, the government did allocate pensions or gratuities to other former rulers and constitutional heads in September and provided allowances for Mutesa's wife and eleven children.[117]

These gestures were offset by the virtual occupation of Buganda, symbolised by the renewal of the State of Emergency in Buganda every six months throughout the remainder of the First Republic, the forced sale in January 1968 of the Buganda government's headquarters (*Bulange*) to the Ministry of Defence for use by the army, and the detention of 50 to 93 persons at any given time. These measures, combined with low coffee prices and the moderate pace of Africanisation, earned Obote the enmity of not only the traditional Baganda aristocracy and chiefs but also the traders and capitalist farmers. The latter perceived that the abolition of the Kabakaship and the end of Buganda's federal autonomy foreshadowed the abolition of the *mailo-kibanja* land-tenure system, the economic basis of Buganda's lead.

Even with such liabilities, the regime's fear of elections was puzzling. In September 1966 it eliminated the 12 elected seats on the 33-member Kampala City Council, reduced elected seats on the 28-member Jinja council from 16 to 6, and on the 24-member Mbale council, from 16 to 8.[118] By postponing national elections from 1967 to 1971, the regime let slip its best opportunity for a popular vote of confidence. Instead, the 'long parliament' became a political liability, as members gained wealth and notoriety, and as 16 seats remained conspicuously vacant.

From February 1968 to the December 1969 assassination attempt, Obote's meet-the-people tours tried to fill the political void between the regime and citizens. The tours did serve as a tactful way of bypassing party notables to assess local support and demands and provided Obote with some opportunities to legitimate his role as head of state, amid pageantry and hoopla. But increasingly the regime relied on three coercive instruments for its survival: the army, the para-military Special Forces within the police, and the General Service Unit (GSU), the 'secret' police headed by Akena Adoko.

Relations between the Obote regime and the Uganda Army, the 4th and 5th battalions of the colonial King's African Rifles (KAR), got off to a rocky start. First, the Uganda-based soldiers in the KAR had played an active role in suppressing the nationalist movement in Kenya during the so-called Mau-Mau Emergency. Second, in early 1962 KAR soldiers massacred Turkana pastoralists on the Uganda-Kenya frontier. Lt. Idi Amin was implicated in one such incident, but, on the advice of Obote, British officers dropped charges and did not dismiss Amin.[119] Third, in early 1964 army mutinies swept through all three East African armies in domino fashion.

The Zanzibar revolution of 12 January triggered the chain of mutinies. At the request of the victorious Afro-Shirazi Party (ASP), President Nyerere of Tanganyika sent a contingent of police from Dar es Salaam to assist ASP in restoring order. Seizing the opportunity afforded by the reduced strength of the police in the capital, Tanganyikan troops staged a mutiny to demand higher pay and Africanisation of the officer corps. A few days later the Uganda Army mutinied at the Jinja barracks; the Kenya Army mutinied at the Lanet and Langata barracks.[120]

The 350 Jinja mutineers demanded the doubling of pay scales for enlisted men. When Felix Onama, then Minister of State for Internal Affairs, went to the barracks to negotiate, the mutineers seized him and held him hostage for 24 hours, forcing him to give a written promise of higher pay. Unlike their Tanganyikan counterparts, the Ugandan mutineers made no attempt to seize strategic positions, probably because the capital was 80 kilometres from the barracks. Obote responded by requesting the assistance of British troops, which were flown in from Nairobi. Following this precedent, the leaders of Tanganyika and Kenya also requested British troop assistance.[121]

Although the mutinies in the three nations resembled each other in the pattern of events and demands, the aftermath diverged in three directions: politicisation of the Tanganyika Army; 'neutralisation' of the Kenya Army; and capitulation to the organisational interests of the Uganda Army. Tanganyikan leaders integrated the army more closely with the ruling party, TANU, and established a balancing force, the para-military National Service.[122] In Kenya the directors of the mutiny were given stiff sentences. The army was further de-politicised along the Western tradition of a politically 'neutral' military and bureaucracy, which proved conducive to the alliance between Kikuyu businessmen and foreign capital. The politicised military and bureaucracy in Tanganyika was conducive to the emergence of peripheral state capitalism.

The Kenyan alternative would have been anathema to the salariat and UPC notables in Uganda; the Tanganyikan alternative was not feasible in 1964, given the UPC-KY alliance. The Obote regime tried to buy time and the loyalty of the military. The day after the mutiny, wages of privates were raised from Shs. 105 to Shs. 265 per month. By July 1964, the officer corps of the army had been Africanised; Col. Shaban Opolot replaced Col. R. Groome as Commander. Only a token number of soldiers were convicted of inciting mutiny, and many of the discharged soldiers were recalled to service during the Congo crisis.[123]

Close collaboration between Obote and Amin started with Uganda's secret intervention in the Congo crisis. Their partnership culminated in Amin's attack on the Kabaka's palace in 1966 and Amin's promotion to Opolot's post after the latter was detained on suspicion of plotting with the UPC right wing. The collaborators drifted apart during their second foreign adventure; funnelling Israeli aid to the Anya Nya rebels in the southern Sudan. Obote ordered Anya Nya assistance ended after Jaafar al-Nimeiry seized control of the Sudanese government in May 1969. Amin (and Onama?) continued to channel Israeli aid to the Anya Nya. The arrest of the West German mercenary Rolf Steiner by Uganda police in August 1970 led to the discovery of Steiner's diary, which revealed Amin's unauthorised collaboration with Israelis in the southern Sudan.[124]

Meanwhile, Obote's reliance on Amin's army carried another price, the cost of meeting the army's demands for a larger share in the budget. Military expenditure rose from 4.4 per cent of the state budget in 1964/65 to 12.3 per cent in 1967/68, then declined in relative terms. To lessen his dependence on the army, Obote began shifting resources from the army to the Special Forces (created in 1968) and to the General Service Unit. The army responded by continuing to spend in the style to which it was accustomed, overrunning its budgetary allocations by 28 per cent or U. Shs. 37.3 million in 1969/70.[125] Although Obote placed personal blame for the 1968/69 and 1969/70 army overspending on Amin, some responsibility also rests with Onama as Minister of Defence.

The murder of Brigadier Pierino Okoya near Gulu on 25 January 1970 increased the enmity between Obote and Amin. Only eight days earlier Okoya had accused Amin of cowardice for fleeing after the 19 December attempt on Obote's life. Okoya's death cast suspicion on Amin.[126] In a television interview in August 1970, Amin pointedly drew a distinction between his support for the office of the President and his support for Obote. After this interview, Amin's political stock rose noticeably among Baganda traders and farmers.

Simultaneously, the new centre-right split in the UPC became more open. Onama was clearly uncomfortable with the 'Move to the Left'. Rumours of an impending coup, led by Onama, Amin, or both, swept Kampala in September. Radio South Africa eagerly reported a coup in progress in Uganda on 29 September. After suspending normal pro-grammes, Radio Kampala gave notice of a special announcement later that evening. The somewhat anti-climactic announcement reported that the Defence Council, chaired by Obote, had approved a number of pro-motions, transfers and a reorganisation. Those promoted included Sandhurst and other educated officers who would be more loyal to Obote than to the enlisted men and NCOs surrounding Amin.[127] The Defence Council also promoted Brigadier Suleiman Hussein to Army Chief of Staff and Colonel Juma Musa to Chief of the Air Force, leaving Amin with less direct control over the military.[128]

Obote's misgivings about Amin were further revealed by the cancelling of the Independence Day celebrations and the military display scheduled for 9 October, ostensibly out of respect for Egypt's President Nasser, who had died more than a week earlier. On 12 October, Amin made a surprise public appearance at Obote's installation as Chancellor of Makerere University, dispelling rumours that Amin was under house arrest. Nervous laughter and scattered applause broke from the audience.

Three months later, while attending the Commonwealth Conference in Singapore to oppose British arms sales to South Africa, Obote's attempts to diversify coercive power through creation of the Special Forces and the GSU came to naught. On the night of 24 January and into the following morning, the sounds of mortars and automatic gun-fire echoed through Kampala. Radio Kampala played music: symphonies, the Beatles, but no martial music; and Kampala residents exchanged rumours as to whether Onama, Amin or someone else was leading the coup. In the afternoon of 25 January 1971, Warrant Officer Wilfred Aswa interrupted the radio music to read the 18-point announcement that the soldiers had taken control of the government.

Notes

1. 'Independence is not an end by itself but a means to a greater struggle
... To the UPC Independence should not mean the mere replacement of White
faces by Black faces in the Government machinery nor the acquisition of
mansions and latest fashionable cars by a few top leaders, while everything in the
countryside continues to be as it was under Imperialism. We must raise the
social and economic status of the Africans to the level which has for long been
enjoyed by the dominant races. No African will remain contented and tolerate
inferior economic status under the flag of Indpendence.' John Kakonge, in UPC,
Second Annual Delegates' Conference, Mbale 4th, 5th and 6th August 1962
(Conference Programme), p. 5. See also A. Milton Obote's 1963 endorsement of
the goal of economic independence in Joseph S. Nye, Jr., *Pan-Africanism and East
African Integration* (Cambridge, Mass.: Harvard University Press, 1965), p. 45.

2. Susanne Bodenheimer, 'Dependency and Imperialism: The Roots of Latin
American Underdevelopment', *Politics and Society*, vol. 1, no. 3 (May 1971),
p. 335.

3. Clive Thomas, 'Industrialization and the Transformation of Africa', *Multinational Firms in Africa*, ed. Carl Widstrand (Uppsala: Scandinavian Institute of
African Studies, 1975), pp. 343-4.

4. Jan Jørgensen and Timothy M. Shaw, 'International Dependence and
Foreign Policy Choices: The Political Economy of Uganda', Paper presented to
the Canadian Association of African Studies, Ottawa, February 1973, p. 45. Cf.
Horace Campbell, *Four Essays on Neo-Colonialism in Uganda* (Toronto: Dumont
Press, 1975), p. 31.

5. Uganda, *Constitution of Uganda* (1962) (Entebbe: Government Printer,
1964), Chapter VII, section 74 (56).

6. Uganda, *The Uganda (Independence) Order in Council, 1962* (Entebbe:
Government Printer, 1964), section 19 (I).

7. Audrey I. Richards, 'Epilogue', *The King's Men*, ed. Lloyd A. Fallers
(London: Oxford University Press for EAISR, 1964), pp. 357-94.

8. Grace Ibingira, *The Forging of an African Nation* (New York: Viking Press,
1973), pp. 92, 114, 182-3. Farmers, particularly Baganda farmers, demanded
that the right of citizenship should not automatically include the right to own
land.

9. Uganda, *Constitution of Uganda (1962)*, Chapter II, sections 7, 8 (5) and
(6), and 12.

10. List of titles compiled from following sources: *Uganda Argus*; Fred Burke,
Local Government and Politics in Uganda (Syracuse, New York: Syracuse
University Press, 1964), p. 167; and Colin Leys, *Politicians and Policies; An
Essay on Politics in Acholi, Uganda, 1962-65* (Nairobi: East African Publishing
House, 1967), p. 19. For an excellent discussion of the conflict between nobles
and commoners within the UPC see Akiiki Mujaju, 'The Role of the UPC as a
Party of Government in Uganda', *Canadian Journal of African Studies*, vol. 10,
no. 3 (1976), pp. 443-67.

11. Richards, 'Epilogue', p. 361.

12. Amos Sempa, Budget Speech, 16 June 1964, p. 3.

13. *Uganda Argus*, 8 January 1964.

14. For the central government's version of the financial dispute, see Milton
Obote, 'The Footsteps of Uganda's Revolution', *East Africa Journal*, vol. 5
(October 1968), p. 11.

15. Uganda, *The Uganda (Independence) Order in Council, 1962*, section
26 (1).

16. Edward Mutesa, *Desecration of My Kingdom* (London: Constable, 1967),

pp. 169-70; Semakula Kiwanuka, 'Diplomacy of the Lost Counties, 1900-1964', *Mawazo*, vol. 4, no. 2 (1974), p. 132; and *Uganda Argus*, 18 January 1964.

17. Mujaju, 'The Role of the UPC', pp. 450-1, 457.

18. *Uganda Argus*, 6 June 1964, and Terence K. Hopkins, 'Politics in Uganda: The Buganda Question', *Boston University Papers on Africa*, ed. Jeffrey Butler and A.A. Castagno (New York: Praeger, 1967), pp. 260-3.

19. Kiwanuka, 'Diplomacy of the Lost Counties', p. 135.

20. Great Britain, Colonial Office, 'Report of a Commission of Privy Coun- sellors on a Dispute Between Buganda and Bunyoro', May 1962 (XI 1119), Cmnd. 1717, Appendix II, pp. 26-7; and Henry W. West, *Land Policy in Buganda* (Cambridge: Cambridge University Press, 1972), pp. 31-3, 48n. and 161.

21. For accounts of these four incidents see the following sources: Nakulabye: *Uganda Argus*, 12, 13 and 14 November 1964; army incident: *Uganda Argus*, 16 February 1965, and special correspondent, 'The Uganda Army: Nexus of Power', *Africa Report*, vol. 11 (December 1966), p. 38; market incident: Mutesa, *Desecration of My Kingdom*, p. 170; Obote, 'The Footsteps of Uganda's Revolu- tion', p. 10; and Akena Adoko, *Uganda Crisis* (Kampala: African Publishers, 1970), pp. 7, 119 and 140; Ndaiga incident: Hopkins, 'Politics in Uganda: The Baganda Question', p. 260.

22. F.M. Dahlberg, 'The Emergence of a Dual Governing Elite in Uganda', *Journal of Modern African Studies*, vol. 9, no. 4 (December 1971), pp. 618-25.

23. As Mujaju notes, Obote himself was linked to a prominent chiefly family through his cousin Akena Adoko. Grace Ibingira, Secretary General of the UPC from 1964 to 1966, was a prince within the traditional hierarchy of Ankole. William Wilberforce Nadiope was a prince within the traditional hierarchy of Busoga and used his position as a political notable within the UPC to regain his former position as traditional or constitutional head (Kyabazinga) of Busoga as well as obtaining the Vice Presidency of Uganda from 1953 to 1966. In addition to being a substantial capitalist farmer, landowner and president of the Bunyoro Growers Co-operative Union, George Magezi, the first Secretary-General of the UPC (before Kakonge and Ibingira), was temporarily linked by marriage to the constitutional head of Bunyoro, the Omukama. As a former KY member, Dr Emmanuel B.S. Lumu, UPC Minister of Health until 1966, had close ties with the Kabaka. Felix Onama, Secretary-General of the UPC and Minister of Defence from 1966 to 1971, was both general manager of the West Nile Co-operative Union and director of a transport company in northern Uganda. Mujaju, 'The Role of the UPC', pp. 450-1; Roger Southall, *Parties and Politics in Bunyoro* (Kampala: MISR, 1972), p. 47; and Selwyn Douglas Ryan, 'Uganda: A Balance Sheet of the Revolution', *Mawazo*, vol. 3, no. 1 (June 1971), p. 60.

24. Joseph S. Nye, Jr., 'TANU and UPC: The Impact of Independence on Two African Nationalist Parties', *Boston University Papers on Africa*, ed. Butler and Castagno, p. 234; and Tertit Aasland, *On the Move-to-the-Left in Uganda, 1969-71*, Research Report No. 26 (Uppsala: Scandinavian Institute of African Studies, 1974), p. 69n.

25. Leys, *Politicians and Policies*, p. 29; and Aasland, *On the Move-to-the- Left*, pp. 70-1.

26. M. Crawford Young, 'The Obote Revolution', *African Report*, June 1966, p. 10.

27. With the break-up of the UPC-KY alliance, a number of KY cabinet members joined the UPC rather than lose their portfolios. Despite Bataringaya's defection, the Democratic Party's extra-parliamentary organisation remained intact, under the leadership of Benedicto Kiwanuka and Paul Ssemogerere.

28. *Uganda Argus*, 5 April and 8, 10, 16 and 19 July 1965. Both Abu Mayanja and Ali Kisekka claimed that the Kabaka had urged the Baganda to join the UPC.

29. Hopkins, 'Politics in Uganda', p. 262.

30. Amos Kalule Sempa in Uganda, *Parliamentary Debates (Hansard); National Assembly Official Report*, vol. 47, Motion on Annual Estimates for 1965/66 Budget, 21 June 1965, p. 2201.

31. Ibingira, *The Forging of an African Nation*, pp. 109-10. Compare Ibingira's stand with Kakonge's above in footnote 1.

32. Akiki Mujaju, 'The Demise of UPCYL and the Rise of NUYO in Uganda', *African Review* (Dar es Salaam), vol. 3, no. 2 (1973), pp. 291-307. Mujaju also notes allegations that UPCYL members were involved in the burning of a European home on Tank Hill, Kampala, following a party at which Europeans ridiculed Uganda's independence and African rule.

33. About 600 people attended a debate between John Kakonge and Adoko Nekyon at the Clock Tower, Kampala, on 30 May 1964, during which Kakonge attempted to defend scientific socialism against Nekyon's anti-Communist barage. *Uganda Argus*, 1 June 1964. In 1970, the UPC newspaper, *The People*, attacked Kakonge for his espousal of scientific socialism and for alleged drunkenness aboard an East African Airways flight.

34. Mujaju, 'The Demise of UPCYL and the Rise of NUYO in Uganda', p. 304.

35. *Uganda Argus*, 30 April and 4 May, 1964; and Mujaju, 'The Role of the UPC', pp. 458-60.

36. Akiiki Mujaju, 'The Demise of UPCYL and the Rise of NUYO in Uganda', p. 306. The Uganda-Vietnam Solidarity Party was banned in December 1969, and again in 1971 by the Amin regime. NUSU was banned in October 1972 for alleged sympathy to the pro-Obote invasion of Uganda from Tanzania. Uganda, *Statutory Instruments 1972*, No. 153.

37. Roger Scott, *The Development of Trade Unions in Uganda* (Nairobi: East African Publishing House, 1966), pp. 11-17, 111, 137-40, and 154.

38. Scott, *The Development of Trade Unions in Uganda,* p. 146; and *Uganda Argus*, 8 and 11 August 1964.

39. *Uganda Argus*, 25 August 1966 and 29 April 1968. Cf. Mahmood Mamdani, *Politics and Class Formation in Uganda* (New York: Monthly Review Press, 1976), pp. 241, 281-5.

40. On the interplay between class and ethnicity within the periphery, see Immanuel Wallerstein, 'Social Conflict in Post-Independence Black Africa: The Concepts of Race and Status-Group Reconsidered', *Racial Tensions and National Identity*, ed. Ernest Q. Campbell (Nashville, Tennessee: Vanderbilt University Press, 1972), pp. 207-26; and Tom Nairn, 'The Modern Janus: Nationalism', *New Left Review*, no. 94 (Nov.- Dec. 1975), pp. 3-29.

41. Ibingira, *The Forging of an African Nation*, p. 204.

42. *Munno*, 25 September 1965; and *Uganda Argus*, 28 July and 4 November 1965, 7 and 17 January, 14 February 1966. Katwe is a Kampala suburb noted for its nationalistic African traders.

43. See, for example, the editorial warning the government not to annoy Tshombe, *Munno*, 26 August 1965.

44. *Uganda Argus*, 15 January 1965; Uganda, *Parliamentary Debates (Hansard); National Assembly*, vol. 58, 4 February 1966; and Uganda, *Report of the L'Estang Commission to Enquire into Gold Allegations*, as summarised in *Uganda Argus*, 18 August 1971.

45. *Munno*, 26 May 1965, and *Uganda Argus*, 26 May 1965.

46. *Munno*, 4 August 1965, contained lengthy critiques of African socialism by KY and DP leaders. *Munno*, 7 August 1965, reported at length Amos Sempa's speech that Obote had abandoned non-alignment and allied himself with the Communist bloc and Tanzania against the people of Kenya and Uganda. Sempa declared that not even all the water in Lake Victoria 'can wash away the big drops

of communism and its bad smell which the Prime Minister has brought to Uganda from his visit to the Eastern bloc'. See also *Munno* editorials, 13 August 1965, 19 August 1965 and 22 September 1965. In September the Lukiko met to discuss steps to deal with alleged centres for Communist training in the forests in Uganda, *Uganda Argus*, 1 October 1965.

47. *Uganda Argus*, 14 February 1966; Southall, *Parties and Politics in Bunyoro*, pp. 46-51; and Young, 'The Obote Revolution', p. 12, for similar party struggles in Sebei.

48. Uganda, *Parliamentary Debates (Hansard); National Assembly*, vol. 58, 4 February 1966, and Emergency Meeting, 15 April 1966.

49. *Uganda Argus*, 18 August 1971.

50. Kirya was an official of the North Mbale Co-operative Union; Ngobi, an official of the Busoga Growers Co-operative Union; and Magezi, leader of the Bunyoro Growers Co-operative Union. As of January 1966, state-guaranteed bank loans to these three co-operatives totalled Shs. 1.9 million or 18.5 per cent of all state-guaranteed loans to co-operatives. Uganda, *The Public Accounts, 1969*, pp. 49-51.

51. *Uganda Argus*, February-May 1966. On a visit to Nairobi, Nadiope may have made inquiries regarding British intervention, Mutesa appealed to Britain and the United Nations for intervention and ordered arms and ammunition from Gailey and Roberts Ltd, a Kampala subsidiary of Unilever.

52. Uganda, *Parliamentary Debates (Hansard); National Assembly Official Report*, Emergency Meeting, 15 April 1966.

53. *Uganda Argus*, 23 April 1966.

54. *Uganda Argus*, 11 May 1966.

55. *Uganda Argus*, May 1966. For other accounts of these events see Obote, 'The Footsteps of Uganda's Revolution'; Milton Obote, 'Constitutional and Political Report of the 1968 UPC Delegates' Conference', June 1968, as cited in Akena Adoko, *Uganda Crisis* (Kampala: African Publishers, 1970), pp. 120-8; Mutesa, *Desecration of My Kingdom*, pp. 9-26, and 181-92; Young, 'The Obote Revolution', pp. 8-13; Hopkins, 'Politics in Uganda', pp. 109-17; Nelson Kasfir, 'Cultural Sub-Nationalism in Buganda', *The Politics of Cultural Sub-Nationalism in Africa*, ed. Victor Olorunsola (Garden City, N.Y.: Anchor Books, 1972), pp. 109-17; and Henry Kyemba, *A State of Blood* (New York: Grosset and Dunlap, 1977), pp. 24-7.

56. Mujaju 'The Role of the UPC', pp. 460-3; and Mamdani, *Politics and Class Formation in Uganda*, pp. 272-8.

57. The major 'parastatal' corporations in Uganda were as follows (date of founding in parentheses): the Uganda Development Corporation (1952); the Uganda Electricity Board (1954); the Lint Marketing Board (1949; Cotton Exporters' Group 1941-9); the Coffee Marketing Board (1953; Coffee Control prior to 1953); the National Housing Corporation (1964); the National Insurance Corporation (1964); the Uganda Commercial Bank (1965; the Uganda Credit and Savings Bank, 1950-65); the Bank of Uganda (1966; East African Currency Board, 1919-66); the National Trading Corporation (1966; African Loans Fund, 1954; and African Business Promotion Ltd of the UDC); the Uganda Tea Growers Corporation (1966); the Dairy Industry Corporation (1967); the Produce Marketing Board (1968); the Apolo Hotel Corporation (1968); the Uganda Co-operative Development Bank (1970); and the Export and Import Corporation (1970). In addition there were the parastatal corporations of the East African Community (1967; East African Common Services Organisation, 1961-7; East African High Commission before 1961): East African Railways Corporation; East African Harbours Corporation; East African Posts and Tele-communications Corporation; the East African Airways Corporation; the East

African Development Bank (1967) and the East African National Shipping Line (1969). Finally there were at least 20 services operated by the East African Community, ranging from the East African Directorate of Civil Aviation and the East African Income Tax Department to the East African Literature Bureau and the East African Trypanosomiasis Research Organisation.

58. Uganda Development Corporation, *Annual Report and Accounts*, 1964 and 1970.

59. Jan Jørgensen, 'Multinational Corporation Involvement in Agricultural Inputs in East Africa: Two Case Studies', paper presented to the Canadian Association of African Studies Annual Meeting, Victoria, British Columbia, February 1976, p. 10.

60. Nye, *Pan-Africanism and East African Integration*, pp. 175-210.

61. Uganda, *Work for Progress; The Second Five-Year Plan, 1966-1971* (Entebbe: Government Printer, 1967), pp. 1-38, 174-5; and Uganda, *Plan III; Third Five-Year Development Plan, 1971/2 – 1975/6* (Entebbe: Government Printer, 1972), p. 125.

62. Obote justified the lack of detailed projects in the First Five-Year Plan by arguing that local details were of little interest to potential donors overseas. Uganda, *Parliamentary Debates (Hansard); National Assembly Official Report, 11 July 1963*. On the regime's concern with political strings attached to foreign aid, see speeches by Obote in *Uganda Argus*, 11 May 1964; 14 June 1966; and 8 December 1966; by Foreign Minister Sam Odaka, *Uganda Argus*, 23 November 1966; and 25 October 1968; and by the Minister for Economic Planning, J.M. Okae, *Uganda Argus*, 12 December 1970. See also the discussion of foreign assistance and tied-aid in Uganda, *Work for Progress*, pp. 36-7.

Despite fears voiced by D.A. Patel and E. Babumba (Hansard, 9 July 1964) that the absence of sectoral restrictions of foreign investment in the Industrial Charter and in the Foreign Investments (Protection) Act would lead to foreign take-overs and the exclusion of local capitalists from the manufacturing sector, there were few new foreign investments and few foreign take-overs in the 1960s. Competition from foreign firm subsidiaries based in Kenya and export restriction arising from management contracts with foreign firms proved to be greater stumbling blocks for locally-based manufacturers.

63. Four of the documents are found in A. Milton Obote, *The Common Man's Charter with Appendices* (Entebbe: Government Printer, 1970), and the fifth, in Obote, *Proposals for New Methods of Election of Representatives of the People of Parliament* (Kampala: Milton Obote Foundation, 1970).

64. *Uganda Argus*, 19 September, 21 November 1970, 13 January 1971; and *The People*, 29 December 1970.

65. Irving Gershenberg, 'Slouching Towards Socialism: Obote's Uganda', *African Studies Review*, vol. 15, no. 1 (April 1972), pp. 79-95.

66. Calculations based on data from Uganda, *Survey of Industrial Production, 1967* (Entebbe: Statistics Division, Ministry of Planning and Economic Development, 1969), pp. 104-5, and Uganda, *Survey of Industrial Production, 1967: Directory of Establishments* (Entebbe: Statistics Division, 1969), which would have been the most recent available statistics prior to Nakivubo. Cotton-ginning, coffee-processing, construction, mining and hydro-electricity were excluded from manufacturing in these calculations. List of firms scheduled for nationalisation taken from Uganda, *Statutory Instrument No. 75 of 1970*.

67. According to one source, the board of directors and shares in the Shell-BP subsidiary were split 50-50 between the parent company and the government. The government nominated the chairman, and Shell the managing director. Shell provided management services for a commission equal to 1 per cent of profits. Although the government made full payment for its shares, 90 per cent of this was

lent back to the government by Shell, to be repaid at 7.5 per cent interest over 5 years. 'Take-Overs: Uganda Faces Bill', *The Standard* (Dar es Salaam), 6 January 1971.

68. T.T. Jeffry-Jones, Shell Transport and Trading Group, interview, London, 12 September 1970.

69. Roman Slawinski, National and Grindlays Bank, interview, London, 22 November 1973; interview with Mr Weait, Barclays Bank, Kampala, 20 April 1971.

70. The eleven additional firms were Standard Bank, Barclays Bank, Bank of Baroda, Bank of India, East Africa General Insurance, Jubilee Insurance, British American Insurance, Motor and General Insurance, Madhvani Sugar Works, Uganda Sugar Factory and East African Steel Corporation. Compensation data found in Uganda, *1973 Statistical Abstract*, p. 85, and Uganda, Plan III, pp. 210, 255, 257-8 and 401.

71. A.R. Dunbar, *A History of Bunyoro-Kitara* (Nairobi: Oxford University Press for EAISR, 1965), p. 211.

72. Uganda, *Parliamentary Debates (Hansard); National Assembly Official Report*, vol. 22, 20 December 1963, pp. 767-9; and Uganda, *The Public Accounts of the Republic of Uganda for the Year Ended 30th June 1969* (Entebbe: Government Printer, 1970), pp. 44-5.

73. Uganda, *1965 Statistical Abstract*, p. 89; *1970 Statistical Abstract*, p. 101; *1973 Statistical Abstract*, p. 106.

74. H.M. Luande in Uganda, *Parliamentary Debates (Hansard); National Assembly Official Report*, 22 October 1968, p. 4271.

75. Until 1953, senior civil service posts were generally reserved for Europeans. Any African or Asian making the grade was paid only three-fifths the salary of a European doing the same work. Edouard Bustin, 'L'Africanisation des cadres administratifs de l'Ouganda', *Civilisations*, vol. 9, no. 2 (1959), p. 135.

76. Data are available only for African males, who in any event comprised 96 per cent of all recorded African employees in 1964 and 93 per cent in 1970. Uganda, *1965 Statistical Abstract*, pp. 93-4, and *1973 Statistical Abstract*, pp. 109-10.

77. Uganda, *1965 Statistical Abstract*, p. 94; *1973 Statistical Abstract*, p. 110; Uganda, *Plan II*, pp. 93-4; and Uganda, *The Patterns of Income and Expenditure of Coffee Growers in Buganda 1962/63* (Entebbe: Statistics Division, Ministry of Planning and Economic Development, mimeograph, January 1967), p. 2 and Appendix II.

78. Leys, *Politicians and Policies*, pp. 13-15.

79. Ali A. Mazrui, 'Social Distance and the Transclass Man', *Cultural Engineering and Nation-Building in East Africa*, ed. Mazrui (Evanston, Illinois: Northwestern University Press, 1972), p. 159.

80. Cyril Ehrlich, 'Some Social and Economic Implications of Paternalism in Uganda', *Journal of African History*, vol. 4, no. 2 (1963), p. 285; Uganda, *1965 Statistical Abstract*, p. 100, and *1973 Statistical Abstract*, p. 115.

81. A. Milton Obote, 'Policy Proposals for Uganda's Educational Needs', *Mawazo*, vol. 2, no. 2 (December 1969), p. 4. See also the thoughtful critique of Obote's educational policies in A.G.G. Gingyera-Pinycwa, 'Political Development and Ideological Void: Uganda under Apolo Milton Obote', paper presented to the International Political Science Association World Congress, Montreal, August 1973, p. 9.

82. Accounts of the Vehicle Advances Fund in Uganda, *The Public Accounts, 1969*, p. 168; Godfrey Kalibala, 'Car Loan Reaction', *Uganda Argus*, 9 October 1970; and A. Milton Obote, 'Communication from the Chair', 20 April 1970, in *The Common Man's Charter with Appendices*, pp. 23-9.

83. See Appendix, Table A.3.

84. By June 1969, state guaranteed loans and promissory notes for growers' co-operative unions totalled U. Shs. 47.4 million. By far the largest was a U. Shs. 11.9 million loan in 1967 by Barclays Bank to the Buganda-based Uganda Growers' Co-operative Union. Uganda, *The Public Accounts, 1969*, pp. 49-51 and 145.

85. Cf. Giovanni Arrighi's definiton, 'International Corporations, Labour Aristocracies, and Economic Development in Tropical Africa', *Imperialism and Underdevelopment; A Reader*, ed. Robert I. Rhodes (New York: Monthly Review, 1970), p. 256.

86. Inflation rate calculations based on price indices and weights for fuel and soap, household goods and clothing for Kampala low-income group, Uganda, *1973 Statistical Abstract*, p. 97. The major price jump for these items occurred in 1968. Median wage for occupational groups from Uganda, *1973 Statistical Abstract*, p. 110. Other data as cited in Jan Jørgensen, 'Structural Dependence and the Move to the Left', *The Politics of Africa; Dependence and Development*, ed. Timothy Shaw and Kenneth Heard (London: Longman and Dalhousie University Press, 1979), pp. 59-60.

87. Uganda, *Survey of Industrial Production, 1968*, pp. 8, 14, 100-1, 106-7. Although these seemingly modest fees were divided among several directors, many directors sat on the boards of several firms. Total directors' fees ranged as high as U. Shs. 173,750 per soft drink firm and U. Shs. 107,800 per firm in distilleries and breweries.

88. Uganda, *Census of Distribution, 1966, Part II* (Entebbe:Statistics Division, 1967), pp. 12 and 25; and *Census of Distribution, 1966, Part II* (Entebbe: Statistics Division, 1969), pp. 4, 7 and 8. As might be expected, the European-owned firms were the largest wholesale firms, accounting for 8 per cent of the number but 21.5 per cent of turnover.

89. Uganda, *Parliamentary Debates (Hansard); National Assembly Official Report*, vol. 100, 20 May 1970, p. 519.

90. Ibid., p. 528.

91. Selwyn D. Ryan, 'Economic Nationalism and Socialism in Uganda', *Journal of Commonwealth Political Studies*, vol. 11, no. 2 (July 1973), p. 150; *The People*, 12 January 1971; *Uganda Argus*, 13 January 1971; and Uganda, *Parliamentary Debates (Hansard)*, vol. 100, 5 May 1970, pp. 304-5.

92. Uganda, *Parliamentary Debates (Hansard)*, vol. 100, 20 May 1970, pp. 524-5.

93. Cases reported to police for the following crimes:

	Murder	Aggravated assault	Robbery	Theft	Burglary
Uganda 1969	2,128	19,496	4,411	27,608	12,414
% Increase 1966-69	39.9	74.4	28.6	32.7	24.5
Rate per 100,000 pop.					
Uganda 1969	22.3	204.2	46.2	289.1	130.0
Kenya 1968	5.7[a]	–[b]	22.3	161.6	68.4

[a] includes attempted murder
[b] treated as attempted murder

Sources: Uganda, *1969 Statistical Abstract*, p. 111; Uganda, *1970 Statistical Abstract*, p. 113; *Kenya Statistical Abstract*, 1972, p. 245. Kenya's 1968 crime rate was chosen, since the 1969 rate was unusually low.

94. Uganda, *1973 Statistical Abstract*, p. 12. As Kabwegyere noted, the British orientation of Asians in Uganda was rooted in colonial history: 'Britain brought them to Uganda. Britain protected them in Uganda, and Britain seemed to promise a better future.' Tarsis Kabwegyere, 'The Asian Question in Uganda', *East Africa Journal*, vol. 9, no. 6 (June 1972), pp. 10-13.

95. H.S. Morris, *Indians in Uganda* (Chicago: University of Chicago Press, 1968), pp. 21, 22, 140-3 and 193; Gardner Thompson, 'The Ismailis in Uganda', *Expulsion of a Minority*, p. 44; and Jessica Kuper, 'The Goan Community in Kampala', *Expulsion of a Minority*, p. 54.

96. J.E. Goldthorpe, *An African Elite: Makerere College Students, 1922-65* (Nairobi: Oxford University Press, 1965), p. 28; and Nelson Kasfir, 'Cultural Sub-Nationalism in Uganda', *The Politics of Cultural Sub-Nationalism in Uganda*, ed. Victor Olorunsola (Garden City, N.Y.: Anchor Books, 1972), p. 130.

97. The obverse of this was that Asians viewed Obote as non-racialist and 'Baganda traditionalists' as anti-Asian. Amar Maini, 'Asians and Politics in Late Colonial Uganda: Some Personal Recollections', *Expulsion of a Minority: Esssays on Ugandan Asians*, ed. Michael Twaddle (London: University of London, Athlone Press, 1975), pp. 112-24. Sugra Visram's membership in the KY was a notable exception of an Asian's co-operation with Buganda neo-traditionalism.

98. Kasfir, 'Cultural Sub-Nationalism in Uganda', p. 127.

99. Kenya enacted a Trade Licensing Act in 1967 to exclude non-citizens from trading in rural areas and to exclude non-citizens from trading in an ever-lengthening list of commodities. Similar measures were not enacted in Uganda until 1969 and were enforced more loosely. Asian firms often continued as commission agents for the National Trading Corporation and existing firms were generally designated cotton and coffee export agents for the Export and Import Corporation. In the period 1970-1, when Kenya was serving quit notices to large numbers of Asian non-citizen firms, the Uganda government was negotiating with Britain to allow a larger number of non-citizen Asians to become Ugandan citizens. Colin Leys, *Underdevelopment in Kenya* (London: Heinemann, 1975), pp. 148-59; Uganda, The Trade (Licensing) Act, 1969, sections 2-4; Michael A. Tribe, 'Economic Aspects of the Expulsion of Asians from Uganda', *Expulsion of a Minority*, p. 148. Colin Legum (ed.), *African Contemporary Record, 1971-72* (London: Rex Collins, 1972), p. B-233.

100. State-owned firms were hardly more progressive than Asian firms in Africanising higher-level positions. In 1968, of 126 senior executive positions within five major parastatal firms (Nyanza Textiles, Kilembe Mines, Agricultural Enterprises Ltd, Uganda Cement Industry and Tororo Chemicals), only 9 (7.1 per cent) were held by Africans, a situation comparable to that in the largest Asian-controlled firms (Mulco Textiles, Steel Corporation of East Africa, other Madhvani firms, Mehta Group and Sikh Saw Mills), where 10 (6.1 per cent) of 165 senior executive positions were held by Africans. Uganda, *Report of the Committee on Africanisation of Commerce and Industry in Uganda* (Entebbe: Government Printer, 1968), p. 19. For more on problems of Africanisation in parastatal firms operated under management contract with foreign firms, see Jørgensen, 'Multinational Corporation Involvement in Agricultural Inputs in East Africa'.

101. As early as 1914, the leader of the Shia Imani Ismaili Muslims, Aga Khan III, had urged his followers in Burma to adapt to nationalism by identifying 'socially and politically' 'as closely as possible' with the local life. After the Second World War he urged his followers in East Africa 'to make English their first language' and to adapt local social customs. His Highness Karim Aga Khan echoed his father's advice when he urged Ismailis in Uganda to take out citizenship in 1962. Aga Khan III, *Memoirs of Aga Khan* (London: Cassell and Company,

1954), pp. 130, 190-1; and Thompson, 'The Ismailis in Uganda', pp. 42-3.

102. Uganda, *Statutory Instruments, 1970*, no. 81 (29 May 1970) and no. 88 (5 June 1970).

103. Douglas Tilbe, *East African Asians* (London: Race Relations Committee, Friends House, 1970), p. 5, as cited in Mamdani, *Politics and Class Formation in Uganda*, p. 280.

104. Nye, 'TANU and UPC', pp. 231-2; and Maini, 'Asians and Politics', pp. 117-18. See also Benedicto Kiwanuka's plea for increased Asian support for the Democratic Party in 1965, *Uganda Argus*, 22 November 1965.

105. Uganda, *Report of the Electoral Commission Under the Chairmanship of Ateker Ejalu* (Entebbe: Government Printer, 1970), pp. 4-5.

106. Selwyn Douglas Ryan, 'Uganda; A Balance Sheet of the Revolution', *Mawazo*, vol. 3, no. 1 (June 1971), p. 56; and *Uganda Argus*, 19 December 1970.

107. Fred Mpanga, Mehta Group Public Relations Consultant, letter, 22 February 1972; and Mehta Group advertisement in City Council of Kampala, *Kampala: The Official Handbook* (Kampala: University Press of Africa, 1970), p. 172.

108. Letter to author from Muljibhai Madhvani & Co. Ltd, 17 March 1972; Madhvani Group, *Enterprise in East Africa* (Nairobi: United Africa Press, 1971); Uganda Development Corporation, *Annual Report and Accounts*, 1967 and 1970.

109. *Uganda Argus*, 3 October 1967, and 4 September 1968.

110. Uganda, *1965 Statistical Abstract*, p. 93; *1973 Statistical Abstract*, p. 109.

111. Kenya, *Statistical Abstract 1972*, pp. 60, 72; Uganda, *1965 Statistical Abstract*, pp. 19, 23, 27, 29-31; and Uganda, *1973 Statistical Abstract*, pp. 26-40. Index for Kenya based on Central Bureau of Statistics distinction between primary and processed goods for SITC categories. Index for Uganda based on Galtung-Hungrø classification of SITC categories, with one exception: Uganda's blister copper exports were treated as raw material export.

112. Kenya, *Statistical Abstract 1972*, p. 211; Uganda, *1965 Statistical Abstract*, p. 93; *1973 Statistical Abstract*, pp. 108-9.

113. Daudi Ocheng (KY-Mityana) charged that the Minister of Agriculture, M.M. Ngobi (UPC-Busoga South) and the Minister of Health, Dr E.B.S. Lumu (UPC earlier KY-Kyandondo North) had used their official positions to gain control of the former Kayanja Estates coffee factory in Kyagwe county. Uganda, *Parliamentary Debates (Hansard); National Assembly*, vol. 35, 3 September 1964, p. 2943.

114. Ironically, Amar Maini's attempts to form joint ventures between Asian and African businessmen in West Nile appear to have only sharpened the latter's desire for Africanisation of trade. Maini, 'Asians and Politics', p. 119.

115. Uganda, *Parliamentary Debates (Hansard); National Assembly*, vol. 35, 29 September 1964, p. 3135.

116. *Uganda Argus*, 17 and 27 February, 4 April 1968.

117. *Uganda Argus*, 22 and 26 August and 11 and 20 September 1967. The five former KY ministers were Dr S.B. Kisekka, Paulo Lubega, A.D. Lubowa, Ntege-Lubwana and Francis Walugembe.

118. *Uganda Argus*, 29 September 1966.

119. David Martin, *General Amin* (London: Faber and Faber, 1974), pp. pp. 17-20. A detailed account of one brutal KAR massacre of Turkana men, women and children may be found in Elizabeth Marshall Thomas, *Warrior Herdsman* (New York: Alfred A. Knopf, 1965), pp. 214-36.

120. *The Times* (London), 24 January 1964, and Henry Bienen, *Armies and Parties in Africa* (New York: Africana, 1978), pp. 138-50.

121. Bienen, *Armies and Parties*, pp. 149-50. According to *The Times* correspondent, 'there was no quarrel with the European officers' at Jinja. *The Times*, 24 January 1964.

122. Bienen, *Armies and Parties*, pp. 150-60.

123. Special correspondent, 'The Uganda Army; Nexus of Power', *African Report*, vol. 11 (December 1966), pp. 37-9; *Uganda Argus*, 25 January, 12 May 1964, and 16 February 1965; and Uganda, *Parliamentary Debates (Hansard); National Assembly*, 1 July 1964.

124. Martin, *General Amin*, pp. 25, 44, 88.

125. Data based on actual expenditures. Uganda, *1970 Statistical Abstract*, pp. 72-5, 78; *1973 Statistical Abstract*, p. 83; Uganda *The Public Accounts, 1970*, p. 40. The 1968/69 army overspending was U. Shs. 24.9 million or 21 per cent over the authorised budget.

126. Martin, *General Amin*, pp. 67-90.

127. *Uganda Argus*, 30 September; and Akiiki Mujaju, Seminar, Political Science, Makerere University, Kampala, 29 July 1971. Mujaju wryly observed that Amin's coup-plotting could date to April 1967, when he first began seriously studying English, as if to prepare for holding news conferences.

128. Martin, *General Amin*, p. 35.

6 THE AMIN REGIME, 1971-9

Explaining the Coup

It is tempting to explain the 1971 coup as a corporatist move by the army to redress its organisational grievances. Four facts support such an explanation: the decline in the army's share of state resources between 1968 and 1970; the prominence of organisational grievances in 5 of the 18 points in the soldiers' manifesto broadcast on the day of the coup; the threat posed by the forthcoming 1971 elections to the privileged political position the army had enjoyed since the 1966 overthrow of the Kabaka; and the rapid increase in state resources allocated to the army in the years after the coup. However, the organisational grievance

Map 3: November 1979 District Names (1974-8 Names in Parentheses)

theory would be far more convincing had the coup been led by senior officers and had the military remained united following the coup. In fact, spearheaded by tanks and armoured vehicles from the Malire Mechanised Regiment near Bombo, the coup was led by a single high-ranking officer – Major-General Idi Amin Dada[1] – in alliance with captains, lieutenants, non-commissioned officers and enlisted men drawn largely from one region in Uganda.

To explain the 1971 military take-over, it is necessary to separate the largely personal and fortuitous causes of the coup from the organisational, ethnic and structural factors which contributed to its success and initial acceptance. The analogy of a fire may be useful. The organisational grievances of the army and ethnic divisions within the army provided some tinder, and the personal predicaments of Idi Amin and Felix Onama, the sparks. Bureaucratic operating procedures help explain why the firemen (officers and troops loyal to Obote) failed to extinguish the initial blaze, while popular discontent with Obote, especially in Buganda and Busoga, provided both fuel and oxygen to sustain the fire.

In the soldiers' manifesto, the five points covering the organisational grievances of the army could be summarised as follows: Obote's failure to provide the army with new accommodations, vehicles, equipment and recruits since 1969; the regime's failure to consult with the army on policy matters and promotions; the alleged downgrading of the army in favour of the General Service Unit; and the regime's alleged discrimination against West Nile and Acholi officers in favour of Langi officers from Obote's home district.[2] But might not the emphasis on corporate grievances be a ploy by the coup-makers to attract maximum support within the army, just as the other points were framed to draw public support? The coup was executed, not by institutionally aggrieved officers and soldiers, but by Amin and his supporters to forestall Amin's imminent arrest in connection with army overspending, unauthorised aid to Anya Nya rebels, and the investigation into Okoya's murder.[3] Minster of Defence Onama assisted the coup-makers by ordering all army officers with accumulated back-leaves to take such leave at once or forfeit it, during Obote's visit to Singapore. David David Martin notes that this order resulted in half the army officers being on leave on 24 and 25 January.[4] We can only speculate whether Onama foresaw the consequences of his order. Onama was at loggerheads with Obote over the Common Man's Charter, army overspending, and aid to the Anya Nya. Indeed, immediately after the coup, a Tanzanian newspaper accused Onama rather than Amin of staging the coup.[5] Whatever his role in the coup, Onama retired thereafter to his lucrative business interests in West Nile. The Onama ruling on back-leaves provides a bureaucratic explanation for the coup's success.

The fact that 13 of 22 officers promoted shortly after the coup were from northwest Uganda provides evidence for the ethnic and regional dimensions of the coup.[6] That another 4 of the 22 were immigrants from the Sudan and Zaire lends credence to allegations that immigrants played a key role in the coup. But these were not newcomer Anya Nya rebels; the Anya Nya had more pressing military objectives at home in the southern Sudan. Rather, the immigrants in the Army were largely 'old' settlers, whose families had arrived in Uganda well before the 1960s. Many were descendants of Emin Pasha's soldiers. By contrast, Muslims were a minority (roughly 20 per cent) among the Anya Nya.[7]

Contrary to the later image of Muslim dominance in the Amin regime, Christians comprised about half of the 22 promoted officers. Although Islam was strong in northwest Uganda (particularly Arua town, Aringa county and Madi district) and stronger still among West Nile and Madi recruits in the Army and police, Christians outnumbered Muslims in the northwest. Indeed, Islam lost ground to Christianity in the 1950s and 1960s because of the lack of Islamic educational facilities beyond the *madrasa* schools for Koranic instruction. The more prosperous and more numerous Shafi'i law Muslims in Buganda neglected their Māliki law co-religionists in the northwest.[8]

The only armed organised groups opposing the coup – the General Service Unit, the Special Forces and the pro-Obote faction within the army – were militarily defeated in the coup itself or were liquidated in uprisings and massacres between January and July, which by Amin's own estimate left more than 1,000 dead.[9]

The desperate tenacity of pro-Obote officers and soldiers in this period was more than matched by the new regime's ruthless efforts to eliminate real and potential enemies within the armed forces. Consider the cohort of approximately 23 army officers who held the rank of Lieutenant Colonel or higher at the time of the coup. Table 6.1 shows the origin and fate of 20 of these men. Five hailed from West Nile, five from Acholi, four from Lango, three from Teso and three from elsewhere, roughly in proportion to the ethnic distribution in the army at the time of the coup (the air force, with higher maths education requirements, tended to be dominated by southerners, who generally welcomed the coup). Eleven of the 20 high-ranking army officers were killed within six months of the coup, either while in custody or while attempting to resist the coup. Of those killed in this early period, seven were from Acholi or Lango.

Table 6.1: Fate of High-ranking Pre-coup Officers in Army after Coup (Lt. Col. Rank or Higher)

	Fate	
Region	Killed within six months	Survived first six months
West Nile	Suleiman Hussein Augustino Akwongo	Idi Amin Barnabas Kili E. Obitre-Gama
Acholi	Albertino Langoya Tom Loyira Hillary Abwola Pirimo Obol	Tito Okello (escaped to Tanzania)
Lango	Meseura Arach Emmanuel Ogwal Oboma Ayumu	David Oyite-Ojok (escaped to Tanzania)
Teso	Ekiring John Ebitu	William Omaria
Other		S. Kakuhire (killed 1973) Charles Oboth-Ofumbi (killed 1977) Bogere

Basic Source: David Martin, *General Amin* (London: Faber and Faber, 1974), pp. 154-7.

While intra-army violence ensured the success of the coup, external factors contributed to its initial popular acceptance.

The salariat, which had objectively benefited from the commanding heights strategy of the Obote regime, generally supported the coup. The coup did not immediately threaten their interests. Moreover, the new regime quickly restored the car loans and annual salary increases which Obote had suspended in 1970.

Despite the fact that Amin had led the 1966 attack on the Kabaka's palace at Mengo, Baganda farmers welcomed the coup. Amin released 55 (of 93) political detainees, including outspoken monarchists and the five cabinet members arrested in 1966.[10] The change of regime opened the possibility of restoring the Kabakaship, banned since 1966 and vacant since Mutesa's 1969 death in exile. Although farmers obtained symbolic satisfaction from the regime's lavish reburial of Edward

Mutesa in April 1971 and the prospect of enhanced local political power with the changeover from appointed to elected *muluka* chiefs, Amin reaffirmed his commitment to a unitary republican state. A unitary state meant uniform land laws. The Land Reform Decree of 1975 abolished the *mailo-kibanja* land-tenure system in Buganda and nationalised all land-holdings in Uganda, though on terms which appeared to favour capitalist tenant-farmers and landlord-farmers against absentee landlords and poor tenant-farmers.[11]

African traders throughout Uganda hailed the coup because of their opposition to Obote's 'socialism' and moderation towards Asian merchants. Somewhat myopically, Asian traders also supported the coup, hoping to obtain trade liberalisation and further renewals of trading licences. Asian merchants and industrialists extended automatic support to the Amin regime as the new party of order. In 1971, Amin rewarded traders and merchants with almost unlimited import licences, but declining foreign exchange reserves and pressure from local manufacturers forced the regime to reintroduce austerity measures and place all imports under control of the State Trading Corporation, formed by merging the Export and Import Corporation with the National Trading Corporation.

Unskilled workers organised into trade unions controlled by white-collar workers were in no position to oppose the coup. Moreover, they had received limited benefits from the Obote regime, which had tried to abolish the right to strike and had barred trade unionists from sitting in Parliament. Unorganised and lacking political consciousness, the migrant workers and poor peasants had won little from the old regime and expected little from the new. None the less, migrant workers from the West Nile and Madi supported the new regime on the basis of regional rather than class solidarity. The lumpenproletariat of urban job-seekers welcomed the coup, both as a retribution against the old regime and as a rupture which might create new openings in the army and bureaucracy.

The students in NUSU who had supported the commanding heights strategy and the Move to the Left were initially silent about the coup. State capitalism offered the students expanded employment opportunities as members of the state salariat.[12] Although the coup leaders heaped scorn on Obote's Move to the Left, the students eventually extended conditional support to the Amin regime and denounced the former regime for paying only lip-service to socialism.

Significantly, the strata and ethnic groups most antagonistic to the Obote regime were situated in or near the capital, Kampala, where their jubilant demonstrations lent the coup an air of legitimacy which was highly visible to the foreign press and embassies. Had the capital been situated in the secondary commodity-producing regions of Acholi or Lango or even Bunyoro, there would have been few, if any, public demonstrations for the coup.

Externally, the coup was welcomed by Great Britain, Israel, Ethiopia and South Africa. Obote had earned the enmity of the British and South African governments for his vocal opposition to British arms sales to South Africa. Despite favourable terms obtained by firms affected by the May 1970 partial nationalisation measures, the British government feared further nationalisation. Once the coup appeared imminent, Israeli advisers to the Uganda Army threw their support behind the coup to retain the support of the new regime.[13] Israel sought to retain sympathetic regimes in Uganda and Ethiopia, the sources of the Nile, and hoped to prolong the Anya Nya rebellion in the southern Sudan. Israel viewed the Israeli-trained Amin as a more malleable leader than Obote, who had complained openly about political strings attached to Israeli aid. As the first African nation to recognise the Amin regime, Ethiopia may have been retaliating against Obote's vehement anti-feudalism campaign, which some had viewed as a slight against Emperor Haile Selassie. Although sympathetic to Obote, the Soviet Union continued to provide economic and military aid to the new regime to counter perceived Chinese influence in neighbouring Tanzania and to train military cadres sympathetic to the Soviet Union. The interests of other countries involved in Uganda – the United States, West Germany, France, Italy, Yugoslavia and Czechoslovakia – were not immediately affected by the coup.[14] The United States could take satisfaction from the overthrow of a regime that had been overtly hostile during its Congo adventures in the 1960s.

The Ultra-right Phase of the Amin Regime, January 1971-February 1972

To the delight of South Africa and pro-South African businessmen in Uganda,[15] the first year of the Amin regime was marked by overtures to South Africa and plans for a Ugandan delegation to South Africa. During the same year, relations with Israel were even more friendly, with several new Israeli-financed projects being started in Uganda. Amin personally made highly publicised friendly visits to Great Britain and Israel, calling on both Queen Elizabeth and Prime Minister Golda Meir.

Within Uganda, Amin allowed Baganda monarchists to campaign openly for the restoration of the Kabakaship. These actions were a reflection of the regime's political, military and economic weakness in its first year.

The ultra-right phase paid off in substantial new public and private loans from Great Britain, Israel and the International Development Agency. A new infusion of $6 million from the IDA for ranches in western and northern Uganda helped to maintain an important form of internal patronage.[16] Politically, the ultra-right phase secured the support of Baganda monarchists during a critical year. The military situation remained unstable. A widespread mutiny in July 1971 culminated in the death or flight of all but a few Langi and Acholi in the Army.[17] Support from Israeli and British military advisers assisted Amin's consolidation of power within the armed forces in the first year.

By October 1971, Amin felt sufficiently secure to start moving against his ultra-right allies and present himself as a populist nationalist. First, he reiterated his opposition to a return to kingdoms in Uganda after meeting with 'the elders of Buganda'.[18] He then extricated himself from the offer to send a delegation to South Africa and later declared his opposition to the racist South African regime.[19] Uganda did not, however, fulfil its financial obligations to the OAU Liberation Committee based in Dar es Salaam. During November Amin retracted his proposal for private commercial broadcasting in Uganda. Between August and November, the regime progressively tightened foreign exchange controls and restricted imports. December marked the first of many warnings to Asians to support the regime and identify with African interests.[20]

After the November 1971 and February 1972 Addis Ababa negotiations ended the Anya Nya rebellion,[21] Amin's ardour for Israel cooled. He flew to Libya and signed a joint communiqué denouncing Zionism. Israel protested and the Israeli press published reports of unrest in Uganda. Amin then expelled all Israeli advisors and broke diplomatic relations with Israel.

By the start of 1972 the Amin regime was secure enough to embark on new policies and to redress the organizational grievances of the armed forces.

Control of the Military and the Means of Coercion

The military's share of state resources grew dramatically after the coup. Military expenditure jumped from U. Shs. 170.2 million in the last full fiscal year of the Obote regime (1969/70) to U. Shs. 565.3 million in the first full fiscal year of the Amin regime (1971/72), from one-tenth to one-fourth of the total state budget. In the official draft estimates for 1975/76, the regime allocated U. Shs. 773.3 million or 40 per cent of the budget for the military, a figure which may be more accurate than the 'actual expenditure' reported later of U. Shs. 678.7 million or 21 per cent of the budget. Figures for 1976/77 and 1977/78 are even more unreliable. In these later budgets only one-fifth of the total expenditure was officially allocated to the military, but mysteriously large sums were allocated in the development budget for finance (U. Shs. 580 million), health (U. Shs. 300 million), agriculture, animal resources and internal affairs, despite the absence of visible signs of new projects in the five areas.[22]

If we total all state expenditures on coercion (military, police, prisons and State Research Bureau) under Amin, we find that coercion accounted for an average 28.7 per cent of reported state expenditures between 1972 and 1978, more than during the two world wars, more than any time since 1907/8 when the primary output of the state was colonial 'pacification'.

The problem of controlling the military was itself a driving force in increasing the military's share of state resources. Amin faced a serious problem in keeping officers and soldiers loyal to the new regime, or if not loyal at least under control. To maintain control, Amin placed arms and ammunition under tightly centralised storage at Magamaga Ordnance Depot. He dispersed military units throughout the country-side, staged frequent alerts and manoeuvres, and established face-to-face contact with soldiers and officers through personal tours of military bases. In speeches to troops he emphasised the importance of loyalty and discipline and voiced his concern for the material comforts of soldiers and their families.

Ruth First observed that armies oust squabbling politicians and proclaim the end of political strife, only to find societal cleavages mirrored in the armed forces.[23] In the Uganda Army ethnic, regional, religious and economic cleavages were particularly acute, leading to rivalry over recruitment, promotion, chains of command and activities outside the barracks.[24] Each ethnic group within the military exerted pressure to increase its own representation, to bring friends and relatives into the military, and to achieve rapid promotion for its representatives. Such internal dynamics help explain the expansion of the Uganda armed forces from 1,000 men in 1962 to 7,680 at the time of the coup and 20,000 by the end of 1974, while the rapid expansion helps explain in turn the lack of discipline within the military.[25]

In addition, Amin entertained grandiose visions of Uganda becoming the strongest military power in the region. The September 1972 invasion by Tanzanian-trained insurgents loyal to Obote strengthened Amin's desire for a strong military force. But by 1974 the Uganda armed forces had swollen to a size twice that of Tanzania and three times that of Kenya, well beyond the optimum size for a force plagued by discipline problems and ethnic/religious rivalry. The internal divisions in the armed forces erupted in an attempted army coup in March and attempted air force putsches in May and October 1974 and June 1977. By 1977 Amin had reportedly cut the effective size of the armed forces from the nominal 22,000 man level to 15,000 through retirements, dismissals, leaves and 'disappearances'.[26]

Through patronage and indulgence, Amin bought loyalty from officers and soldiers. The problem of controlling the military became a problem of wresting sufficient resources from the civilian sector to placate the military. Kondoism and robbery were transferred from the private sector to the state sector by the armed forces. Soldiers and members of the state security forces (the State Research Bureau, the Public Safety Unit and the Military Police) were free to loot, smuggle and extort with little fear of being disciplined by superiors and *no* fear of civilian courts. As Nayenga observed, Decree 8 of 1972 (Proceedings Against the Government (Protection) Decree) granted all government officials immunity from civil proceedings in very broadly defined circumstances.[27] Similarly, Decree 7 of 1972 (Robbery Suspects Decree) gave a licence to kill to all security officers by empowering them to use any force deemed necessary to apprehend anyone suspected of robbery. Finally, Decree 26 of 1972 (Armed Forces Powers of Arrest Decree) gave soldiers and prison officers the right to arrest anyone without a warrant.[28] Although these decrees could have served as the legal foundation for most of the atrocities committed by the agents of the state under Amin, they were seldom invoked. A regime which kidnapped and killed its own Chief Justice had little need for the legal niceties of framing or following its own Nuremberg Laws.[29]

Amin himself filled his pockets with cash from the treasury and drove cars 'abandoned' by expelled Asians.[30] Without detailing his own participation, Health Minister Kyemba noted that by the end of 1973 'it had become established practice for senior officials and ministers to move at will into any such [Asian] property they fancied'.[31]

Economic divisions affecting control of the military took the form of inter-unit rivalry over modern arms, better accommodation, and more amenities, rivalry between professional soldiers and businessmen-soldiers, and rivalry between soldiers and officers. In March 1974, soldiers in several units complained of lack of arms and accused troops in the Malire Mechanised Specialist Reconnaissance Regiment of being overly proud of their modern armoured personnel carriers and tanks. A week later, soldiers at Mubende Tiger Battalion complained of lack of accommodation. Soldiers in the border area of Koboko, near the intersection of the borders of Uganda, Zaire and Sudan, complained about 'all the idle officers in Kampala and Entebbe . . . spending their time driving cars and drinking while those at the border are suffering'. In the aftermath of the economic war, soldiers and officers at Gulu Air Force Base complained about businessmen-soldiers and businessmen-officers who spent too much time in business and too little with military duties.[32] Amin criticised members of the Air and Seaborne Battalion who were involved in smuggling along the Uganda-Kenya border and soldiers and officers engaged in extortion and robbery of civilian victims. Soldiers complained that officers were given government loans for housing their families whereas soldiers with far less pay were given no financial assistance in family housing. Amin acceded to the soldiers' complaints by offering housing loans to soldiers as well as officers.[33]

In handling conflict generated by such economic differentials within the military, the Amin regime followed the Obote regime's pattern of virtual capitulation to the military. Rather than face hard choices and risks involved in denying demands for more arms, accommodation, loans and other amenities, or in redistributing resources within the military, the Amin regime redistributed resources from non-military sectors to the military, thereby increasing the size of the pie available for division among soldiers and officers.

Within the military, the cohort of coup-participants fared considerably better than the cohort of 20 Obote nominees examined earlier. Three months after the coup, 22 soldiers and officers in the Uganda armed forces were promoted with effect retroactive to 25 January, presumably in recognition of their role in the coup.[34] This promotions list was remarkable in several respects. First, it included startlingly rapid promotion jumps of six or even eight ranks: Private Ismail to Captain, Sergeants Yekka and Ambrosio to Captain. Second, a majority of those promoted were from ethnic groups in the labour reserve districts of West Nile and Madi, traditionally a major military recruiting area under British overrule, and almost none from the secondary commodity-producing districts of Acholi and Lango, favoured by Obote for military recruitment. Half were Christian, and half were Muslims, so-called 'Nubians'. The 'Nubi' are not a 'tribe' but a culturally-defined occupational group, embracing the Swahili-speaking, Muslim military caste, originally descended from Emin Pasha's Sudanese troops, but later infused with recruits from other ethnic groups especially those in West Nile (Lugbara, Alur, Lendu, Madi, Kakwa) which span the colonial boundaries of Uganda, Zaire and the Sudan. Of the 22 promoted officers, at least 13 came from this northwestern periphery and labour reserve, and another four from the Sudan and Zaire: six Lugbara, four Madi, one Kakwa (plus Idi Amin), one Alur, one of mixed West Nile background, two Bari (Sudan), one Baka (Sudan) and one Zaire-Kakwa.

Third, as shown in Table 6.2, many in this group played a major role in subsequent years of the Amin regime. As of April-May 1974, six were still in good standing in leading military posts, and another six served elsewhere: cabinet ministers, provincial governors, and managers of parastatal corporations. Two were officially still in the military but on leave, pending investigations (Trete, Musa); one (Marella) was forcibly retired with full pension to return home to Yei, Sudan. Three had been executed (Ochima, Arube, Toloko), and one (Ozi) had fled after being fired as head of the State Research Bureau, but was pardoned and returned. No information was found on the later careers of the remaining three officers. Of the twelve who held military or civilian posts in 1974, one fled the country (Toko), and two were dismissed in 1978 (Ali, Onaah). The image of career stability that emerges from this sample drawn from the inner core of the regime is tinged with violence, betrayal and mystery, but there are also some elements of continuity. Officers who fell from Amin's favour were more likely to be 'kicked upstairs' to a civilian or ambassadorial post than be removed by execution or 'disappearance'.

By contrast, a third cohort, which consisted of officer school graduates, faded into obscurity. The same day that Amin promoted the 22 coup-participants, he commissioned six officers: M.A. Kodili (Sandhurst) from West Nile, N. Obiale (Sandhurst) from Teso, D. Nyankori (Mons Officer Cadet School, Aldershot) from Lango, D. Achia (Mons), B. Akash (Mons) and D. Ntalo (School of Infantry, Jinja).[35] Their later careers could not be traced. Under Obote, the armed forces had sent fewer officers to overseas academies than had Kenya, Zambia or even Tanzania.[36] Under Amin, these officers fared poorly compared with those who rose from the enlisted ranks. One exception was Lt. Col. Sule

Table 6.2: Promotion and Later Career of 22 Coup Participants

PROMOTIONS APRIL 1971 (Source: *UGANDA ARGUS*, 26 April 1971)

Old Rank and Name	New Rank	Rank Difference	Susequent Career
Lt.Isaac Maliyamungu *Kakwa-Zaire* *Protestant*	Major	2	Commander, 2nd Infantry Brigade Masaka (1972), Lt.Col. CO, Magamaga Ordnance Depot, CO of new mechanized battalion (1974), Brig., Chief of Army Training & Operations (1977), fled to Zaire after Amin's overthrow (1979). (*VU* 29/4/74, *ARB* 9/74, 3371, *ACR* 1977-78, B 441)
Capt.Demiro Mondo *Madi-Moyo* *Catholic*	Major	1	Lt.Col., Sec. of Defence (1974), Maj.Gen., Minister of Defence (1978). (*VU* 4/2/74, *ARB* 12/78, 5090)
Lt.Hussein Marella *Baka-Sudan* *Muslim*	Major	2	Brig., Acting Chief of Staff, retired with full pension to Juba, Sudan, after 23rd March 1974 attempted coup by Arube. (*VU* 30/3/74, 1/5/74, and Kyemba, p. 136)
Lt.Kamis Saafi *Madi (Nubianized)* *Muslim*	Major	2	Lt.Col., Leader of Religions in Uganda Armed Forces, Sheikh. (*VU* 25/1/74)
Pvt.Ismail *Lugbara-Aringa* *Muslim*	Captain	8	Major, Kifaru Mechanized Regiment (1974), Deputy Commander Kifaru Batallion, Arua (1977). (*VU* 20/4/74, Kyemba, p. 38)
Lt.Juma A. Oris *Madi/Alur* *Muslim*	Major	2	Acting CO, Malire Mechanized Specialist Regiment (1974), Lt.Col.Min. of Foreign Affairs (1975-78),demoted to Min. of Lands and Water Resources (1978). (*VU* 29/4/74, *ARB* 5/78, 4845)
2/Lt. Francis Itabuka *Busoga* *Christian*	Captain	2	Lt.Col., Chief Intelligence Officer (1974), Director State Research Bureau, dismissed and transferred to 2nd Parachute Regiment, Fort Portal (1977). (*VU* 26/1/74, *ARB* 10/77, 4612)
Sgt.Maj.Moses Ali *Bari-Sudan* *Muslim*	Lt.Col.	8	Brigadier, Minister of Provincial Administration (1974), Min. of Finance (1976-78), dismissed from Cabinet and retired from Army, July 1978. (*VU* 3/5/74, *ARB* 7/78, 4921)
Lt.John D.Onaah *Lugbara-Aringa* *Catholic*	Major	2	Lt.Col. 2nd Paratroopers School, Ft. Portal, then Provincial Governor, Eastern Province (1974), Min. of Tourism and Wildlife (1975-78), forced to retire May 1978. (*VU* 1/1/74, 12/4/74, *ARB* 5/78, 4845)
Capt. Ahmed Suleiman *Indian/Nubi/Lango* *Muslim*	Lt.Col.	2	Managing Director, Peoples Transport Ltd., Managing Director, Uganda Transport Corporation Ltd. (*VU* 13/4/74)
Lt. Wilson Toko *Lugbara-Terego* *Christian*	Major	2	Lt. Col., Acting Commander Air Force (1974), Col., Director-General East African Airways, defected (1976?). (Interview, Nairobi, 16/4/74)
Bashir Juma *Lugbara* *Muslim*	Captain	?	Air Force, Provincial Governor, Southern Province (1974). (*VU* 1/1/74, 12/4/74)
Sgt.Maj.Musa Eyega *Lugbara-Aringa* *Muslim*	Lt.Col.	8	Commander, Malire Mechanized Regiment, sent on leave after Arube's attempted coup (1974), Ambassador to Saudi Arabia (1977). (*VU* 3/4/74, Kyemba, p. 49)
Capt. Charles Arube *Kakwa* *Catholic*	Lt.Col.	2	Brigadier, Army Chief of Staff, died of abdominal gunshot wounds, 24 March 1974, following abortive coup attempt; military spokesman claimed wounds were self-inflicted but doctor's report ambiguous. (*VU* 27/3/74, 3/4/74 and *Observer* 31/3/74)
Sgt.Maj.Baker Trete *Lugbara* *Christian*	Major	7	Chief Signals Officer, sent on leave after Arube's attempted coup (1974), promoted to Lt.Col., arrested and later pardoned and reinstated (1976). (*VU* 3/4/74, *ARB* 12/76, 4262)
Capt.Valentine Ochima *Alur-Jonam* *Christian*	Lt.Col.	2	Briefly Acting Chief of Staff (1971), arrested and accused of plotting to arrest and kill prominent persons in West Nile; executed October 1972. (*UA* 27/7/71, Ravenhill, p. 243, Kyemba, p.10)
Capt. Toloko *Madi* *Catholic*	Lt.Col.	2	Confined to barracks for unscheduled maneuvers and later killed; implicated in murders in Fort Portal area (1974). (Ravenhill, p. 243, Kyemba, p. 10)
Capt. L.M.P.Ozi *Madi* *religion?*	Major	1	Early head of State Research Bureau, dismissed and charged with kidnapping (1974), fled to Sudan, pardoned and returned (1976). (*Observer* 31/3/74, *ACR* 1976-77, B 376, *ARB* 12/76, 4262, and *Commission of Inquiry into Missing Americans*, p. 2)
2/Lt.Hussein Marijan *Bari-Sudan* *Teso settler* *Muslim*	Captain	2	Major, Min. of E.A. Posts and Telecommunications (1977), Lt.Col. CO Simba Mechanized Specialist Reconnaissance Regiment, Min. of Aviation and Communications, May 1978. (*Africa Confidential*, 18, B 15/4/77, *ARB* 5/78, 3845)
Lt. Musa, Paratrooper	Major	2	Later career not known.
Sgt. Ambrosio	Captain	6	Later career not known.
Sgt. Yekka	Captain	6	Later career not known.

Key:

Henry Kyemba, *A State of Blood* (New York: Ace Books, 1977)

F.J. Ravenhill, 'Military Rule in Uganda', *African Studies Review*, vol. 17, no. 1 (April 1974), pp. 229-60

ACR – Colin Legum (ed.), *Africa Contemporary Record*

ARB – *Africa Research Bulletin (Political Series)*

UA – *Uganda Argus*

VU – *Voice of Uganda*

Source: *Uganda Argus*, 26 April 1971.

(Sandhurst), who held several posts: Commander, Malire Mechanised Specialist Reconnaissance Regiment (1974); Acting Commander, Air Force (1976); and Commander, Airborne Regiment (1977). Sule also had the dubious distinction of being the person who announced Idi Amin's elevation to Life-President on 25 July 1975.[37]

With the dissolution of the National Assembly and the suspension of the executive and legislative sections of the 1967 Constitution, President Amin ruled by decree. Formally, there were three governing bodies in the Second Republic: the Defence Council (State Supreme Council), the Cabinet and the National Forum.

The National Forum was a corporatist assembly appointed by the government. First proposed in August 1973, it met only once, in January 1978. Approximately 1,000 delegates attended, of whom only a fourth were 'people's' representatives or 'elders' appointed at the county level by the government. Other delegates included 50 traders, parastatal body chairmen and directors, representatives of the four official religions, chiefs, urban officials, provincial governors, district commissioners, ambassadors, professors, one student, cabinet ministers, permanent secretaries, departmental heads and last but not least, the leaders of the armed forces, including the commander and major from each military regiment.[38] Chaired by Vice-President Maj. Gen. Mustafa Adrisi, the National Forum heard complaints about economic problems, kondoism, smuggling and declining production in agriculture and industry. The forum had no legislative powers, but its four sub-committees (economics, agriculture, transportation and social services) issued written reports.

The cabinet met regularly, but its lack of voice in security matters severely limited its supervision of the state budget. Cabinet ministers did exercise day-to-day responsibility for their respective ministries. Kyemba documented the extent to which day-to-day operations of ministries — even Health or Culture and Community Development — involved catering to the whims of Amin and the demands of the military.[39] Amin infrequently attended the meetings of his own Cabinet,[40] and the Defence Council could overrule the cabinet and dismiss ministers. Serving in the cabinet exposed one to danger. Of 56 individuals who served in Amin's cabinets between 1971 and 1979, six were killed in office or after being dismissed: M. Ondoga, S. Guweddeko, C. Arube, C. Oboth-Ofumbi, Y. Engur and E.W. Oryema. Of these, only Engur was a full-time civilian; the other five were drawn from the military, police and prisons. A seventh cabinet member, Matthew Obado, was killed in April 1978 in what may have

Table 6.3: Cabinets of the Amin Regime, 1971-9

Office/Ministry		1971-72	1973	1974	1975	1976	1977	1978	1979
	At the Beginning of the Year								
President		Idi Amin	Idi Amin	Idi Amin	Idi Amin	Idi Amin	Idi Amin	Idi Amin	Idi Amin
Finance		E.B.Wakhweya	E.B.Wakhweya	M.S.Kiingi	Oboth-Ofumbi	Oboth-Ofumbi	Moses Ali	Moses Ali	J.Masagazi
State for Finance/Sec. to Treasury		--	--	J.Geria	M.S.Kiingi	M.S.Kiingi	M.S.Kiingi	--	
Planning and Economic Development		A.K.Kironde		vacant	E.Wakhweya		I.K.Kabanda	J. Masagazi	
Internal Affairs		Obitre-Gama	Idi Amin	M.L.Obado	Oboth-Ofumbi	Oboth-Ofumbi	Moses Ali	Moses Ali	Farouk Minawa
Foreign Affairs		Wanume Kibedi	Wanume Kibedi	M.Ondoga	Juma A. Oris	Juma A. Oris	Juma A. Oris	M. Adrisi	Idi Amin
State for Foreign Affairs		--	--	P.O.Etiang	--	--	--	Juma A. Oris	--
Defence		Oboth-Ofumbi	Oboth-Ofumbi	F.Nyangweso	Idi Amin	Idi Amin	M. Adrisi	M. Adrisi	Demiro Mondo
State for Defence		--	--	--	M. Adrisi	M. Adrisi	--	I. Lumago	Yusuf Gowon
Air Force Commander		non-cabinet	non-cabinet	S.Guweddeko	S.Guweddeko	S.Guweddeko	S.Guweddeko		
Army Chief of Staff		non-cabinet	non-cabinet	Charles Arube	M. Adrisi	M. Adrisi	M. Adrisi	M. Adrisi	M. Adrisi
Vice President		--	--	--	--	--	--	--	
Local/Provincial Admin.		V.A.Ovonji	J.M.Byagagaire	Moses Ali	Moses Ali	Moses Ali	W.Ali Fadhul	W.Ali Fadhul	W.Ali Fadhul
Public Affairs & Cabinet				J.M.Byagagaire	R.Nshekanabo	R.Nshekanabo	R.Nshekanabo	R.Nshekanabo	R.Nshekanabo
State in the Office of the President		--	--	--	P.O.Etiang	P.O.Etiang	P.O.Etiang	P.O.Etiang	P.O.Etiang
Cooperatives and Marketing		F.L.Okoxare	F.L.Okoxare	M.Ramathan	M.Ramathan	M.Ramathan	M.Ramathan	M.Ramathan	M.Ramathan
Agriculture		W.B.Banage	W.B.Banage	vacant	J.M.Byagagaire	J.M.Byagagaire	J.M.Byagagaire	Ibrahim Garandi	Ibrahim Garandi
Animal Resources		W.Lutara	W.Lutara	vacant	Noah Mohammed	Noah Mohammed	Noah Mohammed	Ismail Sebi	Ismail Sebi
Commerce		W.Lutara	W.Lutara	E.L.Athiyo	Noah Mohammed	Noah Mohammed	Noah Mohammed	Noah Mohammed	Bakhtti
Industry (and Power)			A.K.Kironde		Duemon Saburi	Duemon Saburi	Duemon Saburi	Duemon Saburi	Duemon Saburi
Tourism					John D.Onaah	John D.Onaah	John D.Onaah	John D.Onaah	Idi Amin
Information and Broadcasting		M.Naburi	M.Naburi	M.Ondoga	E.L.Athiyo	E.L.Athiyo	E.L.Athiyo	John D.Onaah	
Works and Housing		M.M.N.Zikusoka	J.M.N.Zikusoka	vacant	S.Lukakamwa	S.Lukakamwa	S.Lukakamwa	S.Lukakamwa	S.Lukakamwa
Transport and Communications		M.M.N.Zikusoka	Obitre-Gama	vacant	M.L.Obado	M.L.Obado	M.L.Obado	P.O.Etiang	P.O.Etiang

Culture and Community Development	Y.Engur	Y.Engur	vacant	*F.Nyangweso*	*F.Nyangweso*	*F.Nyangweso*	Mary Astles Senkatuka	M.A.Senkatuka
Land (Mineral) and Water Resources	*E.W.Oryema*	*E.W.Oryema*	*E.W.Oryema*	*E.W.Oryema*	*E.W.Oryema*	vacant	*Juma A. Oris*	*Juma A. Oris*
Education	A.Mayanja	E.B.Rugumayo	*Barnabas Kili*	*Barnabas Kili*	*Barnabas Kili*	*Barnabas Kili*	*Barnabas Kili*	*Barnabas Kili*
Health	J.H.Gesa	J.H.Gesa	vacant	H.Kyemba	H.Kyemba	vacant	vacant	*Idi Amin*
Labour	J.M.Byagagaire	A.Mayanja	vacant	L.Katagyira	L.Katagyira	L.Katagyira	L.Katagyira	L.Katagyira
Attorney General/Justice	Nkambo-Mugerwa	Nkambo-Mugerwa	G.S.Lule	G.S.Lule	G.S.Lule	vacant	M.B.Matovu	M.B.Matovu
Min. w/o Portfolio or other	--	--	*Oboth-Ofumbi*	--	--	--	--	*Hussein Marijan*

Key: Plain Type — Civilian appointment.
Italics — *Past or present officer in military, police or prisons.*
Not shown: E. Bagaya (Foreign Affairs 1974), S. Nyanzi (Small-scale Industry 1977) and others who served very briefly.
Sources: Great Britain, Foreign and Commonwealth Office, *A Yearbook of the Commonwealth*, 1972-78; and *Africa Research Bulletin*, 1978-79.

been a genuine automobile accident.

The Defence Council enjoyed the status of supreme political body in the Amin regime. Though its membership was secret, it presumably included most military officers at the Lieutenant Colonel rank and above, plus commanding officers of key military units. Members in 1974 included Brig. S. Guweddeko (Muganda), Maj. Gen. Mustafa Adrisi (Lugbara), Maj. Gen. Francis Nyangweso (Bugisu), Lt. Col. Demiro Mondo (Madi-Moyo), Lt. Col. Isaac Maliyamungu (Kakwa-Zaire), Lt. Col. Ibrahim Garandi (Busoga), and Brig. Moses Ali (Bari-Sudan). Moses Ali sat as Minister of Provincial Administrations and acted in a liaison capacity for the Defence Council, provincial governors and the cabinet. Provincial governors were themselves recruited from the officer ranks of the military, police and prisons. As evidenced by soldiers' frequent complaints about lack of access to ammunition, the means of destruction remained under the tight control of Major Maliyamungu, first in his capacity as commander of the Magamaga Ordnance Depot and later as Chief of Operations for the army.

Over time, more and more top posts in the bureaucracy and in business firms were filled by military officers and by individuals from northwest Uganda. The composition of the cabinet illustrates these trends, as shown in Tables 6.3 and 6.4. Including the President, military, police and prison officials held 27.8 per cent of portfolios in 1971-2, 55.6 per cent in early 1974 and a peak of 64.0 per cent in early 1978. The proportion of portfolios held by individuals from West Nile and Madi rose more unevenly from 16.7 per cent in 1971-2 to a peak of 52.0 per cent in early 1978. Cabinet members who had immigrated from the Sudan increased the 1978 and 1979 proportion of 'northwesterners' to 64. 0 per cent.

Amin attempted to sever the military ties of soldier-administrators after Charles Arube's attempted coup of March 1974. At the time, Provicial Governor Lt. Col. Elly Aseni (also a Kakwa Christian) donned his battle dress, returned to his former Malire unit and issued orders to troops which were no longer under his command.[41] Subsequently, the Defence Council decreed that officers and soldiers appointed to civilian posts were to be stripped of military prerogatives.

All members of the armed forces serving outside the armed forces as cabinet ministers, provincial governors, and district commissioners, were required to hand in their uniforms to Secretary of Defence Demiro Mondo. Second, these soldier-administrators were forbidden entry to military barracks without the permission of the Defence Council or a unit's commanding officer. Third, soldier-administrators were denied

Table 6.4: Ethnic Regional Origin of 56 Cabinet Members, 1971-9

South

Buganda	Busoga	Toro	Ankole
S. Guweddeko	W. Kibedi	W.B. Banage	R. Nshekanabo
A. Mayanja	J.M.N. Zikusoka	E.B. Rugumayo	L. Katagyira
A. Kironde	H. Kyemba	E. Bagaya	
P. Nkambo-Mugerwa	S. Lukakamwa		**Bukedi**
M.S. Kiingi	I. Garandi		J.H. Gesa (Gwere)
G.S. Lule			F. Nyangweso (Samia)
I.K. Kabanda	**Bugisu**	**Kigezi**	C. Oboth-Ofumbi (Padhola)
J. Masagazi	E.B. Wakhweya	J.M. Byagagaire	
M.A. Senkatuka			
M.B. Matovu			

North

Acholi	Teso	Karamoja	Lango
E.W. Oryema	F.L. Okwaare	W. Naburi	Y. Engur
W. Lutara	M.L. Obado	E.L. Athiyo	
S. Nyanzi	P. Etiang		

Northwest (West Nile and Madi)

Lugbara	Kakwa	Madi Madi-Moyo	Alur	'Nubi' of Unknown Background
Lugbara-Aringa	Idi Amin	Juma A. Oris	V.A. Ovonji	M. Ramathan
E. Obitre-Gama	Charles Arube	Demiro Mondo	Noah Mohammed	
Barnabas Kili	I. Lumago		Bakhiti	
M. Ondoga	Yusuf Gowon			
J. Onaah				
J. Geria				
Mustafa Adrisi				
Ismail Sebi				

Immigrants (All Muslim)

Bari-Sudan	Other
Farouk Minawa	W. Ali Fadhul (Avukaya-Sudan)
Moses Ali (& Rigbo-Ug.)	Dusman Sabuni (Moru-Sudan)
Marijan (& Teso settler)	

Religious Background of the Northwesterners

Christian (9): Obitre-Gama, Ondoga, Onaah, Arube, Lumago, Mondo, Ovonji, Geria, and Kili.

Muslim (8): Adrisi, Sebi, Amin, Gowon, Oris, Mohammed, Bakhiti, Ramathan.

privileges accorded armed forces officers, such as eating in the officers' mess in Kampala, or shopping in the military commissary, to restrict their contact with other soldiers and officers. Thus the cabinet appeared to go full circle from the technocratic 1971 cabinet, whose civilian members were issued uniforms and inducted into the army,[42] to the 1974 cabinet whose military members were to be exiled into civilian life. As in so many other cases, however, Amin bowed to pressure from the officers and soon reversed his position that officers in civilian posts give up uniforms and military contacts.[43] After Vice-President General Mustafa Adrisi's body guards opened fire on civilian bystanders following a mysterious car accident in May 1978, Amin made another attempt to disarm officers in civilian posts by ordering all members of the government to surrender their weapons to the army.[44] This order was also apparently ignored.

Any account of the regime's means of coercion would be incomplete without mention of the three most notorious institutions, all with head-quarters in the Kampala area: the State Research Bureau at Nakasero, the Public Safety Unit at Naguru, and the Military Police at Makindye. With over 2,000 agents, the State Research Bureau was the largest of the three. It was first headed by Major L.M.P. Ozi (Madi), then by Lt. Col. Francis Itabuka (Busoga) until 1977, and finally Lt. Col. Farouk Minawa (Bari-Sudan), although a Captain Mzee Yosa concurrently held the post of Chief of Operations. Ibrahim Kasule of Buganda was one of the many interrogators employed by the State Research Bureau. Indeed, the three institutions recruited agents from every ethnic and religious group in Uganda to be spies, informers and torturers against fellow citizens. Commissioner M. Kassim (Yusuf) Obura from Lango headed the Public Safety Unit (founded in November 1971), where Deputy Commissioner Ali Towilli (Alur) was a feared figure. The Military Police was headed, until 1974, by Brig. Hussein Marella (Baka-Sudan). British-born Bob Astles achieved notoriety as head of the Anti-Smuggling Unit. In addition, there were individuals such as Waris Ali Fadhul (Avukaya-Sudan) and Abdul Nasur (Alur) who developed repu-tations as ruthless eliminators of suspected civilian foes, while serving as military commanders or as provincial governors.

At the individual level, membership in the armed forces and secret police of the Second Republic served as a means of social mobility – an alternative to the colonial pattern of mobility through education and land tenure. It provided certain individual soldiers and officers with access to high-ranking roles in civilian administration and commerce. At the collective level, the problem of control of the military and the means of coercion contributed to the increasing size of the military establishment at the expense of other strata in the economy. Unfortunately, the embourgeoisement of the military predicted by Mazrui[45] occurred without giving rise to bourgeois law and order.

The Economic War

Demands for increased Africanisation of trade accelerated in the months following the coup. Although Amin claimed that his decision to expel Asians from Uganda came in a dream as a message from God, like most dreams, the major elements could be traced to experiences in waking life − in his case − the growing demands by Baganda bureaucrats and traders for more rapid Africanisation of trade.[46]

Prominent among the exponents of more Africanisation and more state aid to African traders was Joseph Mubiru,[47] Governor of the Bank of Uganda. Using the infant industry argument, Mubiru pointed out that mere provision of credit to African traders would not help them in competition with more experienced non-African traders and that the African trader needed state protection in order to survive and compete. Mubiru argued that the state should provide the African trader with low-cost premises, reserve certain lines of trade to Africans, grant exclusive rights to African firms in provision of goods and services to the state and parastatals, and guarantee Africans easy access to trading licences, working capital and medium- and long-term capital.[48]

Being as aware as Obote that special favours to African traders would, in practice, mean special status for Baganda traders who possessed more experience that their non-Baganda counterparts, Amin initially accorded a lukewarm reception to the demands of Baganda traders and bureaucrats. In his August 1971 address to Baganda 'elders', Amin noted that the Baganda were already advancing rapidly in trade and warned that Ugandanisation of commerce and industry must not lead to tribal discrimination, a veiled warning against Baganda commercial hegemony.[49]

Undeterred, the Baganda businessmen, led by Sam Sebagereka, E.K.K. Ntende and Joseph Mubiru, renewed their campaign for state assistance at a meeting of the Kampala West Rotary Club a week later. They argued that only state intervention could enable African traders to compete with the 'monopoly and malicious competition practised by non-Africans'.[50] The *Uganda Argus* sided with the traders and bureaucrats on the need to give African traders state protection and state-guaranteed monopoly in order to enhance the ability of African traders to obtain loans from commercial banks.[51]

At the same time, government leaders called on Asians to make greater efforts to assimilate themselves into Ugandan society. Foreign Minister Wanume Kibedi urged Asians to 'modify their traditional and communal beliefs that tend to enclose them in certain circles and take an active interest in the social and political affairs of the indigenous communities' of their adopted country.[52] Yet this was an impossible request. The economic buffer role of the Asian minority within the domestic division of labour was predicated on their political and social isolation. Only because the Asians could never translate economic power into political control had the colonial state invited Asians to East Africa to serve as a buffer between Europeans and Africans in the middle rungs of commerce and administration.[53] Only because they, unlike Baganda traders and bureaucrats, could not use economic power to lay claim to governing had the Asian traders and manufacturers been favoured by the Obote regime, and even the Amin regime, until Amin's need to extend his base beyond the salariat made capitulation to Baganda demands necessary.

Amin moved slowly, at first, announcing a review of Asians' citizenship status in August 1971, ordering an Asian census in October, and reiterating African complaints regarding the Asian 'community' to a December conference of Asian 'elders'.[54] But at that conference Amin announced the cancellation of all outstanding applications for citizenship, pending a decision on the status of Asians.[55] By that point the trader-bureaucrat alliance had won its campaign for expulsion of Asians.

The timing and extent of the expulsion remained to be settled. Whereas the accumulation function of the Ugandan state and external legitimation required that the state proceed gradually as in Kenya, serving quit notices on *non-citizen* Asian traders on a dozen by dozen basis, the internal legitimation function required the regime to take more drastic action to win support from African traders.[56] Wholesale expulsions had occurred before in Africa. Ghana had expelled non-citizen Africans (including 100,000 Nigerians) in November and December 1969; Obote had expelled 30,000 Kenyan labourers from Uganda in October and November 1970.[57]

Addressing the troops at Tororo on 4 August 1972, Amin declared that Britain would have to assume responsibility for British subjects of Asian origin. The following day he set a three-month deadline for the departure of British subjects of Asian origin whose presence Uganda no longer required. On 9 August, he expanded the scope of the expulsion order to include citizens of India, Pakistan and Bangladesh.

Having established 8 November as the expulsion deadline, Amin wavered on the questions of exemptions. Here he was buffeted by two opposing forces. African populists demanded the expulsion of all Asians, even the 23,000 who were Uganda citizens. But, to minimise economic disruptions, much of the bureaucracy and cabinet favoured broad exemptions, as reflected in the original exemption list announced on 9 August and repeated on 12 August:

1. All persons in the employment of Government, Government Bodies, Co-operative Movement, East African Community and International Organizations.
2. Professionals such as teachers, practising lawyers, medical practitioners, pharmacists, dentists, chemists, auditors, architects, accountants, surveyors, quantity surveyors, engineers, technicians in industries, commercial and agricultural enterprises, the managers or owners of banks and insurance companies, professionals and technicians engaged in plant, animal, agricutural and forestry production, processing and marketing of those products, and school owners.[58]

These exemptions would have limited the expulsion order to Asian merchants, shopkeepers, artisans (carpenters, brick-layers, plumbers) and their families.

Amin revoked the entire exemption list on 17 August. Two days later, he triggered internal and international protests by ordering the expulsion of Uganda citizens of Asian origin. NUSU objected, members of Cabinet objected, as did leaders of Tanzania, Zambia and other African states. On 22 August, Amin back-tracked: only non-citizen Asians would be expelled. But he opened the door for expulsion of some citizens by warning that Asians with dual citizenship and those who could not prove their citizenship papers were genuine would also be expelled.[59]

Although the regime never enacted a decree for expulsion of citizen Asians, it mattered little in practical terms. Many left rather than endure further intimidation from soldiers and African civilians and rather than face the prospect of being dispersed into rural resettlement schemes, as Amin threatened. Those who had hedged their bets − by having family members opt for citizenship in different countries − had to leave to keep the family united. About 4,000 Asians chose to remain in Uganda. The approximately 49,000 Asians who were expelled went to the following countries: Great Britain, 27,200; India, 4,500; Canada, 6,000 (including the cream of the professionals and technicians); Pakistan, 1,000; West Germany, 1,000; Malawi, 1,000; United States, 1,000; Australia, 500; Sweden, 300; New Zealand, 200; Austria, 100; and Mauritius, 100. Another 3,600 wound up in European refugee camps, and the 2,500 Asian citizens of Kenya and Tanzania simply returned home.[60] The 'missing' 20,000 Asians presumably include uncounted dependants and those who left by their own arrangements.

Support from the African populists who had demanded the Asian expulsion aided the Amin regime in crushing the September 17 invasion launched from Tanzania by 1,000 pro-Obote guerrillas. Amin rallied African support by accusing Obote of staging the invasion to stop the Asian expulsion and to sabotage the economic war.[61] The unsuccessful invasion provided Amin with an excuse to round up dissidents, as well as the opportunity to demand an apology from Nyerere for violating the OAU principles of non-intervention in members' internal affairs.

The Amin regime was quite eloquent in defending the Asian expulsion and economic war in terms of economic nationalism, using language reminiscent of the Common Man's Charter and the original platform of the Uganda National Congress:

> We are determined to make the ordinary Ugandan master of his own destiny, and above all to see that he enjoys the wealth of his country. Our deliberate policy is to transfer the economic control of Uganda into the hands of Ugandans, for the first time in our country's history.[62]

Having pledged to transfer economic control of Uganda into the hands of Ugandans, the Amin regime had to decide into which hands to transfer the 'abandoned' property of the expelled Asians. The spoils of the economic war consisted of 5,655 firms, factories, ranches and agricultural estates, as well as homes, cars and household goods left behind by the Asians.[63] Although Amin's expression of concern for 'ordinary Ugandans' implied that the state should take over ownership of Asian firms and property for the benefit of all ordinary Ugandans, such an outcome would have been contrary to the possessive individualism of the African populists and soldiers whose support Amin deemed essential. Yet, if these firms were to be distributed to individuals, competition was bound to be sharp and the number of disappointed applicants very large. Indeed, the number of 'winners' could be only slightly larger than the number of 'winners' in the Buganda land distribution following the agreement of 1900, notwithstanding a far larger field of competitors in the all-Uganda 'contest' of 1972.

The business of creating rich Ugandans was entrusted to the Business Allocation Committees of the Ministry of Industries and Commerce, which quickly excluded 'ordinary Ugandans' from the competition by setting financial and occupational qualifications which narrowed the field to the African middle class, bureaucrats and soldiers. Not all firms and property were distributed to individuals. All buildings owned by the expelled Asians were nationalised by the state and vested in the Properties Custodian Board as a potential source of state revenue. Industries that were too large or too technically complex to entrust to individual members of the African middle class were awarded to parastatal corporations. For example, the Madhvani group of companies was split in two; the largest component, the sugar plantation and refinery, was made a separate parastatal corporation, while much of the remainder of the group was awarded to the Uganda Development Corporation.[64] The Forestry Department took control of most sawmills formerly owned by Asians.

Prior to the establishment of the Business Allocation Committees, Amin personally distributed 500 businesses to individual friends and supporters. Over time, the military played a larger role in the allocation of the spoils of the economic war. At first, 30 officers from the armed forces were seconded to work with the Business Allocation Committees. Later the civilian chairmen of the sub-committees were dismissed for being 'too slow' and were replaced by military officers. Finally, the military-led sub-committees began reallocating businesses already allocated, from civilians to individuals in the military and their relatives. In the end, individuals connected with the military obtained over half the businesses left behind by the Asians.[65] The official estimates of the final allocation of firms, ranches and estates are shown in Table 6.5.

Nevertheless, apart from plundering the assets of firms for short-term gain, only by operating the firms for long-run profits could the new owners accumulate wealth. In the long run, new owners without business experience, notably the military entrepreneurs, were at a distinct disadvantage. Many of these simply plundered the assets of the newly-acquired firms. Hence, there was another, larger group of 'hidden winners' in the economic war, namely the African-owned firms that had been in business prior to the expulsion of the Asians. While some of

Table 6.5: Allocation of Property of Expelled Asians

Type of property	Business firms and ranches	Estates
Allocated to		
Individuals	5,299	144
Government departments and ministries	169	8
Parastatal bodies	32	1
Charitable organisations	2	0
Total	5,502	153

Source: Uganda, *The Action Programme, 1977/78-1979/80* (Entebbe: Ministry of Planning and Economic Development, 1977), p. 46

these older firms were permanently crippled by poor location and low turnover, the economic war removed their main rivals, for both markets and credit. The elimination of Asian traders and manufacturers as competitors was the structural guarantee, or 'final solution',[66] which these African businessmen had demanded from the state. Older African firms had the lead in experience, credit worthiness and other intangibles in competition with parvenu soldiers and bureaucrats.

Although the vast majority of former Asian firms were allocated to private individuals, the Uganda Development Corporation gained control of the largest of the former Asian businesses. With the exception of the sugar industry, the Uganda Development Corporation assumed control of the bulk of both the Madhvani and Mehta industrial groups.[67] Following the Amin regime's nationalisation of 90-odd British-owned subsidiaries in December 1972, the UDC gained control of additional tea plantations, a cigarette factory, printing firm, hoe factory and brewery.[68] Altogether, the acquisition of former Asian and British firms more than doubled the size of UDC in terms of assets. The potential turnover of UDC's subsidiaries exceeded $100 million by 1973; however, the suddenness of these acquisitions, combined with the expulsion of Asian technicians and managers, placed an enormous strain on the group's capacity in management, engineering, accounting and marketing.

One index of UDC's strained management capacity was the fact that by late 1973, the directors of UDC were unable to obtain financial reports from 14 of 52 subsidiaries.[69] Further difficulties arose from personality conflicts involving the UDC chairman and his associates.[70]

Responding to these problems, the government reorganised the parastatal sector in 1974 and 1975 into nine separate firms organised

Table 6.6: Parastatal Bodies and Subsidiaries, 1975-9

Parastatal body	Number of subsidiaries		Major subsidiaries
	1975	1979	
Produce Marketing Board	80	?	Bakeries.
Uganda Development Corp.	73	23	East African Distilleries, TICAF fertilisers, Lango Development Company, Associated Paper Industries, Papco Industries, Lake Katwe salt, African Ceramics, Bjordal Mines, Uganda Grain Milling Co., Uganda Consolidated Properties, and Kulubya Property Co.
Uganda Tea Authority	26	2	Tea factories and Agricultural Enterprises Ltd.
Wood Industry Corporation	19	9	Saw mills making timber, plywood and particle board.
Lint Marketing Board	17	16	Edible oil and soap factories.
Uganda Steel Corporation	10	7	Steel Manufacturers of East Africa, Uganda Hoes, Uganda Baati (roofing), E.A. Steel Products, Uganda Metal Industries, Tororo Steel, Kalamu Ltd.
Uganda Advisory Board of Trade (external trade)	8	9	Food & Beverages Ltd, General Merchandise Ltd, India-Africa Traders, Textile Marketing Services, Transocean (U) Ltd, Uganda Hardwares, Uganda Industrial Machinery, Uganda Motors, Uganda Pharmaceuticals.
National Textile Board	11	11	Nyanza Textiles, Pamba Textiles, African Textiles, Uganda Rayon Textiles, Blankets, Lebel (E.A.) Ltd, Uganda Garments, Uganda Spinning Mill, Uganda Bags and Hessian Mills.
Uganda Cement Corporation	4	4	Tororo Cement, Universal Asbestos, Spunpipe, Hima Cement.
Min. of Industry and Power	?	20	Uganda Breweries, Nib Breweries, E.A. Glassworks, Kakira Sugar, Lugazi Sugar, Uganda Paper Bag, Uganda Fishnet, Dunlop (EA), Kilembe Mines, Lake Victoria Bottling, Associated Match Co.
Min. of Justice (Nat'l Trust)	?	4	Uganda School Supply, Uganda House, Ugationess, Publishing House.
Uganda Electricity Board	?	2	Cabe Corp. of Uganda, Ruwelex Uganda Ltd.
Independent and unallocated	?	9	Uganda Chibuku, Kampala International Hotel. Uganda Leather (Soroti). R.O. Hamilton (U), Uganda Taxi Services, Uganda Securiko.
Uganda Railways Corp.	—	?	
Uganda Airlines	?	?	
Uganda National Tobacco	?	3	Uganda Tobacco Factories Ltd, Printpack Uganda, Uganda Packaging Ltd.
Uganda Tourist Dev. Corp.	?	3	Uganda Hotels, Uganda Wildlife Development Ltd, Tours and Travel Ltd.
Dairy Corporation	?	?	
Coffee Marketing Board	?	?	
Min. of Information	?	2	Consolidated Printers, International Television Sales Ltd.
Internal Affairs (Prisons)	?	2	Jute and Kenaf, Uganda Meat Packers (Soroti).
Min. of Communication	?	4	Uganda Transport Co., People's Transport Co.
Uganda Livestock Ltd.	?	?	

Sources:
Uganda, *The Action Programme, 1977/78-1979/80*, pp. 4, 95-121; Commonwealth Team of Experts, *The Rehabilitation of the Economy of Uganda* (London: Commonwealth Secretariat, 1979), vol. II, pp. 97, 120-5; and *Croner's Reference Book for World Traders* (Queens Village, N.Y.: Croner, 1978), p. 3 of Uganda section.

along functional lines such as textiles, steel, cement, tobacco and wood. There were 23 separate umbrella parastatal corporations and boards at the end of 1975 operating more than 250 subsidiaries, as shown in Table 6.6. Thirty subsidiaries were removed from the UDC and transferred to the new parastatal bodies. However, the transferred subsidiaries included textile, cement and tea factories which had in the past provided the UDC with the bulk of its earnings for new investments. Furthermore, the transferred subsidiaries did not assume repayment obligation for loans taken out on their behalf by the UDC. Hence, the UDC had to assume the obligation for these debts. By 1977 the once dynamic UDC was experiencing serious financial difficulties.[71]

Amin compounded the uncertainties facing the state sector by repeatedly declaring his long-run commitment to 'privatisation' of the state sector. As the *Voice of Uganda* reported in 1973,

On the suggestion that more business should be given to individuals rather than to Government departments or parastatal bodies, the General said he wanted the people to control business and the country's economy. He wants to see that they own the big hotels like the Kampala International [state owned] ... Those businesses which have been given to Government Departments or parastatal bodies, he said, have been given *temporarily* because at the moment there were no people to take them and when suitable candidates become available, they will take them.[72]

In 1977 the government announced that it would sell off all the assets of the 'Departed Asians' Abandoned Property Custodian Board', which included substantial urban real estate holdings, and the government renewed its intention of divesting itself of many state commercial enterprises.[73] Whether 'privatisation' was a genuine distributive policy or merely a symbolic policy to appease populists is not clear. But such pronouncements, the constant reshuffling of parastatal bodies, and private looting of the output and machinery of parastatals did little to encourage efficient management of parastatal firms.

The political orientation of the economic war was summed up in the frequently used Swahili phrase, *mafuta mingi*, which means abundant lamp oil or kerosene, or dripping with wealth. The goal was the creation of a class of Africans who were *mafuta mingi* (which in turn implied the existence of others less fortunate).

At the level of practice rather than goals, the state bureaucracy controlled the commanding heights of the Ugandan economy to the extent that control was possible at the national level in a peripheral capitalist economy. However, this control was unstable to the extent that the mobility aspirations of individuals within the bureaucracy led them to betray the collective interests of their statist class by acquiring private businesses, appropriating public goods for private gain, and engaging in smuggling and foreign exchange manipulations. They thereby weakened the very state apparatus they sought to use to further their individual and class aspirations.

The state's leaders attempted unsuccessfully to check the very contradictions created by the economic war, pleading for economic restraint and moderation on the part of bureaucrats, soldiers and citizens within the context of a regime whose *mafuta mingi* slogan recalled François Guizot's 'Enrichissez-vous!' Amin urged the new proprietors of former Asian firms to show a large profit. They took him at his word, engaging in hoarding of essential commodities, black-marketing, smuggling, overpricing and looting of assets of confiscated firms and state firms. Complaints were soon voiced that the Asians had been replaced by even worse 'black Asians' and 'black Patels'.[74]

Yet to expect the African shopkeepers to have behaved better than the Asian shopkeepers is to be guilty of reverse racism. Businessmen and traders in a peripheral capitalist economy engage in smuggling, hoarding, overcharging and foreign exchange manipulations as a stratum, not as a race. Even prior to the economic war, a majority of Africans distrusted traders of either race. In a survey of African registered taxpayers in 1969, respondents were asked whether they felt Asian (or African) traders carried out their business honestly. A total of 88 per cent of the respondents felt that Asian traders were never honest or honest only some of the time, while 70 per cent of the same respondents felt that African traders were never honest or honest only some of the time.[75]

On the one hand, the economic war removed the obfuscatory issue of race from what was clearly a class conflict between the commercial strata and lower strata. On the other hand, the economic war lessened class antagonisms in the short run by renewing the illusion of mobility. Even so, the scramble for wealth in Uganda did little to promote capital investment. In commenting on the effects of the economic war on investment, the government newspaper *Voice of Uganda* noted: 'Quite a lot of money is now available to indigenous people whose mode of living and habits are markedly removed from the saving-oriented attitudes of businessmen of Asiatic origin.'[76]

A further paradox was the fact that although the economic war led to the embourgeoisement of the military through corruption and the appropriation of businesses there was no corresponding advance in bourgeois law and order. In the absence of bourgeois law and order, there was little incentive for private businessmen to undertake long-term investments, but great incentive for immediate consumption and export of savings to Nairobi and London havens. Those with sufficient wealth lived in fear of extortion and expropriation by soldiers. Even within the government, there were many who recognised that insecurity of property (and life itself) posed a major barrier to capital accumulation in Uganda. The authors of the 1977 *Action Programme* warned that 'the uncertainty about the ownership of enterprises . . . prevents the allocatees from re-investing profits realised'.[77] The authors noted that government loans allocated to new proprietors of former Asian-owned firms under Operation 'Mafuta Mingi' had been largely spent on consumer goods rather than for business purposes. Although the government pledged to pay compensation to owners of private businesses when businesses were 'reallocated', this was rarely done. Hence insecurity of property continued to be a barrier to reinvestment in both the private and parastatal sectors.

Although the military regime employed selective terror to check the political aspirations of businessmen, particularly Baganda businessmen, its economic policies both whetted the appetite of businessmen for political power and reinforced the economic basis of their claim to political power.

Make the Poor Pay: Allocating the Costs of the Economic War

Both the coup and the economic war led to greater military control over the administrative and commercial spheres, without, however, producing a total eclipse of civilian bureaucrats and businessmen. Together, the soldiers, bureaucrats and businessmen constituted the dominant domestic strata in the Amin period, notwithstanding the grave distrust and internecine violence that soiled the alliance. From a world system perspective, the ethno-religious haemorrhaging of civil society in Uganda occurred within a wider framework of two sets of contradictions: the one structural, the other based on class, each of which had global, regional and domestic dimensions. First, there was the contradiction arising from the vertical division of labour between centre and periphery at the global, regional and national levels. Second, there was the conflict between dominant and dominated strata within and between the three levels. The post-1969 slowdown in the growth of the world economy, the centre's attempts to shift the cost of the post-1973 oil price hikes onto the rest of the world, and the centre's painful adjustment to Japan's entry into the core need only be mentioned in passing as factors which helped to sharpen these contradictions.[78] Within the region, these global discontinuities may have hastened the 1976-7 collapse of the East African Community. The contribution of global and regional factors to Uganda's economic decline was overshadowed by breakdowns in manufacturing, processing and transportation following the expulsion of Asian managers and technicians. Within a shrinking national economy,[79] the dominant domestic strata could maintain and increase their respective shares of resources only by shoving the costs of the economic war onto the dominated strata, especially the poorer peasant growers, migrant agricultural labourers and unskilled workers.

The state attempted to shove the costs onto growers of coffee and cash food crops. The growers' share in coffee export receipts fell from 24.2 per cent (1962-72) to 15.6 per cent (1973-8).[80] Between 1972 and 1974, the growers' share in the Kampala retail price for groundnuts fell from 58 to 17 per cent; for mixed beans, the growers' share dropped from 46 to 18 per cent.[81] Growers, at least those with access to transportation, responded by circumventing both the Coffee and Produce Marketing Boards. As world coffee prices peaked at historic highs in 1976 and1977, growers, soldiers, businessmen and bureaucrats smuggled some 50,000 metric tons each year to Kenya, the equivalent of one quarter to one third of Uganda's output. Additional coffee vanished from the Coffee Marketing Board itself at every stage between processing plants in Uganda and its Mombasa warehouses.[82] Part of the coffee diverted from proper channels was flown to Stanstead, England, each week to buy whisky and other luxury goods for high-level military officers and civilian bureaucrats.

While coffee production centred in Buganda, Bugisu and Sebei suffered only slight declines from the peak in 1972 and 1973, tea production based in the west and southwest fell from 23,400 to 10,900 metric tons (1972-8). But cotton production centred in Busoga, Bukedi, Teso, Lango and Acholi plummeted from 78,600 to 13,800 metric tons of lint between 1972/73 and 1976/77, recovering a bit in the following year to 20,000 metric tons. The drop in cotton output jeopardised (and continues to jeopardise) the long-run prospects for industries relying on cotton lint and seed inputs: textiles, edible oil, soap and cattle feed.[83] Moreover, running the cotton-ginning industry at a fraction of its one-time capacity greatly inflates the overhead which must be borne either by the cotton industry or by other sectors.

The causes of the cotton decline in Lango and Acholi are not difficult to fathom. Elsewhere, the shortage of hoes contributed to the decline, as did perhaps the rapid turnover in chiefs, upon whose 'persuasive' powers cotton production depended heavily in the past. While growers in the more oppressed and more remote areas retreated into subsistence agriculture, growers near the towns switched from cotton to marketable foodstuffs, whose retail prices multiplied under the Amin regime. A grower's ability to benefit from increased foodstuff prices depended on the extent to which the farmer was also a transporter and trader, rather than a mere peasant cultivator selling to the Produce Marketing Board.

While many growers earned higher cash incomes from coffee and food crops, the buying power of the rural population was eroded by sharply higher retail prices for hoes, kerosene, soap, sugar, salt, matches, cloth, blankets and transportation, the supply of which was at best uncertain.

Following the expulsion of Asians, the tax burden shifted increasingly onto the rural population and low income groups. The proportion of state revenue derived from progressive taxes (income tax, licence fees and customs duties on luxury imports consumed by high-income groups) declined from 44.2 to 17.0 per cent between 1971/72 and 1977/78. The proportion of state revenue derived from regressive taxes (export duties, sales tax and excise taxes on locally made mass-consumption goods) increased from 50.7 to 80.1 per cent (mainly the coffee export tax).[84]

Industrial production declined sharply after the economic war. Sugar production fell from 141,266 to 12,436 metric tons between 1971 and 1977. Soap production dropped from 13,600 to 3,600 tons between 1971 and 1975. In 1971 Uganda produced 1.4 million hoes; in 1978, only 333,000.[85]

The production of other goods also fell sharply between 1971 and 1978: cement, -85 per cent; asbestos cement pipes and sheets, -87 per cent; steel ingots, -55 per cent; corrugated iron roofing, -94 per cent; gunny bags and sacks, -80 per cent; matches, -86 per cent; and blankets, -88 per cent. Copper mining and smelting and superphosphate fertiliser production had ceased entirely by 1978.[86]

Against this bleak background, production declines of less than 40 per cent must be considered relative success stories. Cotton and rayon fabric production declined from 46 million square metres (1971) to 40 million (1976) and 28 million (1978), an overall decline of 39 per cent. Beer output decreased by 37 per cent (1971-7), while production of the local 'Waragi' gin from sugar cane declined by 30 per cent (1971-8), and cigarette production dipped only 7 per cent. Between 1972 and 1978 paper production (using imported pulp) declined only 14 per cent. A few new industries actually began production under the Amin regime: Jinja lamps (taken over by UEB), Dunlop tyres (taken over by the Ministry of Industry and Power), Kalamu ball-point pens (Ministry of Industry and Power), the Kinyala sugar works, and the Lake Katwe Salt Company (UDC).[87]

Higher world prices for coffee brought some respite to the beleaguered Amin regime in 1976 and 1977, allowing the government to undertake a fairly large programme of re-equipping factories and improving transportation. This windfall was largely offset by the complete disintegration of the East African Community in 1977. Shs. 1,029 million of the increased revenue from the coffee tax had to be allocated to replace services formerly provided by the EAC.[88] However morally correct, the US ban on Ugandan coffee imports made little impact on Uganda's trade.[89] Uganda found other buyers in a tight market, and may have had some coffee relabelled to enter the US.

The overall slump in industrial production to less than 30 per cent[90] of former capacity was triggered by the shortage of technical and managerial staff following the expulsion of the Asians. The resulting production problems reduced foreign exchange earnings, making it difficult to obtain spare parts. Due to the shortage of spare parts, the transportation sector virtually collapsed in 1974, further compounding production problems and reducing foreign exchange earnings. Prices of domestically manufactured goods sky-rocketed. The initial inflation due to supply shortages was accelerated by massive government borrowing to finance a growing deficit. Government borrowing from domestic sources rose from U. Shs. 568 million to U. Shs. 4,692 million between 1970 and 1976, or 72 per cent of the total credit extended to all domestic borrowers, versus 39 per cent in 1970.[91]

Faced with the uncertainty of dealing with new business owners, foreign suppliers demanded prepayment on goods shipped to Uganda. This put an additional, if temporary, burden on already strained foreign exchange reserves. Faced with tight credit abroad, Ugandan wholesalers and retailers turned to Kenyan suppliers. From 1972 onward, Kenya displaced Britain and the United States as the major source of Uganda's imports. This switch, plus thinly disguised admiration for the expulsion of Asians, explains the positive side of the curious love-hate relationship between the African business elite in Kenya and Idi Amin.

The regime attempted to blame much of Uganda's inflation on rising world prices, particularly petroleum, but the greatest inflation occurred in locally produced foodstuffs.

The *weakness* of the military regime in dealing with inflation was starkly illustrated by a table in the *Action Programme*, which showed the disparity between official retail prices set by the government and actual market prices. Notwithstanding the harsh penalties for 'economic crimes', merchants even charged the government substantially more than the official price (Table 6.7). It is also worth noting that the price

Table 6.7: Official and Actual Retail Prices, 1975

Item	Unit	Official retail price set by government	Average price paid by the government in tendered contracts	Current market price 1975
		All prices shown as Shillings per unit		
Beef (boneless)	Kg	9.00	11.00	20.00
Beef (bone in)	Kg	7.00	10.50	18.00
Eggs	Tray of 30	25.00	45.00	50.00
Dry beans	Kg	1.60	2.50	6.00
Bread, white	500 gm loaf	3.40	4.50	5.00
Matoke (plantain)	Kg	0.50	1.30	2.00
Maize flour	Kg	2.75	3.50	4.00
Sweet potatoes	'Debe'	8.00	–	15.00
Onions	Kg	2.75	4.50	5.50
Fresh milk	500 ml	1.20	1.20	3.50
Sugar	Kg	7.00	7.00	30.00
Rice	Kg	1.75	9.00	9.00
Beer	500 ml	6.00	–	13.50
Charcoal	sack	10.00	28.00	40.00
Soap	bar	11.50	11.50	25.00
Cigarettes (Sportsman)	20	2.80	–	10.00

Source: Uganda, *Action Programme, 1977/78-1979/80*, p. 57.

of beef fillet consumed by upper-income groups rose by a relatively modest 42.5 per cent between 1971 and 1975, while the price of *matoke*, the staple of low-income workers, jumped by 412.8 per cent.[92]

According to the government's statistics, the cost of living for low-income workers in Kampala increased by 531 per cent between 1971 and 1977, while the cost of living for medium- and high-income groups rose by 369 per cent and 234 per cent, respectively.[93] In the same period, the legal minimum wage increased by only 41 per cent, from U. Shs. 170 to U. Sh. 240 per month. Skilled workers fared better – at least up to mid-1974 – winning wage increases proportionate to the rise in the cost of living. Whereas poor peasants could generally retreat into subsistence production to survive, unskilled workers in urban areas had no similar avenue of escape, other than returning to the countryside, which they began doing in large numbers in 1974. By 1978 there were serious labour shortages on sugar and tea plantations. The government even made plans to mechanise sugar harvesting at Kinyala.[94] Paradoxically, capitalist farmers and 'informal sector' employers were able to outbid larger firms in attracting unskilled labour. By paying agricultural labourers U. Shs. 350 per month, outgrowers raided workers from plantations paying only U. Shs. 253. Miners refused to work for less than U. Shs. 450 per month.[95]

Total reported employment rose from 324,500 to 363,000 between 1971 and 1977. The entire increase was in the public sector, which grew from 134,000 to 202,000 in response to the state takeover of Asian and British firms in 1972 and several Kenyan firms in 1976. Reported employment in the private sector declined by 15.5 per cent. Average private sector wages rose from U. Shs. 4,532 to U. Shs. 6,441 per annum; in the public sector, annual average wages rose from U. Shs. 4,098 to U. Shs. 6,748. Although the average wage rose faster than the minimum wage, it did not keep pace with inflation. It should, however, be borne in mind that these are figures for reported employment. The informal sector and illegal sector activities grew remarkably under the regime, escaping both legal and statistical scrutiny. The state thereby lost, but not necessarily the entrepreneurs, who, for example, smuggled as much as US $520 million in coffee from Uganda between 1975 and 1979.[96]

The economic war yielded a mixed harvest for economic nationalists. Ownership of the means of production and distribution shifted from non-citizens and non-African citizens to the state and African citizens. But the structure of the economy became more, not less, dependent.

Despite the state's control of the manufacturing sector and the import-export trade, despite the use of preferential foreign exchange allocations and carefully-planned restrictions on imports, and despite exhortations by leaders for increased self-reliance, Uganda's trade composition index declined from –0.736 to –0.771 between 1970 and 1973, the last year for which detailed trade figures were available.[97] This decline in the Galtung-Hungrø index represents an increase in structural dependence.

The fall in the trade index was obviously caused by severe disruptions in exports of manufactured goods for the East Africa market. The production decline could not be halted despite importation on short-term contracts of managerial and technical cadres from India, Pakistan, Egypt and the Sudan. First, the increased level of personal violence under Amin's regime destabilised the economy and encouraged capital liquidity and capital flight rather than the long-term investment needed for rehabilitating the economy. Second, individuals in the civilian and military bureaucracy betrayed their objective collective interests as managers of state industrial capital by mimicking the acquisitive behaviour of the newly-engaged commercial bourgeoisie. Some looted the equipment, raw materials and output of the state firms to enrich themselves in the *magendo* (black market) trade. Others participated in smuggling goods and secreting wealth to Nairobi, the 'Switzerland' of East Africa. Third, increased inequality in income distribution under the regime fragmented the potential market for domestic mass-consumption goods and expanded the demand for imported consumer goods.

The race for wealth, as much as Amin's capriciousness, explains the increase in personal violence under the regime, the internecine violence of a Hobbesian society devoid of Leviathan. In the name of order, the agents of the state promoted disorder; in the name of self-reliance, individual members of the salariat and the commercial stratum promoted increased dependence on Kenya.

Smuggling, falsification of import and export invoices and the illegal transfers of funds to Nairobi were major factors explaining a second anomaly of the political economy of the Amin regime: the decline of foreign exchange reserves despite substantial positive visible trade balances from 1972 through 1977. According to the data in Table 6.8, between 1966 and 1972, the visible trade surplus averaged U. Shs. 469.4 million, the balance of payments surplus, U. Shs. 15.2 million. Between 1973 and 1977, the visible trade surplus averaged U. Shs. 1,019.5 million, but the balance of payments averaged a *deficit* of U. Shs. 83.0 million annually.

The difference between the visible trade balance reported by the East African Customs and Excise Department and the 'adjusted trade balance' reported by the Uganda Ministry of Finance increased markedly in the 1973-7 period compared with 1966-72.[98] The difference between the customs and excise trade data and the adjusted trade data normally consisted of three elements: (1) valuation adjustments

Table 6.8: Trade and Balance of Payments Data, 1966-78 (U.Shs. million)

Year	Visible trade Exports	Visible trade Imports	Visible trade Net	Merchandise account Exports	Merchandise account Imports	Merchandise account Net merch. A	Net services B	Transfer payments C	Balance of payments account Capital account[a] D	SDR's E	Net balance of payments A+B+C+D+E
1966	1551.1	1188.2	362.9	1470.6	1336.7	133.9	-249.9	7.5	257.5	—	149.0
1967	1562.8	1137.5	425.3	1495.6	1317.3	178.3	-250.6	0.1	143.4	—	71.2
1968	1540.5	1176.0	364.5	1491.4	1323.7	167.7	-186.5	- 3.2	98.0	—	76.0
1969	1661.0	1246.7	414.3	1572.5	1421.9	150.6	-176.9	-16.7	113.0	—	70.0
1970	2012.9	1228.9	784.0	1868.5	1463.7	404.8	-221.1	-38.6	-152.8	38.4	30.7
1971	1857.2	1783.0	74.2	1742.3	2034.0	-291.7	-286.3	-34.1	249.7	36.1	-326.3
1972	2018.6	1158.2	860.4	1884.4	1411.4	473.0	-315.1	-41.6	-113.7	32.9	35.5
1973	2205.6	1139.0	1066.6	1931.5	1416.1	515.4	-202.7	-9.3	-345.9	—	-42.5
1974	2337	1550	787	2165.5	2095.0	70.5	-240.8	-3.5	-89.1	—	-262.9
1975	1977	1470	507	1805.1	1926.8	-121.7	-193.2	114.7	-59.6	—	-259.8
1976	2942	1779	1163	2708	1989	719	-340.9	17.9	-438.7	—	-42.7
1977	4864	3290	1574	4528	3483	1045	-459.7	-21.7	-370.6	—	193.0
1978	n.a.	n.a.	n.a.	2500	2745	-245	-758	-23	578	—	-448

[a] Includes errors and omissions.

Sources: Uganda, *Action Programme*, pp. 34-8; and Uganda, *Budget Speech*, 1977, 1978 and 1979. Obvious typographical errors in the data in the *Action Programme* have been corrected.

arising from transportation costs between the Uganda border and the port of Mombasa; (2) coverage adjustments consisting of the addition of military equipment imports and imports for EAC institutions which are not reported in the customs and excise data; and (3) timing adjustments necessitated by the lag between the physical movement of goods and related movement of payment. The expulsion of Asians altered the timing adjustment. Formerly the Asian merchants had been able to import goods on credit terms extending from 90 to 180 days. Their successors, the *mafuta mingi* businessmen, were required to prepay goods before they were shipped to Uganda. The military regime and the 1972 invasion altered the *coverage* adjustment as more military equipment was ordered to supply the expanded armed forces. However, assuming the published military budget is correct, then military equipment and transport purchases probably did not exceed U. Shs. 320 million in the 1973-4 fiscal year.[99] The prepayment of imports and increased military imports are not sufficient to explain the disparity in trade figures for 1973 and 1974. The remainder of the disparity can only be explained by the increase in illicit trade and foreign exchange manipulations.

In one fairly typical case, a Kampala businessman had exported cotton seed cake to Kenya and instructed the buyer to deposit payment in a Nairobi bank. With these funds the Kampala businessman purchased three automobiles in Nairobi and arranged to have them driven to Kampala with Kenyan registration plates for use in his taxi business.[100] Only the export of the cotton seed cake would have been reported in the visible trade figures. The leniency of the military regime towards such cases was illustrated by the fact that the Ugandan businessman in question was able, by pleading ill-health, to postpone indefinitely his appearance before a military court of inquiry. One assumes the delay was actually occasioned by negotiations over the needed bribe.

Alternatively, a Ugandan merchant might smuggle locally produced cloth, hoes or coffee into Kenya, return to Uganda with proceeds of the sale in Kenyan currency, exchange this currency for Ugandan currency on the black market at double or more the official rate, and thereby double his original working capital. The new holder of the Kenyan currency would probably be a petty trader who used the foreign exchange to buy a motor vehicle in Kenya for a transport business or to buy consumer goods from African merchants on River Road in Nairobi, to be smuggled back into Uganda for sale at the vastly inflated *magendo* prices necessary to recoup the original outlay for foreign exchange. In this commodity circulation cycle none of the transactions would have been recorded by the East African Customs and Excise Department. While the merchant and petty trader gained, the Ugandan economy would have had to export twice the necessary value of goods in return for imports from Kenya.[101]

Hence, the winners of the economic war included African traders, the salariat (and the military), some skilled workers and farmers with access to transportation. The losers, aside from the expelled Asians, included most unskilled workers and the peasants who lacked the transport to turn higher food prices to their advantage. But continued lawlessness made victory ephemeral for many winners in the economic war.

The Politics of Survival: The Dynamics of Ethnicity

Survival was a constant preoccupation, both for the regime and for its subjects. Supporters and opponents became ensnared in self-fulfilling ethnic and religious stereotypes: the 'capitalist' Baganda; the 'socialist' Langi; the 'mercenary' Sudanese; the 'blood-thirsty' Nubians; the 'foreign' West Nilers; the 'anti-Muslim, anti-Amin' Christians; and the 'anti-Christian, pro-Amin' Muslims.

Although he sometimes falls into the stereotype trap, particularly regarding the Sudanese and the Nubians, Holger Bernt Hansen has made a valuable contribution toward understanding the dynamics of ethnic and religious conflict in Uganda under both Obote and Amin.[102] To paraphrase Hansen, Obote's attempt to foster even development between the north and the south was branded by southern and eastern opponents as an attempt to foster Langi hegemony. Opposition led to polarisation and, perforce, to hegemony in the coercive sphere. The one side included Lango and Acholi, with Bunyoro as a tacit ally after 1964; the other side included Buganda, Busoga and Ankole, with Teso (the 'East') as a tacit ally. Neglected in the northern 'catch-up' project and threatened by Obote's buttressing of Acholi and Langi positions in the coercive sphere (which was the West Nile's sole high-status role within the domestic cultural division of labour), the West Nile swung toward the southern camp, signalled by Amin's switch from the pro-Obote Muslim organisation (the National Association for the Advancement of Muslims) to the pro-Buganda Muslim organisation led by Prince Badru Kakungulu of Kibuli Mosque.[103]

In turn, the Amin coup began as an attempt to redress the grievances of the northwest *vis-à-vis* the rest of Uganda. In gratitude for the over-

throw of Obote and the expulsion of Asians, Buganda became a tacit
ally of the northwest. Amin's claim to ethnic impartiality was, however,
undermined from the start by two documents propagated by the
regime: the 18-point manifesto and the 'Lango Development Master
Plan of 1967'.[104] Points 15 and 16 in the manifesto accused the former
regime of deciding that 'all key positions in Uganda's political, commercial, army and industrial life have to be occupied and controlled by
people from Akokoro County, Lango District'. The 'Lango Development Master Plan' was either an outright forgery or a crank letter to
Obote from a Langi constituent, urging Langi dominance. The Amin
regime propagated it as its own 'Protocols of the Elders of Zion' to
divide Acholi from Langi and to rouse antagonisms against the Langi.
Even Oboth-Ofumbi, who should have known better, travelled around in
May 1971, accusing the Langi of springing up from nowhere to hold 'all
responsible positions in the Ministries in 1969'.[105] In response to
massacres at Mbarara, Kampala and Karuma Falls, Acholi and Langi
soldiers staged mutinies in Moroto and Jinja in July 1971. About 1,000
soldiers and police, led by Tito Okello and David Oyite-Ojok, escaped
to Tanzania to form the core of the movements which invaded Uganda
in 1972 and 1979.[106]

Within West Nile tensions surfaced between Amin and the Alur. Subsequently, the Lugbara and Madi Christians fell out with Amin. This
reduced the inner core of the regime to Kakwa, Lugbara (from the
largely Muslim Aringa county), Madi Muslims, Nubians throughout
Uganda, immigrants from Zaire and the Sudan, plus individual non-
Nubian, non-West Nile Ugandans who served in the regime. As Hansen
correctly notes, the Lugbara and Madi Christians and the Alur moved
to the outer core of the regime, rather than being expelled completely.
They still stood to gain from the West Nile 'catch-up' project;
moreover, others in Uganda regarded them as pro-Amin West Nilers
anyway, propelling them back to the fold.[107]

Hansen has more problems with the Nubians and the immigrants,
labelling the latter as mercenaries.[108] The 'Nubians' are a uniquely
Ugandan phenomenon, a product of the history of Uganda. They form a
culturally-defined occupational case of 'de-tribalised' Muslim Ugandans
in the army, police and prisons. If we accept the argument of those who
would deny the Ugandan birthright of the Nubians, then we fall into
the trap of requiring that a Ugandan be first a member of a 'tribe'
before being accepted as a Ugandan. In any event, most 'Nubians' can
easily trace their internal Uganda origins. Amin's error in projecting
the 'Nubians' as a universal Ugandan tribe was the fact that, in a strict

sense, only Muslims could be Nubian. Not all Ugandans wished to be Muslim, and not all Muslims wished to be Nubian.

As for the immigrants, Uganda's farmers and planters had long been only too happy to employ migrant labourers from Rwanda, Zaire and the Sudan. In 1965, Sudanese and Zairian labourers comprised 36.4 per cent of the plantation work force on the Madhvani sugar estate at Kakira.[109] Sudanese women laboured for very low wages on UDC plantations in 1970. The Bari from the Sudan and the Kakwa from Zaire (and the Sudan) did not regard themselves as mercenaries when they responded to the opportunities presented by a fellow Kakwa's rise to power in Uganda. (Both Kakwa and Bari are part of the Bari cluster of Eastern Sudanic languages, while Baka, Avukaya and Moru in the Sudan and Madi in Uganda are part of the Moru-Madi sub-groups of Central Sudanic languages.) The proportion of Sudanese and Zairians in the Uganda armed forces eventually peaked at no more than 10 per cent, if that high. For their part, West Nilers eventually held as much as 35 to 50 per cent of the posts in the Army.[110] If the higher figure was correct, army recruitment represented a considerable drain on West Nile manpower (equivalent to 1 in 10 West Nile males between the ages of 18 and 52).[111]

The 'greater West Nile co-prosperity sphere' had other limits, as Amin discovered in March 1974, when resentment against Hussein Marella and other Sudanese officers sparked the mutiny led by Charles Arube and Elly Aseni (both Kakwa Christians). Marella (Baka) was forced to retire to Yei, Sudan. Charges were dropped against Lt. James Ayoma (Lugbara Christian), who was accused of ordering the murder of three Baka officers and soldiers in retaliation for Arube's death. For leading the armoured attack on Marella's headquarters at Makindye, Aseni was tried by a military tribunal, which accepted the argument of the defence that there was no case to answer and freed him. Amin later appointed Aseni Uganda's Ambassador to Moscow (1978). Two weeks after Kampala fell to the Uganda National Liberation Front (UNLF), Amin phoned Aseni in Moscow to plead for assistance from Ugandan cadets training in the USSR.[112] Amin's careful handling of the West Nile officers who participated in the March 1974 coup attempt contrasts sharply with the way the regime treated civilian opponents from elsewhere in Uganda.

If language were all that mattered in Amin's search for ethnic allies, he could have directed his attention to other Eastern Sudanic language groups in Uganda: Teso and Karimojong. There is some evidence that he did so. Cabinet members from Teso and Karamoja served longer than

most, and the Teso continued to be well-represented in the Army led
by Lt. Col. William Omaria, a carry-over from Obote. Ironically, even the
Acholi and Langi languages are part of the Eastern Sudanic group and
are thus technically closer cousins to Kakwa than is, say, Madi, a fact
that should also be borne in mind by the post-Amin regimes.[113]

Hansen observed that, whereas Amin had problems maintaining a
winning ethnic coalition, his opponents faced even greater obstacles in
the quest for unity. Baganda and Langi anti-Amin movements were not
above betraying each other's plots to Amin. Was Amin's dictatorship
really more bearable than victory by the 'other side' from the bitter
contest of the 1960s?

Politics of Survival: The Religious Factor

Religion was also important in alliances and cleavages. Understandably,
Amin tried to reverse the effects of colonial rule, during which the
British bias against Muslims and state subsidies to mission schools had
steadily eroded the status of Islam from its late nineteenth-century
peak.[114] Whereas the Obote regime had united Protestants and Muslims
(as very junior partners) against the Catholic DP, the Amin regime
attempted to forge a Muslim-Catholic alliance (with Catholics the junior
partner) against Protestants. Even in West Nile the alliance proved
shaky. Although Christians (mostly Catholic) outnumbered Muslims
among the 17 West Nilers who served in Amin's Cabinet, the Christian
'majority' was an illusion. Christians simply experienced a high
turnover, whereas Muslims enjoyed staying power. In 1974, five of the
seven portfolios held by West Nilers were held by Christians. By 1979,
of twelve portfolios held by West Nilers, Christians held only two, and
Muslims ten. Furthermore, although Zairian and Sudanese immigrants
included both Christians and Muslims, it so happened that all five immigrants who served in the Cabinet were Muslims.

Religious affiliations became increasingly politicised under Amin, so
much so that Muslims were automatically presumed to be Amin
supporters, and Christians, especially Protestants were assumed to be
opponents. Amin ordered a census of missionaries in November 1972
and expelled at least 74 of the 1,455 missionaries between then and
July 1975. Father Clement Kiggundu, editor of the Catholic newspaper
Munno, was killed in January 1973. In September 1977, the regime
curbed the growth of Protestant sects by banning 27 religious groups,
leaving Islam, Roman Catholicism, the (Anglican) Church of Uganda

and the Greek Orthodox Church as the only legally sanctioned religious organisations.[115]

The 1977 Centenary Celebration of the Anglican Church in Uganda acquired a political dimension which was further magnified by the forceful open letter to President Amin, signed by Archbishop Luwum and 17 Bishops and Assistant-Bishops in early February. The letter protested the search conducted by state security forces in the homes of the Archbishop and Yona Okoth, Bishop of Bukedi. The letter went on to protest the intimidation of civilians by the security forces and by the State Research Bureau, the war against the educated, and the threat to life and property posed by agents of the state. Three of the Centenary Celebration organisers — Luwum, Oryema and Oboth-Ofumbi — were killed on 17 February, following the disclosure of a pro-Obote plot, in which one of the alleged plotters was tortured into naming Archbishop Luwum as a participant.[116]

As shown by the public execution of a group of alleged conspirators during Ramadan, AH 1397 (September 1977 AD) and by his frequent quarrels with the Muslim Supreme Council, Idi Amin was hardly a model Muslim.[117] Nevertheless, his promotion of Islam in Uganda and his ringing post-1971 denunciations of Zionism helped the regime to obtain external assistance which offset the fall-off in Western aid after the Asian expulsion and the nationalisation of British firms. In 1968-73 official aid to Uganda from all sources (mainly OECD members and multilateral agencies) averaged US $25.5 million per annum; in 1974-8 official aid from all sources (mainly Arab and OPEC sources) averaged US $26.1 million per annum.[118] But, because of inflation, the real value of aid declined.

The Politics of Survival: Administrative Innovations

The Amin regime instituted a number of administrative innovations beyond such wholly negative measures as the suspension of Parliament and the elimination of political parties.

At the local level, the regime instituted the election of chiefs first promised by Obote in 1970. Following the coup, popular agitation arose in Buganda for the replacement of all chiefs appointed by the former regime. Amin observed that pressure took the 'form of threats not to pay Graduated Tax until such chiefs were removed'.[119] The threat was carried out in the Buganda districts: East Mengo, West Mengo, Masaka and Mubende. A spokesman for the Ministry of Public

Service and Local Administrations reported 'extremely appalling' low levels of graduated tax collection in the first three months of 1971.[120] However, whatever their loyalty to the new regime, Amin could at least count on the Obote chief's loyalty to the policy of no restoration of the monarchy. Furthermore, wholesale dismissal of these chiefs would have undermined the morale and loyalty of the entire salariat by raising the spectre of mass dismissals of Obote appointees at all levels of the bureaucracy. In the first year, Amin needed the support of the salariat from the top down. Finally, wholesale appointments of new chiefs would have plunged the new regime into the murky and treacherous waters of internal Baganda factionalism.

Even so, the expulsion of the Asians increased the regime's dependence on graduated tax revenues. Elections for chiefs were held in March 1973. Election of chiefs presented several advantages to the regime: it removed unpopular chiefs; it insulated the central government from local factionlism; and it provided an outlet for political ambitions of capitalist farmers. The central government reserved the right to screen candidates and to override election results which it found unpalatable. Many of the elected chiefs were dismissed: 24 of 34 chiefs in Madi. In May, the regime appointed 728 low-ranking soldiers to become chiefs.[121] It is unclear whether these soldier-chiefs remained part of the military, and whether the practice of appointing soldiers as chiefs continued throughout the regime, which would indicate that the election of chiefs had ceased almost as soon as it started.

A more lasting reform was the new system for taxing businesses introduced following the expulsion of the Asians. In a manner somewhat reminiscent of the French tax system, businessmen were assessed taxes on the basis of the type of business and the location of the business rather than on the basis of self-reported income. The so-called provisional income tax was introduced in 1976. Traders in medium-size towns paid a flat rate of Shs. 3,000 per annum, those in small villages, Shs. 2,000. Jaggery manufacturers paid Shs. 30,000 per annum. Cinema owners paid a tax based on the number of seats. Commercial vehicle owners paid a tax based on the number of seats in buses or the gross weight of lorries, ranging up to Shs. 30,000 for 15-ton lorries and Shs. 20,000 for buses with more than 20 seats.[122] The post-Amin UNLF regime found the provisional income tax system to be very efficient. It raised most rates and extended the system to fishermen and fishmongers. Owners of buses with more than 20 seats were now assessed a tax of Shs. 50,000.[123]

Another lasting innovation was the introduction of the *Nyumba*

Kumi (ten house) system of social control and surveillance, which was itself adapted from the Cuban and Tanzanian models. For every ten houses in a village, one person was selected to report to the local chief on the coming and going of inhabitants and to watch for smuggling, tax evasion and unfounded rumours. The UNLF regime kept the *Nyumba Kumi* system, ordering the *Nyumba Kumi* members to expose all forms of tax evasion.[124]

At the regional level, the regime replaced centrally-administered District Councils with a new system of 10 semi-autonomous Provincial Administrations ruled by Governors recruited from the military, police and prisons. Each Province contained several of the old districts. The position of Secretary-General at the district level, created by the former regime, was abolished. District boundaries were redrawn.

Although the official rationale for the reorganisation was the need for decentralisation of administration and decision-making, the creation of new provincial-level posts and bureaucracies provided patronage posts for ambitious officers and new opportunities for the civilian salariat. Posting an overly ambitious officer to be governor of a province was a cheaper alternative than a diplomatic assignment.

The creation of new districts served two other purposes. First, it met local demands for separate status, arising from conflicts pre-dating independence, as in the case of East and West Acholi or the desire of the Bwamba and Bakonjo for districts separate from Toro. Second, it contributed to a policy of divide and rule — many small districts were easier to control than a few powerful districts. The divide and rule policy underwent some modifications. The initial August 1972 plan called for nine provinces, organised so that Buganda would be divided into five districts, two of which (North and South Masaka) were to be amalgamated with districts in Kigezi and Ankole to form the Southern Province, while the three remaining districts formed the truncated Buganda Province.[125] The plan evidently encountered stiff resistance from Baganda notables, because the final plan published in March 1974 preserved the territorial 'purity' of Buganda by dividing it into nine districts organised into three Buganda provinces (North Buganda, South Buganda and Central Province). Part of West Acholi was transferred from the Northern Province to the Nile Province.[126]

Politics of Survival: Violence

Whereas kondoism constituted the most feared form of personal

Table 6.9: Prominent Disappearances and Murders Under Amin. A
Selected List

Name	Position or other information (year of death)
Benedicto Kiwanuka	Chief Justice of Uganda (1972)
Michael Kagwa	President, Industrial Court, and businessman (1971)
Raphael Sebugwawo Amooti	President, Industrial Court, and chairman of the organising committee for the Catholic Church Centenary (1978)
Joseph M. Mubiru	Governor of Bank of Uganda (1972)
32 Army officers	Blown up in cell at Malire Barracks, 8 March 1971
Lt. Col. Ogwal	Killed in shelling of Dr Ebine's Nakasero home (1971)
Dr George W. Ebine	Gynaecologist, Mulago Hospital. Seized in OR (1971)
Dr Vincent Pim Emiru	Professor of Opthalmology, Makerere (1971)
Al-Hajji Shaban Nkutu	Obote's Min. of Works, Communications and Housing, former leader of National Association for Advancement of Muslims (NAAM) (1973)
Al-Hajji Ali Kisekka	Former Deputy Minister in East African Community
Martin A. Okello	Former Member of Parliament for West Nile and Madi (1971)
Ahmed Oduka	Director of Music, Uganda Police (1971)
Mr Rwamashonge	President of the Uganda Mine Workers' Union (1971)
Janan Luwum	Archbishop, Church of Uganda (Anglican) (1977)
Charles Oboth-Ofumbi	Amin's Minister of Internal Affairs (1977)
Lt. Col. Erinayo Oryema	Amin's Min. of Land and Water Resources (1977)
Yekosfati Engur	Amin's former Min. of Culture and Community Development (1977)
Lt. Col. Michael Ondoga	Amin's Min. of Foreign Affairs (1974)
Brig. S. Guweddeko	Air Force Commander under Amin (1977)
167 to 258 soldiers	Mbarara Barracks massacre, July 1971
120 soldiers	Moroto Barracks massacre, July 1971
About 400 soldiers	Jinja uprising, July 1971
50 soldiers	Magamaga Ordnance Depot massacre, July 1971
245 to 295 soldiers	Executions at Mutukula Prison, January 1972
Mr Mulekezi	District Commissioner, Bukedi (1972)
Samson Ddungu	Businessman and President, Uganda Guide Post (1973)
Nr Nshekanabo	Manager, Rock Hotel, Tororo (1972)
William Kalema	Obote's Minister of Commerce and Industry (1972)
Anil Clerk	Asian Member of Parliament (1972)
Basil Bataringaya	Obote's Minister of Internal Affairs (1972)
Alex Ojera	Obote's Min. of Information, Broadcasting and Tourism, member of 1972 invasion force, captured and killed
Brig. Suleiman Hussein	Obote's Army Chief of Staff, killed at Luzira (1971)
Joshua Wakholi	Obote's Min. of Public Service (1972)
John Kakonge	Obote's Min. of Agriculture and Co-operatives (1972)
James Ochola	Obote's Min. of Local Administration (1972)

Frank Kalimuzo	Vice-Chancellor of Makerere University (1972)
Peter Oketta	Assistant Commissioner of Prisons (1972)
Ben Otim	Local administration, Lango District (1972)
Simayo Peter Oryem	Administrative Secretary, Acholi District (1972)
Mr Tibayungwa	Administrative Secretary, Acholi District (1972)
Nekemia Bananuka	Former Secretary-General, Ankole District (1972)
George Kamba	Director, E.A. Posts and Telecommunications, and former ambassador to India and West Germany (1972)
Francis Walugembe	Businessman and former mayor of Masaka (1972)
James Buwembo	Chemist and brother-in-law of Obote (1972)
Martin A. Rubanga	Secretary for Defence (1972)
Lt. Col. Valentine Ochima	Amin's aide-de-camp (1972)
Capt. Avudria	Lugbara Christian (1972)
Wakuma Maeno	Chief Grader, Coffee Marketing Board (1972)
David Ocaya	Secretary, Lint Marketing Board
John Kasasa	Insurance agent (1972)
Patrick Ruhinda	Lawyer (1972)
Henry Berunga	Uganda Director, EA Railways (1973)
James Bwogi	Commercial manager, Uganda Television (1971)
John Okech-Omara	Regional Supplies Officer, EA Railways (1973)
Auwar Owuor	Regional Personnel Officer, EA Railways (1973)
Mr Tomusange	Industrial Relations Officer, EA Railways (1973)
Father Clement Kiggundu	Editor, *Munno* (Catholic newspaper) (1973)
Dr F.G. Sembeguya	Former Member of Parliament (1973)
Dr Edward Kizito	Acting head of Dental School, Makerere (1973)
Lt. Col. Kakuhikire	President's Office (1973)
'Jolly' Joe Kiwanuka	Former politician, former detainee under Obote (1973)
James Karuhanga	Maths teacher accused of plotting against Amin (1973)
Mrs Ogwang	Jinja businesswoman
Godfrey Kiggala	Official in Foreign Ministry (1973)
Paul Bitature	Mbarara businessman and former official of EAC (1973)
Mr Nakibinge	Personnel Manager, Lugazi Sugar Works, and former Mayor of Kampala (1973)
Bulasio Kavuma	Former politician, Buganda
Stephen Epanau	Manager, Barclays Bank, Kabale
Capt. Justin Sam Aswa	Soldier who first read the 18-point manifesto (1973)
Brig. Charles Arube	Army Chief of Staff, alleged leader of 1974 coup attempt
Al Hajji Balunywa	Administrative Secretary, Busoga
Abdalla Anyuru	Chairman, Public Service Commission (1977)
Daniel Nsekero	Assistant Commissioner of Police (1977)
Y.Y. Okot	Chief Inspector of Schools (1977)
Augustine Kamya	Chairman of National Chamber of Commerce and Industry, founder of Uganda National Movement (1972)
Byron Kawadwa	Director, National Theatre. His play *St Charles Lwanga* depicted Mwanga's 1885 persecution of Christians (1977)
Jimmy Parma	Photographer, *Voice of Uganda*, angered regime by investigating Dora Bloch's murder (1976)

John Serwaniko	Editor, *Munno* (1976)
Al-Hajji Shaban M. Kaloddo	Masaka businessman, murdered by anti-Amin forces for alleged role in State Research Bureau (1977)
24 Tanzanians	Six students and 18 farmers. Uganda later admitted responsibility for deaths in exchange for de facto recognition of the regime by Tanzania (1972)
Kaman Gitau	Kenya businessman
Dora Bloch	Airline hostage at Entebbe (1976)
Nick Stroh & Robert Siedle	Journalist and University lecturer, respectively (1971)
Robert Scanlon	Businessman and close associate of Bob Astles (1977)
Bruce McKenzie	Chief executive of Cooper Motor Corp., Nairobi, killed when plane exploded on flight from Entebbe to Nairobi (1977)

Sources: International Commission of Jurists, *Violations of Human Rights and the Rule of Law in Uganda*, ed. Michael Posner (Geneva: ICJ, 1974); Henry Kyemba, *State of Blood*; Colin Legum (ed.), *Africa Contemporary Record*, various years; *Africa Research Bulletin*, 1971-79; and Joseph Kamau and Andrew Cameron, *Lust to Kill* (London: Corgi, 1979).

violence under Obote's regime, murders and disappearances were the most feared forms of personal violence under Amin's. Table 6.9 presents a partial list of prominent disappearances and murders between 1971 and 1979.

Amin claimed complete innocence in the disappearances, which he blamed on outside agents intent on embarrassing the regime. Justice Mohamed Saied's commission of inquiry into the disappearances of 308 prominent persons specifically exonerated President Amin of directing any disappearances or the annihilation of any ethnic groups.[127] Bob Astles maintained that Amin himself never personally participated in executions (not even the killing of Archbishop Janan Luwum).[128] Amin had a knack for having alibis during waves of repression; he was either out of the country or in hospital. Nevertheless, Amin's public threats to individuals — that they might be sent to Makindye, that they might end up swimming in the Nile, and that they might be detained under cold water — attest to Amin's personal involvement in disappearances and murders.[129]

In the short summary of findings released in June 1975, Justice Saied's commission of inquiry did implicate a number of other officials in the disappearances: Deputy Commissioner of Police Ali Towilli (Public Safety Unit), Commissioner Kassim (Yusuf) Obura (PSU), Lt. James Byansi Obbo, Lt. Nalumosos, Capt. Juma, Lt. Muavu, Warrant Officer Abdul Ismail, Capt. Kiryona Magasi, Lt. Col. Toloko, and Said Umar. Of the 308 'disappearances' investigated, 109 occurred in 1971,

134 in 1972, 55 in 1973 and 10 in 1974. The victims consisted of 153 civilians, 93 soldiers and officers, 49 police staff and 13 prisons staff. The 7,000 pages of testimony before the commission of inquiry were never made public. Towilli and Obura were subsequently brought to trial for the disappearance of a policeman accused of extortion, but were acquitted when the defence argued there was no evidence to counter their claim that the man had been released.[130] Similarly, Justice David Jeffreys Jones's commission of inquiry into the disappearance of two Americans (journalist Nicholas Stroh and lecturer Robert Siedle) at Mbarara had implicated Major Juma Aiga in their murder and Col. Waris Ali Fadhul in the cover-up of the murder, yet no action was taken against either officer. Instead, the government attacked the impartiality of the judge; it did, however, allow the findings to be published, which could be purchased from the government printer even in 1974.[131]

The Amin regime appeared to relish illegal and covert actions, much like the Nazi regime described by Hannah Arendt (though the Amin regime in no way approached the brutal efficiency of the Hitler regime which Amin claimed to admire).[132] Opponents usually disappeared or were summarily killed rather than being arrested and tried before a court. The regime denied involvement in disappearances, yet for a fee agents of the state could often direct relatives to the location of the bodies of the 'disappeared'. As a token gesture of concern, the regime reduced the period after which a missing person could legally be presumed dead from seven to three years and issued the Missing Persons Decree in 1973 to allow relatives to manage the estates and businesses of missing persons. Widows of 'missing persons' were sometimes allocated 'abandoned' Asian homes, but the state also evicted Mrs Maxencia Zalwango Kiwanuka (widow of Benedicto Kiwanuka) and Mrs Alex Ojera from their homes in June 1975.[133]

It would be a mistake to attribute all violence in Uganda under the Amin regime to agents of the state. The Amin regime provided a perfect cover for private individuals who wished to settle the score with personal enemies.[134] In some cases, it was only necessary to denounce one's rival to the State Research Bureau; in other cases, personal murders might be staged to implicate the State Research Bureau or Military Police. Even in such murders the regime should bear ultimate responsibility for the breakdown in law and order.

The pitfalls of concentrating on the disappearances of prominent individuals are illustrated by a comment by a wealthy Kenyan businessman, interviewed in Nairobi in April 1974: 'If Amin weren't killing so many educated people and would simply put them in jail for a few

years, then everyone would salute him for what he has done.' By 'everyone', the Kenyan meant the African bourgeoisie. If Amin had only
contented himself with killing uneducated soldiers. oppressing
uneducated poor peasants and malnourishing uneducated labourers,
then all would have been well. The focus on personal violence masked
the underlying escalation of structural violence: the rise in kwashiorkor,
the absence of medicine, the shortage of doctors, the disrepair of rural
bore-hole wells. More may have died from structural violence than from
personal violence.

But how many did die from personal violence? Estimates range from
80,000 in the first two years of the regime to 300,000 to 500,000 by
the end.[135] If so many died, why did so few flee? Even the 80,000
deaths estimate must be treated with some scepticism. Such a figure
represents 0.8 per cent of the total population of Uganda. Carnage by
the stage apparatus in a short period at that magnitude should have
resulted in massive emigration. When approximately the same proportion of citizens actually died in ethnic conflict in Burundi and when a
far smaller proportion of inhabitants died in the southern Sudan, tens
of thousands of ordinary citizens fled to neighbouring countries.[136]
Official UN refugee statistics at the end of 1976, showed 2,200
Ugandan refugees in Tanzania, 700 in Kenya and 500 in the Sudan.[137]
We might have to triple these figures to account for those who wished
to avoid the stigma of official refugee status and also add another
thousand or so who found it prudent to go to Europe and North
America on extended educational or work visits. The number of official
refugees from Uganda jumped sharply during 1977; 3,700 were in
Tanzania, 4,000 in Kenya by the end of the year.[138] Even so, the
refugee totals appear low. Ordinary peasants tended to remain in
Uganda. For the most part, members of the African bourgeoisie voted
with their feet to remain in Uganda, indicating that the calculus of
violence and enrichment was such that the opportunities for wealth
outweighed the risks of death or disappearance. By outward signs of
loyalty or compliance to the regime, each businessman sought to reduce
the chance of permanent elimination from the race for wealth. Few, if
any, businessmen took seriously the March 1975 introduction of the
death penalty for economic crimes: fraud, embezzlement, hoarding
and smuggling.

Certainly, many did die under the Amin regime, but the high
estimates appear to be the result of treating peaks of violence as
averages. What were the peaks of violence? The first was the initial
six months of the regime, during which as many as 1,500 soldiers were

killed, plus an unknown number of civilians, some of which were killed by fellow civilians in revenge for supporting the former regime. The second peak was 1972-3 during and following the first invasion from Tanzania, which provided an excuse for eliminating opponents of the regime as well as captured invaders. A third, less severe, peak centred on the 1974 coup attempt. The Israeli raid to free hostages at Entebbe in July 1976 sparked a new round of violence. The success of the raid revealed that the Uganda armed forces were vulnerable, which inspired fresh coup attempts, while the regime's counter-measures culminated in the repression from February to September 1977. Finally, the outbreak of mutinies during the 1978 Ugandan invasion of the Kagera Salient and the counter-invasion by Tanzania led to a new wave of repression, culminating in indiscriminate killing of civilians in eastern and northern Uganda by fleeing soldiers following the UNLF's capture of Kampala.

In addition to these peaks, there was the background violence perpetrated by the state security apparatus: the State Research Bureau, the Public Safety Unit and the Military Police. Here we generally only have peak figures. Rev. George William Lukwiya, who was imprisoned for three months at the State Research Bureau, Nakasero, for a traffic violation, estimated that 30 to 60 prisoners died each day during 1978.[139] Matthew Kakambe of the Kampala Mortuary stated that up to 15 bodies were dumped at the mortuary each night by unknown parties, and that mortuary employees assumed those with smashed skulls or gunshot wounds had died at the hands of the Public Safety Unit whereas those with smashed chests or strangulation marks had died at the hands of the State Research Bureau. Records seized from the Military Police indicate that of 38 prisoners held at one time in July 1975 11 died, while of another group of 89 held in 1977, 46 died.[140] A sign in the State Research Bureau carried the ominous slogan, 'Secret what you do here; secret what you leave here.'

On the basis of the low refugee figures and in the absence of more substantial evidence, I estimate that the total number killed at the hands of state agents under Amin ranged from 12,000 to 30,000 (1,500 to 3,750 per annum), plus another 16,000 to 20,000 'ordinary' murders by civilians (2,000 to 2,500 per annum). However, if we blame the 'ordinary' civilian crimes on the regime – which we should – we should in fairness also blame the UPC and UNLF regimes for their high crime rates (1,500 to 2,000 murders per year under the UPC).

International and Regional Dimensions of Amin's Survival and Ultimate Defeat

From February 1972 onward, militant anti-Zionism in foreign policy and the strengthening of Islam within Uganda smoothed the way for Amin's growing links with the Arab world. In return, his regime obtained assistance from both Arab moderates (Saudi Arabia and Kuwait) and radicals (Libya and the Palestine Liberation Organisation). But the Arab/OPEC economic aid that materialised was less than what had been expected, and Amin's attempts to win preferential petroleum prices from OPEC failed.[141] While the Arab League welcomed Uganda's support for the Palestinians, OPEC nations demanded cash rather than anti-Zionism as payment for oil. Aside from Saudi Arabia's gift of Shs. 105 million to the Uganda armed forces in February 1974, almost all Arab military aid to the Amin regime came from the radicals. Libyan military advisers arrived in 1972, and PLO advisers in 1974.[142] Libya sent military aid to Amin during the September 1972 invasion from Tanzania and during the 1978-9 border clash with Tanzania. Libyan troops, said to number anywhere between 300 and 3,000, bore the brunt of the final April 1979 assaults on Entebbe and Kampala by the combined Tanzanian-UNLF forces which overthrew Amin.

Amin's recklessness in pursuing his pro-Palestinian foreign policy contributed to his downfall. In stark contrast to his handling of the March 1974 hijacking of an East African Airways plane, in which he personally persuaded the two Ethiopian hijackers to surrender, Amin collaborated with the PFLP (Popular Front for the Liberation of Palestine) hijackers who seized control of an Air France plane on 27 June 1976. In the early hours of 4 July, Israeli commandos freed more than 100 hostages in the Entebbe raid which resulted in the deaths of 20 to 45 Ugandan soldiers, 7 hijackers and 4 Israelis (including Dora Bloch, who was murdered in retaliation for the raid).[143] By revealing the regime's military vulnerability and its unpopularity (some Kampala residents were killed for laughing at Amin's misfortune), the raid set in motion the train of events which culminated in Amin's overthrow nearly three years later.

Contrasted with the warm ties between Idi Amin and Muammar el-Qaddafi, the relations between Uganda and the USSR were very formal, despite Soviet military aid to Amin's regime. In becoming the key military backer of Uganda and the post-1977 Ethiopian regime, the USSR appeared to inherit the 'headwaters of the Nile' strategy pursued earlier by Israel and earlier still by Britain. But it was ideology which forged the alliance between the Soviet Union and the Menigistu regime in Ethiopia, while Soviet geo-political interests in Uganda had less to do with the Nile Basin than with East Africa itself, where three states provided just the right number to enable the United States, the Soviet Union and the People's Republic of China to each have a friend. Uganda had enjoyed friendly relations with the Soviet Union since 1965, while Kenya had become increasingly pro-American, and Tanzania, in the eyes of Moscow, pro-Chinese following the 1969 agreement with China for the building of the Tan-Zam railway (TAZARA). The overthrow of Obote led to more formal relations between Uganda and the Soviet Union, but the military aid continued. The Soviet Union, as usual, was taking the long view. Only twice did the Soviet Union openly exert pressure on Amin. First, it forcefully dissuaded him from erecting a statue to honour Hitler. Second, in a series of moves punctuated by a six-day suspension of diplomatic relations and military aid, it persuaded Amin, as 1975-6 chairman of the OAU, to recognise the MPLA regime in Angola over the competing claims of the FNLA and UNITA.[144] Significantly, the Soviet Union turned a deaf ear to Amin's pleas for assistance during the 1978-9 border dispute with Tanzania.[145]

The British and American roles in Uganda after Amin's initial right-wing phase were less clear. Were they taking the long view or simply muddling through? Britain was the target of many of Amin's more outrageous barbs, just as Amin was the butt of British journalists. Britain suspended most of its aid to Uganda following the 1972 expulsion of Asians and broke off diplomatic relations in 1976 over the death of Dora Bloch, who was also a British subject. In addition to seizing the assets of the Asians with British passports, Amin nationalised most British firms in Uganda, with such notable exceptions as the banks and Shell-BP. Amin used the Denis Hills affair to force British Foreign Secretary James Callaghan to bow before him (1975). Yet it was Britain which allowed the Stanstead flights that supplied the duty-free shops for the elite of the Amin regime. It was Britain which allowed its firms to supply communications and security equipment to the State Research Bureau.[146] As for the United States, it broke diplomatic relations with Amin in 1973, not over the deaths of Americans Siedle and Stroh, nor over the detention of American Peace Corps volunteers, but over Amin's cocky telegrams to Nixon regarding Watergate.[147] American firms supplied Amin's regime with security equipment, helicopters and Amin's personal jet, and, in turn, bought most of Uganda's coffee up to the October 1978 embargo imposed by the US Congress. The autobiographical account by CIA agent Jay Mullen portrays Amin's Uganda as simply another, slightly more dangerous, playground for sophomoric pranks and bugging escapades by CIA agents against their Russian and Chinese counterparts.[148] It suited Britain and the United States to depict Amin as the object lesson of what emerged from Soviet collaboration with Arab radicals in Africa.[149] This view coyly neglected British and American contributions to the maintenance of Amin's regime.

Nevertheless, although the Arab-Israeli conflict and the rivalries among the United States, the USSR and the People's Republic of China clearly had an impact on events in Uganda, the shifting fortunes of the Amin regime were more closely shaped by strains within the East African Community (EAC). As Green has observed, maintenance of the EAC from 1967 onward depended on counter-balancing two economic dyads (Kenya-Tanzania; Kenya-Uganda), in which Kenya was stronger, with a political coalition (Tanzania-Uganda). The hostility between the Tanzanian and Ugandan regimes after the 1971 overthrow of Obote eliminated the political counter-balance. The deterioration of the Ugandan economy after the 1972 expulsion of Asians reduced the Kenya-Uganda economic dyad to one of complete Kenyan dominance and Ugandan dependence. Uganda under Amin, according to Green, was thereby reduced to a politically and economically impotent bystander in the growing conflict between 'free-enterprise' Kenya and 'socialist' Tanzania over the division of EAC gains and costs.[150] Despite the overdrawn nature of these ideological stereotypes, research on the attitudes of EAC employees towards income inequalities has shown the existence of significant differences between Tanzanian respondents on the one hand and Kenyan and Ugandan respondents on the other.[151]

Whereas the 1974-6 international recession had jeopardised the EAC by making the partner states increasingly anxious to hoard foreign exchange by slowing and even blocking transfers from local EAC operations to the headquarters of EAC corporations, the 1976-7 coffee price boom suddenly made both Kenya and Tanzania more willing to face the costs of an EAC collapse. Moreover, events in Mozambique and Zambia had broadened Tanzania's alternatives to the south, just as Kenya's horizons had widened to the north (the Arab world) from its base in the Kenya-Uganda 'domestic' market. Hence, what began as a familiar scenario, the suspension of East African Airways services on 28 January 1977 due to the slow remittances to its Nairobi head office, suddenly departed from the normal script as Tanzania closed its border with Kenya on 3 February to call the Kenyan bluff. Unfortunately, by impounding private Kenyan vehicles, detaining Kenyan travellers and denying Tanzanian airspace to Kenyan planes, the Tanzanians made the closure so severe that Kenya had no face-saving route back to the conference table.[152] The EAC died in disputes over the July budget, though the process of carving up its remains had begun as early as 1975 with the Kenyan seizure of the Lake Victoria shipping fleet. The timing and mechanics of the EAC collapse were such that both Kenya and Tanzania could bask in unexpected short-term gains which hid the longer-term costs of replacing lost EAC services and markets.[153] As for Uganda, the EAC's demise sealed its fate as a neo-colonial appendage of Kenya. The collapse coincided with Amin's February-September purges and thereby prevented the resuscitation of the Uganda-Tanzania political coalition at a time when landlocked Uganda needed it to offset Kenya's economic hegemony and control of Uganda's access to the ocean.

What are less clear are the effects of the EAC collapse on the two opposing camps of anti-Amin exiles centred primarily in Nairobi and Dar es Salaam. For the conservative exiles in Kenya, the United States and Britain, collaboration with the radical factions now seemed more palatable, with Uganda locked in the Kenyan orbit and with the EAC-imposed need for alliances with Tanzania no longer a factor. Though the conservatives were favourably disposed towards Kenya's ideological orientation, they were by no means lackeys of Kenya. Indeed as a well-educated group of experienced administrators, they posed a significant threat to continued Kenyan domination of Uganda's economy and were often harrassed by Kenyan authorities whose official policy of neutrality towards Amin hardly squared with the magnitude of the Kenyan elite's business dealing with Amin's cronies. For the more radical exiles based in Tanzania and Zambia, collaboration with the conservatives was now all the more urgent in order to remove Uganda from the Kenyan orbit. Even so, the first attempt at collaboration in Lusaka in August 1977 was boycotted by several key groups.[154]

What finally broke the deadlock was the escalation of the border conflict between Uganda and Tanzania over the Kagera Salient, which began 27 October 1978. A secret meeting of most exile groups was held in Nairobi in late December, after Nyerere dropped hints that the Tanzanian counter-attack would not be limited to driving Ugandan troops from the Kagera Salient. The meeting, which included representatives from the Organisation for Free Uganda, Uganda Freedom Union, Uganda Human Rights Group, Uganda Action Committee, the UPC and the DP, agreed to support the Tanzanian incursion into Uganda.[155] Following the capture of Mbarara and Masaka by Tanzanian troops and Ugandan exile forces, a new meeting was held in Moshi, Tanzania, in late March 1979 to form the Uganda National Liberation Front (UNLF) as the government-in-exile headed by Yusuf Lule, former head of Makerere University. The UNLF served as umbrella organisation for 18 different exile groups. On 11 April 1979 Tanzanian troops and UNLF forces took control of Kampala, and Lule announced the formation of the new government.

The Kenyan response to these events was ambiguous. The government had arrested 30 of the exile representatives en route to the Moshi conference. Even on 11 April, when the outcome was no longer in doubt, the *Standard* (Nairobi) continued to refer to the invading force as 'rebels' and the Amin forces as the 'loyalists'. By 28 April, however, the UNLF/Tanzanian force had been relabelled 'freedom fighters'. The reasons for Kenyan misgivings were both economic and strategic. The fallen regime owed Kenyan firms Shs. 300 million, according to estimates by the Kenya National Chamber of Commerce and Industry, which illustrated the extent of the Amin regime's dependence on Kenya.[156] Equally important, the successor regime(s) to Amin, regardless of ideological orientation, were likely to adopt a foreign policy more favourable to Tanzania than any time since 1971. The era of Kenyan hegemony over Uganda had ended; that of Tanzania had begun.

Notes

1. Idi Amin Dada was born around 1925. His mother was of mixed Kakwa-Lugbara descent. His Kakwa father had been christened into the Catholic faith as Andrea Dada, but was converted to Islam by Ali Kenyi Midia, who was the Kakwa chief in Koboko, West Nile, between 1910 and 1920. On conversion to Islam, Idi Amin's father took the name Amin Dada. In the 1920s Amin Dada rose to the rank of Sergeant in the Uganda Police and served at Katwe. His superiors nicknamed him Simon. Idi Amin Dada was himself nicknamed Andrea by soldiers familiar with his father's background. Idi Amin Dada joined the King's African Rifles, served in Burma in the Second World War, in the Kenya anti-Mau-Mau campaign in the 1950s, and in anti-cattle-raiding expeditions in Karamoja and Turkana around 1961-2. Details on early life provided by Omari Kokole.

2. 'The Eighteen Points' or 'First Statement by the Soldiers', *Uganda Argus*, 26 January 1971, and Uganda, *The Birth of the Second Republic* (Entebbe: Government Printer, 1971), pp. 26-8. Of special interest is Point 13, which cited the lack of Defence Council meetings since July 1969. This would contradict the reported Defence Council meeting in September 1970 which promoted Idi Amin into a largely ceremonial post.

3. David Martin, *General Amin* (London: Faber and Faber, 1974), pp. 31-90. After sifting through the conflicting evidence of alleged involvement by Amin

versus alleged framing of Amin by Obote, the 1971 inquest headed by Justice Arthur Dickson concluded that Okoya was murdered by a person or persons unknown.

4. Martin, *General Amin*, p. 45.

5. Editorial, 'Uganda Coup', *The Nationalist* (Dar es Salaam), 26 January 1971.

6. *Uganda Argus*, 26 April 1971. An annotated list of the promotions can be found in Table 6.2 below.

7. Cf. Martin, *General Amin*, pp. 28-44; and John Howell, 'Horn of Africa: Lessons from the Sudan Conflict', *International Affairs* (London), vol. 54, no. 1 (July 1978), p. 432. Howell's article (pp. 421-36) presents a valuable and provocative analysis of the regional dimensions of the Anya Nya rebellion. For an earlier overview of the Sudanese situation, see Keith Kyle, 'The Southern Problem in the Sudan', *The World Today*, vol. 22, no. 12 (December 1966), pp. 512-20.

8. Noel King, Abdu Kasozi and Arye Oded, *Islam and the Confluence of Religions in Uganda, 1804-1966* (Tallahassee, Florida: American Academy of Religion, 1973), pp. 35-9; and F.B. Welbourn, *Religion and Politics in Uganda, 1952-62* (Nairobi: East African Publishing House, 1965), pp. 66-9. According to the 1959 census figures cited by Welbourn, 12.4 per cent of the adult population in West Nile and Madi were Muslim versus 7.3 per cent in Buganda. In absolute numbers, however, there were three times as many Muslims in Buganda as in the northwest.

9. *Uganda Argus*, 27 April and 31 July 1971.

10. *Uganda Argus*, 29 January 1971 and 12 January 1971 (for number in detention).

11. Uganda, 'The Land Reform Decree, 1975: A Decree to Provide for the Vesting of Title to All Land in Uganda in Trust for the People of Uganda, to Facilitate the Use of Land for Economic and Social Development and for Other Matters Connected Therewith', Decree No. 3 of 1975. Section 4 specifically abolished the following: the Busulu and Envujo Law, the Ankole Landlord and Tenant Law, and the Toro Landlord and Tenant Law. All land-holdings in Uganda were converted to leaseholds for a period of 99 years for individuals and 199 years for public bodies, religious organisations and charitable organisations. The extent to which the decree took effect is unclear. Land was still bought and sold, and resistance to expropriation for social use under the decree was strongly resisted, as shown by a Radio Kampala broadcast on 23 October 1977 which complained about landlords standing in the way of government land development schemes. Colin Legum, *Africa Contemporary Record (ACR)*, 1977-8, B-459.

12. Of 1,481 African students who entered Makerere in the 1922-53 period, over 60 per cent found employment in the state salariat. J.E. Goldthorpe, *An African Elite; Makerere College Students, 1922-60* (Nairobi: Oxford University Press, 1965), p. 61. If anything, this tendency became stronger during the Africanisation of the salariat after 1953.

13. Israeli military advisers were very much in evidence in the days and weeks following the coup. Some were given VIP seats in the Nakivubo Stadium celebrations on 6 February 1971. Personal observation.

14. Yugoslavia's main interests in Uganda were the Energoprojekt construction firm and the troubled Soroti Meat Packing Company. Czechoslovakia's main interest lay in the supply of trainer jet planes to the Uganda Air Force. The other countries listed had aid programmes and/or investments in Uganda.

15. In an interview in Kampala, 20 April 1971, a British banker expressed satisfaction bordering on glee at the turn of events and declared his willingness to assist Amin in his proposed visit to South Africa.

16. Interview with Australian, FAO ranching expert, Aswa Ranch, Acholi

District, July 1971. The IDA scheme under Obote is described in Bank of Uganda, *Annual Report, 1969-70*, pp. 51-2.

17. At the time of the coup, approximately one-third of the 7,150 members of the army were from Acholi or Lango. At least 1,000 soldiers and officers were killed in the first six months after the coup, most in July. The author photographed blood stains on the bridge at Karuma Falls, site of some of the July executions. Another 1,000 ex-soldiers and police fled to the Sudan from where they posed a serious threat to the new Ugandan regime. Howell suggests that it was this threat which sparked the expulsion of Israelis from Uganda in 1972 as part of a package deal between Uganda and the Sudan to cease supporting rebel groups based in each other's territory. The Sudanese government removed the pro-Obote forces from the border area shortly after the signing of the February accord ending the Anya Nya rebellion. By June 1972 the pro-Obote forces had been reassembled in Tanzania. Howell, 'Horn of Africa', p. 434; and Martin, *General Amin.*

18. *Uganda Argus*, 11 October 1971.

19. The visit to South Africa was strongly opposed by NUSU in September 1971. By November the goodwill mission had been transformed into a critical fact-finding mission, which led South Africa to reconsider the invitation. By December Amin was openly critical of the white regimes in South Africa and Southern Rhodesia. Radio Kampala, 14 December 1971; and *Uganda Argus*, 20 December 1971. Oddly enough, it was the combined effort of the Mobutu regime in Zaire and the Kenyatta regime in Kenya which apparently succeeded in persuading Amin to drop the pro-South African policy, much to the relief of Wanume Kibedi, the progressive Ugandan Foreign Minister and son-in-law of Amin.

20. Idi Amin, 'Speech to the Asian Conference, 8 December 1971', *East Africa Journal*, vol. 9 (February1972), pp. 2-5.

21. M. Louise Pirouet, 'The Achievement of Peace in the Sudan', *Journal of Eastern African Research and Development* (Nairobi), vol. 6, no. 1 (1976). Pages 24-38 in the pre-publication typescript.

22. Uganda, *Summary of Draft Estimates of Recurrent and Development Expenditures*, 1973-4 through 1977-8; and Uganda, *1973 Statistical Abstract*, p. 83.

23. Ruth First, *The Barrel of a Gun; Political Power in Africa and the Coup d'Etat* (London: Allen Lane, Penguin Press, 1970), p. 436.

24. In a ceremony in February 1974, Amin took pains to stress that the seven officers being promoted were chosen 'on merit and not on tribal basis'. *Voice of Uganda*, 6 February 1974. In April, Amin urged the troops 'to work as a team and avoid any discrimination based on tribal or religious differences'. *Voice of Uganda*, 8 April 1974. Given the events of March (the Arube attempted coup), we should, for once, vouchsafe his sincerity.

25. Estimates of the army's size in 1970 begin with the official 6,000 figure and continue upward. Michel Martin gives the figure of 7,150 for the army plus 450 in the air force and 80 in the navy (Lake Patrol?). Michel L. Martin, 'The Uganda Military Coup of 1971; A Study of Protest', *Ufahamu*, vol. 3, no. 3 (Winter 1972), p. 104; and Holger Bernt Hansen, *Ethnicity and Military Rule in Uganda*, Research Report No. 43 (Uppsala: Scandinavian Institute of African Studies, 1977), pp. 75, 107-8.

26. Legum, *ACR*, 1977-8, B-442. Another source puts the figure at 20,000 plus 1,000 in the air force. Gregory R. Copley (ed.), *Defence and Foreign Affairs Handbook* (London: Copley and Associates, 1978), p. 528.

27. Peter F.B. Nayenga, 'Myths and Realities of Idi Amin's Uganda', *African Studies Review*, vol. 22, no. 2 (September 1979), p. 132.

28. Uganda, *1972 Decrees* (Entebbe: Government Printer, 1973), pp. 31, 33, 200-2. Decree 26 (Powers of Arrest) was modified in August 1973 to restrict the powers of arrest to the police and the military police, but the modification had little real effect. *Africa Research Bulletin (ARB)*, August 1973, p. 2959. The 'top secret' Cabinet Minute Paper 131 of 14 March 1972 empowered Cabinet members to shoot to kill if they felt their lives threatened by crowds or individuals, Joseph Kamau and Andrew Cameron, *Lust to Kill* (London: Corgi, 1979), p. 343.

29. Chief Justice Benedicto Kiwanuka was kidnapped by State Research Bureau agents from the High Court on 21 September 1972 and killed shortly thereafter. On the Nuremburg Laws in Nazi Germany, see Hannah Arendt, *The Origins of Totalitarianism* (New York: Hartcourt, Brace and World, 1966), p. 394.

30. Henry Kyemba, *A State of Blood* (New York: Ace Books, 1977), pp. 52, 97.

31. Ibid., p. 102.

32. *Voice of Uganda*, 30 March, 8 April and 20 April 1974.

33. Ibid., 11 April, 20 April 1974. The airing of complaints lasted a month after the attempted March coup.

34. *Uganda Argus*, 26 April 1971.

35. Ibid., 26 April 1971. p. 3.

36. M. Martin, 'The Uganda Military Coup of 1971', p. 95.

37. *ARB*, June 1975, p. 4054.

38. Ibid., January 1978, pp. 4711-12.

39. Kyemba, *State of Blood*, pp. 60-107, 128-44.

40. Ibid., p. 101.

41. *Voice of Uganda*, 27 March 1974.

42. *Uganda Argus*, 7 August 1971.

43. Kyemba, *State of Blood*, p. 101.

44. *ARB*, May 1978, p. 4845.

45. Mazrui, 'The Rise of the Lumpen-Militariat', *Soldiers and Kinsmen*, p. 144.

46. When asked if he often had such dreams, Amin is reported to have replied, 'Only when necessary'. David Martin, 'Inside Amin's Prisons', *Observer* (London), 15 August 1976, p. 15.

47. A Muganda Catholic, Joseph Mubiru began his career as an economist for the UN. In the early 1950s he worked in the Masaka branch of National and Grindlays Bank. He then joined the Uganda Commercial Bank and rose to the position of Managing Director before being called to the chairmanship of the Bank of Uganda shortly after its establishment. In the 1950s he was an avid supporter of foreign investment in Uganda. His 'Foreign Capital' letter to the *Uganda Argus* (6 July 1959) contained a homily about an African with a gold deposit on his five-acre plot who invites foreign investors to bring the necessary skills and machines in to mine the deposit. The government takes the royalties; the African becomes a wage-earner in the mine and saves enough money so that his son gets an education to become a clerk in the mine. And one day perhaps a neighbour's son will rise to become general manager of the mine, while the hero goes on, according to Mubiru, to become a labour leader in a new mine. A year after Mubiru's July-August campaign on behalf of the populist alliance, he was dismissed by Amin and ordered not to talk to the press unless he wished to be 'detained under cold water'. *The People*, 25 September 1972. Shortly thereafter, Mubiru joined the ranks of the 'missing persons' in Uganda.

48. Speech at Mbarara as reported in *Uganda Argus*, 27 July 1971.

49. *Uganda Argus*, 6 August 1971.

50. H. Nsambu, 'African Traders Must be Protected', *Uganda Argus*, 12 August 1971. Two of the three speakers had a base in state corporations to use for advocating individual African control of commerce. Sebagereka, a prominent

businessman in his own right, was then a director of the parastatal Export-Import Corporation and chairman of Mackenzie Technical Services (Uganda) Ltd, a subsidiary of Inchcape, and offshoot of the original Smith-Mackenzie/IBEA group. During the economic war, the European managing director of Mackenzie sternly warned that any African employees of the firm who acquired a business from the allocation committees would face dismissal. *Voice of Uganda*, 16 January 1973.

51. *Uganda Argus*, 10 August 1971. The editorial none the less went on to criticise traders of all races for exploiting consumers in the sale of sugar and other scarce commodities.

52. *Uganda Argus*, 27 July 1971.

53. From the inception of the capitalist world system, rulers have recognised the value of having a non-indigenous commercial bourgeoisie, since an indigenous bourgeoisie would lay claim to a major role in internal politics. Immanuel Wallerstein, *The Modern World System* (New York: Academic Press, 1974), p. 151.

54. *Uganda Argus*, 7 August 1971; *The People*, 16 October 1971; and Idi Amin, 'Speech to the Asian Conference, 8 December 1971'.

55. About 12,000 applications for citizenship were pending as of December 1971. *Keesing's Contemporary Archives*, 1972, p. 25023. Most of the unprocessed applications had been stalled since the 1964 expiration of the constitutional guarantee of automatic citizenship to applicants.

56. The accumulation/legitimation model of the state is elaborated in James O'Connor, *The Fiscal Crisis of the State* (New York: St Martin's Press, 1973).

57. *ARB* (economic series), 1969, p. 1535; and *Facts on File*, 1970, 897E3.

58. Idi Amin, 'Message to the Nation on British Citizens of Asian Origin and Citizens of India, Pakistan and Bangladesh Living in Uganda', 12-13 August 1972, *Speeches by . . . President General Idi Amin Dada* (Entebbe: Government Printer, 1973), p. 1.

59. *ARB*, August 1972, pp. 2568-70.

60. *Keesing's Contemporary Archives*, 1972, pp. 25599-600, 1973, p. 25776.

61. Uganda, *The Second Year of the Second Republic* (Entebbe: Government Printer, 1973), p. 74.

62. Idi Amin, 'Mid-Night Address to the Nation', 17 December 1972, *Speeches Speeches by . . . Idi Amin* (1973), p. 25.

63. Uganda, *The Action Programme, 1977/78-1979/80* (Entebbe: Ministry of Planning and Economic Development, 1977), p. 46.

64. *Uganda Argus*, 24 November 1972, lists members of the management committees of the sugar works at Kakira, Lugazi and Kinyala.

65. *Uganda Argus*, 30 November 1972; *Voice of Uganda*, 16 January 1973; and interview with Horace Campbell, Kampala, 16 February 1974.

66. Jack Parson, 'Africanizing Trade in Uganda: The Final Solution', *Africa Today*, vol. 20, no. 1 (Winter 1973), pp. 59-72.

67. *Uganda Argus*, 27 September, 9 November and 24 November 1972.

68. Idi Amin, 'Mid-Night Address to the Nation', 17 December 1972, pp. 25-6. In the same address Amin changed the names of a number of national parks and Kampala streets to replace colonial names with the names of anti-imperialists: Kabalega, Lumumba, Nkrumah, Kimanthi, etc.

69. Uganda Development Corporation, 'Managing-Director's Report to Directors', no. 123 (September-October 1973)', Kampala, 10 January 1974.

70. Commonwealth Team of Experts, *The Rehabilitation of the Economy of Uganda*, (London: Commonwealth Secretariat, 1979), vol. II, p. 113, in an obvious reference to Semei Nyanzi. Nyanzi was later replaced by S. Lukwago in one of the five o'clock Radio Kampala news bulletins which periodically announced government appointments (and disappearances) to the surprise of

appointees (and the soon-to-disappear).

71. Uganda, *The Action Programme*, p. 47.

72. 'Businessmen Assured of Assistance', *Voice of Uganda*, 16 January 1973.

73. Uganda, *The Action Programme*, pp. 4, 45-6.

73. *Uganda Argus*, 22 November 1972; and *Voice of Uganda*, 8 April 1974.

75. M. Crawford Young, 'Agricultural Policy in Uganda: Capability and Choice', *The State of the Nations: Constraints on Development in Independent Africa*, ed. Michael Lofchie (Berkeley: University of California Press, 1971), p. 150.

76. *Voice of Uganda*, 30 March 1974.

77. Uganda, *The Action Programme*, pp. 52-3.

78. Samir Amin, 'Towards a New Structural Crisis of the Capitalist System?', *Multinational Firms in Africa*, ed. Carl Widstrand (Uppsala: Scandinavian Institute of African Studies, 1975), pp. 3-21; Geoffrey Barraclough, 'The North-South Debate on the New International Economic Order', *New York Review of Books*, vol. 25, no. 16 (26 October 1978); and Robert W. Cox, 'Ideologies and the New International Economic Order', *International Organization*, vol. 33, no. 2 (Spring 1979), pp. 257-302.

79. The gross domestic product not only failed to keep pace with an annual population increase of 2.8 per cent (1969-80), but actually declined in real terms after the economic war: 1972, +3.1%; 1973, -1.2%; 1974, -2.0%; 1975, -2.2%; 1976, +0.7%; and 1977, +1.5%. Uganda, *Budget Speeches*, 1973-8.

80. Appendix A.3.

81. Uganda, *Quarterly Economic and Statistical Bulletin*, September 1974, pp. 19 and 21.

82. Commonwealth Team, *Rehabilitation of the Economy*, vol. II, pp. 62-4.

83. Commonwealth Team, *Rehabilitation of the Economy*, vol. II, pp. 70, 76, 130. The production of 46 million square metres of cotton cloth requires about 12,000 metric tons of cotton lint (65,000 bales).

84. Uganda, *Revised Financial Statement and Revenue Estimates*, 1973-4 and 1979-80. By 1977-8, the coffee export tax accounted for 57.4 per cent of all government revenue, leading to the sentiment that Buganda and Bugisu were subsidising other regions. This view neglected the migrant worker's contribution.

85. Uganda, *The Action Programme*, p. 31; Uganda, *The Budget Speech, 24 June 1978*, p. 5; and Commonwealth Team, *Rehabilitation of the Economy*, vol. II, p. 142.

86. Uganda, *The Action Programme*, p. 31; and Commonwealth Team, *Rehabilitation of the Economy*, vol. II, pp. 133-48, 167.

87. Uganda, *The Action Programme*, p. 31; and Commonwealth Team, *Rehabilitation of the Economy*, vol. II, pp. 83, 129-59. A.H. Fawcett has surveyed the history of the Lake Katwe project from the technical and economic angles in 'Katwe Salt Deposits', *Uganda Journal*, vol. 37 (1973), pp. 63-80.

88. The founding of the Uganda Railways Corporation took the bulk of this expenditure. The rest went to strengthen the already existing Uganda Airlines and to establish the Uganda Posts and Telecommunications and to build an earth satellite station. Uganda, *Budget Speech, 24 June 1978*, p. 10.

89. Robert Keeley, US State Department, interviewed on MacNeil/Lehrer Report, PBS Television, 17 April 1979. A strong case for the boycott is set forth in Richard H. Ullman, 'Human Rights and Economic Power: The United States Versus Idi Amin', *Foreign Affairs*, vol. 56, no. 3 (April 1978), pp. 529-43.

90. Uganda, *The Action Programme*, p. 95.

91. Uganda, *1973 Statistical Abstract*, p. 73; and Uganda, *Budget Speech, 16 June 1977*, p. 7.

92. Uganda, *Quarterly Economic and Statistical Bulletin*, September 1974,

p. 21; and Uganda, *The Action Programme*, p. 57.

93. Uganda, *Quarterly Economic and Statistical Bulletin*, September 1974, p. 20; Uganda, *Budget Speech, 12 June 1975*, p. 4; *Budget Speech, 16 June 1977*, p. 5; and *Budget Speech, 24 June 1978*, p. 6.

94. Uganda, *Budget Speech, 24 June 1978*, p. 5.

95. Commonwealth Team, *Rehabilitation of the Economy*, vol. II, pp. 84-5, 165.

96. Uganda, *1973 Statistical Abstract*, p. 113; Uganda, *Budget Speech, 24 June 1978*, p. 6; and *Budget Speech, 4 December 1979*, p. 4.

97. Uganda, *1973 Statistical Abstract*, pp. 26-44; and East African Customs and Excise Department, *Annual Trade Report of Tanzania, Uganda and Kenya, 1973.*

98. Plotting the visible trade balance against the merchandise account trade balance reveals a discontinuity between the two time periods. The 1966-72 data lie on a regression line quite distinct from the line for the 1973-7 data.

99. This is a very generous estimate of military imports which includes *all* expenditures on stores, equipment, transportation and development. Assuming that the share of the military budget for these items was the same in 1973-4 as in 1968-9 (60 per cent versus 33 per cent for the military wage-bill) and assuming that the published figure for 1973-4 military expenditures of U. Shs. 528.5 million is correct, then the maximum spent on military imports would be U. Shs. 317 million. The real figure was probably less. Uganda, *The Public Accounts, 1968-69*, pp. 135-6; and Uganda, *Summary of Draft Estimates of Recurrent and Development Expenditures*, 1975-6, pp. 1, 3. It may be argued that arms ship-ments on credit from the Soviet Union do not appear in the budget, but nor do shipments on credit impose an immediate charge on foreign exchange reserves.

100. Based on an actual case discovered by the author in April 1974 interviews in Kampala.

101. See the letter by C.B. Abdu Mosoke questioning the presence in Kampala of large numbers of Mercedes, Fiat, Alfa Romeo and Datsun 240Z cars bearing Kenyan registration plates, *Voice of Uganda*, 29 April 1974, p. 4. See also the story on the trial of a Ugandan merchant, arrested on the Kenyan side of the border with a full lorry of Ugandan cloth, edible oil and other commodities whose export was then forbidden because of Ugandan shortages, *Daily Nation* (Nairobi), 4 April 1974, p. 5. The merchant undoubtedly considered his K. Shs. 3,000 fine as a minor business expense. The merchandise was confiscated, but not the lorry.

102. Hansen, *Ethnicity and Military Rule*, passim.

103. Akiiki Mujaju, 'The Political Crisis of Church Institutions in Uganda', *African Affairs* (London), vol. 75, no. 298 (1976), pp. 76-8.

104. Both can be found in Uganda, *The Birth of the Second Republic* (Entebbe: Government Printer, 1971), pp. 26-8, 37-9.

105. *The People*, 13 May 1971, as cited in Jeffrey T. Strate, *Post-Military Coup Strategy in Uganda* (Athens, Ohio: Ohio University Center for International Studies, 1973), pp. 35-6.

106. As Hansen observes, the Amin regime's occasional pogroms in Acholi and Lango districts led to a vicious circle in which still more Acholi and Langi made their way to Tanzania to join the anti-Amin forces under Obote, Oyite-Ojok, and Okello. The Tanzanian threat provoked still more pogroms. Hansen, *Ethnicity and Military Rule*, p. 105

107. Hansen, ibid., p. 118.

108. Cf. Hansen, ibid., pp. 79-80, 108-11; and Dennis Pain, 'The Nubians', *Expulsion of a Minority*, ed. Michael Twaddle (London: University of London, Athlone Press, 1975), pp.176-92. Although he recognises the fluidity of the

Nubian label, Hansen occasionally views them as an immigrant community. This was only partially true even in the 1890s (due to recruitment of Lendu and others into the Nubian fold), and not true in the 1960s and 1970s.

109. Azarius Baryaruha, *Factors Affecting Industrial Employment; A Study of the Ugandan Experience, 1954 to 1964* (Nairobi: Oxford University Press for EAISR, 1967), p. 69.

110. Omari Kokole, personal communication to author, 2 June 1980; and Hansen, *Ethnicity and Military Rule*, p. 108.

111. Uganda, '1969 Population Supplement', *Quarterly Economic and Statistical Bulletin*, March 1971, S-5.

112. *Voice of Uganda*, 25, 26, 27 and 30 March, 3 April, 3 May 1974; *ARB*, May 1974, p. 3234, June 1974, p. 3272, May 1979, p. 5271; and Omari Kokole, personal communication, 2 June 1980. The Defence Council thanked Marella for his 21 years of service in the military. His brother, Captain Johnson, a Christian, was also retired.

113. According to Greenberg's classification, Kakwa, Bari, Teso, Karimojong, Lotuho, Acholi, Lango and Alur are all Eastern Sudanic languages, whereas Madi, Moru, Lugbara, Lendu, Mvuba, Baka and Avukaya are Central Sudanic languages. Joseph H. Greenberg, *The Languages of Africa*, 3rd edn. (Bloomington: Indiana University Press, 1970).

114. The planter-dominated Development Commission of 1920 had urged the establishment of a government primary school for Muslims. Uganda, *Report of the Uganda Development Commission, 1920*, p. 35. The colonial state eventually provided some aid to Muslim schools for Africans. In 1945 these included the secondary school at Kibuli, 2 fully-aided primary schools in Buganda, 19 partially-aided vernacular primary schools and 17 sub-grade primary schools. But there were no government-aided teacher-training centres for African Muslims. Uganda, *Blue Book 1945*, pp. 125-37. The fact that pupil-teacher ratios were lower in Muslim than in Christian schools may support the colonial state's claim that the demand for education was lower among Muslims, but it may also have resulted from the poor training for Muslim teachers. Muslims were allowed to attend Protestant schools without conversion.

115. *Keesing's Contemporary Archives*, 1973, p. 25774; Legum, *ACR*, 1972-3, B-281, 1975-6, B-358; and *ARB*, September 1977, p. 4570. On the other hand, Amin lavished praise on mission hospitals in August 1974, and, at the dedication of the Namugongo Martyrs' Shrine in June 1975, he took time to note that 40 Muslims as well as 22 Catholics had been martyred for their faith on that site in 1886. Idi Amin, *Development on the Basis of Self-Reliance*, 4 August 1974, p. 10; and Uganda High Commission (Ottawa), *Uganda News Bulletin*, no. 4, July 1975, p. 8.

116. Nayenga, 'Myths and Realities', p. 136; Legum, *ACR*, 1976-7, B 376-84; and Kyemba, *State of Blood*, pp. 179-92. Kyemba reprints Archbishop Luwum's open letter to Amin (pp. 271-8). For Amin's documentary 'evidence' for the plot see Uganda, *Obote's War Call to Langis and Acholis* (Kampala, Ministry of Information, 1977).

117. Feigning coma, Amin ignored pleas from Muslim leaders that the executions be postponed. Nayenga, 'Myths and Realities', p. 136; and *ARB*, September 1977, p. 4569. As for the ups and downs of Amin's relations with the Muslim Supreme Council (which replaced both the Uganda Muslim Community and NAAM), see Amin's lecture to the council as reported in *Voice of Uganda*, 6 February 1974; and Legum, *ACR*, 1974-5, B 316, 1975-6, B 358, 1977-8, B 449.

118. Based on data in the Organisation for Economic Co-operation and Development, *Development Co-operation Review* (Paris: OECD), 1970-79.

119. Idi Amin, 'Speech at the Opening of the Conference of Buganda Elders', 5 August 1971, *Speeches by . . . Idi Amin* (1972), p. 27.

120. Augustin Apecu, 'Tax Collection in Buganda Region Disappointing', *The People*, 26 April 1971. Ironically, Lango reported very high tax compliance in the first two years of the Amin regime.

121. Legum, *ACR*, 1973-4, B 291; and F.J. Ravenhill, 'Military Rule in Uganda: The Politics of Survival', *African Studies Review*, vol. 17, no. 1 (April 1974), p. 239. For example, Private Soro of the Masindi Artillery Regiment rose from chief in Bunyoro to District Commissioner of South Karamoja, while still a Private. He later was promoted to Captain and became Governor of Northwest Nile, but was suspended in 1976. *Voice of Uganda*, 14 and 16 January 1974; and *ARB*, December 1976, p. 4262.

122. Uganda, *Budget Speech, 16 June 1977*, pp. 15-17; and *Budget Speech, 24 June 1978*, pp. 11-13. On the French tax system, see Arnold J. Heidenheimer, 'Taxation: Administration, Allocation and Compliance', *Comparative Public Policy*, by Heidenheimer, Hugo Heclo and Carolyn Adams (New York: St Martin's Press, 1975), pp. 237-8.

123. Uganda, *Budget Speech, 4 December 1979*, pp. 14-15.

124. Peter Enaharo, *Africa* (London), May 1977, as cited in Legum, *ACR*, 1977-8, B 439; and Uganda, *Budget Speech, 4 December 1979*, p. 13.

125. Idi Amin, 'Address to District Representatives on the Transfer of the Economy into the Hands of Ugandans', 29 August 1972, *Speeches by . . . Idi Amin* (1972), pp. 15-16.

126. Uganda, *Uganda's 10 Provinces and 38 Districts* (Ministry of Information and Broadcasting, 22 March 1974); and Uganda, *Map of Uganda Administrative Boundaries* (Department of Lands and Surveys, 1975, reprinted 1977). The UNLF regime abolished provinces and reduced the number of districts to 33 (see Map 3).

127. Uganda High Commission (Ottawa), *Uganda News Bulletin*, no. 4, July 1975, p. 6.

128. Bob Astles, interviewed by Bob Lomax in Nairobi, 'Sunday Morning', Canadian Broadcasting Corporation Radio, 10 June 1979.

129. See for example Amin's threat against Mubiru that he would be detained under cold water if he spoke with the press, as reported in *The People*, 25 September 1972, p. 3. Similarly, Radio Kampala announced Frank Kalimuzo's disappearance before Kalimuzo disappeared. The regime's indifferent investigation of murders and disappearances and threats against private individuals who attempted to investigate disappearances attest to complicity at the highest level of government.

130. Uganda High Commission (Ottawa), *Uganda News Bulletin*, no. 4, July 1975, pp. 5-7, 13; Legum, *ACR*, 1975-6, B 353; *ARB*, July 1975, p. 3700; and Michael Gillard, 'Inside Amin's Terror Machine', Granada TV International, broadcast on TV Ontario, 26 October 1979.

131. Uganda, *Commission of Inquiry into the Missing Americans, Messrs. Stroh and Siedle* (Entebbe: Government Printer, 1972). I did find one case in which a civilian court tried and sentenced a military officer for committing atrocities against civilians. Corporal Rashid Bahemuka was sentenced to 12 years imprisonment for cutting the ears off two persons accused of witchcraft and ordering them to eat their ears. Bahemuka was then a Jago (sub-county) chief in Padyere county, West Nile. The case was under appeal. *Voice of Uganda*, 29 January 1974, p. 3.

132. Arendt, *The Origins of Totalitarianism*, p. 394.

133. Legum, *ACR*, 1974-5, B 314; Kyemba, *State of Blood*, p. 119; and *ARB*, June 1975, pp. 3657-8. The Legal Notice for Mrs Maxencia Kiwanuka's

application to manage her 'missing' husband's estate was published in the *Voice of Uganda*, 4 February 1974, p. 4.

134. In January 1978 Amin accused businessmen of hiring 'ex-soldiers' to murder business rivals. *ARB*, January 1978, p. 4712.

135. The estimates are presented in International Commission of Jurists, Report on Uganda, February 1977, as reported in *ARB*, Febraury 1977, p. 4332.

136. In Uganda alone there were 181,000 refugees at the end of 1971, including 75,000 from the Sudan, 72,000 from Rwanda, and 33,500 from Zaire. United Nations, Report of the UN High Commissioner for Refugees (UNHCR), 27th Session of the General Assembly (1972), Supplement 12 (A/8712). The Sudanese began returning home in 1972, and by the end of 1973 there were less than 6,000 Sudanese refugees in Uganda. Of the 114,000 refugees in Uganda at the end of 1973, most were from Rwanda and Zaire. UNHCR Report (1974), A/9612.

137. UNHCR Report (1977), A/32/12.

138. UNHCR Report (1978), A/33/12. At the end of 1978 the figure had risen to 4,600 Ugandans in Kenya, 4,100 in Tanzania, plus some in the Sudan, and an unknown number in Europe and North America. Yet even at the end of 1978, Uganda was a net importer of refugees, with 112,400, mainly from Rwanda and Zaire. UNHCR Report (1979), A/34/12. By contrast, over a year after the fall of the Amin regime, there were 50,000 pro-Amin Ugandan refugees in Zaire and another 39,000 in the Sudan. UNCHR estimates reported in *Africa* [newsmagazine], no. 108 (August 1980), p. 12.

139. Rev. George William Lukwiya, interviewed by Peter Kent, 'The National', Canadian Broadcasting Corporation Television, 1 May 1979.

140. Gillard, 'Inside Amin's Terror Machine'.

141. Howell, 'Horn of Africa', p. 434; and *Voice of Uganda*, 9 April 1974.

142. Yasir Arafat interviewed by Mike Wallace, 'Sixty Minutes', CBS Television, 18 March 1979; and *Voice of Uganda*, 9 February 1974.

143. *Voice of Uganda*, 25 March 1974; and William Stevenson and Uri Dan, *90 Minutes at Entebbe* (New York: Bantam Books, 1976).

144. *ARB*, November 1975, p. 3840; December 1975, p. 3860; and January 1976, p. 3926. Earlier (1974) Uganda had sent military aid to Holden Roberto's FNLA, probably as a result of Amin's friendship with Mobutu, a key FNLA backer. *Voice of Uganda*, 14 February 1974.

145. *ARB*, February 1979, p. 5155; March 1979, p. 5185; and May 1979, p. 5271.

146. Gillard 'Inside Amin's Terror Machine'.

147. Robert Keeley, US State Department, interviewed on MacNeil/Lehrer Report, PBS Television, 17 April 1979. Keeley was head of the US mission in Uganda in 1973.

148. Jay Mullen, 'I Was Amin's Basketball Czar', *Oregon Magazine*, vol. 9, no. 5 (May 1979), pp. 55-65 (Part I), and no. 6 (June 1979), pp. 66-77 (Part II).

149. Howell notes the Israeli use of this tactic in the southern Sudan. Howell, 'Horn of Africa', pp. 428 and 431. For a British example, see Colin Legum, 'How Russia Found a Friend in Amin', *Observer*, 29 June 1975.

150. Reginald H. Green, 'The East African Community: The End of the Road', *ACR*, 1976-7, A 59-67; and Green, 'The East African Community: Death, Funeral, Inheritance', *ACR*, 1977-8, A 125-37.

151. Tanzanians tended to favour smaller pay increases for those in the top scales and larger pay increases for manual workers than did their Kenyan and Ugandan counterparts. Moreover, respondents working in Tanzania (regardless of nationality) were more likely than those working in Kenya (again, regardless of nationality) to favour reducing income inequalities throughout East Africa.

Patricia Fosh, 'Attitudes of East African White-Collar Workers to Income Inequalities', *International Labour Review*, vol. 117, no. 1 (January-February 1978), pp. 99-109.

152. Green, 'EAC: Death, Funeral, Inheritance', pp. A 125-6.

153. Ibid., p. A 129.

154. *Africa Confidential*, vol. 18, no. 22 (4 November 1977), pp. 4-5; and *Keesing's Contemporary Archives*, 27 January 1978, p. 28798.

155. Gemini News Service reports cited in *ARB*, February 1979, pp. 5156-7.

156. *Africa Confidential*, vol. 20, no. 9 (25 April 1979), p. 6; *The Standard* (Nairobi), 11 April 1979, pp. 1 and 4; 28 April 1979, p. 1.

7 EPILOGUE

The Quest for Stable Civilian Rule

As envisaged by the Tanzanian government and by Ugandan exiles, freeing Uganda from Amin was to be a straightforward task: first, the seizure of Masaka and Mbarara in retaliation for Uganda's foray into the Kagera Salient; second, a holding action to allow disaffected troops and popular revolts to topple the Amin regime in Kampala; third, the hand-over of power to a government of national reconciliation which would hold the first parliamentary elections since 1962; fourth, the massive influx of overseas aid to rebuild the economy; and fifth, the rapid withdrawal of Tanzanian troops, who by then would have earned the eternal gratitude of the Ugandans and the OAU for their selfless intervention.

Only the first step went according to plan, and only after extensive fighting in late February and early March (1979) which destroyed hospitals, barracks, schools, offices, coffee works, cotton ginneries, shops, communications facilities and homes in Masaka, Mbarara and surrounding areas.[1] There were some troop mutinies in the early stages, but popular uprisings occurred only in Masaka and Tororo. The Tororo uprising proved premature and met with bloody reprisals from the retreating Amin forces. The Tanzanian force grew to 46,000,[2] including militia, and eventually had to fight its way to Entebbe and Kampala. To everyone's relief, the Amin forces withdrew eastward to Jinja and did not blow up the hydro-electric dam and the Nile bridge to cover their retreat. From Jinja, they were chased through Tororo to the Kenyan border, which was sealed, then northward to Soroti and Moroto (where the armoury was looted of 12,000 rifles), and finally westward through Lira, Gulu (the scene of heavy fighting) and Arua. The pro-Amin forces, numbering some 100,000 including dependants, fled into Zaire and the Sudan. Amin escaped to Libya and later moved to Saudi Arabia.

The liberation of Kampala was accompanied by a wave of looting, first by retreating Amin supporters, then by citizens and invading forces. In a pattern that was repeated in most towns, looters stripped shops, factories, go-downs, hospitals, schools, government offices and homes of every moveable object: desks, chairs, filing cabinets, books, files, records, beds, tools and inventory. Safes in banks and other institutions were blown open and looted, causing extensive structural damage to buildings.[3] The storming and ransacking of the State Research Bureau might have been anticipated and even applauded, but the looting of everything else? The apology offered by Ugandans — that citizens had suffered greatly and, fearing Amin's return, sought to destroy the instruments of the state — is unconvincing. Even after the overthrow of the regime was ensured, few came forward to return what had been taken. More disturbingly, the invading forces themselves participated in the looting. The 'grab-what-you-can' political culture of the Amin regime proved more resilient than the regime itself. As late as August 1979, some Tanzanian soldiers were relieving Ugandans of watches and other belongings.[4]

On 11 April 1979, following the capture of Kampala, the Uganda National Liberation Force announced its new government, headed by President Yusuf K. Lule, former Principal of Makerere University. The 30-member UNLF National Consultative Council, selected at Moshi and chaired by Edward Rugumayo, functioned as a surrogate parliamentary body and ruling party.[5] Members of the NCC held 15 of 21 posts in the first Lule cabinet. This fact, and the announcement that elections would be delayed for two years, aroused concern that the UNLF would remain a government of exiles ruling over those who had stayed behind and endured the hardships of Amin's regime. Exclusion from the UNLF was especially galling to internal members of underground organisations such as SUM (Save Uganda Movement), which had waged a valiant sabotage campaign against the old regime.

The 'stayee/returnee' division was grounded in mutual suspicion. Each side had endured its own hardships. Those who had remained inside Uganda suspected the exile groups of harbouring persons who had lined their pockets either before fleeing or while in exile. Acknowledging an element of truth in these charges, an NCC member pointed to another concern of the stayees. Under Amin, the flight of experienced professionals had accelerated promotions for those who dared to stay. Some parvenus were more qualified than those who had fled; but others were less so. With the sudden overthrow of Amin, these people faced the threat of being ousted by the former incumbents of posts in government, the university, parastatals and the private sector. For their part, the returnees tended to view anyone who had stayed behind as a covert Amin supporter, until proven otherwise.

These problems were overshadowed by divisions within the NCC. President Lule ran afoul of the NCC by not consulting the full body when he reshuffled the cabinet June 7. His appointment of Grace

Ibingira (member of the former Nkore royal family) to Information
and Robert Serumaga, a staunch monarchist playwright from Buganda,
to Commerce and Industry upset the balance within the cabinet and
offended the republican majority in the NCC. Lule attempted a partial
retreat on 19 June. He dropped Ibingira and restored the ethnic if not
the political balance of the cabinet, but again insisted on the right to
make appointments without consulting the full NCC. The NCC
responded the next day by dismissing Lule and installing Godfrey
Binaisa as president.

Was Lule a monarchist and Muganda sub-nationalist, as claimed by
both supporters and opponents? His economic conservatism clearly
attracted the neo-traditional monarchists. Nevertheless, consistent with
his academic background, a person's education mattered more to Lule
than did business acumen or royal lineage. This partly explains the
cerebral flavour of both the April and June cabinets, though one could
argue that the large number of authors, scholars and physicians was a
reflection of the composition of the NCC itself. It certainly explains
Lule's 30 April plan for army recruitment, which guaranteed propor-
tional representation for all regions, but set seven years of primary
school as the minimum entry standard for privates and O-levels and A-
levels as requirements for officers.[6]

Lule's removal and ignominious incarceration, first at Entebbe and
later at State House in Dar es Salaam, unleashed a wave of protests,
strikes and violence in Kampala. Tanzanian troops fired on pro-Lule
demonstrators. In retaliation, the Internal Joint Underground
Liberators (IJUL) sprang into existence to organise strikes, roadblocks
and attacks on both officials and offices of the new government. Rioters
freed Amin supporters from the Katwe police station on 27 June, and
Amin supporters joined in the violence and demonstrations.[7] Doctors,
nurses and other professionals were victims of a wave of murders by
unknown attackers in July and August, which triggered another exodus
to Kenya. At least 89 persons were killed in fresh violence in late
September and early October. One of the murder squads used
Tanzanian uniforms in raids to discredit the government's continued
reliance on 20,000 Tanzanian troops. The 23-strong squad was partly
financed by 'a European company with ties to men in Mr Lule's administration'.[8] Political detainees soon numbered over 200, in addition to
the more than 3,000 former officials and soldiers of Amin. By October
detainees included Sam Njuba, chairman of the Uganda Law Society;
Luke Kazinja, general manager of the government-owned *Uganda
Times*; Simon Mwebe, former editor of *Munno*; Sebatiani Kibuka, one-

time DP official and employee of the *Citizen*; Walusimbi Mpanga, former mayor of Kampala; and Charles Senabulya, a lawyer. Later that month the Kampala security situation improved, and many of the detainees were released.[9] It was ironic that Binaisa should rely on preventive detention, for he had resigned as Obote's Attorney-General in 1967 over that issue and the continuation of the state of emergency in Buganda.

Having weathered the storm over Lule's dismissal, President Binaisa began the task of consolidating his power within the UNLF, the economy, the military and the country as a whole. He announced in August that for two years all political activity would be restricted to the UNLF to the exclusion of parties within and outside the UNLF. This move did not sit well with DP members of the UNLF such as Paul Ssemogerere, who had already signalled his displeasure with Binaisa by filing a court suit on Lule's behalf. It also sparked protests from the UPC and the Uganda Liberation Group (Zambia).[10] A group of 'stayees' led by A. Olaya, David Onen Oyera, C. Rwaheru and L.B. Ntambi formed the Uganda National Union (UNU) with the expressed intention of joining the UNLF to break the monopoly of the 'returnees'.[11] UNU failed in its bid to join the UNLF, but Binaisa wisely resisted the temptation to ban it. UNU's formation did spur Binaisa to implement the UNLF pledge to widen the NCC membership. Aware of his narrow political base, Binaisa wished to widen the NCC through appointments, but the UNLF remained committed to election of new members by the 33 district councils acting as electoral colleges. The early October elections resulted in the selection of 61 new NCC members from a field of 728 candidates short listed from the nearly 1,300 who chose to run.[12] The new members plus 10 military appointees and the cabinet raised the NCC membership to 127.

To rehabilitate the economy, the government sought external aid from the West and the return of old firms via joint ventures with the state. The unstable political climate slowed the inflow of aid, but Finance Minister Jack Ssentongo succeeded in negotiating the return of Madhvani, Mehta, Rallie Brothers, Mitchell-Cotts and Massey-Ferguson (a newcomer).[13] Controversy broke over Binaisa's rather brazen attempts to use his patronage powers to place personal followers in top parastatal posts. He named Roger Mukasa, his brother-in-law, to head the UDC, ousting Sam Lukwago, who had nursed the ailing parastatal through the final years of the Amin regime. But the NCC vetoed his appointment of Bukombe Mpambara to chair the Coffee Marketing Board.[14]

Binaisa attempted to undermine the power of those, especially on the left, who opposed him: Yoweri Museveni, Ateker Ejalu, and Paulo Muwanga. In a major cabinet reorganisation on 19 November, Ejalu was demoted from Regional Co-operation to an ambassadorial post, and Museveni from Defence to Regional Co-operation. Like Lule, Binaisa failed to seek advance NCC approval for the changes, but he did seek, and narrowly won, *ex post facto* NCC approval. Ejalu remained in Uganda, however, and Museveni continued to control his own section of the Uganda National Liberation Army, which he had recruited while in exile and during the liberation war. In early February (1980), Muwanga was dismissed from Internal Affairs, but he too refused to take up his diplomatic assignment and appealed instead to the NCC and to the Tanzanian government for a reversal. By late February Muwanga was back in cabinet in the less visible post of Labour Minister. Attacking the left had a salutary effect on Binaisa's popularity among more conservative elements around Kampala and abroad. For the first time he was able to move in public. In mid-February he addressed an outdoor rally of 15,000 supporters in Kampala.[15] The hard core of Lule's supporters continued to despise Binaisa, however, and now added widespread corruption to charges against Binaisa's government.

In military matters and internal security, the government's dependence on Tanzanian troops and 1,000 Tanzanian police became increasingly burdensome, both politically and financially. Uganda's share of the Tanzanians' upkeep was put at Shs. 87 million per month (including food and housing allowances). The total cost of all security expenditures including Uganda's own badly fragmented forces was even higher: U. Shs. 192 million per month in 1979/80.[16]

The security/intelligence forces of the police had especially murky cleavages. Some units and individuals were pro-Binaisa; others were pro-Muwanga and thus, it was argued, pro-Obote; some may have been pro-Museveni. Layered over this was the network of external alliances and intrigue: the Kenya-Israel connection, the Tanzania connection, plus the usual sprinkling of CIA, British, KGB, Chinese, South African and French interests.[17] When Binaisa failed to win NCC approval in January (1980) for a special Shs. 35 million allocation for security/intelligence forces, it was a sign of growing UNLF mistrust of his intentions.[18]

As for the Uganda National Liberation Army, it consisted of at least four armies, each composed of soldiers with sub-national loyalties. Some were loyal to David Oyite-Ojok (Lango) who supported Obote; some were loyal to Tito Okello (Acholi) who had long supported Obote but drifted now towards the DP; some were loyal to Museveni (Ankole) who forged his own energetic blend of ethnic, youth and radical politics in his effort to emulate FRELIMO; some were loyal to William Omaria (Teso) who remained politically neutral, though his men displayed antipathy towards the Karimojong. Oyite-Ojok and Omaria, both career military men, were reportedly unhappy with Museveni, the student-turned-guerrilla, who none the less demonstrated considerable organisational skills.[19] Significantly, there was no pro-Binaisa force within the UNLA.

Binaisa's political position became increasingly brittle in March and April. Tanzania threatened to withdraw its troops if elections were not moved up from 1981 to 1980. At Binaisa's urging, the UNLF executive committee drafted a plan for December 1980 elections in which all candidates would run under the UNLF label rather than separate party banners. The NCC approved the plan in April, but UPC and DP members angrily charged that Binaisa had called the meeting knowing several opponents could not be present. Earlier Binaisa had sought Tanzanian approval for the retirement of Okello and the elevation of Oyite-Ojok to a non-command post. When Dar refused, Binaisa turned in March to Kenyan President Daniel Arap Moi for advice and support. Meanwhile, Binaisa's opponents travelled to Dar to seek support for replacing Binaisa by Rugumayo or Martin Aliker. Animosity between Binaisa and the military escalated with the publication of intelligence reports in the right-wing *Citizen* and *Economy* weeklies. The military held Binaisa supporters responsible for the leaks and arrested James Namakajo, Binaisa's Press Secretary, and Roland Kakoza, editor of *Economy*. When President Binaisa announced the dismissal of Oyite-Ojok on 10 May 1980, the army seized power in what it termed 'an action' rather than a coup and handed power over to a six-member Military Commission headed by Paulo Muwanga (Table 7.1). Binaisa was placed under house arrest. His fall was mourned by many, though by no means all, of the groups that had castigated Binaisa for helping to oust Lule.[20]

The Military Commission's assumption of power embarrassed Tanzania, and was also opposed by Edward Rugumayo, NCC chairman, and the group of Marxist intellectuals around him (Yash Tandon, Dan Nabudere and Omwony Ojok) who had voiced their commitment to human rights.[21] Winners in the coup, apart from Oyite-Ojok and Muwanga, were the UPC, the DP and Museveni, all of whom preferred to run under separate party banners rather than the UNLF.

The Military Commission appeared to be a step backward. Nevertheless, by allowing separate parties to contest the election, it cleared away the secrecy and shifting personal allegiances which had buffeted the NCC. Henceforth, candidates had to proclaim openly their loyalties. This alone facilitated the formation of more lasting coalitions. However, logistical problems eventually forced the Military Commission to postpone the election day from 30 September to 10 December.

Four parties announced their intention to contest the election. The UPC was headed by Milton Obote, who returned from exile on 27 May. After some manoeuvring, the DP selected Paul Ssemogerere, its former Publicity Secretary, as standard bearer. Lule made an effort to win the nomination, but lacked long-standing DP ties and was barred from returning to Uganda until he apologised to the UNLF for his scathing criticism of the organisation he once headed. Yoweri Museveni launched his own party, the Uganda Patriotic Movement (UPM), pledging social justice and an end to corruption. Finally, the Katikiro of Buganda during the 1966 crisis, J.S. Mayanja-Nkangi, launched the Conservative Party to fight for a return to a federal form of government.[22]

Going into the election, the parties' regional strongholds appeared to be as follows: UPC – Lango, Teso, Sebei and Kigezi; DP – Buganda, Acholi, West Nile and Busoga; UPM – Ankole and Toro; and the Conservative Party, only scattered support in Buganda and the other former kingdoms. Whereas the Conservative Party took some support from the DP in Buganda, the UPM reduced DP support in Ankole and Toro, but lessened UPC support in urban areas, and among students, trade unionists and civil servants.[23] In overall support, the DP enjoyed a plurality.

The platforms of the two leading parties were not strikingly different; both were contesting for the centre. The DP claimed to have the broadest ethnic, regional and religious appeal. It softened its earlier championing of free enterprise to praise the virtues of the mixed economy. It did eschew any talk of income redistribution, basing its appeal to workers and the rural poor on a pledge to install effective price controls and to introduce co-determination (state, management and worker control) in state-owned enterprises, presumably on the West German model. It would only encourage co-determination in the private sector. As the victim of the 1969 suspension of political parties, the DP pledged vigorous support for a multi-party system and promised to revise the 1967 constitution to curb the powers of the president. For its part, the UPC pledged reconciliation, no more nationalisation, respect for free enterprise and foreign investment, and a government of

Table 7.1: Cabinets of the Uganda National Liberation Front, 1979-1980, and Uganda People's Congress, 1980

Office/Ministry	11 April 1979	7 June 1979	25 June 1979	19 November 1979	18 May 1980	1 December 1980
President	Yusuf K. Lule	Yusuf K. Lule	Godfrey Binaisa	Godfrey Binaisa	MILITARY COMMISSION[5]	A. Milton Obote
Vice-President	--	--	--	--	--	Paulo Muwanga
Prime Minister	--	--	--	--	--	Otema Allimadi
State in the Office of the President	--	--	--	B.M.Y.Galla	Raphael Bitamazire	Christopher Rwakasisi
State in the Office of the Vice-President	--	--	--	--	--	Peter Otai
State in the Office of the Prime-Minister	--	--	--	--	--	Edward Rurangaranga
Presidential Affairs/ Min. without Portfolio	--	--	--	B. Kununka	--[4]	Shafiq Arain
Finance	Sam Sebagereka	Sam Sebagereka	Jack Ssentongo	Jack Ssentongo	Lawrence Sebalu	A. Milton Obote
Planning and Economic Development			Anthony Ocaya	Anthony Ocaya	Anthony Ocaya	Sam Odaka
Deputy Finance						Milton B. Makmot
Internal Affairs	Paulo Muwanga	P. Muwanga	Paulo Muwanga	Paulo Muwanga	Sam Tewungwa	Luwuliza Kirunda
State for Internal Affairs	Andrew Kayiira	Andrew Kayiira				William Omaria
Deputy Internal Affairs	Otema Allimadi	Otema Allimadi			Christopher Okoth	
Foreign Affairs	--	Otema Allimadi	Godfrey Binaisa	Otema Allimadi	Otema Allimadi	A. Milton Obote
State for Foreign Affairs	--					A. Picho Owinyi
Deputy Foreign Affairs	Sam Karugire	Sam Karugire	Sam Karugire	Sam Karugire	Sam Karugire	Sam Tewungwa
Regional (E.A.) Cooperation		Ateker Ejalu	Ateker Ejalu	Yoweri Museveni	A. Picho Owinyi	Paulo Muwanga
Defence	Yusuf K. Lule	Yusuf K. Lule	Yoweri Museveni	Godfrey Binaisa	MILITARY COMMISSION[5]	
Deputy Defence	William Omaria	William Omaria	William Omaria			
State for Defence	Yoweri Museveni	Yoweri Museveni				
Army Commander	Tito Okello	Tito Okello	Tito Okello	Tito Okello	Tito Okello	Tito Okello
Chief of Staff	D. Oyite-Ojok	D. Oyite-Ojok	D. Oyite-Ojok	D. Oyite-Ojok	D. Oyite-Ojok	D. Oyite-Ojok
Police Inspector-General		David Barlow	David Barlow		Luke Ofungi	L. Kalule-Ssetala
Local Government	Mathias Ngobi	Mathias Ngobi	Bidandi Ssali	Bidandi Ssali	Bidandi Ssali	Patrick Rwandha
Deputy Local Government						Wilson Okwenje
Cabinet and Public Service			Wilson Okwenje	Wilson Okwenje	Wilson Okwenje	Masete Kuuya
Reconstruction and Rehabilitation	Andrew Adimola	Andrew Adimola	Andrew Adimola	P. Kaboha	Masete Kuuya	
Co-operatives and Marketing			Yona Kanyomozi	Yona Kanyomozi	J. Obua-Otua	Yona Kanyomozi
Culture and Community Development	Dan Nabudere	Dan Nabudere	Dan Nabudere	Dan Nabudere	A. Tiberondwa	James Rwanyarare
Deputy Culture & Comm. Dev.						A. Olanya Olenge
Agriculture	J. Dungu	J. Dungu	Mathias Ngobi	Mathias Ngobi	Mathias Ngobi[4]	Sam Mugisa
Forestry and Fisheries				Y. Kyesimira		John J. Otim
Animal Industry		H.S.K. Msubuga	H.S.K. Msubuga	E.R. Mkwasibwe	E.R. Mkwasibwe	

Portfolio						
					Sam Mugiswa	Patrick Rubaihayo
State for Agriculture						Patrick Rubaihayo
Deputy Agriculture						Okello I. Okwakol
Deputy Animal Industry	A. Byaruha	R. Serumaga				Jofi Oyara Aliro
Commerce	A. Byaruha	R. Serumaga	P. Kaboha	Ephraim Kamuntu	Eriya Kategaya	A. Tiberondwa
Industry			Y. Kyersimira	Lawrence Sebalu	Obonyo	Ronald Badanyanya
Deputy Industry						
Power Posts & Communications	Akena P'Ojok	Akena P'Ojok	Akena P'Ojok	Akena P'Ojok	Akena P'Ojok	Akena P'Ojok
Information & Broadcasting	Ateker Ejalu	Grace Ibingira[1]	A. Picho Owinyi	A. Picho Owinyi	David Anyoti	David Anyoti
Deputy Information						Matia P. Kissembo
Housing & Urban Development						Abraham Waligo
Works	Abraham Waligo	Abraham Waligo	Abraham Waligo	Abraham Waligo	Abraham Waligo	Abener Rangwale
Deputy Housing/Works		Mungate				Ben Etonu
Transport					Kintu Musoke	Yosam Mugenyi
Supply					Moses Apiliga	Moses Apiliga
Deputy Transport						Joshua Akol
Land and Natural Resources	T. Kabwegyere	T. Kabwegyere	T. Kabwegyere	T. Kabwegyere	T. Kabwegyere	Max Choudry
Deputy Land and Resources						Amon Basira
Tourism and Wildlife	A. Mandira	A. Mandira	J. Obua-Otua	J. Obua-Otua	Ephraim Kamuntu	Ntege Lubwama
Education			G.M. Bitamazire	G.M. Bitamazire	G.M. Bitamazire	Isaac Ojok
State for Education						
Deputy Education						Philimon Watea
Health	Arnold Bisase	Arnold Bisase	Arnold Bisase[2]	P.H. Sebuwufu	Max Choudry[6] / Ntege Lubwama	A.A. Nkwasibwe
Deputy Health	P. Senabulya	R. Rugunda	R. Rugunda	R. Rugunda	R. Rugunda	Theresa Odong-Oduka
Labour	Paulo Muwanga	Paulo Muwanga	Paul Ssemogerere[3]	Badru Wegulo	J.Luwuliza-Kirunda	Anthony Butele
Deputy Labour					Matiya Kasaija	Henry Tungakwo
Justice	Dan Mabudere	G. Kanyethamba	Stephen O. Ariko	Stephen O. Ariko	Stephen O. Ariko	Stephen O. Ariko
Attorney-General	G. Kanyethamba	G. Kanyethamba	Stephen O. Ariko	Stephen O. Ariko	Stephen O. Ariko	Stephen O. Ariko

[1] Dropped from Cabinet in Lule's cabinet reshuffle of 19th June, and replaced by Charles Magala.

[2] Dismissed 25th July, and replaced by P.H. Sebuwufu.

[3] Refused post, replaced by B. Kununka.

[4] Ngobi soon promoted to Minister for Presidential Affairs, and Sam Mugiswa named Minister of Agriculture. Ngobi resigned from Cabinet for family reasons 27th June 1980.

[5] Government run by Military Commission: Paulo Muwanga, Chairman; Yoweri Museveni, Vice-Chairman; Maj. Gen. Tito Okello; Brig. D. Oyite-Ojok; Col. William Omaria; and Col. Zeddi Maruru.

[6] Replaced by Ambrose Okullu in September 1980.

[7] Not shown: Ali Senyonga and Ephraim Kamuntu, both Ambassadors Extraordinary and Plenipotentiary, President's Office.

Sources: *Africa Research Bulletin; Africa Confidential;* and Uganda High Commission, Ottawa.

national unity. Its chief asset and main liability, Milton Obote, expressed continued private belief in a one-party state as an abstract goal. For the moment, however, Obote saw the rural sector to be his first priority, followed closely by the rehabilitation of industry to replace imported goods and increase exports. Ugandans and foreigners were to be encouraged to invest their money in the Ugandan economy.[24]

It was in their views on the make-up of the post-election government that Ssemogerere and Obote clearly diverged. Obote argued that the elections should lead to the formation of a broad-based government, formed by accord rather than by bargaining. Since neither party was likely to emerge with a clear majority, the Military Commission should call on the party with the most experience to head a coalition government. This suggestion by Obote (via Muwanga) was unacceptable to Ssemogerere. He firmly opposed any coalition government (or any replay of the 1962-4 UPC/KY alliance), arguing that the party winning the most seats should be called upon to form a national government, inviting *individual* members from minority parties to participate in the government.[25]

Military and security problems continued to cloud Uganda's future. Leonard Mugwanya, a prominent DP member, was killed at his home near Kampala on 21 August in what was widely believed to be a politically-motivated assassination.[26] Violence flared near the capital as the election campaign gained momentum. Earlier, the Military Commission ran into criticism over the 1980-1 budget, which increased the defence and security allocation by U. Shs. 440 million — more than the total amount allocated to agriculture. This increase in security expenditures from 27 per cent to 31 per cent of the total budget led NCC member Israel Mayengo to lament that 'we do not have a shortage of money, only a shortage of common sense'.[27]

In the northeast, security deteriorated steadily, partly due to the drought and famine, partly due to the escalation of cattle-raiding in Karamoja after the 1979 looting of the Moroto armoury. Starving Karimojong evoked little sympathy among the largely Iteso soldiers in the region, who were their traditional rivals in cattle raids. The drought did reveal the rationale behind what one European had termed the Karimojong's 'inane' attachment to cattle.[28] In a region in which insects and erratic rainfall caused total or partial failure of the sorghum crop in 14 years out of 29, cattle represented the ultimate granary and security against starvation.[29] When the UNLF government proved unable or unwilling to alleviate the effects of the 1979-80 famine in Karamoja, the French government won permission to use military aircraft to fly relief supplies to Catholic missions in the region.

In the northwest, the border situation had improved following the Sudanese government's September 1979 decision to disarm pro-Amin exiles.[30] New fighting was reported in West Nile in October 1980. Obote charged that Amin supporters had seized control of Arua and Koboko. From his exile in Kenya, Moses Ali countered that the disturbances were only the by-product of skirmishes between UNLA troops and refugees coming home to register for the elections. Ali accused Obote of exaggerating the incidents to delay the elections indefinitely (a replay of 1966-7). Clearly the Sudan had no interest in any adventure that would legitimate the continued presence of 10,000 Tanzanian troops in Uganda. As for Zaire's regime, it had the motive but lacked the means to back pro-Amin raids, given its own tenuous hold on that corner of Zaire.

Reconstruction placed third in the Military Commission's hierarchy of concerns, behind the elections and the security problem. Pending stabilisation of the political situation, the rehabilitation of roads, transportation fleets, wells, and factories received scant official attention and only a trickle of external aid, although the slow economic recovery was as much cause as effect of the political instability.

Successive UNLF regimes did find time to grapple with the reallocation of booty from Amin's economic war. Among the NCC's complaints against Lule was his failure to establish a system for the allocation and reallocation of businesses. There were several linked problems: (a) the desire to make amends to citizen Asians who had lost property; (b) the desire to return large scale factories and plantations to production as quickly as possible; (c) the lack of resources to establish a fund for the compensation of departed Asians; (d) the need to do something with shops and other businesses abandoned by Amin's supporters; (e) the need to regularise the ownership of homes and other 'abandoned' property vested in the Departed Asians Property Custodial Board; (f) the desire of outsiders to punish insiders who had profited from the Amin regime; and (g) the desire of certain elements within the NCC to turn the clock back and re-establish the Asian commercial group as a political buffer between the state bureaucracy and the African businessmen.

Within two days of the liberation of Kampala, some Asians returned to reclaim their homes. Because expropriated homes had generally remained under state custody, this caused few problems. The Lule administration announced that factories and large firms would be returned to their former owners, but retail shops and medium-size firms would remain in African hands. This policy appeared to change in September 1980. In order 'to create a healthy society in which property was respected,' all expropriated property was to revert to former owners, provided they were Ugandan citizens. Even property that had changed hands legally after expropriation was to be returned.[3] Whether the decree extended beyond dwellings to include shops, shares and moveable assets was not clear. Moreover, what would happen if the Asians (in many cases, after eight years, citizens of other countries) failed to return? Uncertainty would discourage current owners from reinvesting profits. The explosive political implications of the wholesale return of the commercial sector to Asian ownership does not seem to have been considered by the Military Commission in its quest for restitutive justice. Compensation might have been cheaper in the long run. Many shops in Uganda have by now three or more 'rightful' owners, whose exercise of property rights depends on the regime in power that day. The sole consolation (?) is that many in Uganda have now some experience in the management (or mismanagement) of business.

The Road Ahead

Going into the 1980s Uganda stands at three crossroads, of which the domestic political crossroad is merely the most obvious. The second is geo-political; the third, economic.

As in the 1890s Uganda finds itself at the centre of rival regional and great power strategies for carving a corridor of friendly territory through Africa. In the 1890s it was France which sought to win Uganda and the Upper Nile to complete a corridor of French territory from west to east across Africa, whereas Britain pursued Cecil Rhodes' Cape to Cairo dream on the north-south axis. Britain won the military face-off at Fashoda and the religious/political intrigue in Uganda.

Going into the 1980s it is the NATO bloc and conservative states in the OAU which seek to win Uganda's allegiance to complete the east-west axis linking Kenya and Zaire (a *cordon sanitaire* between the pro-Soviet regimes in Ethiopia and Angola), whereas the Warsaw Pact and radical states in the OAU view Uganda as a much-needed link in the north-south corridor from Ethiopia to Mozambique and Zimbabwe. Just as Belgium, Germany and Egypt complicated matters in the late nineteenth century, so the People's Republic of China, South Africa and the Arab world make the 1980s contest more complex. Regardless of which side wins, Soviet military aid will probably continue to be offered to Uganda and will not be lightly refused, though the DP might use Karamoja famine relief from the French military to legitimate a larger French military presence in Uganda (a strong echo from the nineteenth century). Should the Tanzanians be forced to continue their military presence in Uganda, one might anticipate renewed parallels with the Vietnamese presence in Cambodia, namely increased covert Western support for supporters of the discredited ousted regime in northwest border adventures to destabilise the successor regime.

In terms of alignments, the DP and the Conservative Party clearly favour the east-west corridor, whereas the UPC and UPM favour slightly different variations of the north-south corridor. Obote's main regional allies on the north-south axis are Tanzania and Zambia, whereas Museveni's models are Mozambique and Zimbabwe. Whether an objective view or a self-fulfilling prophecy, Obote is viewed as leaning toward the Soviet Union; Museveni toward China.

The economic crossroad, though linked with the geo-political and domestic political alternatives, is a distinct entity. The UPC would use the north-south alliance as a bargaining counter to pressure Kenya into reviving the East African Community (possibly on an enlarged basis). Two dangers face the UPC. The first is that for a supposedly progressive party, its economic strategy has a nostalgic air: forward to the golden era of 1969-70! Given present circumstances, recovery to those levels would certainly be a step forward, but Uganda has the resources to do far better. Aside from import substitution within a revived EAC framework and a return to export-oriented development, where is the UPC's vision of Uganda's economic future beyond 1970? The second danger is that the UPC's stated commitment to egalitarian principles may not extend to party notables any more this time than last. Obote's own Mercedes entourage and Max Choudry's alleged mishandling of famine relief give scant grounds for optimism.

The DP might use the east-west alignment as a spring-board for modest economic sub-imperialism in which Uganda's landlocked position would be turned to advantage to gain markets in eastern Zaire, southern Sudan, Rwanda, Burundi, northwestern Tanzania and possibly western Kenya. This strategy has the advantage of luring the pro-Amin exiles back into the mainstream of Ugandan life with Arua as the commercial gateway to the west and north. The pitfall in the scenario is that Kenya is presently better equipped industrially to play the economic sub-imperial role.

The UPM economic strategy might envisage using the entire north-south group of radical states as the basis for pursuing regional autonomy and collective self-reliance. Whether socialist regimes can embark on such a broad redivision of labour without succumbing to the temptations of sub-imperialism remains an open question.

Needless to say, all of the foregoing strategies require stable government as a prerequisite. That alone would satisfy most Ugandans in the 1980s.

Notes

1. Colin Legum (ed.), *Africa Contemporary Record, 1978-79* (New York and London; Africana, 1980), pp. B 426-34, outlines the course of the war.

2. *Africa Research Bulletin (ARB)*, September 1979, p. 5413.

3. Details of the damage to the Ugandan economy caused by neglect, looting and the war (in that order of importance) can be found in Commonwealth Team of Experts, *The Rehabilitation of the Economy of Uganda*, vol. II (London: Commonwealth Secretariat, 1979), passim.

4. Interview, Godfrey Okoth, October 1979; and *ARB*, July 1979, p. 5337.

5. Legum lists 29 members: Edward Rugumayo, Omwony Ojok, Tarsis Kabwegyere, Ayei Kweya, H.M.B. Makmot, Father Christopher Okoth, J.W.M. Luwuliza-Kirunda, Stephen Ariko, W.W. Ankbonggo, Osinde Wangwor, Paul Ssemogerere, Vincent Okot, Olara Otunnu, Kefa Sempangi, J. Magezi, B.M. Buzabo, Paul Bisase Kibuka Musoke, I. Mayengo, L. Komakec, Yona Kanyamozi, Paul Wanoola, Eriya Kategaya, Jack Maumbe, Denis Echou, E.R. Kamuntu, Fred Ssempebwa, L. Kayiira and Omara Atubo. Legum (ed.), *ACR, 1978-79*, p. B 445.

6. *ARB*, May 1979, p. 5261.

7. *The Standard* (Nairobi), 28 July 1979.

8. *ARB*, November 1979, p. 5468.

9. Ibid., August 1979, p. 5384; October 1979, pp. 5447-8.

10. Ibid., August 1979, p. 5372.

11. Ibid.

12. Ibid., October 1979, p. 5440.

13. *Africa Confidential*, vol. 21, no. 5 (27 February 1980), p. 6.

14. Ibid., vol, 20, no. 4 (28 November 1979), p. 5.

15. See George Byaruhanga's scathing attack on Binaisa as a puppet of pro-Communist forces, unable to show his face in public, *The Standard* (Nairobi), 7 September 1979, p. 5. Compare that with reports of his public rally five months later, *ARB*, February 1980, p. 5585.

16. *ARB* (Economic Series), 15 June-14 July 1980, p. 5586.

17. *Africa Confidential*, vol. 21, no. 5 (27 February 1980), p. 7.

18. *ARB* (Economic Series), 15 January-14 February 1980, p. 5404.

19. *Africa Confidential*, vol. 20, no. 20 (3 October 1979), p. 4; and vol. 21, no. 5 (27 February 1980), p. 6.

20. Ibid., vol. 21, no. 7 (26 March 1980), pp. 7-8; *ARB*, March 1980, p. 5610; April 1980, p. 5654; May 1980, pp. 5682-4; and Magina Magina, 'State of Unrest', *Africa*, no. 106 (June 1980), pp. 20, 25.

21. *Africa Confidential*, vol. 21, no. 5 (27 February 1980), p. 6.

22. Ibid., vol. 21, no. 15 (16 July 1980), pp. 5-8.

23. UPC notables (as of July-August 1980): Milton Obote, Paulo Muwanga,

Otema Allimadi, Sam Tewungwa, J. Luwuliza-Kirunda, Akena p'Ojok, David Anyoti, Ado Tiberondwa, Stephen Ariko, Moses Apiliga, Ben Bella Ilakut, D. Oyite-Ojok, Sam Mugiswa and Max Choudry.

DP notables: Paul Ssemogerere, Adoko Nekyon, Martin Aliker, Laurence Sebalu, Anthony Ocaya, Andrew Adimola, A.K. Lubega, Tiberio Okeny, Ambrose Okullu, Yoweri Kyesimira, Mikombe Mpambara, Wilson Lutara, Francis Wazarwahi-Bwengye, and Zach Olum.

UPM notables: Yoweri Museveni, Bidandi Ssali, Eriya Kategaya, Kinto Mosoke, C. Kiyunga, Sam Karugire, Zeddi Maruru, Erisa Kironde, Jeremiah Opira, Ruhakana Rugunda, Rhoda Kalema, Matiya Kasaija, Christopher Okoth, Raphael Bitamazire, and David Wogute. Source: *Africa Confidential*, especially vol. 21, no. 15 (16 July 1980), pp. 5-8.

24. Magina Magina, 'Uganda at the Crossroads', *Africa*, no. 109 (September 1980), pp. 12-19.

25. Ibid.

26. *ARB*, August 1980, p. 5779.

27. *ARB* (Economic Series), 15 June-14 July 1980, p. 5586.

28. J.M. Watson, 'Some Aspects of Teso Agriculture', *East African Agricultural Journal*, vol. 6, no. 4 (April 1941), p. 209.

29. Rough estimate based on 1924-57 data (incomplete) in Neville Dyson-Hudson, *Karimojong Politics* (Oxford: Clarendon Press, 1966), pp. 76-80.

30. *ARB*, September 1979, p. 5414.

31. *ARB*, May 1979, p. 5261; June 1979, p. 5298; and Uganda High Commission (Ottawa), *Uganda Bulletin*, No. 6 (July-September 1980), pp. 5-7.

APPENDICES

Table A.1: Peoples of Uganda, 1959 Census

African Ethnic Groups	Number	%			Number	%
1) Baganda	1,044,878	15.99	17) Bakonjo (Konjo)		106,890	1.64
2) Iteso (Teso)	524,716	8.03	18) Jo-Padhola (Badama)		101,451	1.55
3) Banyankure (Nkore)	519,283	7.94	19) Banyole (Nyoli)		92,642	1.42
4) Basoga (Soga)	501,921	7.68	20) Madi		80,355	1.23
5) Bakiga (Kiga)	459,619	7.03	21) Kuman		61,459	0.94
6) Banyaruanda (Ruanda)	378,656	5.79	22) Samia		47,759	0.73
7) Langi (Lango)	363,867	5.57	23) Kakwa		37,828	0.58
8) Bagisu (Gisu)	329,257	5.04	24) Sebei		36,800	0.56
9) Acholi	284,929	4.36	25) Gwe		36,130	0.55
10) Lugbara	236,270	3.61	26) Mwamba (Amba)		34,506	0.53
11) Batoro (Toro)	208,300	3.19	27) Kenyi		23,707	0.36
12) Banyoro (Nyoro)	188,374	2.88	28) Pokot (Suk)		21,850	0.33
13) Alur-Jonam	150,820	2.31	29) Labwor		10,042	0.15
14) Rundi	138,749	2.12	30) Lendu		4,744	0.07
15) Karimojong	131,713	2.02	31) Topeth (Tepes)		4,363	0.07
16) Bagwere	111,681	1.71	Others*		176,079	2.69
			Total		6,449,558	98.67

Non-African Ethnic Groups	Number	%
1) "Bahindi" (Indo-Pakistani)	71,933	1.10
2) "Bazungu" (Europeans)	10,866	0.17
3) Arabs	1,946	0.03
Others	2,313	0.04
	87,058	1.33

	Number	%
Total Population 1959	6,536,531	100.00

Notes:

*Includes immigrants from Kenya, Tanzania, Zaire, Sudan and elsewhere.

The following peoples were not enumerated separately: Hororo (Mpororo), Jo-Palwo (Chopi), Dodoth (Dodos), Jie, Teuso (Ik), Napore, Nyakwai, Kebu, Kuku, Mening, Koki, Igara, and others.

Source:

Uganda, *Atlas of Uganda*, 2nd edn (1967), p. 40; and *1967 Statistical Abstract*, pp. 5 and 7.

Table A.2: Government Revenue and Expenditure, 1901-1980

Year	Total Revenue	Total Expenditure	Coercion A	Agriculture B	Education C	Health D	Ratio A/(B+C+D)	Ratio (A+B+C+D)/Total
	(Shs. '000)							
1901-02	1,480	4,574	2,046	42	0	213	8.02	0.50
1902-03	823	4,075	1,727	18	0	234	6.85	0.49
1903-04	1,029	3,736	1,470	23	0	370	3.74	0.50
1904-05	1,194	3,461	1,297	28	0	282	4.18	0.46
1905-06	1,556	3,823	1,470	41	2	349	3.75	0.49
1906-07	1,935	3,830	1,293	51	3	315	3.51	0.43
1907-08	2,278	3,911	1,170	71	3	375	2.60	0.41
1908-09	2,051	5,137	1,199	175	4	636	1.47	0.39
1909-10	3,303	4,803	1,188	244	25	448	1.66	0.40
1910-11	3,822	5,523	1,277	183	22	436	1.99	0.35
1911-12	4,070	7,644	1,171	289	25	392	1.66	0.25
1912-13	4,773	6,364	1,302	212	25	452	1.89	0.31
1913-14	5,131	6,858	1,188	276	25	563	1.38	0.30
1914-15	5,657	6,813	1,111	256	25	576	1.30	0.29
1915-16	5,741	6,087	1,202	293	25	540	1.40	0.34
1916-17	6,309	5,952	1,322	239	25	570	1.59	0.36
1917-18	6,527	5,858	1,312	240	25	557	1.60	0.36
1918-19	7,037	6,619	1,361	279	42	607	1.47	0.35
1919-20	9,911	9,952	1,596	530	44	872	1.10	0.31
1920 (9 mo)	15,542	12,323	1,935	897	94	996	0.97	0.32
1921	16,063	20,285	2,460	756	146	1,572	0.99	0.24
1922	16,407	22,192	3,954	810	164	1,640	1.51	0.30
1923	19,995	21,581	2,572	912	258	1,744	0.88	0.25
1924	24,796	21,318	2,938	1,014	350	2,120	0.84	0.30
1925	29,586	24,069	3,104	1,644	492	2,366	0.69	0.32
1926	27,793	26,607	3,124	1,546	854	2,630	0.62	0.31
1927	25,846	28,919	3,336	1,574	960	2,698	0.64	0.30
1928	30,385	27,469	3,156	1,678	992	2,896	0.57	0.32
1929	33,658	32,111	3,432	1,734	1,124	3,174	0.57	0.29
1930	28,245	32,806	3,128	2,262	1,302	3,288	0.46	0.30
1931	27,998	29,135	3,248	1,924	1,342	3,338	0.49	0.34
1932	28,051	25,978	2,928	1,860	1,370	2,956	0.47	0.35
1933	26,101	28,406	2,748	1,862	1,432	2,884	0.44	0.31
1934	30,553	27,653	2,904	1,996	1,456	2,814	0.46	0.33
1935	31,334	29,240	2,904	1,898	1,522	2,978	0.45	0.32
1936	34,259	33,188	3,114	2,128	1,614	3,296	0.44	0.31
1937	39,191	35,082	3,106	2,306	1,786	3,530	0.41	0.31
1938	37,277	40,751	3,672	2,454	2,102	3,700	0.44	0.29
1939	34,359	54,791	3,954	2,466	7,890	3,880	0.28	0.33
1940	37,418	41,319	7,038	2,516	3,000	3,546	0.78	0.39
1941	43,566	38,895	6,500	2,432	2,798	4,062	0.70	0.41
1942	43,801	41,386	6,042	2,570	2,738	4,192	0.64	0.38
1943	48,573	42,777	8,278	2,934	3,080	5,320	0.73	0.46
1944	53,165	52,030	9,460	3,302	4,146	6,126	0.70	0.44
1945	67,328	64,033	13,400	3,100	5,670	6,678	0.87	0.43
1946	81,000	71,484	14,428	5,184	7,196	6,624	0.76	0.47
1947	106,624	89,475	6,732	6,623	9,551	9,092	0.27	0.36
1948	128,101	130,609	10,591	9,175	11,473	12,458	0.32	0.33
1949	161,888	133,737	10,064	11,157	9,936	13,026	0.30	0.33
1950	220,734	160,008	17,117	20,823	14,047	12,420	0.36	0.40
1951	316,526	246,910	21,807	21,912	16,051	16,254	0.40	0.31
1952	345,780	319,020	29,307	45,765	33,207	21,201	0.29	0.41
1953	354,701	348,636	29,857	36,053	46,210	22,627	0.28	0.39
1954 (6 mo)	206,972	172,554	15,282	13,265	31,474	11,063	0.27	0.41
1954-55	416,717	418,413	38,610	33,768	78,862	29,852	0.27	0.43
1955-56	431,958	459,932	53,522	32,518	82,908	30,780	0.37	0.43
1956-57	473,793	480,160	55,190	39,372	88,896	33,620	0.34	0.45
1957-58	448,820	510,357	62,000	39,564	91,624	43,682	0.35	0.46
1958-59	482,112	513,676	66,092	40,036	91,808	52,474	0.36	0.49
1959-60	438,743	497,919	70,258	43,256	115,366	60,860	0.32	0.58
1960-61	528,001	623,672	70,930	48,366	120,674	70,176	0.30	0.50
1961-62	653,589	762,580	73,215	102,522	144,212	69,352	0.23	0.51
1962-63	780,481	863,951	82,240	130,594	154,562	61,304	0.24	0.50
1963-64	917,868	932,284	111,674	136,261	189,072	72,126	0.28	0.55
1964-65	1,065,340	1,107,671	155,817	79,852	234,135	87,120	0.39	0.50
1965-66	1,143,445	1,247,946	221,321	87,055	232,097	98,630	0.53	0.51
1966-67	1,050,904	1,091,185	202,996	99,205	133,145	84,817	0.64	0.48
1967-68	1,065,963	1,143,401	249,244	105,717	186,628	91,688	0.65	0.55
1968-69	1,311,421	1,511,606	263,731	112,417	274,012	215,619	0.44	0.57
1969-70	1,235,097	1,615,105	300,351	170,937	321,168	159,276	0.46	0.59
1970-71	1,461,067	2,037,236	349,298	199,164	361,646	175,576	0.47	0.53
1971-72	1,719,511	2,512,107	718,322	229,567	373,329	128,099	0.98	0.58
1972-73	1,240,606	1,825,470	508,504	222,148	354,934	127,256	0.72	0.66
1973-74	1,301,838	2,174,411	660,731	270,147	412,082	115,602	0.83	0.67
1974-75	2,491,000a	3,430,000a	499,896*	217,626*	327,681*	109,580*	0.76	n.c.
1975-76	2,336,502*	3,227,199	1,023,252	274,516	568,638	210,856	0.97	0.64
1976-77	4,322,800a	5,202,400a	1,357,582a	705,640a	734,406a	609,854a	0.66	0.65
1977-78	6,062,500a	7,761,064a	1,310,819*	708,150*	862,072*	353,219*	0.68	n.c.
1978-79	3,402,000*	5,232,000*	n.a.	n.a.	n.a.	n.a.	n.a.	n.a.
1979-80	5,100,000*	6,699,800*	1,808,946*	468,986*	1,045,200*	418,000*	0.94	0.56

Symbols:
*   –   Draft budget estimate (often very inaccurate) rather than actual figure.
a.   –   Revised estimate (somewhat inaccurate) rather than actual figure.
n.a. –   Not available.
n.c. –   Not calculated because of multiple sources.
Definitions and notes:
a)   Total revenue includes both recurrent and development (extraordinary) revenue.
b)   Total expenditure includes both recurrent and development (extraordinary) expenditure.
c)   Expenditure on coercion includes recurrent and development (extraordinary) expenditure on the following: military, defence, war, police, prisons, war bonuses and punitive expeditions.
d)   Expenditure on agriculture includes recurrent and development (extraordinary) expenditure on the following: crop production, veterinary services, tsetse and locust control, forestry, hunting and fishing.
e)   Expenditure on education includes recurrent and development (extraordinary) expenditure on education at all levels.
f)   Expenditure on health includes expenditures on the health department and hospitals.
g)   Except as noted by symbols, all figures are for actual revenue and expenditure.
h)   Expenditure totals do not include transfers to reserve funds (e.g. Shs. 8 million in 1930 and Shs. 677,140 in 1932), but do include the servicing of loans.
i)   The coverage of local government revenue and expenditure is sketchy prior to 1960/61. The 1960/61-1965/66 series amalgamates central and local government revenue (and expenditure) in a way different from the post-1965/66 series.
j)   The 1972/73-1979/80 series is based on a patchwork of sources and must be used with great caution.
Sources:
1901/02-1945   *Blue Books*; and Thomas and Scott, *Uganda*, p. 504.
1946   Colonial Office, *Annual Report on Uganda, 1946.*
1947-1971/72   *Statistical Abstracts;* and Douglas Harris, *Development in Uganda, 1947 to 1955/56.*
1972/73-1979/80 *Budget Speeches; Financial Statement and Revenue Estimates;* and *Summary of Draft Estimates of Recurrent and Development Expenditures.*

Table A.3: Cotton and Coffee Data, 1910/11-1978

	COTTON LINT EXPORTS					RAW COFFEE EXPORTS				
	Value	Quantity	Price (fob) Mombasa	Grower price seed cotton	Ratio	Value	Quantity	Price (fob) Mombasa	Grower price for robusta*	Ratio
Year	Shs.'000	Metric tons	Shs. per metric ton A	Shs. per metric ton B	A/B	Shs.'000	Metric tons	Shs. per metric ton C	Shs. per metric ton D	C/D
1910/11	3,308	2,427	1,453a	n.a.	n.a.	8	13	580	n.a.	n.a.
1911/12	4,617	3,707	1,226a	196.87¢	6.23	51	86	594	n.a.	n.a.
1912/13	5,088	4,689	1,085a	234.13¢	4.63	179	170	1,054	n.a.	n.a.
1913/14	6,354	5,002	1,258a	230.16¢	5.47	463	622	744	n.a.	n.a.
1914/15	7,023	5,903	1,178a	110.23¢	10.69	820	1,072	765	n.a.	n.a.
1915/16	4,909	4,758	1,033a	230.60¢	4.48	1,744	2,197	794	265	3.00
1916/17	6,978	3,961	1,762	268.30¢	6.57	2,279	2,469	923	265	3.49
1917/18	10,742	5,050	2,127	378.97¢	5.61	791	1,008	785	728	1.08
1918/19	19,319	4,988	3,873	357.15¢	10.84	2,120	2,759	768	728	1.06
1919/20	24,193	6,628	3,650	616.63¢	5.92	3,234	2,996	1,079	750	1.44
1920 (9 mo)	75,579	8,654	8,734	1,190.00 (peak)	7.34	1,807	1,219	1,483	n.a.	n.a.
1921	25,627	14,763	1,736	176.37	9.84	1,881	2,482	758	n.a.	n.a.
1922	17,553	8,762	2,003	n.a.	n.a.	1,985	2,604	762	n.a.	n.a.
1923	40,536	15,975	2,538	n.a.	n.a.	2,170	2,079	1,044	n.a.	n.a.
1924	69,731	34,334	2,988	617.00	4.84	2,354	2,088	1,127	n.a.	n.a.
1925	93,720	35,569	2,635	551.00	4.78	2,789	1,518	1,837	n.a.	n.a.
1926	61,036	32,815	1,860	397.00	4.69	2,958	1,687	1,753	n.a.	n.a.
1927	33,817	23,901	1,415	353.00	4.01	3,408	2,211	1,542	n.a.	n.a.
1928	49,507	25,127	1,970	441.00	4.47	3,284	2,050	1,602	882 -1,323	1.82 -1.21
1929	66,253	37,024	1,789	397.00	4.51	3,543	2,093	1,693	n.a.	n.a.
1930	31,107	23,428	1,328	331.79	4.00	3,100	2,482	1,249	n.a.	n.a.
1931	30,066	34,277	877	237.66	3.69	3,228	3,556	908	n.a.	n.a.
1932	31,683	37,617	842	236.55	3.56	4,463	4,424	1,009	n.a.	n.a.
1933	53,644	53,493	1,003	193.56	5.18	4,213	5,103	826	n.a.	n.a.
1934	58,556	51,826	1,130	223.55	5.05	4,645	7,801	749	n.a.	n.a.
1935	54,455	45,948	1,229	258.60	4.19	4,619	6,385	723	n.a.	n.a.
1936	66,538	58,305	1,141	209.66	5.44	7,623	11,617	656	n.a.	n.a.
1937	85,386	61,397	1,391	291.45	4.77	8,410	13,104	642	n.a.	n.a.
1938	68,559	72,945	939	181.66	5.17	6,553	14,232	460	132	3.48
1939	53,111	59,808	888	167.38¢	5.31	8,741	17,388	503	132	3.80
1940	75,202	55,076	1,365	227.41¢	6.00	9,390	17,426	539	132	4.07
1941	85,245	66,398	1,284	194.45	6.60	11,945	19,785	604	132	4.56
1942	57,202	42,829	1,336	169.31	7.89	14,057	17,473	804	287	2.81
1943	64,756	22,283	2,906	276.90	10.49	22,863	19,993	1,144	309	3.71
1944	100,868	34,386	2,933	290.57	10.09	20,252	18,518	1,094	309	3.54
1945	140,515	34,982	2,928	326.94	8.96	22,864	19,991	1,144	350	3.27
1946	112,402	39,770	2,826	361.55	7.82	34,565	31,920	1,083	331	3.27
1947	142,379	45,919	3,101	406.75	7.62	30,995	21,371	1,450	375	3.87
1948	149,152	31,617	4,717	450.18	10.48	64,937	38,413	1,690	419	4.04
1949	346,860	70,806	4,899	652.78	7.50	57,820	24,284	2,381	463	5.14
1950	333,960	63,186	5,285	699.96	7.55	166,640	32,361	5,149	551	9.34
1951	574,843	62,778	9,157	951.51	9.62	273,080	44,351	6,157	882	6.98
1952	599,080	68,584	8,735	1,048.51	8.33	246,900	40,083	6,160	1,102	5.59
1953	336,040	60,646	5,541	1,071.44	5.17	230,860	36,273	6,364	1,543	4.12
1954	417,540	71,351	5,852	1,089.07	5.37	269,560	35,206	7,657	3,307	2.32
1955	327,720	55,566	5,898	1,296.53	4.55	402,680	75,645	5,323	n.a.	n.a.
1956	385,700	68,312	5,646	1,148.82	4.91	314,420	62,640	5,019	1,653	3.04

Year									
1957	349,520	61,100	5,721	1,175.93	4.87	431,740	85,400	5,056	1,764	2.87
1958	362,680	70,308	5,160	1,210.33	4.26	416,540	79,964	5,209	1,764	2.95
1959	308,560	67,722	4,556	974.43	4.68	373,760	89,819	4,161	1,499	2.78
1960	298,600	59,975	4,987	987.88	5.05	339,740	118,675	2,863	1,235	2.32
1961	334,320	63,186	5,291	1,151.46	4.60	279,580	104,857	2,666	1,102	2.42
1962	165,200	32,750	5,044	1,147.71	4.39	403,480	133,053	3,032	1,213	2.50
1963	286,600	59,739	4,798	1,180.78	4.06	543,620	147,582	3,684	1,058	3.48
1964	317,140	64,501	4,917	1,245.60	3.95	707,560	139,657	5,066	1,257	4.03
1965	334,233	69,093	4,852	1,190.48	4.08	608,427	157,786	3,856	950	4.06
1966	306,892	69,802	4,397	1,235.18	3.56	695,665	167,288	4,158	880	4.73
1967	303,224	71,959	4,214	761.87	5.53	715,010	159,481	4,339	880	4.93
1968	295,673	61,653	4,796	933.54	5.14	715,929	151,955	4,705	880	5.35
1969	250,955	52,903	4,744	1,130.56	4.53	779,929	190,725	4,089	880 - 1,060	4.65 - 3.86
1970	350,985	78,117	4,493	974.99[c]	4.61	1,014,464	191,244	5,305	1,060 -1,190	5.00 - 4.46
1971	352,105	68,753	5,121	1,130.56[c]	4.53	982,338	174,621	5,626	1,190	4.73
1972	370,733	66,584	5,567	1,123.09[c]	4.96	1,128,294	214,183	5,268	1,190	4.43
1973	336,010	64,692	5,194	1,170.49[c]	4.44	1,346,728	226,874	5,936	1,190	4.99
1974	272,300	36,200	7,522	1,493.65[c]	5.04	1,650,500	201,500	8,761	1,250	7.01
1975	210,900	25,400	8,303	1,724.47[c]	4.81	1,501,200	188,400	7,968	1,400	5.69
1976	182,400	n.a.	n.a.	n.a.	n.a.	2,510,400	163,414	15,362	2,500	6.14
1977	132,000	n.a.	n.a.	n.a.	n.a.	4,538,000	131,843	34,420	3,500	9.83
1978	148,000	n.a.	19,859	2,733.00[c]	7.27	2,332,000	103,922	22,440	3,500	6.41

Notes:

* Whereas the grower price for seed cotton is the average price obtained by all growers for all grades and types of cotton, the grower price for robusta is the set grower price in Buganda for unhulled *kiboko* robusta coffee. The data for coffee exports, however, includes both robusta and kiboko coffee in various degrees of processing: husked, parchment, etc.

ɑ Up through 1915/16, part of the cotton was shipped to Kisumu, Kenya, for ginning. The quantity shown is for the ginned equivalent, but the export price shown is only for cotton ginned in Uganda.

ϵ Estimate based on extrapolating all-Uganda grower price for cotton from one or more of the following: the Buganda grower price, the set price for good (*saff*) cotton, average of district prices weighted by acreage in each district, or conversion of lint price statistics to seed cotton statistics by multiplying the lint weight by 3.12656 to obtain the seed cotton weight equivalent.

n.a. Not available.

I have not computed the grower share in the export price, as is usually done. For cotton, the problem with such a statistic is that, over time, the cotton seed which comprises nearly two-thirds of the weight of the seed cotton becomes increasingly valuable in its own right as a source for edible oil and animal feeds. For coffee, the problem is that the series contains only robusta grower prices, whereas the export prices are a combination of all types and grades of coffee.

Sources:

Blue Books; Annual Trade Reports; Statistical Abstracts; Report of the Commission of Enquiry into the Cotton Industry, 1929; Report of the Uganda Cotton Commission, 1938; Cyril Ehrlich, 'The Marketing of Cotton in Uganda, 1900-1950,' pp. 288 and 304; *Department of Agriculture Annual Reports, 1924, 1960; The Action Programme, 1977/78-1979/80; Budget Speeches;* and Commonwealth Team, *The Rehabilitation of the Economy of Uganda.*

Table A.4: Key Exports and Imports, 1905-1975 (Shs. '000)

	1905-06	1915-16	1925	1935	1945	1955	1965	1973	1975
Exports: Total	1,797	10,074	101,944	72,620	198,784	995,640	1,448,820	2,205,616	1,977,000
Cotton lint	22	4,909	93,720	56,455	140,515	327,720	335,233	336,010	210,900
Coffee	3	1,744	2,789	4,619	22,864	402,680	608,427	1,346,728	1,501,200
Copper	-	-	-	-	-	-	159,878	109,520	69,500
Tea	-	2	-	38	2,411	21,680	48,429	109,505	120,800
Cotton seed	-	195	2,456	2,716	2,845	15	-	-	-
Cottonseed oil	-	-	-	-	-	8,660	23,262	3,573	-
Cotton textiles	-	-	-	-	-	-	48,429	31,260	3,100
Animal feedstuffs	-	-	-	-	-	29,640	41,457	48,181	11,400
Chillies	381	337	59	45	815	1,142	1,122	1,001	-
Electricity	-	-	-	-	-	-	8,362	11,989	9,918
Fertilizer	-	-	-	-	-	-	6,868	5,985	-
Hides and skins	731	1,290	677	617	2,816	13,940	25,163	33,318	16,600
Ivory	531*	612*	571*	369*	754*	670*	n.d.	5,051	n.d.
Margarine/shortening	-	-	-	-	-	1,300	10,293	2,289	-
Rubber	266	113	1,374	408	973	381	-	-	-
Soap	-	-	-	-	-	-	8,473	604	-
Steel rods & bars	-	-	-	-	-	-	6,792	4,987	-
Sugar & confectionery	26	12	154	3,367	3,960	16,700	19,479	106	-

Imports									
Tobacco & cigarettes		—	31*	616	13,714	116,320	25,024	13,916	15,900
Imports: Total	2,860	34,167	53,555	32,879	65,625	758,820	1,151,100	1,139,038	1,470,000
Cloth (including blankets and synthetics)	1,060	5,261	18,945	7,624	25,956	81,680	98,640	35,582	
Of which, grey unbleached Americani	(480)	(2,036)	(4,669)	(1,779)	(6,471)	n.d.	n.d.	(1,270)	
Bicycles		—	87	3,160	1,023	675	20,180	3,380	1,395
Hoes		—	67	1,560	550	1,338	3,340	5,700	n.d.
Galvanized roofing		—	52	980	619	168	30,680	5,460	n.d.
Medicine		—	n.d.	n.d.	n.d.	1,508	6,460	13,480	28,132
Automobiles		—	n.d.	816	n.d.	720	30,980	41,700	4,801
Lorries and buses		—	n.d.	1,710α	n.d.	1,532	44,820	67,260	28,766
Tractors / agr. machinery		—			n.d.	483	8,700	16,540	7,668

Notes:
* Includes goods imported and subsequently re-exported.
α Includes agricultural tractors.
n.d. Data probably available, but not collected by author.
Sources:
Kenneth Ingham, *The Making of Modern Uganda*, p. 284; *Blue Books*, 1905/06, 1915/16, 1945; *Annual Trade Report of Kenya and Uganda*, 1925, 1935, 1945; *Statistical Abstracts 1957, 1967*; *Annual Trade Report of Tanzania, Uganda and Kenya, 1973*; and *The Action Programme, 1977/78-1979/80*.

Table A.5: External Barter Terms of Trade: Cotton Lint Exports Versus Grey Cloth Imports, 1906-1973

Year	Export price (fob) Mombasa Cotton lint £ / 100 lb. A	Import price (cif) Mombasa "Americani" Unbleached grey cloth £ /1,000 yd. B	Ratio A/B	Index (1911-12= 100)
1906/07	3.26	16.51	.197	103
1910/11	3.29	14.66	.224	117
1911/12	2.78	14.53	.191	100
1913/14	2.85	14.30	.199	104
1915/16	2.34	14.09	.166	87
1916/17	4.00	16.81	.238	125
1922	4.55	29.38	.155	81
1923	5.76	25.40	.227	119
1924	6.79	27.19	.250	131
1925	5.99	24.67	.243	127
1926	4.22	23.69	.178	93
1927	3.21	17.81	.180	94
1928	4.47	17.53	.255	134
1929	4.06	17.64	.230	120

Year	Export price (fob) Mombasa Cotton lint £ / 100 lb. A	Import Price (cif) Mombasa "Americani" Unbleached grey cloth £ /1,000 yd. B	Ratio A/B	Index (1911-12= 100)
1941	2.91	16.84	.173	91
1942	3.03	28.21	.107	56
1943	6.60	60.10	.110	58
1944	6.67	58.19	.115	60
1945	6.66	44.89	.148	77
1946	6.42	47.90	.134	70
1947	7.05	60.09$^{\alpha}$	.117	61
1948	10.73	70.21	.153	80
1955	13.42	46.59$^{\omega}$	.288	151
1958	11.74	46.24^{k}	.254	133
1959	10.36	50.88	.204	107
1960	11.34	58.28	.195	102
1961	12.04	57.98	.208	109
1962	11.47	56.29	.204	107

Year				Year			
1930	3.01	12.97	.232	121	1963	10.91	49.93	.219	115
1931	1.98	11.25	.176	92	1964	11.18	47.74	.234	123
1932	1.90	10.18	.187	98	1965	11.04	45.64	.242	127
1933	2.27	9.11	.249	130	1966	10.00	46.77	.214	112
1934	2.56	9.35	.274	143	1967	9.58	49.49	.194	102
1935	2.78	9.39	.296	155	1968	10.91	52.37	.208	109
1936	2.58	9.37	.275	144	1969	10.79	75.55	.143	75
1937	3.15	10.36	.304	159	1970	10.22	93.62	.109	57
1938	2.12	9.76	.217	114	1971	11.64	99.61^k	.117	61
1939	2.01	9.08	.221	116	1972	12.66	65.68^u	.193	101
1940	3.10	12.05	.257	135	1973	11.82	75.68^u	.156	82

Notes:

α Before 1947, the price is per linear yard; from 1947 onward, the price is per square yard.

ω Estimate based on average price per yard for all types of imported cloth and relationship between grey cloth price and that average.

k The 1958-1971 series is based on Kenyan import price statistics for grey cloth.

u Based on Ugandan price statistics for imported grey cloth.

Observervations:

The external barter terms of trade index above shows the variation in the amount of cotton cloth Uganda could purchase with a given amount of cotton lint. For example, in 1911-12 Uganda had to export 523 lbs. of cotton lint to import 1,000 yards of unbleached grey cloth. In 1935, Uganda needed only 338 lbs. of lint to purchase the same amount of cloth, or could purchase 55 per cent more. By contrast, in 1942 Uganda required 931 lbs of lint to purchase 1,000 yards of cloth, or could purchase only 56 per cent of what it could in 1911-12.

SELECT BIBLIOGRAPHY

A useful overview of the files in the National Archives at Entebbe may be found in Tarsis Kabwegyere, *The Politics of State Formation* (q.v. below), pp. 259-68. An extensive list of government publications and other sources relating to Uganda in the colonial period may be found in Harlow, Chilver and Smith (eds.), *[Oxford] History of East Africa,* vol. II, pp. 700-25; and Low and Smith (eds.), *[Oxford] History of East Africa,* vol. III, pp. 614-58.

Abbreviations:

CAAS   Canadian Association of African Studies
CUP   Cambridge University Press
EAISR East African Institute of Social Research
EALB   East African Literature Bureau
EAPH   East African Publishing House
MISR   Makerere Institute of Social Research (formerly EAISR)
OUP   Oxford University Press
SIAS   Scandinavian Institute of African Studies
UGP   Uganda Government Printer
USSC   Universities of East Africa Social Sciences Council
CJAS   *Canadian Journal of African Studies*
JAH   *Journal of African History*
JMAS   *Journal of Modern African Studies*
UJ   *Uganda Journal*

Aasland, Tertit, *On the Move-to-the-Left in Uganda, 1969-71.* Research Report No. 26. Uppsala: SIAS, 1974

Adoko, Akena, *Uganda Crisis.* Kampala: African Publishers, 1970

Alibaruho, George. 'The Impact of Marketing Board Policy on the Level and Variability of Cotton Producer Prices in Uganda, 1945-1969.' Discussion Paper No. 199. Nairobi: Institute for Development Studies, 1974

Alpers, Edward, A. *Ivory and Slaves in East Central Africa.* London: Heinemann, 1975

Amin, Idi. *Development on the Basis of Self-Reliance, 4 August 1974.* Entebbe: UGP, 1974

—— 'Speech to the Asian Conference, 8 December 1971.' *East Africa Journal* 9 (February 1972): 2-5

—— *Speeches by His Excellency the President General Idi Amin Dada.* Vol. 1 (1972). Vol. 2 (1973). Entebbe: UGP

Amnesty International. *Human Rights in Uganda.* London: AI, June 1978. (AFR 59/05/78)

Anyang-Nyongo, Peter. 'The Civil Servant in Uganda.' *East Africa Journal* 8, no. 4 (April 1971): 9-19

Apter, David. *The Political Kingdom in Uganda.* 2nd edn. Princeton: Princeton University Press, 1967

Aranow, Philip Thompson. 'Alien Entrepreneurs: The Indians in Uganda, 1958-68.' BA Honours Thesis, Harvard College, 1969

Atanda, J.A. 'The Bakopi in the Kingdom of Buganda, 1900-1912.' *UJ* 33, no. 2 (1969): 151-62

Atkinson, Ronald Raymond. 'A History of the Western Acholi of Uganda, circa 1675-1900.' PhD Thesis, Northwestern University, 1978

Badenoch, A.C. 'Graduated Taxation in the Teso District of Uganda.' *Journal of Local Administration Overseas* 1, no. 1 (January 1962): 15-22

Baker, S.J.K. 'The Population Map of Uganda.' *UJ* 1, no. 2 (April 1934): 134-44

Baryaruha, Azarias. *Factors Affecting Industrial Employment; A Study of the Ugandan Experience, 1954 to 1964.* Nairobi: OUP for EAISR, 1967

Beattie, John. *Bunyoro: An African Kingdom.* New York: Holt, Rinehart and Winston, 1960

—— 'The Kibanja System of Land Tenure in Bunyoro.' *Journal of African Administration* 6, no. 1 (January 1954): 18-28

—— *The Nyoro State.* Oxford: Clarendon Press, 1971

Bienen, Henry. *Armies and Parties in Africa.* New York: Africana, 1978

Bowles, B.O. 'Economic Anti-Colonialism and British Reaction in Uganda, 1936-1955.' *CJAS* 9, no. 1 (1975): 51-9

Brett, E.A. *Colonialism and Underdevelopment in East Africa; The Politics of Economic Change, 1919-39.* London: Heinemann, 1973

Burke, Fred. G. *Local Government and Politics in Uganda.* Syracuse, NY: Syracuse University Press, 1964

—— 'The New Role of the Chief in Uganda.' *Journal of African Administration* 10, no. 3 (July 1958): 153-60

Bustin, Edouard. 'L'Africanisation des cadres administratifs de l'Ouganda.' *Civilisations* 9, no. 2 (1959): 133-50

Campbell, Horace, *Four Essays on Neo-Colonialism in Uganda*. Toronto: Dumont Press, 1975

Cohen, David William. *The Historical Tradition of Busoga*. Oxford: Clarendon Press, 1972

—— 'Misango's Song: Adventure and Structure in the Precolonial African Past.' Paper presented to Centre of African Studies, Dalhousie University, Halifax, Nova Scotia, 29 February 1980

Coles, Diana M.S. *The Vegetable Oil Crushing Industry in East Africa*. Nairobi: OUP for MISR, 1968

Commonwealth Team of Experts, *The Rehabilitation of the Economy of Uganda*. 2 vols. London: Commonwealth Secretariat, 1979

Cook, Albert R. 'Further Memories of Uganda.' *UJ* 2, no. 2 (October 1934): 97-115

—— 'Kampala During the Closing Years of the Last Century.' *UJ* 1, no. 2 (April 1934): 83-95

Crazzolara, J.P. 'The Lwoo People.' *UJ* 5, no. 1 (1937/38): 1-21

Dahlberg, F.M. 'The Emergence of a Dual Governing Elite in Uganda.' *JMAS* 9, no. 4 (December 1971): 618-25

Decalo, Samuel. *Coups and Army Rule in Africa; Studies in Military Style*. New Haven and London: Yale University Press, 1976

Denoon, D.J.W. 'Agents of Colonial Rule; Kigezi, 1908-1930.' USSC Paper, Kampala, 1968

Doornbos, Martin, 'Images and Reality of Stratification in Pre-Colonial Nkore.' *CJAS* 7, no. 3 (1973): 477-95

—— 'Protest Movements in Western Uganda: Some Parallels and Contrasts.' USSC Conference Paper, Nairobi, December 1966

Driberg, J.H. 'The Lango District.' *Geographical Journal* 58, no. 2 (1921): 119-33

Dunbar, A.R. *A History of Bunyoro-Kitara*. Nairobi: OUP for EAISR, 1965

Dyson-Hudson, Neville. *Karimojong Politics*. Oxford: Clarendon Press, 1966

Edel, May Mandelbaum. *The Chiga of Western Uganda*. New York: OUP, 1957

Ehrlich, Cyril. 'Cotton and the Uganda Economy, 1903-1909.' *UJ* 21, no. 2 (1957): 169-72

—— 'The Economy of Buganda, 1893-1903.' *UJ* 20, no. 1 (1956): 17-26

—— 'The Marketing of Cotton in Uganda, 1900-1950.' PhD Thesis, University of London, 1958

—— 'Some Social and Economic Implications of Paternalism in

Uganda.' *JAH* 4, no. 2 (1963): 275-85

—— 'The Uganda Economy, 1903-1945.' in *[Oxford] History of East Africa.* Vol. II: 395-475. Edited by Harlow, Chilver and Smith (q.v.)

Elkan, Walter. *An African Labour Force: Two Case Studies in East African Employment.* Kampala: EAISR, 1956

—— 'A Half Century of Cotton Marketing in Uganda.' *Indian Journal of Economics* 38, no. 4 (April 1958): 365-74

——*Migrants and Proletarians; Urban Labour in the Economic Development of Uganda.* London: OUP for EAISR, 1960

—— 'Regional Disparities of Income and Taxation in Uganda.' EAISR Conference Paper, Moshi, 1957

Emwanu, G. 'The Reception of Alien Rule in Teso, 1896-1927.' *UJ* 31, no. 2 (1967): 171-82

Engholm, G.F. 'Decline of Immigrant Influence on the Uganda Administration, 1945-62.' *UJ* 31, no. 1 (1967): 73-88

Fallers, Lloyd A. *Bantu Bureaucracy; A Century of Political Evolution Among the Basoga.* 2nd edn. Chicago: University of Chicago Press, 1965

——, ed. *The King's Men; Leadership and Status in Buganda on the Eve of Independence.* London: OUP, 1964

Fawcett, A.H. 'Katwe Salt Deposits.' *UJ* 37 (1973): 63-80

Flint, John. 'The Wider Background to Partition and Colonial Occupation.' In *[Oxford] History of East Africa.* Vol. 1: 353-90. Edited by Oliver and Mathew (q.v.)

Frank, Charles S. *The Sugar Industry in East Africa.* Nairobi: EAPH for EAISR, 1965

Frederick, Kenneth D. 'The Role of Market Forces and Planning in Uganda's Economic Development, 1900-1938.' *Eastern Africa Economic Review* (n.s.) 1, no. 1 (June 1969): 47-62

Fuller, Thomas, 'African Labour and Training in the Uganda Colonial Economy.' *International Journal of African Historical Studies* 10, no. 1 (1977): 77-95

Furley, O.W. 'The Sudanese Troops in Uganda.' *African Affairs* (London) 58, no. 233 (October 1959): 311-28

Galbraith, John S. *Mackinnon and East Africa, 1878-1895.* Cambridge: CUP, 1972

Gartrell, Beverley. 'The Ruling Ideas of a Ruling Elite: British Colonial Officials in Uganda, 1944-52.' PhD Thesis, City University of New York, 1979

Gee, T.W. 'Uganda's Legislative Council Between the Wars.' *UJ* 25 (March 1961): 54-63

Gershenberg, Irving. *Commercial Banking in Uganda.* Kampala: MISR, 1973

—— 'Slouching Towards Socialism: Obote's Uganda.' *African Studies Review* 15, no. 1 (April 1972): 79-95

Gertzel, Cherry. 'How Kabaka Yekka Came to Be.' *Africa Report* 9 (October 1964): 9-13

——*Party and Locality in Northern Uganda, 1945-1962.* London: University of London, Athlone Press, 1974

Ghai, Dharam P. 'Concepts and Strategies of Economic Independence.' *JMAS* 11, no. 1 (1973): 21-42

Gingyera-Pinycwa, A.G.G. *Apolo Milton Obote and His Times.* New York and Lagos: NOK Publishers, 1978

Girling, F,K. *The Acholi of Uganda.* London: HMSO, 1960

Goldschmidt, Walter. *Culture and Behavior of the Sebei.* Berkeley: University of California Press, 1976

Goldthorpe, J.E. *An African Elite; Makerere College Students, 1922-65.* Nairobi: OUP, 1965

Gray, John. 'Kakunguru in Bukedi.' *UJ* 27, no. 1 (1963): 31-59

—— 'Mutesa's Caravan to Zanzibar, 1870-72.' *UJ* 11, no. 1 (1947): 96-7

Gray, Richard, and Birmingham, David, eds. *Pre-Colonial African Trade; Essays on Trade in Central and Eastern Africa Before 1900.* London: OUP, 1970

Green, Reginald Herbold. 'The East African Community: The End of the Road.' In *Africa Contemporary Record, 1976-77,* pp. A 59-67. Edited by Colin Legum. New York: Africana, 1977

—— 'The East African Community: Death, Funeral, Inheritance.' In *Africa Contemporary Record, 1977-78,* pp. A 125-37. Edited by Colin Legum. New York: Africana of Holmes & Meier, 1979

Greenberg, Joseph H. *The Languages of Africa.* 3rd edn. Bloomington: Indiana University Press, 1970

Gukiina, Peter M. *Uganda; A Case Study in African Political Development.* Notre Dame, Indiana: University of Notre Dame Press, 1972

Gulliver, Pamela, and Gulliver, P.H. *The Central Nilo-Hamites.* London: International African Institute, 1953

Gutkind, Peter C.W. *The Royal Capital of Buganda.* The Hague: Mouton and Company, 1963

Gwyn, David. *Idi Amin.* Boston: Little, Brown and Company, 1977

Hailey, Lord. *Native Administration in the British African Territories: Part I, East Africa.* London: HMSO, 1950

Hancock, I.R. 'Patriotism and Neo-Traditionalism in Buganda: The

Kabaka Yakka ("The King Alone") Movement, 1961-62.' *JAH* 11, no. 3 (1970): 419-34

Hansen, Holger Bernt. *Ethnicity and Military Rule in Uganda.*. Research Report No. 43. Uppsala: SIAS, 1977

Harlow, Vincent; Chilver, E.M.; and Smith, Alison, eds. *[Oxford] History of East Africa*. Vol. II. Oxford: Clarendon Press, 1965

Harmsworth, Josephine. 'Cows for Christmas.' USSC Paper, Dar es Salaam, January 1963

—— 'Dynamics of Kisoga Land Tenure.' USSC Paper, Limuru, Kenya, January 1962

Harris, Douglas, *Development in Uganda, 1947 to 1955-56*. Wisbech, England: Balding and Mansell for the Government of Uganda, n.d. [1955?]

Hattersley, C.W. *The Baganda at Home.* London: Religious Tract Society, 1908; reprinted London: Frank Cass, 1968

Hayley, T.T.S. *The Anatomy of Lango Religion and Groups.* Cambridge: CUP, 1947

Hazlewood, Arthur. 'Trade Balances and Statutory Marketing in Primary Export Economies.' *Economic Journal* 67 (March 1957): 73-82

Herring, Ralph. 'Centralization, Stratification and Incorporation: Case Studies from Northeastern Uganda.' *CJAS* 7, no. 3 (1973): 497-514

Holt, P.M. *The Mahdist State in the Sudan, 1881-1898*. Oxford: Clarendon Press, 1958

Hopkins, Anthony G. 'Imperial Business in Africa; Part II. Interpretations.' *JAH* 17, no. 2 (1976): 267-90

Hopkins, Terence K. 'Politics in Uganda: The Buganda Question.' In *Boston University Papers on Africa*, pp. 251-90. Edited by Jeffrey Butler and A.A. Castagno. New York: Praeger, 1967

Howell, John. 'Horn of Africa: Lessons from the Sudan Conflict.' *International Affairs* (London) 54, no. 1 (July 1978): 421-36

Hoyle, W.E. 'Early Days in Kampala.' *UJ* 21, no. 1 (March 1957): 91-8

Ibingira, Grace. *The Forging of an African Nation.* Kampala: Uganda Publishing House, and New York: Viking Press, 1973

Imlah, Albert H. *Economic Elements in the Pax Britannica*. Cambridge, Mass.: Harvard University Press, 1958

Ingham, Kenneth. *The Kingdom of Toro in Uganda*. London: Methuen, 1975

—— *The Making of Modern Uganda.* London: George Allen and Unwin, 1958

International Bank for Reconstruction and Development (World Bank) Mission to Uganda. *The Economic Development of Uganda*. Baltimore: Johns Hopkins University Press, 1962

International Commission of Jurists. *Violations of Human Rights and the Rule of Law in Uganda*. Edited by Michael Posner. Geneva: ICJ, 1974

Jamal, Valimohamed. 'The Role of Cotton in Uganda's Economic Development.' In *Commodity Exports and African Economic Development*, pp. 135-54. Edited by Scott R. Pearson and John Cownie. Lexington, Mass.: Lexington Books, 1974

Job, A.L. 'Mining in Uganda.' *UJ* 31, no. 1 (1967): 43-61

Johnston, Harry. *The Uganda Protectorate*. 2 vols. London: Hutchinson and Company, 1902

Jones, H. Gresford. *Uganda in Transformation*. London: Church Missionary Society, 1926

Jørgensen, Jan. 'Multinational Corporation Involvement in Agricultural Inputs in East Africa: Two Case Studies.' CAAS Conference Paper, Victoria, British Columbia, February 1976

—— 'Structural Dependence and the Move to the Left.' In *The Politics of Africa; Dependence and Development*, pp. 43-72. Edited by Timothy Shaw and Kenneth Heard. London: Longman for the Dalhousie University Press, 1979

Kabwegyere, Tarsis. 'The Asian Question in Uganda.' *East Africa Journal* 9, no. 6 (June 1972): 10-13

—— 'The Dynamics of Colonial Violence: The Inductive System in Uganda.' *Journal of Peace Research* 9, no. 4 (1972): 303-14

—— *The Politics of State Formation; The Nature and Effects of Colonialism in Uganda*. Nairobi: EALB, 1974

Kagwa, Apolo. *The Kings of Buganda*. Translated and edited by M.S.M. Kiwanuka. Nairobi: EAPH, 1971

Kajubi, W. Senteza. 'Coffee and Prosperity in Buganda: Some Aspects of Economic and Social Change.' *UJ* 29, no. 2 (1965): 135-47

Kamau, Joseph, and Cameron, Andrew. *Lust to Kill; The Rise and Fall of Idi Amin*. London: Corgi, 1979

Karugire, Samwiri Rubaraza. *A History of the Kingdom of Nkore in Western Uganda to 1896*. Oxford: Clarendon Press, 1971

Kasfir, Nelson. 'Cultural Sub-Nationalism in Uganda.' In *The Politics of Cultural Sub-Nationalism in Uganda*, pp. 51-148. Edited by Victor Olorunsola. New York: Anchor Books, Doubleday, 1972

Kennedy, T.J. 'Study of Economic Motivation Involved in Peasant Cultivation of Cotton.' *East African Economics Review* 10, no. 2

(December 1963): 88-95

King, Anne. 'The Yakan Cult and Lugbara Response to Colonial Rule.' *Azania* (Nairobi) 5 (1970): 1-25

King, Noel; Kasozi, Abdu; and Oded Arye. *Islam and the Confluence of Religions in Uganda, 1840-1966*. Tallahassee, Florida: American Academy of Religion, 1973

Kiwanuka, Semakula. 'Diplomacy of the Lost Counties, 1900-1964.' *Mawazo* 4, no. 2 (1974): 111-41

——*A History of Buganda from the Foundation of the Kingdom to 1900*. London: Longman, 1971

Kiyaga-Mulindwa, David. 'Social Change in Pre-Colonial Buganda.' CAAS Conference Paper, Halifax, Nova Scotia, February 1974

Kjekshus, Helge. *Ecology Control and Economic Development in East African History; The Case of Tanganyika, 1850-1950*. London: Heinemann, 1977

Kyemba, Henry. *A State of Blood; The Inside Story of Idi Amin*. New York: Grossett & Dunlap, Ace Books, 1977

Ladefoged, Peter; Glick, Ruth; and Criper, Clive. *Language in Uganda*. London: OUP, 1972

La Fontaine, J.S. *The Gisu of Uganda*. London: International African Institute, 1959

Lamphear, John. *The Traditional History of the Jie of Uganda*. Oxford: Clarendon Press, 1976

——, and Webster, J.B. 'The Jie-Acholi War; Oral Evidence from Two Sides of the Battle Front.' *UJ* 35, no. 1 (1971): 23-42

Langlands, Bryan. 'Students and Politics in Uganda.' *African Affairs* (London) 76, no. 302 (January 1977): 3-20

Lawrance, J.C.D. *The Iteso*. London: OUP, 1957

——'A Pilot Scheme for Grant of Land Titles in Uganda.' *Journal of African Administration* 12, no. 3 (July 1960): 135-43

——'The Position of Chiefs in Local Government in Uganda.' *Journal of African Administration* 8, no. 4 (October 1956): 186-92

Legum, Colin, ed. *Africa Contemporary Record*. 1971-2 through 1977-8. London: Rex Collings; and New York: Africana of Holmes and Meier

——*Must We Lose Africa?* London: W.H. Allen, 1954

Leys, Colin, *Politicians and Policies; An Essay on Politics in Acholi, 1962-65*. Nairobi: EAPH, 1967

Low, Donald Anthony. *Buganda in Modern History*. Berkeley and Los Angeles: University of California Press, 1971

——'The Composition of the Buganda Lukiko in 1902.' *UJ* 23 (March

1959): 64-8

—— 'Uganda: The Establishment of the Protectorate, 1894-1919.' In *[Oxford] History of East Africa.* Vol. II: 57-120. Edited by Harlow, Chilver and Smith (q.v.)

—— 'Uganda Unhinged.' *International Affairs* (London) 49, no. 2 (April 1973): 219-28

——, ed. *The Mind of Buganda; Documents of the Modern History of an African Kingdom.* Berkeley and Los Angeles: University of California Press, 1971

——, and Pratt, R. Cranford. *Buganda and British Overrule, 1900-1955.* London: OUP, 1960

——, and Smith, Alison, eds. *[Oxford] History of East Africa.* Vol. III. Oxford: Clarendon Press, 1976

Loxley, John. 'The Development of the Monetary and Financial System of the East African Currency Area, 1950-64.' PhD Thesis, University of Leeds, 1966

Lugard, Frederick. *The Diaries of Lord Lugard.* Edited by Margery Perham. Evanston: Northwestern University Press, 1959

—— *The Dual Mandate in Tropical Africa.* 4th edn. Edinburgh and London: William Blackwood and Sons, 1929

—— *The Rise of Our East African Empire: Early Efforts in Nyasaland and Uganda.* Edinburgh and London: William Blackwood and Sons, 1893

Lury, D.A. 'Dayspring Mishandled? The Uganda Economy 1945-60.' *[Oxford] History of East Africa.* Vol. III: 212-50. Edited by D.A. Low and Alison Smith (q.v.)

McMaster, David N. *A Subsistence Crop Geography of Uganda.* Bude, Cornwall: Geographical Publications, 1962

Madhvani Group, *Enterprise in East Africa.* Nairobi: United Africa Press, 1971

Magina, Magina. 'Uganda at the Crossroads.' *Africa* [newsmagazine] no. 109 (September 1980): 12-19

Mamdani, Mahmood. *Politics and Class Formation in Uganda.* New York: Monthly Review Press, 1976

—— Review of *Colonialism and Underdevelopment in East Africa*, by E.A. Brett. *African Review* (Dar es Salaam) 3, no. 4 (1973): 635-44

Martin, David. *General Amin.* London: Faber and Faber, 1974

Martin, Michel L. 'The Uganda Military Coup of 1971; A Study of Protest.' *Ufahamu* 3, no. 3 (Winter 1972): 81-121

Masefield, G.B. 'Agricultural Change in Uganda, 1945-1960.' *Stanford University Food Research Institute Studies* 3, no. 2 (May 1962):

87-124

Matson, A.T. 'Baganda Merchant Venturers.' *UJ* 32, no. 1 (1968): 1-15

Mazrui, Ali A. *Soldiers and Kinsmen in Uganda.* Beverly Hills: Sage, 1975

—— , ed. *Cultural Engineering and Nation-Building in East Africa.* Evanston, Illinois: Northwestern University Press, 1972

Mettam, R.W.M. 'A Short History of Rinderpest with Special Reference to Africa.' *UJ* 5, no. 1 (1937/38): 22-6

Mettrick, Hal. *Aid in Uganda: Agriculture.* London: Overseas Development Institute, 1967

Middleton, John. *The Lugbara of Uganda.* New York: Holt, Rinehart and Winston, 1965

Mitchell, Philip. *African Afterthoughts.* London: Hutchinson, 1954

Mohiddin, Ahmed. 'Changing of the Guard.' *Mawazo* 2, no. 4 (December 1970): 19-28

Morris, H.F. *A History of Ankole.* Nairobi: EALB, 1962

Morris, H.S. *Indians in Uganda.* Chicago: University of Chicago Press, 1968

Motani, Nizar A. *On His Majesty's Service in Uganda; The Origins of Uganda's African Civil Service, 1912-1940.* Syracuse: Maxwell School of Citizenship and Public Affairs, Syracuse University, 1977

Mounteney-Jephson, A.J. *Emin Pasha and the Rebellion at the Equator.* New York: Charles Scribner's Sons, 1890

Moyse-Bartlett, H. *The King's African Rifles.* Aldershot: Gale and Polden, 1956

Mudoola, Dan. 'Colonial Chief-Making: Busoga, A Case Study 1900-1940.' USSC Conference Paper, Dar es Salaam, December 1970

—— 'The Politics of Higher Education in a Colonial Situation: Uganda, 1920-1941.' Unpublished paper, University of Dar es Salaam, 1978

Mujaju, Akiiki. 'The Demise of UPCYL and the Rise of NUYO in Uganda. *African Review* (Dar es Salaam) 3, no. 2 (1973): 291-307

—— 'The Political Crisis of Church Institutions in Uganda.' *African Affairs* (London) 75, no. 298 (1976): 67-85

—— 'The Role of the UPC as a Party of Government in Uganda.' *CJAS* 10, no. 3 (1976): 443-67

Mukherjee, Ramkrishna. *The Problem of Uganda; A Study in Acculturation.* Berlin: Akademie-Verlag, 1956

Mukwaya, A.B. *Land Tenure in Buganda; Present Day Tendencies.* Kampala: EAISR, 1953

—— 'The Rise of the Uganda African Farmers' Union in Buganda, 1947-1949.' EAISR Conference Paper, Moshi, Tanganyika, June 1957

Mulira, E.M.K. *Troubled Uganda*. London: Fabian Society, Colonial
Bureau Pamphlet, 1950

Musazi, I.K. 'Strikes and Disturbances in Uganda: Their Origins and
Results.' In Milton Obote Foundation, *Labour Problems in Uganda*,
pp. 17-25. Kampala: Milton Obote Foundation, 1966

Mutesa, Edward, *Desecration of My Kingdom*. London: Constable,
1967

National Christian Council of Kenya. *Who Controls Industry in Kenya?;
Report of a Working Party*. Nairobi: EAPH, 1968

Nayenga, Peter F.B. 'Myths and Realities of Idi Amin Dada's Uganda.'
African Studies Review 22, no. 2 (September 1979): 127-40

Ngologoza, P. *Kigezi and Its People*. Nairobi: EALB, 1969

Njala, A.S., and Obura, S.A. 'Evolution of the East African Currencies.'
Bank of Uganda Quarterly Bulletin 3, no. 2 (March 1971): 51-4

Nyakatura, J.W. *Anatomy of an African Kingdom* (Abakama ba
Bunyoro-Kitara). Edited by Godfrey N. Uzoigwe and translated by
Teopista Muganwa. Garden City, NY: Anchor Books, Doubleday,
1973

Nye, Joseph S., Jr. 'TANU and UPC: The Impact of Independence on
Two African Nationalist Parties.' In *Boston University Papers on
Africa*, pp. 224-50. Edited by Jeffrey Butler and A.A. Castagno.
New York: Praeger, 1967

——*Pan-Africanism and East African Integration*. Cambridge, Mass.:
Harvard University Press, 1965

Obote, A. Milton. *The Common Man's Charter with Appendices*.
Entebbe: UGP, 1970

—— 'The Footsteps of Uganda's Revolution.' *East Africa Journal* 5
(October 1968): 7-13

—— 'Policy Proposals for Uganda's Educational Needs.' *Mawazo* 2,
no. 2 (December 1969): 3-9

——*Proposals for New Methods of Election of Representatives of the
People to Parliament*. Kampala: Milton Obote Foundation, 1970

Ocheng, D.O. 'Land Tenure in Acholi.' *UJ* 19, no. 1 (March 1955):
57-61

O'Connor, A.M. *Railways and Development in Uganda*. Nairobi: OUP
for EAISR, 1965

Odada, M.A.E. 'The Kumam: Langi or Iteso?' *UJ* 35, no. 2 (1971):
139-52

Odhiambo, E.S. Atieno. 'The Paradox of Collaboration: The Uganda
Case.' *East Africa Journal* 9 (October 1972): 19-25

Ogot, B.A., ed. *Zamani; A Survey of East African History*. 2nd edn.

Nairobi: EAPH and Longman, 1974

Oliver, Roland, and Mathew, Gervase, eds. *[Oxford] History of East Africa*. Vol. 1. Oxford: Clarendon Press, 1963

Olivier, Henry. 'Some Aspects of the Owen Falls Scheme.' *UJ* 17, no. 1 (March 1953): 28-37

Pain, Dennis. 'The Nubians.' In *Expulsion of a Minority*, pp. 176-92. Edited by Michael Twaddle. London: University of London, Athlone Press, 1975

Parson, Jack, 'Africanizing Trade in Uganda: The Final Solution.' *Africa Today* 20, no. 1 (Winter 1973): 59-72

Perlman, M.L. 'Land Tenure in Toro.' USSC Conference Paper, Limuru, Kenya, January 1962

Pirouet, M. Louise. 'The Achievement of Peace in the Sudan.' *Journal of Eastern African Research and Development* (Nairobi) 6, no. 1 (1976)

Posnansky, Merrick. 'Kingship, Archeology and Historical Myth.' *UJ* 30, no. 1 (1966): 1-12

Powesland, Philip Geoffrey. *Economic Policy and Labour*. Edited by Walter Elkan. Kampala: EAISR, 1957

Pratt, R. Cranford. 'Administration and Politics in Uganda, 1919-45.' In *[Oxford] History of East Africa*. Vol. II: 476-541. Edited by Harlow, Chilver and Smith (q.v.)

—— 'Nationalism in Uganda.' *Political Studies* 9, no. 2 (1961): 157-78

Purseglove, J.W. 'Re-settlement in Kigezi.' *Journal of African Administration* 3, no. 1 (January 1951): 13-21

Ramchandani, R.R. *Uganda Asians; The End of an Enterprise*. Bombay: United Asia Publications, 1976

Ravenhill, F.J. 'Military Rule in Uganda; The Politics of Survival.' *African Studies Review*, 17, no. 1 (April 1974): 229-60

Redford, Arthur. *Manchester Merchants and Foreign Trade*. Vol 2: *1850-1939*. Manchester: Manchester University Press, 1956

Richards, Audrey I., ed. *East African Chiefs*. London: Faber and Faber, 1959

——, ed. *Economic Development and Tribal Change; A Study of Immigrant Labour in Buganda*. Cambridge: W. Heffer and Sons for EAISR, 1954

Roberts, Andrew. 'Evolution of the Uganda Protectorate.' *UJ* 27, no. 1 (1963): 95-106

—— 'The "Lost Counties" of Bunyoro.' *UJ* 26, no. 2 (September 1962): 194-9

—— 'The Sub-Imperialism of the Baganda.' *JAH* 3, no. 3 (1962):

435-50

Robinson, Ronald; Gallagher, John; and Denny, Alice. *Africa and the Victorians; The Climax of Imperialism*. New York: St Martin's Press, 1961

Rowe, John A. *Lugard at Kampala*. Makerere History Paper No. 3. Kampala: Longmans of Uganda, 1969

—— 'Pattern of Political Administration in Pre-Colonial Buganda.' CAAS Conference Paper, Halifax, Nova Scotia, February 1974

—— 'Revolution in Buganda 1856-1900; Part One: The Reign of Kabaka Mukabya Mutesa, 1856-1884.' PhD Thesis, University of Wisconsin, 1966

Ryan, Selwyn. 'Economic Nationalism and Socialism in Uganda.' *Journal of Commonwealth Political Studies* 11, no. 2 (July 1973): 140-58

—— 'Uganda: A Balance Sheet of the Revolution.' *Mawazo* 3, no. 1 (June 1971): 37-64

Saul, John. 'The Unsteady State: Uganda, Obote and General Amin.' *Review of African Political Economy*, no. 5 (January-April 1976): 12-38

Schnitzer, Eduard [Emin Pasha]. *Emin Pasha in Central Africa*. Edited by G. Schweinfurth and others. London: George Philip and Son, 1888

Scott, Roger. *The Development of Trade Unions in Uganda*. Nairobi: EAPH, 1966

Shepherd, George, Jr. *They Wait in Darkness*. New York: John Day Company, 1955

Sheriff, Abdul. 'The Rise of a Commercial Empire; An Aspect of the Economic History of Zanzibar, 1770-1873.' PhD Thesis, University of London, 1971

Shiroya, Okete. 'Northwestern Uganda in the Nineteenth Century; Inter-ethnic Trade.' USSC Conference Paper, Dar es Salaam, December 1970

Short, Philip. 'Uganda; Putting it in Perspective.' *Africa Report* 18 (March-April 1973): 34-8

Southall, Aidan, W. *Alur Society*. Nairobi: Oxford University Press, 1953

—— 'General Amin and the Coup: Great Man or Historical Inevitability?' *JMAS* 13, no. 1 (1975): 85-105

—— 'Micropolitics in Uganda; Traditional and Modern Politics.' EAISR Conference Paper, Dar es Salaam, January 1963

——, and Gutkind, Peter C.W. *Townsmen in the Making; Kampala and its Suburbs*. Kampala: EAISR, 1957

Southall, Roger. *Parties and Politics in Bunyoro*. Kampala: MISR, 1972

Special Correspondent, 'The Uganda Army: Nexus of Power.' *Africa Report* 11 (December 1966): 37-9

Steinhart, Edward I. *Conflict and Collaboration: The Kingdoms of Western Uganda, 1890-1907*. Princeton: Princeton University Press, 1977

Stemler, A.B.L.; Harlan, J.R.; and Dewet, J.M.J. 'Caudatum Sorghums and Speakers of Chari-Nile Languages in Africa.' *Journal of African History* 16, no. 2 (1975): 161-83

Stonehouse, John. *Prohibited Immigrant*. London: Bodley Head, 1960

Stoutjesdijk, E.J. *Uganda's Manufacturing Sector*. Nairobi: EAPH, 1967

Strate, Jeffrey T. *Post-Military Coup Strategy in Uganda*. Athens, Ohio: Ohio University Center for International Studies, 1973

Sundström, Lars. *The Exchange Economy of Pre-Colonial Tropical Africa*. London: C. Hurst and Company, 1974

Sutton, J.E.G. 'The Settlement of East Africa.' In *Zamani*, pp. 70-97. Edited by B.A. Ogot (q.v.)

Thomas, Elizabeth Marshall. *Warrior Herdsmen*. New York: Alfred A. Knopf, 1965

Thomas, Harold Beken. 'Capax Imperii: The Story of Semei Kakunguru.' *UJ* 6, no. 3 (January 1939): 125-36

——, and Scott, Robert. *Uganda*. London: Humphrey Milford and OUP, 1935

Tosh, John, *Clan Leaders and Colonial Chiefs in Lango, Circa 1800-1939*. Oxford: Clarendon Press, 1978

—— 'Lango Agriculture During the Early Colonial Period; Land and Labour in a Cash-Crop Economy.' *JAH* 19, no. 3 (1978): 415-39

—— 'Small-Scale Resistance in Uganda: The Lango Rising at Adwari in 1919.' *Azania* (Nairobi) 9 (1974): 51-64

Tothill, J.D., and the Staff of the Department of Agriculture, Uganda. *Agriculture in Uganda*. London: Humphrey Milford, OUP, 1940

Trowell, H.C. 'Food Protein and Kwashiokor.' *UJ* 21, no. 1 (March 1957): 81-90

Trowell, Margaret, and Wachsmann, K.P. *Tribal Crafts of Uganda*. London: OUP, 1953

Twaddle, Michael. 'The *Bakungu* Chiefs of Buganda under British Colonial Rule, 1900-1930.' *Journal of African History* 10, no. 2 (1969): 309-22

——, ed. *Expulsion of a Minority*. London: University of London, Athlone Press, 1975

Twining, E.F. 'Uganda Medals and Decorations.' *UJ* 2, no. 3 (January 1935): 209-25

Uchendu, V.C. 'Traditional Work Groups in Economic Development.' USSC Conference Paper, Dar es Salaam, December 1970

Ullman, Richard H. 'Human Rights and Economic Power; The United States Versus Idi Amin.' *Foreign Affairs* 56, no. 3 (April 1978): 529-43

Uzoigwe, G.N. 'Pre-Colonial Markets in Bunyoro-Kitara.' USSC Conference Paper, Dar es Salaam, December 1970

—— *Revolution and Revolt in Bunyoro-Kitara.* Makerere History Paper No. 5. Kampala: Longman Uganda, 1970

—— , ed. *Tarikh* (Ibadan) 3, no. 2: *The Peoples of Uganda in the Nineteenth Century.* London: Longman, 1970

Vail, David Jeremiah. *A History of Agricultural Innovation and Development in Teso District, Uganda.* Syracuse, NY: Maxwell School of Citizenship and Public Affairs, Syracuse University, 1972

Van Zwanenberg, R.M.A., and King, Anne. *An Economic History of Kenya and Uganda, 1800-1970.* Atlantic Highlands, NJ: Humanities Press, 1975

Vansina, Jan, 'Inner Africa: A.D. 500-1800.' In *The Horizon History of Africa*, pp. 261-73. Edited by Alvin M. Josephy, Jr. New York: American Heritage Publishing Co., 1971

Vincent, Joan. *African Elite; The Big Men of a Small Town.* New York and London: Columbia University Press, 1971

—— 'Colonial Chiefs and the Making of Class; A Case Study from Teso.' *Africa* 47, no. 2 (1977): 140-58

Wallis, H.R. *The Handbook of Uganda.* 2nd edn. London: Crown Agents for the Colonies, 1920

Watson, J.M. 'Some Aspects of Teso Agriculture.' *East African Agricultural Journal* 6, no. 4 (April 1941): 209-12

Webster, J.B. 'The Civil War in Usuku.' in *War and Society in Africa*, pp. 35-64. Edited by Bethwell A. Ogot. London: Frank Cass, 1972

—— 'Noi! Noi! Famines as an aid to Interlacustrine Chronology.' In *Chronology, Migration and Drought in Interlacustrine Africa*, pp. 1-37. Edited by J.B. Webster. London: Longman for Dalhousie University Press, 1979

Welbourn, F.B. *Religion and Politics in Uganda, 1952-62.* Nairobi: EAPH, 1965

West, Henry W. *Land Policy in Buganda.* Cambridge: CUP, 1972

—— , ed. *The Transformation of Land Tenure in Buganda Since 1896.* Leiden: Afrika Studiecentrum, 1971

Wild, J.V. 'Note on the Busuulu and Envujjo Law.' In *The Transformation of Land Tenure in Buganda*, pp. 79-86. Edited by H.W. West
(q.v.)

Wilson, E.G., ed. *Who's Who in East Africa, 1965-66*. Nairobi: Marco
Publishers, 1966

Winter, Edward H. *Bwamba Economy*. Kampala: EAISR, 1955

——*Bwamba; A Structural-Functional Analysis of a Patrilineal
Society*. Cambridge: W. Heffer and Sons, 1955

Wrigley, Christopher C. 'Buganda: An Outline Economic History.'
Economic History Review (2nd Series) 10, no. 1 (1957): 69-80

—— 'The Changing Economic Structure of Buganda.' In *The King's
Men*, pp. 16-63. Edited by Lloyd A. Fallers (q.v.)

——*Crops and Wealth in Uganda; A Short Agrarian History*. Kampala:
EAISR, 1959

Yoshida, M., and Belshaw, D.G.R. 'The Introduction of the Trade
Licensing System for Primary Products in East Africa, 1900-1939.'
EAISR Conference Paper, January 1965

Young, M. Crawford. 'Agricultural Policy in Uganda: Capability and
Choice.' In *The State of the Nations*, pp. 141-64. Edited by Michael
Lofchie. Berkeley: University of California Press, 1971

—— 'The Obote Revolution.' *Africa Report* (June 1966), pp. 8-14

INDEX

Acholi 38; agriculture 98-9;
as labour reserve 56, 110, 122;
capitalist farmers 99; Ganda
agents 82; land tenure 97-9;
political parties in 195, 197-8,
199, 337; religious composition
199
Adoko, Akena 254
Adrisi, Mustafa 279, 284
African Development Fund 188
Africanisation: commerce and trade
187-90, 248, 252, 285;
employment 251; ginneries 158,
186, 198; in Kenya 251;
military 120; salariat 178, 179,
188, 192, 222, 237-41; *see also*
Ugandanisation
African Loans Fund 187, 188, 189,
198
agriculture 103; animal epidemics
58-9; Buganda 48; Busoga 96;
cash crops 60, 85, 96, 97, 141,
155; cattle 93, 94, 102, 105;
commercialisation 93, 97, 106;
cycles 100; dairy products 189;
education 166; extension services
166-7; food crops 34, 37, 60,
61, 96, 98, 100-1, 113; non-
indigenous crops 34; plough use
104-5; pre-colonial 34, 37,
68n19, 93, 94, 96, 98-100;
research 125n41, 166, 175n117;
soil fertility 91, 103-4; wholesale
traders 157-8; *see also* coffee;
cotton; sugar
Aiga, Juma 313
Ali, Moses 280-1, 282, 283, 341
Aliker, Martin 336
Allimadi, Otema 195, 338-9
Amin Dada, Andrea 320n1
Amin Dada, Idi 120, 144, 215, 254,
256; alliance with Obote 232, 255;
and military in government 282-4;
anti-Zionism 273, 307, 316;
commitment to 'privatisation'
292; coup 267-8; cuts military
275; early life 320n1; expels
Asians 285-318 *passim*; expels

missionaries 306; investigated 229;
overthrow 316, 319-20, 331;
supports Islam 307, 316; weapons
purchases 228
Amin Regime (1971-9) 267-330;
bans protestant sects 306;
borrowing 297; cabinets 279-82,
283, 284; cost of living during
296, 297, 298-9; dependence on
Kenya 320; disappearances and
deaths 269-70, 277, 279-82, 306,
307, 310-15; ethnic dimensions
282, 283, 303-6; foreign policy
316-17; new industries 297;
redistricting during 309; religious
dimensions 306-7; ultra-right
phase 272-3
Anglo-French Convention (1898) 40
Ankole: as labour reserve 110, 113;
Bairu cultivators and Bahima
pastoralists 67n8; Ganda agents 82;
land allocation 79; political parties
in 199, 337; religious composition
199
Ankole Agreement (1901) 125n35
Ankole Landlord and Tenant Law
321n11
Anya Nya Rebellion 255, 268, 269,
272, 273
Arube, Charles 279, 282, 305
Aseni, Elly 282, 305
Asians 136, 224; Amin warns 273;
assimilation 286; 'black' 293;
boycott against 190; citizenship
246-7, 249, 286, 287-8; economic
nationalism 160; expulsion
285-318 *passim*; in industry 57-8,
160, 249, 252; in Parliament 249;
in salariat 81, 247, 248; intimidation 246; make-up 247; measures
against 248; monopolies 179;
Obote alliance with 232; property
allocation 288-9, 290; return
341-2; sugar barons 159; traders
189, 190, 192, 198; welcome coup
271
Astles, Bob 284, 312
Aswa, Wilfred 256

371

For Product Safety Concerns and Information please contact our
EU representative GPSR@taylorandfrancis.com Taylor & Francis
Verlag GmbH, Kaufingerstraße 24, 80331 München, Germany